Marxism and history

MANCHESTER
UNIVERSITY PRESS

Even with philosophers who gave their works a systematic form, e.g. Spinoza, the real inner structure of his system is, after all, wholly different from the form in which he consciously presented it.

K. Marx, *Grundrisse*
(Harmondsworth, 1974), p. 60.

Marxism and history
A critical introduction
Second edition

S. H. Rigby

Manchester University Press
Manchester and New York
distributed exclusively in the USA by Palgrave

The right of S. H. Rigby to be identified as the author of this work has been asserted by him in accordance with the Copyright, Designs and Patents Act 1988.

First edition published 1987 by Manchester University Press

This edition published 1998 by
Manchester University Press
Oxford Road, Manchester M13 9NR, UK
and Room 400, 175 Fifth Avenue, New York, NY 10010, USA
www.manchesteruniversitypress.co.uk

Distributed exclusively in the USA by
Palgrave, 175 Fifth Avenue, New York,
NY 10010, USA

Distributed exclusively in Canada by
UBC Press, University of British Columbia, 2029 West Mall,
Vancouver, BC, Canada V6T 1Z2

British Library Cataloguing-in-Publication Data
A catalogue record for this book is available from the British Library

Library of Congress Cataloging-in-Publication Data applied for

ISBN 0 7190 5612 8 paperback

This edition first published 1998

05 04 03   10 9 8 7 6 5 4 3

Typeset in Joanna
by Northern Phototypesetting Co. Ltd, Bolton
Printed in Great Britain
by Bell & Bain Ltd, Glasgow

Contents

Preface to the first edition vi
Preface to the second edition vii
Introduction 1

PART ONE Marx as a productive force determinist 5

Chapter 1 Marx's ambiguous legacy 7
2 Forces and relations of production 17
3 Marx's productive force determinism 27
4 Productive force determinism as Marxist orthodoxy 60
5 The origins of productive force determinism 71

PART TWO Productive force determinism:
a critique and an alternative 81

6 Productive force determinism and functional
explanation 84
7 Productive force determinism: a critique 92
8 Productive force determinism: an alternative 143

PART THREE 'Base and superstructure' in historical
materialism 175

9 'Base and superstructure': definition and determination 177
10 Modes of production: variant forms of the 'base' 208
11 The political superstructure 251
12 The 'idealistic superstructure' 275

Conclusion: Marxism, politics and history 299
Bibliography 302
Index of names and subjects 311

Preface to the first edition

Recent years have seen a revival of interest in the nature and the utility of Marx's historical theory. Debate amongst historians and philosophers on Marx's claims for the social primacy of the productive forces, his functional explanation and his metaphor of 'base and superstructure' continues apace, so that a number of works appeared too late to be considered by the present volume. These include R. W. Miller, *Analyzing Marx* (Princeton, 1984); T. Bell and J. Farr (eds.), *After Marx* (Cambridge, 1984); R. H. Hilton, 'Feudalism in Europe: problems for historical materialism', *New Left Review* 147 (September–October 1984); E. M. Wood, 'Marxism and the course of history' (*ibid.*) and J. Roemer (ed.), *Analytical Marxism* (Cambridge, 1986). I have, where possible, made use of J. Elster, *Making Sense of Marx* (Cambridge, 1985), although this work also appeared when the bulk of the present book had already been written.

Thanks are owed to a number of members of Manchester University: to I. J. Prothero and C. L. M. Evans for their encouragement in the early stages of writing; to members of the History Discussion Group for their comments on papers used to prepare Chapters 3, 6 and 7; to members of the Social Transformation seminar for their comments on a draft version of Chapter 8; to M. E. Rose for his advice on the Poor Law; to J. Dyson, whose ideas form the basis for my discussion of working-class reformism; to J. Bergin, for his comments on absolutism; to A. L. Hughes for her comments on Protestantism; to J. Breuilly for his comments on ideology; to R. C. Nash for advice on Wallerstein; to I. Steedman for his comments on the labour theory of value and to N. Geras for comments on Althusser and on exploitation. In particular I would like to thank G. P. Burton and R. Brown-Grant, who suggested many improvements to earlier drafts of this book. They are, of course, absolved of all responsibility for the final outcome.

Preface to the second edition

The first edition of this book proceeded from the assumption that Marx and Engels's intellectual legacy was far too important to abandon it to the Marxists. The problem with the Marxists is that they want us to adopt Marxism as an identity. It is for this reason that the labour theory of value has assumed such totemic value for them: it is the one piece of theory which distinguishes Marxism from all of its radical rivals. In this book, by contrast, I preferred to assess Marxism not as an identity to be embraced or discarded in its entirety but rather as a series of propositions, some of which could be accepted and others rejected. Although in the 'Introduction' I coquetted with poststructuralist modes of expression (Marx as a 'space where a multiplicity of discourses intersect' etc.), the book was intended as a contribution to the decidedly non-poststructuralist historical project of determining which aspects of Marx's theories were most helpful to us in understanding the societies of the past. After all, of Marx and Engels's intellectual heritage, their politics, based on the conception of the proletariat as a revolutionary class, now seems like wishful thinking; their economics, premised on the labour theory of value, is now rejected by all but a handful of fundamentalists; their philosophy of dialectical materialism is an intellectual museum-piece. What remains of interest in Marx and Engels's work is their social and historical theory: historical materialism. Marx may have wanted to change the world rather than simply to interpret it in a new way but, in practice, Marxism has actually been rather more successful at comprehending the world than it has at changing it. Marx and Engels deserve more to be remembered for their social science than for their 'scientific socialism'.

The starting point of my analysis was the apparent divergence between, on the one hand, historical materialism as defined by Marxist philosophers and exegetes, such as Cohen, Shaw and McMurtry, and, on the other, the form of Marxism actually used to interpret the past by Marxist historians whom I admired, such as Rodney Hilton and Robert Brenner. First, whilst the philosophers emphasised the determination of society's class relations (or 'relations of production') by its productive forces (in crude terms, by its technology and level of social productivity), Marxist historians emphasised the importance of class relations in determining the form and pace of development of the productive forces. Second, whilst Marxist philosophers tended to see Marxism as an over-arching, universal philosophy of human history based on the relentless growth of the productive forces, Marxist historians preferred to emphasise the divergent historical paths taken by particular societies and the role of class struggle in determining which path was taken. Third, whilst the philosophers saw Marxism as providing us with a model of historical progress, Marxist historians saw it as a source of hypotheses and concepts. In short, Marxist philosophers saw historical materialism in 'convergent' terms, as a set of answers, whilst Marxist historians saw it in 'divergent' terms as a source of inspiring questions.[1]

One response to these two readings of historical materialism would be to scour Marx's works in order to find which of the two approaches corresponds most closely with Marx's 'real meaning'. The problem when we do this is that we find Marx's works themselves are profoundly contradictory, thus allowing both schools of thought to claim scriptural authority for their reading of Marx. In particular, there tended to be a gap between the explicit, programmatic statements of Marx's social theory, such as the 'Preface' to his *A Contribution to the Critique of Political Economy* (1859), most of which are based on the social primacy of the productive forces (Chapter 3, below), and the implications of many of his actual historical analyses which tend to emphasise the primacy of society's relations of production and the importance of class struggle as a motor of historical change (Chapter 8, below). Since both approaches could claim legitimacy from Marx and Engels's own works, it made little sense to ask which approach was 'most Marxist' (a question Marxists tend to confuse with the issue of which approach is 'most correct'). Instead, the key issue is which reading of Marx was most useful for the actual study of history. I argued that Marxist claims for the social primacy of the productive forces were open to a variety of logical and empirical criticisms and that it was the alternative Marxist tradition, the one emphasising class and class conflict, which was the most useful to historians. However, acceptance of this alternative Marxist tradition of historical writing by no means entailed an acceptance of Marx's communism. However much Marxists might chant the mantra of the 'unity of theory and practice', Marxist historical theory was substantially in advance of Marx's revolutionary politics.

Although the first edition of the book received some positive responses,[2] I am now inclined to agree with those reviewers who complained that the book overly concentrated its fire on Marxist claims for the primacy of the productive forces and that, as a result, other, equally problematical Marxist claims escaped criticism or were adopted a little too lightly.[3] Of the two key theses of historical materialism set out in the 'Introduction' of the book, it was the claim that 'the level of the productive forces explains the nature of society's relations of production' which was most critically examined whilst the second major thesis, that society's relations of production constitute an 'economic base' which determines its 'political and ideological superstructure', was subject to less rigorous questioning. For instance, my assessment of Marx's theory of ideology (Chapter 12, below) tended to accept rather uncritically the idea that 'it is not the consciousness of men that determines their existence, but their social existence that determines their consciousness'.[4] Yet, Marxist social theory can be criticised for its tendency to equate social existence with class position. It is sociologists in the Weberian tradition who have argued that economic class is simply one possible ground of 'social exclusion' and that other forms of exclusion, such as race, gender, status, and order, which are by no means reducible to class inequalities, can be just as important. There are thus a number of forms and grounds of social power (economic, political and ideological), giving rise to a variety of forms of social groups (or 'systacts'), none of which can be assumed to have an automatic, universal or necessary social primacy.[5]

It is not that Marxists have neglected such non-class forms of inequality. On the contrary, Marx and Engels themselves distinguished the estates and orders of pre-capitalist societies from the economic classes of capitalism[6] whilst Marxist social theorists have produced a number of studies of non-class inequalities, particularly those of gender.[7] The problem is rather that, as feminist historians and sociologists have argued, Marxists have tended to present gender relations in class societies as 'dominated by', secondary to, or subordinated to property relations.[8] Marxists thus often provide a functional explanation of gender relations in terms of their benefits for the reproduction of particular modes of production.[9] Patriarchy is thus viewed as secondary and derivative from society's mode of production rather than being presented as an autonomous form of social inequality in its own right.[10] Alternatively, Marxists simply tag non-class forms of social inequality on to their analysis in an *ad hoc* fashion, lapsing implicitly into a pluralist account of social structure. In my own empirical historical work written after the appearance of *Marxism and History*, I have tried to emphasise, in Weberian fashion, the ways in which individuals are constituted by a multiplicity of different axes of inequality and are thus members of a variety of over-lapping social groups: classes, genders, orders, estates, status-groups and so on. In medieval England, for instance, the specific privileges enjoyed by the clergy or the social disabilities faced by the Jews cannot be reduced to class inequalities.[11] Such social differences 'have a reality *sui generis*', a reality not equatable with or reducible to the relations arising from society's mode of production as defined in Marxist terms.[12]

Second, much of my discussion of Marx and Engels's conceptualisa-tion of society in terms of the metaphor of 'economic base' and 'politi-cal and ideological superstructure' (Chapter 9, below) sought to show that the work of Maurice Godelier provided a response to those critics of Marxism, such as Acton, Plamenatz, Leff and Lukes, who raised the issue of the '*interpenetration*' of base and superstructure. For these critics, so-called 'superstructural' phenomena, such as politics and ideas, do not merely reflect society's economic base or even interact with it; they are actually a constitutive part of society's economic 'base'. But, if the Marx-ist distinction between base and superstructure is untenable, it then becomes illegitimate to derive the latter from the former: one cannot say that x produces y if y is actually a part of x in the first place.[13] In fact, although I still believe that Godelier's reformulation of historical mate-rialism provides a successful defence of Marxism against this very sophisticated level of criticism, I would now argue that Marxist social theory actually comes to grief on the far more straightforward issue of the *interaction* of base and superstructure.[14] Why is this the case?

Although Marxism's opponents frequently attack it for its supposed neglect of the active historical role performed by society's so-called political and ideological 'superstructure', Marx and Engels themselves referred to the 'reciprocal action' of base and superstructure as early as *The German Ideology* (1845–6) and it was this 'dialectical interaction' of base and superstructure which Engels invoked in his famous letters of the 1890s in order to reject the accusation of economic reductionism made by Marx's critics.[15] The problem for Marxists is how to maintain this awareness of the active role of politics and ideas without abandon-ing their claims for the primacy of society's mode of production, claims which, after all, give Marxism its distinctiveness as a theory of the social world and of history. This dilemma can be seen in the structuralist ver-sion of historical materialism offered by Louis Althusser. Ironically, whilst Althusser's theory was attacked by E. P. Thompson for its economic reductionism, it would be truer to say that Althusser's theory actually founders (at least as a form of Marxism) in its recognition of the complex interaction involved in historical explanation. Far from reducing society to its mode of production, Althusser redefined the mode of production to include economic, political and ideological levels (or practices), each of which is 'relatively autonomous' and possesses its own chronology of development. Instead of positing a one-way determination of politics and ideology by economics, Althusser argues that specific relations of production may presuppose elements of the legal, political and ideological 'superstructure' as a condition of their existence.[16] Many historians and social theorists would be inclined to accept such a view. It is simply that it is rather difficult to see what is distinctively Marxist about it. In other words, the problem of reductionism cannot be solved simply by invoking the concept of the 'relative autonomy' of the state and ideology[17] (even if qualified by a determination by the economic 'in the last instance').[18] Neither is it a solution simply to abandon the metaphor of base and superstructure, perhaps by blaming it on Engels rather than on Marx himself.[19] It is not the *metaphor* of base and superstructure which is the problem but rather the idea which it seeks to express, i.e. the claim for a hierarchy of social elements or causal asymmetries which gave Marxism its specificity and separate identity as a form of social theory.[20]

Thus, in rejecting reductionism, Marxist theorists constantly slip towards an implicit pluralism by which Marxism dies the death of a thousand qualifications. This tendency is even more pronounced in the complex historical analyses offered by Marxist historians. For instance, Brenner's account of why the eastern European peasantry was enserfed in the late medieval and early modern periods when the peasantry in the west was winning its freedom, an account which I present below as a model of the value of the Marxist approach (Chapter 8, below), rejects traditional historical explanations in terms of population change and offers instead an analysis which is explicitly based on a Marxist claim for the primacy of class struggle. Brenner argues that it was the strength of the western European peasant community which allowed it to resist the seigneurial offensive of the late medieval period and thus to win its freedom, whereas the weakness of the peasant communities in the east meant that they were unable to counter the landlords' pressure, thus opening the way to serfdom. The problem is that when he comes to explain why the peasant community was weaker in the east than in the west, Brenner lists a host of particular historical factors which cannot be reduced to expressions of class structure or of class struggle, such as the absence of common land in the east, the prevalence there of individualistic methods of farming rather than of highly evolved common-field systems, the small size of eastern villages, the lack of villages of divided lordship, the effects of political conquest, and the emergence of particular state-forms. The outcome of class struggle thus ceases to be simply an explanation and itself becomes something to be explained in terms of a variety of factors.[21] There is a comparable pluralism at work in Brenner's account of how strong peasant property and the absolutist state developed in early modern France 'in mutual dependence upon one another', which suggests that absolutism was more than simply the 'expression' of social change, as Brenner elsewhere claims in more orthodox Marxist fashion, but was itself an active agent in bringing such change about.[22]

Such pluralism is not confined to the works of Brenner but pervades much of recent Marxist historiography.[23] It can, for instance, be seen in Corrigan and Sayer's explanation of why modern capitalism first triumphed in England in terms of 'the singularity of English state formation and state forms' and in Genovese's attempt to square the circle by claiming that the social superstructure is 'generated' by the base but that this superstructure also develops according to a logic of its own and, in turn, reacts back upon the base.[24] Similarly, Parker, in an essay explicitly intended to defend the metaphor of base and superstructure, argues that the motor of historical change in the early modern period was not to be found in class struggle or in any aspect of the economy 'but in the activities of the state', in particular, the rise of the absolutist state under the pressure of warfare and religious antagonisms.[25] In practice, such accounts present us with a multiplicity of interacting forces, an 'infinite variety of local factors',[26] which together bring about a particular historical outcome, a picture of history which is familiar from non-Marxist historiography and from Weberian sociology, but which sits uneasily with the Marxist claims for the primacy of the economic base (even when redefined in Godelier's terms). As Kitching put it, commenting on the high quality of Marxist historiography: 'Engaging in a professional practice which is more sophisticated than its theorization is in fact very likely to coexist with a trained inability to either recognize or express that sophistication formally or explicitly.'[27]

The threat which such pluralism poses for Marxism cannot be avoided merely by changing historical materialism from a claim for the

primacy of a narrowly defined 'economic' level to a more broadly conceived 'class determination'.[28] Nor is explanatory pluralism only implicit
in the Marxist tradition which emphasises the historical role of the relations of production and of class struggle rather than of the productive
forces.[29] Rather, pluralism is an insoluble problem for *any* brand of Marxism which rejects reductionism and which seeks to explain historical
change in terms of the interaction of a variety of historical forces.[30] As
philosophers in the tradition of John Stuart Mill have argued, it is impossible to claim an objective explanatory primacy for any of the multiple
factors which bring about a particular event. Causes have an objective
existence in the real world but which we choose to emphasise and
which we take as given will largely depend upon our own subjective
purposes, upon the knowledge which we think we can assume on the
part of our audience, or on the identification of some new piece of the
historical jigsaw to which we wish to draw our readers' attention.[31] In
this perspective, it is not just the Marxist claim for the primacy of the
economic which is doomed but *any* attempt to ascribe objective primacy
in historical explanation.[32] In other words, whatever our explicit theory
may be, we cannot help, in practice, but be pluralists. It is precisely this
fact which allows the pieces of the historical jigsaw discovered by Marxist historiography to be so easily subsumed into orthodox history.

As the high quality of Marxist historical writing suggests, Marxists
have easily avoided the Scylla of reductionism, upon which its critics
have usually seen it as foundering. Yet this danger has only been avoided
at the expense of being drawn into the Charybdis of pluralism. It would
seem then that there is no way in which Marxism can successfully nav-
igate between these two fates. That historical materialism and Marxist
historiography are open to such criticism does not mean that Marx and
Engels's work has to be 'abandoned' by historians.[33] Our task is rather to
incorporate their insights into a multi-dimensional conception of social
structure and a pluralist account of historical change. Each generation
creates its own version of Marx and Engels's thought to revere, to
demonise or to plunder. Even where we disagree with them, their work
provides many of the central questions and issues with which historians
and social theorists continue to wrestle. In history, as in sociology, 'there
is more to be learned from a major author who is wrong, than a nonen-
tity who is right'.[34]

Notes

1 For the convergent/divergent distinction, see L. Hudson, Contrary Imaginations: A Psychological Study of the English Schoolboy (Harmondsworth, 1967).

2 See, for instance, A. G. Meyer in American Historical Review, 95 (1990), pp. 453–4 and P. Davies in Philosophy Today, 7 (1991), pp. 7–8.

3 R. N. Berki in Political Studies, 36 (1988), pp. 392–3; J. C. Isaac in Philosophy of the Social Sciences, 19 (1989), pp. 514–15.

4 K. Marx, A Contribution to the Critique of Political Economy (London, 1971), p. 21.

5 M. Weber, Economy and Society (2 vols, Berkeley, 1978), vol. I, p. 577, vol. II, p. 926; G. Neuwirth, 'A Weberian outline of a theory of community: its application to the "Dark Ghetto"', British Journal of Sociology, 20 (1969), pp. 148–63; R. Murphy, Social Closure (Oxford, 1988); R. Collins, Conflict Sociology (New York, 1975); F. Parkin, 'Strategies of social closure in class formation', in F. Parkin, The Social Analysis of Class Structure (London, 1974), pp. 1–18; F. Parkin, Marxism and Class Theory: A Bourgeois Critique (London, 1979); F. Parkin, 'Social stratification', in T. Bottomore and R. Nisbet, A History of Sociological Analysis (London, 1979); F. Parkin, Max Weber (London, 1982), pp. 100–2; W. G. Runciman, 'The three dimensions of social inequality', in A. Béteille, ed., Social Inequality (Harmondsworth, 1969), pp. 45–63; W. G. Runciman, 'Towards a theory of social stratification', in Parkin, The Social Analysis of Class Structure, pp. 55–101; W. G. Runciman, A Treatise on Social Theory, vol. II (Cambridge, 1989), pp. 2–24; M. Mann, The Sources of Social Power, vol. I (Cambridge, 1986); A. Giddens, A Contemporary Critique of Historical Materialism (London, 1981).

6 K. Marx and F. Engels, Collected Works, vol. V (London, 1975), pp. 69, 73, 89–90; M. Godelier, The Mental and the Material (London, 1988), pp. 245–52.

7 See, for instance, C. Middleton, 'The sexual division of labour in feudal England', New Left Review, 113–14 (1979), pp. 147–68; C. Middleton, 'Peasants, patriarchy and the feudal mode of production in England', Sociological Review, 29 (1981), pp. 105–54; C. Middleton, 'Women's labour and the transition to pre-industrial capitalism', in L. Charles and L. Duffin, Women and Work in Pre-Industrial England (London, 1985), pp. 181–206; R. H. Hilton, Class Conflict and the Crisis of Feudalism (London, 1985), chapters 15 and 16; R. H. Hilton, The English Peasantry in the Later Middle Ages (Oxford, 1975), chapter 6; E. J. Hobsbawm, The Age of Empire, 1875–1914 (London, 1989), chapter 8. Many Marxist accounts of gender inequalities form an implicit or explicit debate with F. Engels, The Origin of the Family, Private Property and the State (Moscow, 1968). For a bibliography on this issue, see S. H. Rigby, Engels and the Formation of Marxism: History, Dialectics and Revolution (Manchester, 1992), pp. 198–204.

8 Marx and Engels, Collected Works, vol. V, p. 43; Engels, The Origin of the Family, Private Property and the State, p. 6.

9 Middleton, 'Peasants, patriarchy and the feudal mode of production in England', pp. 151–2; O. Adamson et al., 'Women's oppression under capitalism', Revolutionary Communist, 5 (1976); M. Gimenez, 'Marxist and non-Marxist elements in Engels' views of the oppression of women', in J. Sayers, M. Evans and N. Redclift, eds, Engels Revisited (London, 1987), p. 48; M. Barrett, Women's Oppression Today (London, 1984), pp. 132–3; C. Cockburn, 'The relations of technology: what implications for theories of sex and class?', in R. Crompton and M. Mann, eds,

Gender and Stratification (Cambridge, 1986), pp. 81–2.

10 S. de Beauvoir, *The Second Sex* (Harmondsworth, 1974), p. 87; S. Firestone, *The Dialectic of Sex* (London, 1979), p. 15; K. Millett, *Sexual Politics* (London, 1985), p. 38; C. Delphy, *Close to Home* (London, 1984), pp. 38–9, 74–5; R. McDonough and R. Harrison, 'Patriarchy and relations of production', in A. Kuhn and A. Wolpe, eds, *Feminism and Materialism* (London, 1978), pp. 31–2; A. Davin, 'Feminism and labour history', in R. Samuel, ed., *People's History and Socialist Theory* (London, 1981), p. 180.

11 S. H. Rigby, *English Society in the Later Middle Ages: Class, Status and Gender* (Basingstoke, 1995) and S. H. Rigby, 'Approaches to pre-industrial social structure', in J. H. Denton, ed., *Orders and Hierarchies in Late Medieval and Renaissance Europe* (Basingstoke, 1998).

12 Parkin, *Marxism and Class Theory*, pp. 4–5.

13 H. B. Acton, *The Illusion of the Epoch* (London, 1955), pp. 164–8, 177, 258; J. Plamenatz, *Man and Society*, vol. II (London, 1963), pp. 283–9, 345; G. Leff, *The Tyranny of Concepts* (London, 1969), pp. 144–51; R. Wokler, 'Rousseau and Marx', in D. Miller and L. Siedentop, eds, *The Nature of Political Theory* (Oxford, 1983), pp. 231–7; S. Lukes, 'Can the base be distinguished from the superstructure?', *ibid.*, pp. 103–19; K. Graham, *Karl Marx: Our Contemporary* (Hemel Hempstead, 1992), pp. 52–4.

14 S. H. Rigby, 'Historical causation: is one thing more important than another?', *History*, 80 (1995), pp. 227–42.

15 Marx and Engels, *Collected Works*, vol. V, pp. 40, 52–3; K. Marx and F. Engels, *Selected Correspondence* (Moscow, 1975), pp. 390–402, 433–5, 441–3.

16 E. P. Thompson, *The Poverty of Theory* (London, 1978), pp. 254, 355, 360; T. Lovell, *Pictures of Reality* (London, 1980), pp. 27–8; L. Althusser and E. Balibar, *Reading Capital* (London, 1975), pp. 97, 100, 104–5, 177–8, 183, 187, 220–4; L. Althusser, *For Marx* (London, 1977), pp. 96–101, 113; M. Gordy, 'Reading Althusser: time and the social whole', *History and Theory*, 22 (1983), pp. 1–21; R. Blackburn and G. S. Jones, 'Louis Althusser and the struggle for Marxism', in D. Howard and K. E. Klare, eds, *The Unknown Dimension: European Marxism Since Lenin* (New York, 1972), pp. 369–74; S. Hall, 'Re-thinking the base and superstructure metaphor', in J. Bloomfield, ed., *Class, Hegemony and Party* (London, 1977), pp. 43–71; T. Bennett, *Formalism and Marxism* (London, 1979), pp. 40–1; P. Anderson, *Arguments Within English Marxism* (London, 1980), pp. 66–77; P. Q. Hirst, *Marxism and Historical Writing* (London, 1985), pp. 22–3; A. Milner, 'Considerations on English Marxism', *Labour History*, 41 (1981), p. 8.

17 R. Miliband, *Class Power and State Power* (London, 1983), pp. 56–62; Bennett, *Formalism and Marxism*, pp. 40–1; Althusser and Balibar, *Reading Capital*, pp. 100–1; T. Eagleton, *Ideology* (London, 1991), p. 153; G. Williams, '18 Brumaire: Karl Marx and defeat', in B. Matthews, ed., *Marx: A Hundred Years On* (London, 1983), pp. 12–13, 32–3.

18 Marx and Engels, *Selected Correspondence*, pp. 393–6, 399, 401–2, 441–2; K. Kautsky, *The Materialist Conception of History* (New Haven, 1988), pp. xlii, 3–4, 227, 232–3; Althusser and Balibar, *Reading Capital*, pp. 97, 177–8, 220–4.

19 L. Colletti, *From Rousseau to Lenin* (London, 1972), p. 65; M. Rader, *Marx's Interpretation of History* (New York, 1979), pp. xx, 70, 75–6, 78, 82 181, 183–4; Thompson, *The Poverty of Theory*, pp. 79–85, 119–21; D. Sayer, *The Violence of Abstraction*

(Oxford, 1987), pp. 91–2, 148; E. Genovese, *The World the Slaveholders Made* (London, 1970), p. ix; H. J. Kaye, *The British Marxist Historians* (Cambridge, 1984), pp. 117, 191–2, 205, 234.
20 K. Korsch, *Karl Marx* (London, 1938), pp. 225, 230; T. Lovell, *Pictures of Reality* (London, 1980), p. 28; N. Geras, 'Seven types of obloquy: travesties of Marxism', in R. Miliband, L. Pantich, and J. Saville, eds, *The Socialist Register* (London, 1990), pp. 9–11; Anderson, *Arguments Within English Marxism*, pp. 66, 81; E. Genovese, *In Red and Black* (New York, 1972), pp. 19, 323–4; Genovese, *The World the Slaveholders Made*, p. ix; J. Haldon, 'The Ottoman state and the question of state autonomy: comparative perspectives', *Journal of Peasant Studies*, 18 (1991), p. 28; K. McDonnell and K. Robins, 'Marxist cultural theory: the Althusserian smokescreen', in S. Clarke et al., eds, *One-Dimensional Marxism* (London, 1980), p. 215; A. W. Wood, *Karl Marx* (London, 1981), pp. 64–5; R. P. Miller, 'Social and political theory: class, state and revolution', in T. Carver, ed., *Cambridge Companion to Marx* (Cambridge, 1991), pp. 101, 324; P. van Parijs, 'From contradiction to catastrophe', *New Left Review*, 115 (1979), pp. 87, 91; V. G. Kiernan, 'Problems of Marxist history', *New Left Review*, 161 (1987), p. 107; E. Hobsbawm, 'Marx and history', *New Left Review*, 143 (1984), pp. 44–6; E. O. Wright, A. Levine and E. Sober, *Reconstructing Marxism* (London, 1992), chapters 3 and 6.
21 R. Brenner, 'Agrarian class structure and economic development in pre-industrial Europe', *Past and Present*, 70 (1976), pp. 57–60; Brenner, 'The agrarian roots of European capitalism', *Past and Present*, 97 (1982), pp. 72–6. Guy Bois complains about Brenner's implicit pluralism in 'Against the neo-Malthusian orthodoxy', *Past and Present*, 79 (1978), p. 67.
22 Brenner, 'Agrarian class structure and economic development in pre-industrial Europe', p. 71; Brenner, 'The agrarian roots of European capitalism', p. 81.
23 See S. H. Rigby, 'Marxist historiography', in M. Bentley, ed., *Companion to Historiography* (London, 1997), pp. 889–928.
24 P. Corrigan and D. Sayer, *The Great Arch: English State Formation as Cultural Revolution* (Oxford, 1985), p. 85; Genovese, *In Red and Black*, pp. 322–3.
25 D. Parker, 'French absolutism, the English state and the utility of the base–superstructure model', *Social History*, 15 (1990), pp. 287, 297–8; D. Parker, *The Making of French Absolutism* (London, 1983), pp. 60–4, 74, 147–9. Parker thus recommends the application to western Europe of Anderson's account of the rise of eastern absolutism in terms of international rivalry. *The Making of French Absolutism*, pp. 297–8; P. Anderson, *Lineages of the Absolutist State* (London, 1979), pp. 195–202, 212–16. See also Chapter 11, below.
26 Haldon, 'The Ottoman state and the question of state autonomy', pp. 88–9. This variety of local factors can be seen in the treatment of the role of 'great men' in history, where the emphasis of Marxist historians on the indispensable role of particular individuals provides a contrast with Engels's (untestable) claim that 'if Napoleon had been lacking, another would have filled the place'. Marx and Engels, *Selected Correspondence*, p. 442; I. Deutscher, *The Prophet Armed: Trotsky, 1879–1921* (Oxford, 1954), p. vii; M. Rodinson, *Mohammed* (Harmondsworth, 1973), pp. ix–x, 298.
27 G. Kitching, *Karl Marx and the Philosophy of Praxis* (London, 1988), p. 225. Breuilly makes a similar point about the pluralist-Marxist accounts of the making of the German working class offered by Jürgen Kocka and Hartmut Zwahr

in J. Breuilly, 'The making of the German working class', *Archiv für Sozial Geschichte*, 27 (1987), pp. 44–52.

28 E. M. Wood, *Democracy Against Capitalism: Renewing Historical Materialism* (Cambridge, 1995), p. 175; Genovese, *The World the Slaveholders Made*, pp. ix, 19, 103; Genovese, *In Red and Black*, pp. 323–4; H. J. Kaye, 'Totality: its application to historical and social analysis by Wallerstein and Genovese', *Historical Reflections/Réflexions Historiques*, 6 (1979), pp. 415–19; S. Clarke, 'Socialist humanism and the critique of economism', *History Workshop*, 8 (1979), p. 144; G. Williams, 'In defence of history', *History Workshop*, 7 (1979), p. 118; Kaye, *The British Marxist Historians*, pp. 232–41; E. P. Thompson, *The Making of the English Working Class* (Harmondsworth, 1972), pp. 9–11; Thompson, *The Poverty of Theory*, pp. 85, 298–9. When class becomes an economic, social, political, psychological and cultural phenomenon (Genovese, *In Red and Black*, pp. 323–4), there is a danger that this concept 'turns into a synonym for the social structure itself, occasionally masquerading as one of its principal parts' (Parkin, *Marxism and Class Theory*, p. 8).

29 G. McLennan, 'The historical materialism debate', *Radical Philosophy*, 50 (1980), pp. 39–40; G. McLennan, *Marxism, Pluralism and Beyond* (Cambridge, 1989), pp. 70–7.

30 L. Johnston, *Marxism, Class Analysis and Socialist Pluralism* (London, 1986), pp. 8, 50, 66–7, 69, 80–1, 122. Since 'reductionism' is a term of abuse which no one applies to themselves, this means, in effect, all versions of Marxism. After all, even Stalin emphasised the 'reciprocal' influence of the social superstructure on the economic base and argued that, far from denying the role of the state and ideology in history, Marxism 'stresses the important role and significance of these factors in the life of society'. See J. V. Stalin, *Dialectical and Historical Materialism* (Moscow, 1951), pp. 26–7.

31 J. S. Mill, *A System of Logic* (London, 1970), pp. 214–17; J. Hospers, *An Introduction to Philosophical Analysis* (London, 1973), pp. 292–6; A. Ryan, *J. S. Mill* (London, 1974), pp. 74–9; J. Skorupski, *John Stuart Mill* (London, 1989), pp. 175–7; A. Ryan, *The Philosophy of John Stuart Mill* (London, 1987), pp. 41–50; H. L. A. Hart and T. Honoré, *Causation in the Law* (Oxford, 1985), pp. xxxiii, 15–22, 28, 33–7; G. Ryle, *The Concept of Mind* (London, 1963), pp. 50, 88–9, 113–14; W. G. Runciman, *A Treatise on Social Theory*, vol. I (Cambridge, 1983), p. 193; S. Gorovitz, 'Causal judgements and causal explanations', *Journal of Philosophy*, 62 (1965), pp. 701–2; P. Veyne, *Writing History* (Manchester, 1984), pp. 91–2, 101; P. Gardiner, *The Nature of Historical Explanation* (Oxford, 1961), pp. 10–11, 99–112; W. Dray, *Laws and Explanation in History* (Oxford, 1957), pp. 98–101; H. Putnam, *Meaning and the Moral Sciences* (London, 1979), pp. 41–4; H. Putnam, *Philosophical Papers*, vol. III (Cambridge, 1983), pp. 211–15; A. Garfinkel, *Forms of Explanation* (New Haven, 1981), pp. 3–5, 21–34, 138–45, 156–74; R. J. Anderson, J. A. Hughes and W. W. Sharrock, *Philosophy and the Human Sciences* (Beckenham, 1986), p. 171; M. Brodbeck, 'Explanation, prediction and "imperfect knowledge"', in H. Feigl and G. Maxwell, eds, *Minnesota Studies in the Philosophy of Science*, vol. III (Minneapolis, 1962), p. 239; F. L. Will, *Induction and Justification* (London, 1974), pp. 24, 273–5; R. F. Atkinson, *Knowledge and Explanation in History* (London, 1989), pp. 159–64; A. Heller, *A Theory of History* (London, 1982), pp. 159–60; C. Behan McCullagh, *Justifying Historical Descriptions* (Cambridge, 1984), pp. 208–11; K. Popper, *The Poverty of Historicism* (London, 1969), p. 151; M. Scriven, 'Causes, connections and conditions in history', in W. H. Dray, ed., *Philosophical Analysis and History* (New York, 1966), pp. 254–8.

32 Rigby, *Engels and the Formation of Marxism*, pp. 177–82; Rigby, *English Society in the Later Middle Ages*, pp. 141–3; Rigby, 'Historical causation: is one thing more important than another?', pp. 227–42.

33 S. L. Waugh, 'Medieval England and closure theory', *New Left Review*, 226 (1997), p. 127.

34 W. G. Runciman, *A Critique of Marx Weber's Philosophy of Social Science* (Cambridge, 1972), p. 1.

Introduction

Recent years have seen the publication of a number of works on Marxism and history, works which form the starting point of the present analysis of Marxist historiography. These studies have produced much of value, yet are often marred by a common failing, the belief that the meaning of a text is best seen in terms of the purposes of the author who produced it. The task of criticism, or exegesis, is then to construct the author of the text by establishing the unity of the author's works. This approach to textual analysis has been abandoned in many quarters[1] but remains dominant in studies of Marx. Critics thus attempt to discover what Marx 'really said'; to offer 'a less untidy version of some of his major thoughts than he himself provided'. Marx is allowed the 'occasional inconsistency' but, overall, it is assumed that it is possible and profitable to interpret his works in terms of the unity of his intentions. It is the critic's task to reconstruct these intentions and, from such reconstructions, to deduce what, for instance, Marx would have said about the state (if he had ever got around to writing an extended book on the subject) or about recent theories of oriental despotism.[2]

An author's intentions are, of course, one of the constraints on the interpretation of a text or a body of work. A text cannot, after all, mean anything and everything. Certainly, Marx's intentions are evident in the contrast between the stirring opening of *The Communist Manifesto* (world history as class struggle) and the less revolutionary tone adopted by his 'Preface' to *A Contribution to the Critique of Political Economy*, a text written with a wary eye on the Prussian censor.[3] Nevertheless, even where an author's intentions can be reconstructed they cannot be taken as a guarantee of the text's sense or as the limit of its meaning. The meaning of a text is not some essence inherent within it, but is the result of a specific reading

1

If the writing of history is a 'continuous process of interaction between the historian and his facts', so the interpretation of an author is the product of the unending dialogue between text and reader.[4]

This shift of attention away from the author, and towards the reader's creation of meaning, opens up the number of possible interpretations of a given text. The author, in our case Marx, ceases to be an 'imaginary unity' and becomes instead 'a space where a number of discourses intersect, an unstable and shifting configuration of discourses produced by the interaction of a specific group of works with particular historically and socially locatable ways of reading those works'.[5] To interpret a text is not merely to reconstruct the unity of its author's intentions. It is also to identify the text's contradictions, absences and silences, the problems which the text papers over or leaves unresolved. Marx's works then cease to be cogent, rounded wholes from which it is possible to distil what he 'really said'. The significance of his work will lie as much in the differences between its meanings as in its unity.[6] This does not merely imply that there was a young, a mature and an old Marx, but rather that his individual texts are themselves contradictory and problematical. Such difficulties are frequently revealed through an author's choice of metaphors. An unravelling of Marx's metaphors reveals the problems inherent in any attempt to impose a single, coherent meaning on his texts.

The desire to locate incoherence within an author's texts can, however, become as much of a critical orthodoxy as the previous search for the unity of meaning guaranteed by the presence of the author.[7] Marx is portrayed in the present work not merely as a mass of contradictions, nor as a single unity. Rather we identify a number of internally coherent but mutually contradictory Marxes. For Draper, such contradictions do not lie in Marx's works themselves, but are simply the result of sterile quotation mongering. In order to find out 'what Marx really taught' about, for example, the nature of the state, we need to bring together all of Marx's quotations on the subject. Only then can we locate the real, consistent Marx. Certainly it is sterile to bandy quotations about in order to discover what Marx 'really said', but there is no reason why extensive quotation from Marx's works will reveal the coherence of his works, rather than their contradictions. The possibility of identifying contradictions is further compounded by Draper's desire to allow the reader to 'form an independent opinion' of Marx's views. If readers bring their own concerns and priorities to a text (as is inevitable), then the chances of discovering silences and inconsistencies would seem to be increased, rather than diminished. In this sense Marxology is not, as Draper claims, 'one of the most curious of industries', it is the inevitable result of a variety of readers making sense of Marx's extensive works concerning the most controversial issues in social theory.[8]

Our central task is thus not to reconstruct some single, coherent Marx, but, rather, to determine which of Marx's contradictory claims are useful in the analysis of social structure and of historical change. Putting Marx to work is a rather better way of assessing his contribution to historiography than the futile labour of attempting to discover what he really meant. In order to assess Marx's historical theory, it is thus vital, but not sufficient, to establish the philosophical validity of his concepts and forms of explanation. We must also consider the methodological implications of the history which Marx himself wrote, implications which often pose a challenge to Marx's own explicit message.

It is important too, in assessing the value of Marx's contribution to historiography, to consider the history produced by modern 'Marxist' historians, in order to determine to what extent Marx's historical claims have proved useful in practice. The implications of the works of historians such as Christopher Hill, or Robert Brenner, may prove as valuable here as the explicit exegesis of historical materialism by philosophers such as Lukács or Althusser. Marxist historiography is often seen as the study of industrial capitalism, partly because of the influence of Capital, and partly because of the well-known works of historians such as Foster, Thompson and Hobsbawm, works with an obvious relevance to the modern labour movement. Yet much of the most interesting recent Marxist historical writing has been on pre-industrial societies: Godelier on primitive societies; De Ste-Croix on the ancient world; Hilton, Bois and Kula on feudalism; Brenner on the transition to capitalism. It is these studies of pre-industrial society, and particularly of the era of the transition to capitalism, which will be used as test-cases for Marx's claims in the following pages.

Any exercise in historiography is necessarily parasitic on other texts. This is certainly true of the present work in its assessment of historical materialism from Marx and Engels to Cohen and Brenner. Yet, in a broader sense, all texts are formed through the integration and disintegration of other texts and Marx and Engels's works are no exception. Marx's thought developed in a prolonged encounter with Hegel, Proudhon and Ricardo. Who would ever have heard of Herr Eugen Dühring, if it were not for Engels's critique of his 'revolution in science'? This book takes as its starting point G. A. Cohen's account of historical materialism, an account 'whose intellectual force supersedes virtually all previous discussion'.[9] Cohen defines historical materialism through two central theses:

(1)   the level of the productive forces explains the nature of society's relations of production;

(2)   the nature of society's relations of production (the 'economic base') determines the nature of the social 'superstructure' (law, politics and [perhaps] ideology).[10]

Part I of this book establishes the meaning of the first of these claims in Marx's works and discusses the origin and development of this claim for the social primacy of the productive forces. Part II offers an alternative account of the relationship between the productive forces and the relations of production. Part III assesses the value of Marx's metaphor of 'base and superstructure'.

Notes

1 See J. Caughie (ed.), *Theories of Authorship* (London, 1981). Althusser's concept of a 'symptomatic reading' of Marx opened up the possibility of constructing a number of Marxes whilst, in practice, producing a new orthodoxy. See L. Althusser & E. Balibar, *Reading Capital* (London, 1975), pp. 24–30.

2 G. A. Cohen, *Karl Marx's Theory of History: A Defence* (London, 1978), p. ix; W. H. Shaw, *Marx's Theory of History* (London, 1978), p. 149; M. Rader, *Marx's Interpretation of History* (New York, 1979), pp. 14, 41; B. Hindess & P. Q. Hirst, *Pre-Capitalist Modes of Production* (London, 1975), p. 219.

3 A. M. Prinz, 'Background and ulterior motive of Marx's Preface of 1859', *Journal of the History of Ideas* XXX (1969), pp. 437–50.

4 E. H. Carr, *What is History?* (Harmondsworth, 1970), p. 30.

5 S. Jenkins (ed.), *Fritz Lang: The Image and the Look* (London, 1981), p. 7.

6 T. Moi, *Sexual Textual Politics* (London, 1985), p. 94.

7 S. Connor, *Charles Dickens* (Oxford, 1985), p. 89.

8 H. Draper, *Karl Marx's Theory of Revolution*, vol. I (New York, 1977), pp. 20–1.

9 P. Anderson, *Arguments Within English Marxism* (London, 1980), p. 82.

10 Cohen, *Karl Marx's Theory of History*, pp. 134, 216–17.

PART ONE

Marx as a productive force determinist

Whilst many commentators are willing to admit the general influence which Marx has had on historical thought, it is rather more difficult to specify his precise contribution (Chapter 1). Even the basic concepts of 'Marxist' historiography are open to conflicting interpretations, but it is possible to give a coherent sense to the terms which Marx uses to describe the production process and society's class relations (Chapter 2). One way in which to specify the nature of Marx's historical thought is to present him as a technological or, to be more precise, a productive force determinist. Other writers would deny this interpretation of Marx's works. Extensive quotation from Marx reveals that he did offer an explicitly productive force determinist account of historical change (Chapter 3). This philosophy was taken to be the orthodox reading of historical materialism by the theoreticians of the Second and Third Internationals (Chapter 4), and was deeply rooted in Marx's intellectual heritage and in the economic and social conditions of the first half of the nineteenth century (Chapter 5). Part II of this book offers a critique of Marx's productive force determinism and analyses an alternative Marxist tradition based on the primacy of society's relations of production.

CHAPTER 1

Marx's ambiguous legacy

The general influence of Marx on modern historical writing is rarely denied, even by his sternest critics: 'He has profoundly affected our understanding of history and it is hard to deny that without him our researches would be less complete and less accurate than they are . . . he made a tremendous contribution by altering the whole fashion of historical thought.'[1] The precise nature of Marx's contribution to modern historical analysis is, however, rather more difficult to specify. Too often Marx's theory of history is reduced to an emphasis on class, or to the omnipotent role of the 'economic factor'. Marxism, like psychoanalysis, has had such an immense impact on contemporary thought partly *because* it was perceived in an over-simplified fashion.[2] Much of the motivation for this over-simplification, it must be said, came from a political animus to Marx and his theories.[3] Yet this is not the only reason why Marxism has been perceived as a form of economic determinism. Marx and Engels's own legacy was contradictory and ambiguous. It is pointless to search for a single theory of history in the works of Marx and Engels, let alone in the interpretation and development of their work by their later followers. There *was* an economic determinist 'Marx', just as there was a 'Marx' who can be invoked to provide a critique of economic determinism. The point is not to attempt to identify what Marx 'really' meant. Even if it were possible to contact the ghost of Marx through a spirit medium all we would receive would be more words, more texts, for us to interpret and to put to work. We can leave the task of deciding what Marx 'really' meant to the political dogmatists. The key point is which of the many ideas which Marx put forward do we wish to use in an analysis of historical and contemporary societies?

Part I of this book argues that Marx may legitimately be presented as

7

a 'productive force determinist' who saw the growth of society's productive forces as the main determinant of social evolution. Part II of this book argues that Marx's own work may be invoked to provide an alternative to productive force determinism. In this chapter we argue that it is not only on the issue of productive force determinism that Marx's legacy has been an ambiguous one. On the contrary, on a number of the key issues of historical materialism it is impossible to identify a single 'Marxist' approach.

The most common conception about Marx's theory of history (or historical materialism) is that it is a form of economic reductionism, a mono-causal account of historical development in which only economics has an active role. Even a writer as perceptive as Collingwood could claim that Marx believed that if people held certain philosophical views 'they had no philosophical reasons for holding them but only economic reasons'.[4] Certainly there have been Marxists who have erred in this direction, often to correct what they perceived as an opposite imbalance in orthodox historiography. Mehring's claim that the Reformation, one of the decisive events in the formation of modern Europe, was 'only the ideological reflection of an economic development' encapsulates the 'vulgar Marxism' which portrays ideas as merely a passive reflection of a real, active economic base.[5] At times Marx and Engels themselves lapsed into this 'vulgar' Marxism. In the 1873 'Postface' to volume I of *Capital*, for instance, Marx refers to his conception of the process of thinking as opposite to that of Hegel. For Hegel the process of thinking is converted into an independent historical factor which creates the real world: 'With me the reverse is true: the ideal is nothing but the material world reflected in the mind of man, and translated into forms of thought.'[6] English political economy is similarly said to be the 'scientific reflection' of English economic circumstances, modern socialism is the 'reflection' of the conflict between the productive forces and the relations of production found in modern capitalist society.[7]

To refer to ideas as 'reflections' of material reality suggests their passivity and historical impotence. Yet Engels himself described the belief that ideas have no historical influence as 'fatuous'. He and Marx had merely meant to deny that ideas had an *independent* historical role. Indeed, Engels described the claim that the economic factor was the only determining factor in historical change as 'meaningless, abstract and absurd'.[8] Nor can Engels's denials of the charge of economic reductionism be seen as merely a late correction to historical materialism. As early as 1845 Marx had criticised Feuerbach's materialism because it presented material reality as having a one-way influence over the ideal. Consciousness does not only reflect reality; there is also a reciprocal relationship between the objective world and the activity of 'man', between material reality and human consciousness.[9] Consciousness is not to be ignored, but neither is it to be seen as an autonomous historical force existing independently from real living individuals.[10]

Associated with the belief that historical materialism is a form of economic reductionism is the claim that Marx saw history as being 'structurally limited to the point of being inevitable'.[11] Certainly, Marx can be quoted to support this belief. For instance, Marx told the German readers of volume one of *Capital* that they should heed the example of England, since 'the country that is more developed industrially shows to the less developed the image of its own future'.[12] Marx even applied this model to India and claimed that all lands drawn into the market of European capitalism would follow in the footsteps of advanced Europe.[13] He similarly argued that the extension of large-scale industry and the growth of the industrial proletariat would eventually undermine the society which had produced them. The fall of the bourgeoisie and the victory of the proletariat were thus 'equally inevitable'.[14]

Yet, by the end of his life, Marx was protesting against those who took his sketch of the development of capitalism in western Europe as an inevitable path of development, 'imposed by fate on all peoples, whatever the historical circumstances in which they find themselves'. Marx and Engels argued that Russia, for instance, need not follow the path of the west and could bypass the capitalist mode of production: 'Russia's peasant communal landownership may serve as the point of departure for a communist development.'[15] If Marx suggested alternative paths to future communist society, then he also outlined alternative historical paths from the earliest stage of human society, primitive communism. From this mode of production, which Marx defined by its tribal-communal appropriation of surplus labour, Marx outlined three possible roads: the Asiatic mode of production based on the village community with surplus labour appropriated by the state in the form of taxation; the Ancient mode based on slavery and the city-state; and a Germanic mode based on relatively self-sufficient peasant households.[16]

Later Marxists have also stressed the diversity of historical evolution. Trotsky's theory of permanent revolution, for instance, was explicitly designed to show why 'backward' countries such as Russia would not have to inevitably follow in the footsteps of the west and pass through a prolonged capitalist period before socialist revolution was possible.[17]

Whatever the historical value of Marx and Trotsky's theories of Russian development, they can hardly be cited to support the view that historical materialism sees historical evolution as that of some necessary or unilinear development. 'Inevitabilism' is not an inevitable part of Marxist historiography.

At the heart of all historical and sociological writing are the problems of structure and of agency. In other words, how can we reconcile a belief in purposeful individual action with a belief in the social determination of human thoughts and acts?[18] Marxism, as we have seen, is often presented as a form of economic determinism in which human agency is said to have no role. Individuals are merely the puppets of economic forces whose inevitable course they are powerless to influence.[19] In volume one of *Capital*, for instance, Marx claims that he treats individuals merely as the 'personifications of economic categories, the bearers of particular class-relations and interests'.[20] Yet Marx and Engels themselves also criticised those thinkers who presented people as merely the bearers of some metaphysical 'History'.[21]

'History does nothing, it possesses no immense wealth, it wages no battles. It is man, real living man who does all that, who possesses and fights; "history" is not, as it were, a person apart, using man as a means to achieve its own aims, history is nothing but the activity of man pursuing his aims.'[22] In other words Marx stressed that 'men' make their own history but, of course, added that 'they do not make it just as they please; they do not make it under circumstances chosen by themselves but under circumstances encountered, given and transmitted from the past'.[23] Later Marxists have also stressed that it is real humans, not 'economic forces', who make history. Non-Marxist historians have argued, for example, that the ability of the English peasantry to win its freedom in the later Middle Ages was the result of economic circumstances: the peasant's strong bargaining position given the shortage of tenants following the Black Death and later plagues.[24] It is the Marxists, Rodney Hilton and Robert Brenner, who argue that this shortage of tenants could equally have led to the strengthening of feudal bonds. The eventual freedom of the English peasantry was not only the result of economic circumstances but also of the peasants' own actions, their local and national struggles, which prevented the reimposition of feudal restrictions.[25]

The claim that Marxists see humans as puppets of economic forces is associated with the belief that Marxism allows no room for the influence of 'great men' on historical change.[26] Yet Marxist historiography has not found it difficult to deal with the role of important individuals in major historical events. Isaac Deutscher, for instance, stressed the objective factors which led to the victory of Stalin over Trotsky and the development of a new ruling bureaucracy in post-revolutionary Russia (the chaos resulting from years of war, the dispersal of the working-class vanguard, the social weight of the Russian peasantry, the international isolation of the Revolution and so on), but he was also concerned to ask 'to what extent did Trotsky himself contribute to his own defeat?'[27] Neither did Trotsky's own history of the Russian Revolution ignore the role of the individuals caught up in it. The personality of Nicholas II, for instance, was, of necessity, a historical force since 'the monarchy by its very principle is bound up with the personal'. Similarly, he argued that Lenin made a decisive personal contribution to the Revolution in April 1917, when he persuaded the Bolsheviks to adopt an independent political position, and again in October 1917, when he successfully urged the Bolsheviks to adopt a policy of insurrection at a time when the victory of the Revolution depended on a crucial two or three days.[28]

Finally, those who see Marxism as a form of economic reductionism claim that it has no room for the importance of politics and the state in historical change. Marxism, it is argued, holds that the state and politics are mere superstructural reflections of society's economic base.[29] Marx's account of the transition to capitalism is thus said to overemphasise economic factors and to ignore the decisive role of politics in bringing about the transition.[30] Certainly, Marx may be cited to support the view that politics is merely a reflex of economics. In The Poverty of Philosophy, for example, he claims that 'legislation, whether political or civil, never does more than proclaim, express in words, the will of economic relations'.[31] Yet, as always, it is possible to quote Marx against his reductionist self. It is hard to see how Marx can be said to ignore the role of politics in the transition to capitalism. His account of this process in England contains chapters on the use of the law to expropriate the peasantry, to discipline vagabonds and to keep down wages. It concludes that the culmination of the transition process may be seen in the colonial system and in the development of modern forms of taxation. All of these changes 'employ the power of the state, the concentrated and organized form of society, to hasten, as in a hothouse, the process of the transformation of the feudal mode of production into the capitalist mode'.[32] Conversely, Robert Brenner has argued that in France the development of the absolutist state and its guarantee of peasant property rights were a key obstacle to the development of capitalist agriculture.[33] More generally, recent writers

11

have stressed 'how large a place' the idea of the autonomy of the state possesses in the writings of Marx and Engels.[34]

The point is not to force a uniform theory of the state on Marx, but rather to decide which of his approaches, if any, is of use to those who wish to understand social structure and historical change. Again and again we are forced not to choose for or against Marxism, but to decide which components of Marx we wish to retain and employ. As E. P. Thompson remarked: 'Marx is on our side; we are not on the side of Marx.'[35] It is often said that when you attack a castle you attack its weakest points, but when you attack a body of ideas you attack its strongest points. Attack the weakest points of a castle and it will fall; attack the weakest points of a body of ideas and its strengths remain. This is certainly true of Marx's ambiguous and contradictory works. We may reject his economic reductionist formulations, but would-be critics still have to come to terms with an impressive body of sociological concepts and historical analysis.

In an attempt to go beyond the enduring misconceptions and over-simplifications of Marxist historical theory, recent writers have attempted to offer a more precise and detailed reading of Marx's account of historical change which goes beyond a simple emphasis on class, or on the 'economic factor'. Commentators such as Cohen, Shaw and McMurtry have presented Marx's thought as a form of technological or 'productive force determinism'. In this reading of Marx's works, society's productive forces (i.e. in sum, the organisation of the labour process which creates a certain level of productivity) are said to bring into being specific forms of class relations. These productive forces are held to have developed throughout history and have periodically required new forms of class relations (relations of production). The growth of society's productivity is thus not only a key *theme* of human history, but also an *explanation* of that history. The growth of the productive forces is held to be society's dynamic and primary element which, through its creation of specific forms of class relations, brings into being new forms of the state and ideology.[36]

This interpretation of historical materialism has much that will recommend it to many readers of Marx. It is firmly based on Marx's 1859 'Preface' to A Contribution to the Critique of Political Economy, Marx's most famous and explicit statement of his theory of history.[37] Many readers of Marx will find congenial a theory of history in which society is presented as a structure of relations in which certain elements (the productive forces) have a privileged explanatory role. Productive force determinism offers an attractive emphasis on historical change and an account of that change through the growth of the productive forces. It also stresses the existence of inherent tensions and conflicts within the social structure (as society's class relations became fetters on the growth of new productive forces), a key element in any Marxist theory of history.

It is the aim of this book to show that Marx's views of historical change and of the role of the productive forces were rather more complicated than writers such as Shaw and Cohen would suggest. We argue that:

(1) A productive force determinist reading of Marx is totally valid given Marx and Engels's quite explicit claims on the matter. We defend this point in Chapter 3 against those who wish to deny Marx's productive force determinism.

(2) To Marx and Engels's successors in the Second and Third Internationals (Kautsky, Plekhanov, Lenin, Trotsky and so on) historical materialism was essentially a form of productive force determinism. These writers did little more than reformulate the assertions which Marx and Engels had made but had never systematically defended (Chapter 4).

(3) There were strong historical and intellectual pressures which led Marx and Engels to their productive force determinism (Chapter 5).

(4) The most systematic elaboration and defence of productive force determinism has appeared in the works of recent writers such as Shaw and Cohen. An assessment of their claims shows productive force determinism to be logically untenable and historically invalid (Chapters 6 and 7).

(5) Marx's works contain an interpretation of social structure and historical change very different from that of productive force determinism. This alternative rejects deductive philosopies of history (such as productive force determinism) and provides the concepts which open the way to the empirical investigation of concrete hypotheses. It is an alternative based not on the thesis that the productive forces create social relations, but rather on the claim that production is itself a form of social activity (Chapter 8, Part a).

(6) Marxist historians have been able to make little use of the claims of productive force determinism. The transition from feudalism to capitalism, a key test of the claims of productive force determinism, is used to show the redundancy of the theories of Shaw and Cohen. An alternative approach is outlined in which the development of the productive forces is not the fundamental explanation of social change. On the contrary, change in the productive forces

13

is itself the result of changes in society's relations of production (Chapter 8, Part b).

There may be two immediate reactions to these claims. Firstly, do we really need to identify yet more versions of what Marx 'really said' or 'almost thought'? The issue of whether Marx held two contradictory theories of history (Chapters 3 and 8) is, however, a relatively minor one. Even if we conceded that Marx held only one, productive force determinist, theory of history (the theory outlined in Chapter 3), we would still be entitled to ask:

(1)   Is this theory valid (Chapter 7)?
(2)   If it is not valid, which alternative accounts of social change do we prefer? (Chapter 8).

The second reaction to our six main points may be 'why bother?' Can a study of Marx's historical theory have any practical relevance? Chapter 7 of this book considers the political implications of Marx's productive force determinism. Of course, there cannot be a one-to-one correspondence between politics and historical interpretation. R. H. Tawney's *Religion and the Rise of Capitalism*, for example, could fairly be described as a classic work of Marxist history, even though Tawney was not a Marxist in his political views.[38] Paul Sweezy, on the other hand, is a revolutionary Marxist in his politics, yet his interpretation of the transition from feudalism to capitalism owes more, theoretically, to Adam Smith than to Karl Marx.[39] Similarly, an acceptance of the interpretation of Marx's theory of history offered in this book does not automatically commit the reader to its analysis of working-class reformism.

Nevertheless, historical theories do have political implications and Marxist political analysis is closely linked to more general theories of historical development. Productive force determinism certainly has important political implications, since it offers an explanation of social revolution and an account of the problems involved in the construction of a post-revolutionary socialist economy.[40] The role of the productive forces in historical change touches on nearly every aspect of Marxist, and thus of much non-Marxist, social science: the dynamic of historical change, the causes of revolution, the emergence of new class structures and the limits of political choice and action. For these reasons an assessment of productive force determinism is of importance far beyond the limited ranks of Marxists and Marxologists.

To many readers the most familiar aspect of Marx's theory of history will not be his claims for the primacy of the productive forces, but, rather, his metaphor of 'base and superstructure', in which the nature of society's economic foundation determines the form taken by its state and by its ideology. Once more, Marx grapples with the central problems of social and historical theory: why does the state have a particular form at a particular time? Why do certain groups of people adopt specific ideologies and outlooks? Both Marx's productive force determinism and his social explanation of the political and ideological superstructure take a 'functional' form, i.e. just as society's relations of production exist to promote the development of the productive forces, so the existence of the state and of society's dominant ideology can be explained by their stabilising effect on the relations of production. Both the relations of production and the social superstructure are thus accounted for in terms of their benefits (for, respectively, the productive forces and the relations of production). Any assessment of Marx's historical materialism must, therefore, come to terms with the logical and empirical problems involved in this form of explanation. But before we can assess Marx's claims concerning social determinism we must first define the meaning of the key concepts in his historical theory.

Notes

1 L. Kolakowski, Main Currents of Marxism, vol. I (Oxford, 1978), pp. 369–70.

2 E. J. Hobsbawn, 'Karl Marx's contribution to historiography', in R. Blackburn (ed.), Ideology in Social Science (London, 1973), p. 269.

3 See, for instance, R. N. Carew Hunt, The Theory and Practice of Communism (Harmondsworth, 1969, 1st edn 1950).

4 R. G. Collingwood, The Idea of History (Oxford, 1976), p. 123.

5 F. Mehring, On Historical Materialism (London, 1975), p. 15.

6 K. Marx, Capital, vol. I (Harmondsworth, 1976, Pelican edn), p. 102. My emphasis.

7 T. B. Bottomore & M. Rubel, Karl Marx: Selected Writings in Sociology and Social Philosophy (Harmondsworth, 1970), p. 114; F. Engels, Herr Eugen Dühring's Revolution in Science (London, Lawrence & Wishart, n.d.), p. 301.

8 K. Marx & F. Engels, Selected Correspondence (Moscow, 1975), p. 435 (letter of 14.7.1893).

9 K. Marx, Early Writings (Harmondsworth, 1975), pp. 421–3 (Theses on Feuerbach); A. Giddens, Capitalism and Modern Social Theory (Cambridge, 1979), pp. 20–1.

10 K. Marx & F. Engels, Collected Works, vol. V (London, 1975), p. 37 (The German Ideology).

11 C. Wright Mills, The Marxists (Harmondsworth, 1969), p. 120.

12 Marx, Capital, vol. I (Pelican), p. 91.

13 K. Marx, *Surveys from Exile* (Harmondsworth, 1973), pp. 24–5; 319–35.
14 Marx & Engels, *Collected Works*, vol. V, p. 439 (*The German Ideology*); K. Marx & F. Engels, *The Communist Manifesto* (Harmondsworth, 1970), p. 94; Marx, *Capital*, vol. I (Pelican), p. 930.
15 T. Shanin (ed.), *Late Marx and the Russian Road* (London, 1983), especially pp. 134–9.
16 K. Marx, *Pre-capitalist Economic Formations* (London, 1975), pp. 32–5.
17 L. Trotsky, *The Permanent Revolution, and Results and Prospects* (London, 1971), pp. 115–19; Mills, *The Marxists*, pp. 268–70.
18 P. Abrams, *Historical Sociology* (Shepton Mallet, 1982), p. xiii.
19 Carew Hunt, *The Theory and Practice of Communism*, pp. 72–3.
20 Marx, *Capital*, vol. I (Pelican), p. 92.
21 K. Marx & F. Engels, *Collected Works*, vol. IV (London, 1975), p. 79 (*The Holy Family*).
22 Ibid., p. 93. See also K. Marx, *The Poverty of Philosophy* (Moscow, 1973), p. 100.
23 Marx, *Surveys From Exile*, p. 146.
24 M. M. Postan, *The Medieval Economy and Society* (London, 1972), pp. 105–7, 151–3.
25 R. H. Hilton, *The Decline of Serfdom in Medieval England* (London, 1969), p. 57; R. Brenner, 'Agrarian class structure and economic development in pre-industrial Europe', *Past and Present* 70 (1976), pp. 51–2.
26 Carew Hunt, *The Theory and Practice of Communism*, pp. 72–3.
27 I. Deutscher, *The Prophet Armed* (Oxford, 1954), p. vii.
28 L. Trotsky, *The History of the Russian Revolution* (London, 1967), vol. I p. 65; vol. III, pp. 148; 310–11.
29 Carew Hunt, *The Theory and Practice of Communism*, p. 77.
30 J. Baechler, *The Origins of Capitalism* (Oxford, 1975), p. 24.
31 Marx, *The Poverty of Philosophy*, p. 72.
32 Marx, *Capital*, vol. I (Pelican), Chs. 27–31. (Quotation from pp. 915–16.)
33 R. Brenner, 'Agrarian class structure', pp. 68–9.
34 R. Miliband, *Class Power and State Power* (London, 1983), Ch. 1; H. Draper, *Karl Marx's Theory of Revolution*, volume I (New York, 1977), Chs. 11–23.
35 E. P. Thompson, *The Poverty of Theory* (London, 1978), p. 384; R. Johnson, 'Reading for the best Marx: history writing and historical abstraction', in R. Johnson, G. McLennan, B. Schwarz and D. Sutton (eds.), *Making Histories* (London, 1982), pp. 153–201.
36 G. A. Cohen, *Karl Marx's Theory of History: A Defence* (Oxford, 1978); W. H. Shaw, *Marx's Theory of History* (London, 1978); W. H. Shaw, ' "The handmill gives you the feudal lord": Marx's technological determinism', *History of Theory* XVIII (1979), pp. 155–76; J. McMurtry, *The Structure of Marx's World View* (Princeton, 1978).
37 K. Marx, *A Contribution to the Critique of Political Economy* (London, 1971), pp. 19–23.
38 R. H. Tawney, *Religion and the Rise of Capitalism* (Harmondsworth, 1972, first edn 1926).
39 P. Sweezy, 'A rejoinder', in R. H. Hilton et al., *The Transition from Feudalism to Capitalism* (London, 1976), pp. 33–56; R. Brenner, 'The origins of capitalist development: a critique of neo-Smithian Marxism', *New Left Review* 104 (July–August 1977), pp. 38–53.
40 See, for instance: C. Bettelheim, *Class Struggles in the U.S.S.R., 1917–23*, (Hassocks, 1976), pp. 23–9.

CHAPTER 2

Forces and relations of production

The first step in our argument must be to establish the meaning of the key terms in Marx's theory of social structure and social change. Marx's own use of these terms was notoriously casual and, as a result, his followers and interpreters have had to offer their own definitions, which have differed considerably. Given the variety of definitions available and the range of opinion about the casual links between the elements of the social structure, it often seems as if being a 'Marxist' involves a commitment to a certain vocabulary, rather than to a distinct body of 'scientific' concepts. The range of Marxisms on offer makes a mockery of any simple choice between Marxist and 'bourgeois' history.

The productive forces

The works of Cohen and McMurtry have clearly established the meaning of the 'productive forces' in Marx's writings. A productive force is 'anything that is, or can be, used to make a material use value', the latter being any product with utility.[1] A productive force is thus a facility 'capable of use by a producing agent in such a way that production occurs (partly) as a result of its use'.[2] The nature of the productive forces may be clearly seen in three main elements of the labour process outlined by Marx in volume I of *Capital*:

1 Instruments of production

An instrument of production is anything that a producer works with in order to alter the form of a raw material. This category includes tools (such as looms or fulling mills), but also fuels used to power these instruments and the buildings which contain the instruments of

17

production. An instrument of production is thus a 'thing or complex of things which the labourer interposes between himself and the object of his labour which serves as a conductor, directing his activity into that object'.[3]

2 Raw materials

Together with the instruments of production, raw materials may be labelled as means of production, as distinct from work, the third component of the productive forces. Raw materials are, of course, the elements of the production process whose nature is intentionally changed in order to produce a material use value. Raw materials may have a number of alternative uses. 'Corn, for example, is a raw material for millers, starch manufacturers, distillers and cattle breeders.'[4] A particular productive force may serve as both a raw material and an instrument of production. Thus in the fattening of cattle the animal is both a raw material and 'an instrument for the production of manure'.[5] Similarly the product of one labour process may become an instrument of production for another process. Machine tools, for instance, are both produced by and, in turn, function as instruments of production. 'Whether a use value is to be regarded as raw material, as an instrument of labour or as a product, this is entirely determined by its function in the labour process ... as its position changes, so does its determining characteristics.'[6]

3 Work

Marx defines the labour process as 'purposeful activity aimed at the production of use values'.[7] The labour process thus not only involves the use of means of production (instruments of labour and raw materials), but also human action, 'purposeful activity of man, that is work itself'.[8] Physical labour is an obvious candidate for inclusion in the productive forces; skills, particularly technological and scientific knowledge, are more problematical. Some commentators see science, along with all other ideas, as part of society's superstructure, as opposed to the 'material' base.[9] Yet Marx himself was quite explicit in including science and ideas as elements in the production process, as a 'direct force of production' and even as the 'most solid form of wealth'.[10] Indeed, for Marx it is the role of consciousness which is the distinguishing feature of human labour. 'A bee puts to shame many an architect in the construction of her cells. But what distinguishes the worst architect from the best of bees is this, that the architect raises his structure in imagination before he erects it in reality. At the end of every labour process we get a

18

result that already existed in the imagination of the labourers at its commencement.'[11] In other words, the fact that technological knowledge is made up of ideas does not mean that it is part of the superstructure. The distinction between 'base' and 'superstructure' is not the distinction between the material and the mental, nor is it a distinction between distinct institutions. The difference between the two is that of function. In so far as scientific knowledge serves as part of the production process it may be regarded as part of the productive forces, as separate from society's superstructure.[12]

Relations of production, surplus labour and exploitation

Relations of production may be defined in two main ways. Firstly, they determine access to society's productive forces. For instance, modern wage labourers only have access to the means of production when they are employed by a capitalist. The medieval craftsman, by contrast, would often own his own tools and raw materials. Secondly, society's relations of production determine the form of redistribution of the product of the labour process, i.e. society's wealth. We may imagine two craftsmen carrying out identical tasks, such as making furniture. One may be an employee in a workshop, the other an independent craftsman selling his own products on the market. The relations of production in which the employee is involved give him access to society's wealth in the form of wages; the independent craftsman, by contrast, is the owner of the goods which he produces and his income consists of profit from his sales. As a result, society's relations of production may have two forms. They may be relations between a person (or group of persons) and another person (or group of persons), or they may be between a person (or group of persons) and a productive force (or group of productive forces). The relations between a capitalist employer and his employees is a relation of production of the first type; the employer's ownership of raw materials or of a factory is a relationship of the second type.[13]

Marx distinguishes between relations of production by the specific form of appropriation of surplus labour which they involve. The meaning of surplus labour is clearly illustrated by the example of the Wallachian peasant given in volume I of *Capital*. In this example the land was divided into two parts, the demesne lands held by the lords, and the land occupied by the peasantry. In return for their holdings, the peasants were obliged to work three days a week on the lord's demesne. Surplus labour was not distinguished from necessary labour by the type of work involved. On the contrary, the tasks were similar on the land of both lord and peasant. The distinction lies in who obtained the benefit of the peasant's labour. For three days the peasant works on his own land 'for his own maintenance', for three days he works on the demesne, work which 'yields no equivalent to the labourer himself'. The work done for the lord, the surplus labour, is distinguished from the labour necessary for the peasant's own maintenance by time and place. Surplus labour thus appears in its most obvious 'independent and palpable form'.[14] The feudal mode of production not only involves the production of surplus labour, it is defined by the dominance of a specific form of surplus labour, feudal rent. This rent can take three forms, labour rent, rent in kind or rent in money. In all three forms the peasant hands over a proportion of his time for the lord's benefit.[15] Under capitalism Marx claims that the distinctive form of surplus labour is that of surplus value. For part of the week the worker produces commodities which, when sold, will produce the money needed to pay the capitalist's wage bill. During the remaining part of the week the labourer produces goods which, when sold, will form the basis of the capitalist's profit.[16] We may imagine a capitalist tenant-farmer employing wage labour to produce grain which is sold at a profit on the market. From his profits the tenant-farmer will be required to pay rent to a landlord. Under feudalism rent is surplus labour, under capitalism rent is a redistribution of the surplus value produced by capitalist relations of production.[17] The fact that 'rent' exists in both cases is of little importance. The form of surplus labour in each case is quite distinct.

Three warnings are necessary at this point. Firstly, Marx did not define necessary labour time in terms of the time needed to produce the minimum required for biological existence. On the contrary, he stressed that the number and extent of the labourer's wants are the products of social development and include a 'historical and moral element'.[18] The means of subsistence needed to reproduce labour-power will thus vary, according to time and place. Secondly, Marx did not only include the time needed to maintain the individual labourer in the time spent on necessary labour, but also the time needed to reproduce labour-power for future employment. Thus if we imagine a male labourer earning a family wage, this wage must not only cover the costs of his own subsistence (at a given historical level), but also the costs of maintaining a family and thus of reproducing the commodity of labour-power.[19] Finally, Marx claimed that his analysis of exploitation was not a moral criticism.

Exploitation under capitalism could be objectively expressed as a ratio between the time spent on necessary and on surplus labour.[20] This is the most problematic part of his argument since it is not apparent that 'surplus labour' is really a surplus. Feudal rent, for example, can be seen as a payment by the peasant for the public goods of justice and protection, rather than as a surplus over and above the peasant's needs. Capitalist profits can be seen as a payment for the use of the factor of capital, for the capitalist's management expertise, or as an incentive for the capitalist to risk investment, i.e. as a cost of production, rather than as a social surplus.[21] The problems involved in defining surplus labour are discussed in detail below.[22] For the moment we will use the phrase to mean the form taken by the income of the ruling class: feudal rents, capitalist profits, and so forth.

Finally, it should be noted that in his early writings Marx used the phrase 'forms of intercourse' to refer to the relations of production. In The German Ideology (1845–6), it is society's forms of intercourse which are said to act as fetters on the growth of the productive forces, thus creating social revolution. In the 1859 'Preface' Marx repeats the same claim, but refers to the social fetters on the productive forces as 'relations of production', the term adopted by later Marxists and commentators on Marx.[23]

Work relations

The first major problem of definition of Marx's concepts comes with work relations, i.e. the division of labour within a factory or other unit of production. Should these relations be included in the relations of production? Or in the forces of production? Or are they a separate category? For Shaw, work relations are part of the relations of production. This 'would seem to be implied by the term (work relation) itself'.[24] However, we are not discussing the literal implications of 'terms', but rather attempting to establish how certain concepts may be used in historical analysis. In this light it is not useful to categorise work relations as a relation of production. It is true that Marx may certainly be quoted to this effect, as in The Communist Manifesto, where he says that 'the bourgeoisie cannot exist without constantly revolutionizing the intruments of production and thereby the relations of production and with them the whole relations of society'.[25] In this instance Marx certainly uses the phrase 'relations of production' to refer to the work relations transformed by the advent of new instruments of production. But he also

21

distinguishes these work relations of production from the 'relations of society', which they are said to influence. There is no doubt that in production people enter relations with one another. It is of little use to merge these relationships, entered into during production, with the social relations of production, defined by the appropriation of a specific form of surplus labour. We are dealing with two quite distinct concepts. To use the same 'term' for both concepts can only lead to confusion.

There is a similar confusion in Balibar's claim that the productive forces are 'a connexion of a certain type within the mode of production, in other words, they, too, are a relation of production'.[26] Balibar argues that the productive forces 'are not really things' such as a hand mill or steam mill. Rather a society's productive forces can be defined as its whole mode of appropriation of nature, the system whereby raw materials are transformed into products. The productive forces are not the elements which make up the labour process (as defined above), but rather *how* these elements are combined. Thus it is the manufacturing system of early modern Europe, or the modern industrial system, which are productive forces, not any particular tool or element used within the system. Balibar's argument has a strong element of truth, although it is possible to combine a view of the productive forces as an entire system with one that identifies the elements which go to make up the system (instruments, raw materials and work). Also useful is Balibar's claim that the most interesting aspect of the productive forces is not their composition, but rather 'the rhythm and pattern of their development', although again we do not have to counterpose one view against the other.[27] Given that Balibar distinguishes the appropriation of nature (the productive forces) from the appropriation of surplus labour (the relations of production), it is strange that he should wish to assert that productive forces are a relation of production. In practice, Balibar continues to distinguish between the two concepts. He separates the earliest phase of capitalist industry, manufacture, based on human labour, from that following the Industrial Revolution where machinery, not human labour, determines the nature of the production process. Only in the latter case is there a 'correspondence' between the relations of production and specifically capitalist forces of production.[28] The validity of this view does not concern us here. We need simply notice that it makes little sense to talk of a 'correspondence' (or non-correspondence) between the productive forces and the relations of production, if the productive forces *are* a relation of production. The two categories are separate.

Cohen agrees that the work relations of production (which he labels 'material relations of production') must be clearly distinguished from the social relations of production, i.e. relationships between classes.[29] Cohen works with a three-storey model of society in which society's superstructure (the state, ideology) is determined by its relations of production. These relations of production are, in turn, determined by the more fundamental element of the productive forces. Cohen clearly distinguishes work relations from relations of production when he argues that the former 'belong alongside the productive forces as a substratum of the social relations of production'.[30] However, Cohen does not believe that the work relations should be included within the category of productive forces. For Cohen, the productive forces are the elements *owned* and *used* in the production process, rather than the entire way that the production process is organised, as it is for Balibar. He argues that a specific form of division of labour is not a productive force, although 'the *knowledge* of ways of organizing labour is a productive force', since that knowledge is an element which is owned by whoever owns the labour power which incorporates that knowledge. The division of labour itself is neither owned nor used in the production process.[31]

There are two possible objections to Cohen's view that the work relations are not part of the productive forces. Firstly, in what sense is knowledge 'owned' by those who use it and why must this be a requirement for something to be described as a productive force? In Adam Smith's famous example of the division of labour involved in pin-making does the employer actually *own* the knowledge of how the tasks are divided? Surely this would only be the case if the employer had a monopoly or patent on this particular idea?[32] Secondly, why can't we say that a specific division of labour is 'used' in the production of these pins? Cohen rightly argues that both steam mills and the knowledge of how to build steam mills are productive forces.[33] In that case why can't we allow that both the knowledge of a division of labour and the division of labour itself are productive forces? We are offered a choice between seeing the work relations as productive relations (Shaw, Balibar), as a distinct concept (Cohen), or as part of the productive forces, as McMurtry has argued.[34] The work relations of production are a fundamentally different concept from the social relations of production involved in the appropriation of surplus labour. Work relations are an inherent part of the organisation of the labour process and a vital influence on the productivity of labour. There seems to be no reason why work relations should not be included in the category of society's productive forces, as one of the elements used in the production process.

Mode of production

The concept of a mode of production has been central in recent debates on Marxist historiography, indeed the concept has been described as 'a base camp in the Arctic of theory from which the explorers may not depart for more than a hundred yards for fear of being lost in an ideological blizzard'.[35] Yet, despite this centrality, Marx himself used the term in at least two quite distinct ways. Firstly, 'mode of production' can simply mean a manner of producing, the way in which production is carried out. Thus Marx refers to the Mongols' mode of production as 'cattle breeding'.[36] In volume III of *Capital* Marx refers to the 'constant and daily revolutions in the mode of production' under capitalism.[37] Whether we like it or not, there are no daily revolutions in capitalism's class relations and it is clear that Marx is referring, here, to the organisation of the labour process. In a similar vein Marx refers to a mode of production as an 'industrial stage' and even to the mode of production 'in one sphere of industry'.[38]

However, Marxists do not normally use the term mode of production simply to refer to the technical manner of producing. Mode of production is more commonly used by Marxists to describe the wider 'social character of production'.[39] In *The Poverty of Philosophy*, for instance, Marx uses mode of production as a synonym for the '*relations* in which productive forces are developed' whereas in the examples given above mode of production is used to refer to the *forces* not the relations of production.[40] It is in this wider sense that Marx defines capitalism as a mode of production in which commodities are produced by means of the commodity of labour-power and where the production of surplus value is the aim and determining motive of production. It is this social definition of capitalism which allows us to distinguish it from the feudal mode of production.[41] The capitalist mode of production involves both the production of commodities and the production of surplus value, in other words the capitalist mode of production is a combination of productive forces with the specific type of relation of production which defines it.

It has been argued here that it is possible to give a coherent and consistent meaning to the basic terms of Marx's social theory. The key problem facing us is thus not that of definition, but rather that of determination and, in particular, the relationship between society's productive forces and its class relations. It is to this problem that we must now turn.

Notes

1 J. McMurtry, *The Structure of Marx's World View* (Princeton, 1978), p. 55.
2 G. A. Cohen, *Karl Marx's Theory of History: A Defence* (Oxford, 1978), p. 32.
3 K. Marx, *Capital*, vol. I (Harmondsworth, 1976, Pelican edn), p. 285.
4 Ibid., p. 288.
5 Ibid.
6 Ibid., p. 289.
7 Ibid., p. 290.
8 Ibid., p. 284.
9 M. M. Bober, *Karl Marx's Interpretation of History* (Cambridge, Mass., 1962), pp. 20–1; R. N. Carew Hunt, *The Theory and Practice of Communism* (Harmondsworth, 1969), p. 70.
10 K. Marx, *Grundrisse* (Harmondsworth, 1974), pp. 540; 699; 706; K. Marx, *Theories of Surplus Value*, Part III (London, 1972), pp. 266–7.
11 K. Marx, *Capital*, vol. I (London, 1977, Lawrence & Wishart edn), p. 174 (this translation is used here in preference to the Pelican edn, p. 284).
12 M. Godelier, 'Infrastructures, society and history', *New Left Review* 112 (November–December 1978), pp. 84–96.
13 Cohen, *Karl Marx's Theory of History*, p. 31.
14 Marx, *Capital*, vol. I (Pelican), pp. 345–8.
15 K. Marx, *Capital*, vol. III (London, 1979, Lawrence & Wishart edn), Ch. 47. Labour rent is the most palpable form of feudal surplus labour; rent in kind also hands over a proportion of the peasantry's crop, and hence labour time, to the lord. Money rent is only rent in kind in money form, the produce embodying the surplus labour time having been sold on the market.
16 Marx, *Capital*, vol. I (Pelican), pp. 324–5.
17 Marx, *Capital*, vol. III, pp. 625–6.
18 Marx, *Capital*, vol. I (Pelican), p. 275.
19 Ibid., p. 718.
20 Ibid., p. 326.
21 D. C. North & R. P. Thomas, 'The rise and fall of the manorial system', *Journal of Economic History* XXXI (1971), pp. 777–803; B. J. McCormick *et al.*, *Introducing Economics* (Harmondsworth, 1977), pp. 429–31.
22 See below, pp. 209–14.
23 K. Marx & F. Engels, *Collected Works*, vol. V (London, 1976), pp. 74, 82 (*The German Ideology*).
24 W. H. Shaw, *Karl Marx's Theory of History* (London, 1978), p. 25.
25 Ibid., pp. 30–1; K. Marx & F. Engels, *The Communist Manifesto* (Harmondsworth, 1970), p. 83.
26 L. Althusser & E. Balibar, *Reading Capital* (London, 1975), p. 235.
27 Ibid.
28 Ibid., pp. 236–41.
29 Cohen, *Karl Marx's Theory of History*, pp. 35; 111–14.
30 Ibid., p. 113.
31 Ibid. My emphasis.
32 A. Smith, *The Wealth of Nations*, books I–III (Harmondsworth, 1970), pp. 109–10.

33 Cohen, *Karl Marx's Theory of History*, pp. 32; 41.
34 McMurtry, *The Structure of Marx's World View*, p. 72.
35 E. P. Thompson, *The Poverty of Theory* (London, 1978), p. 346.
36 K. Marx, *A Contribution to the Critique of Political Economy* (London, 1971), p. 203.
37 Marx, *Capital*, vol. III, p. 263.
38 Ibid., p. 622; Marx & Engels, *Collected Works*, vol. V, pp. 43; 53 (*The German Ideology*); Marx, *Capital*, vol. I (Pelican), p. 505.
39 K. Marx, *Capital*, vol. II (Harmondsworth, 1978, Pelican edn), p. 196.
40 K. Marx, *The Poverty of Philosophy* (Moscow, 1973), p. 106. My emphasis.
41 Marx, *Capital*, vol. III, pp. 879–80. See also K. Marx, *Theories of Surplus Value*, part II (London, 1968), pp. 429–30.

CHAPTER 3

Marx's productive force determinism

The first step of our argument is to establish that Marx did assert the primacy of the productive forces in historical development, i.e. that 'the nature of the production relations of a society is explained by the level of development of the productive forces'.[1] We later proceed to offer a critique of Marx's position and of recent defences of it (Chapter 7) and then go on to give an alternative reading of Marx and of historical change (Chapter 8). Given the 'truly obsessional preoccupation' of recent theorists with doing up and undoing the concept of a mode of production, it may seem strange that it should be necessary to establish the nature of Marx's thought on the relationship between the productive forces and the relations of production.[2] Yet there are a number of conflicting opinions on this issue, differences which, we argue below, are the result of Marx's own contradictory views. For writers such as Bukharin, Cohen and McMurtry, productive force determinism is the essence of Marx's whole theory of history.[3] For others the problem is worth only a passing mention when outlining Marx's contribution to historical thought.[4] Other Marxists have gone further and denied both the validity of a productive force determinist reading of Marx and of productive force determinism as an explanation of historical change.[5] For Shaw, The Communist Manifesto is evidence that Marx held a technological or productive force determinist interpretation of history; for Rosenberg, the Manifesto is 'a definitive refutation of the view that Marx was a technological determinist'.[6] Given such denials of Marx's productive force determinism we will, unfortunately, need extensive quotation to show Marx did have an explicit productive force determinism and that it amounted to much more than a few passing comments and aphoristic assertions.[7]

The essence of productive force determinism is that the level of development of a society's productive forces explains the nature of its relations of production so that as the productive forces develop so society is obliged to change. Rather than going through Marx's works chronologically in order to illustrate his views, it is more useful to define the seven major elements of his productive force determinism as it is formulated from The German Ideology (1845–6) onwards. These seven points are then used as the outline for the critique of productive force determinism offered in Chapter 7. Throughout this discussion we need to distinguish two quite separate issues:

(1)   Was Marx a productive force determinist?
(2)   Is productive force determinism a logically tenable and empirically proven explanation of social structure and of historical change?
       We should not confuse these issues and argue that:
(a)   because Marx was a productive force determinist, the theory must be correct (Marx is always right) or
(b)   because this theory is not correct, Marx could not have held it (Marx is never wrong).

1 Human existence and human society are impossible without production.

> The first premise of all human existence, and therefore of all history … (is) that men must be in a position to live in order to 'make history'. But life involves before everything else eating and drinking, housing, clothing and various other things. The first historical act is thus the production of the means to satisfy these needs, the production of material life itself. And this is indeed an historical act, which today, as thousands of years ago must daily and hourly be fulfilled merely in order to sustain human life.[8]

> The writers of history have so far paid little attention to the development of material production which is the basis of all social life.[9]

The implication is, of course, that because the satisfaction of such needs is the fundamental pre-condition of human existence, they are somehow fundamental in historical causation.

2 Humans produce in a distinctive manner, a manner which distinguishes them from other animals.

> Men can be distinguished from animals by consciousness, by religion, or anything else you like. They themselves begin to distinguish themselves as soon as they begin to produce their means of subsistence.[10]

28

The use and construction of instruments of labour, although present in germ among certain species of animals, is characteristic of the specifically human labour process, and Franklin therefore defines man as a 'tool-making animal'.[11]

Labour is first of all, a process between man and nature, a process by which man, through his own actions, mediates, regulates and controls the metabolism between himself and nature. ... We are not dealing here with those first instinctive forms of labour which remain on the animal level. ... We presuppose labour in a form in which it is an exclusively human characteristic. A spider conducts operations which resemble those of a weaver and a bee would put many a human architect to shame by the construction of its honeycomb cells. But what distinguishes the worst architect from the best of bees is that the architect builds the cell in his mind before he contructs it in wax. ... Man not only effects a change in form in the materials of nature, he also realizes his own purpose in those materials.[12]

Engels put it more concisely:

The essential difference between human and animal society consists in the fact that animals at most collect while men produce.[13]

The first point of productive force determinism implied that production is the fundamental element in historical development because 'man' must produce before he can make history; this second point implies that because 'man' may be defined as a tool-making animal then production must have some causal primacy.

3.1 In general society's relations of production (or 'forms of intercourse') are determined by the level of development of the productive forces (the 'primacy thesis').

If points 1 and 2 merely imply the fundamental importance of production for human society then point 3.1 makes a more specific claim, i.e. that the nature of the production process calls into being certain specific relations of production. It is this concept which Cohen labels the 'primacy thesis'.[14] As this thesis is the essence of productive force determinism it requires the most detailed supporting quotation. The German Ideology (1845–6) is the first work in which Marx develops this systematic productive force determinist reading of historical development:

Definite individuals who are productively active in a definite way enter into these definite social and political relations. Empirical observation must in each separate instance bring out empirically, and without any mystification and speculation, the connection of the social and political structure with production. The social structure and the state are continually evolving out of the life process of definite individuals, however of these individuals, not as they may appear in their own or other people's imaginations but as they *actually* are i.e. as they act, produce materially and hence as they work under definite material limits, presuppositions and conditions independent of their will.[15]

Marx here suggests that we can conceive of individuals in production, who then enter into social relations. Later he was to suggest, however, that 'whenever we speak of production ... what is meant is always production at a definite stage of social development – production by social individuals'.[16] That it is impossible to conceive of a moment of pure production which anticipates man's entry into social relations is one of the main criticisms of productive force determinism offered below. We must, however, first establish Marx's productive force determinism before giving a critique of it.

One of Marx's most famous claims is that his conception of history 'relies on expounding the real process of production – starting from the material production of life itself – and comprehending the form of intercourse connected with *and created by* this mode of production i.e. civil society in its various stages'.[17] In other words, the material production of life (here described as the mode of production) creates distinct forms of social intercourse, or civil society. Marx is quite specific that it is the 'aggregate of productive forces accessible to men (which) determines the condition of society, hence the "history of humanity" must always be studied and treated in relation to the history of industry and exchange'.[18] Again and again Marx stresses that certain forms of social relations correspond to a definite stage of the productive forces:

> What appears accidental to a later age as opposed to an earlier ... is a form of intercourse which corresponds to a definite stage of development of the productive forces. The relation of the productive forces to the forms of intercourse is the relation of the form of intercourse to the occupation or activity of the individuals.[19]

> Civil society embraces the whole material intercourse of individuals within a given stage of the development of the productive forces.[20]

> Rent of land, profit, etc., these actual forms of existence of private property are social relations corresponding to a definite stage of production.[21]

> In small scale industry and all agriculture up till now property is the necessary consequence of the existing instruments of production.[22]

Marx thus has a three-tier model of society in which the productive forces create certain relations of production to which correspond, in turn, specific forms of the state.[23] Similarly:

> Men are the producers of their conceptions, ideas etc., real active men as they are conditioned by a definite development of their productive forces and of the intercourse corresponding to these.[24]

Marx goes on to criticise those thinkers who divorce society's ruling ideas 'from the ruling individuals and, above all, from the relations which result from a given stage of the mode of production'.[25] Again Marx distinguishes the mode of production (meaning here the production process) from the social relations produced by it.

The German Ideology remained unpublished during Marx and Engels's lifetimes and Marx later remarked that, having achieved self-clarification, he and Engels left the manuscript to the gnawing criticism of the mice. ('In fact the manuscript as it survives does bear considerable traces of mice's teeth.')[26] We may be tempted to disregard the claims of this early, unpublished manuscript (although the failure to have the manuscript published was not through lack of effort on the part of Marx and Engels), particularly as Engels later remarked that this work only proved 'how incomplete our knowledge of economic history still was at that time'.[27] Unfortunately the productive force determinism of The German Ideology cannot be dismissed as a youthful aberration as Marx continued to repeat these claims throughout his intellectual career.

Having come to terms with Feuerbach and the Young Hegelians in The German Ideology Marx next took issue with the works of the French socialist Proudhon. His critique of Proudhon, The Poverty of Philosophy (1847), and the letters associated with it, are amongst the clearest expressions of productive force determinism and it is in The Poverty of Philosophy that Marx gives one of the most famous statements of his theory:

> M. Proudhon the economist understands very well that men make cloth, linen or silk materials in definite relations of production. But what he has not understood is that these definite social relations are just as much produced by men as linen, flax etc. Social relations are closely bound up with productive forces. In acquiring new productive forces men change their mode of production and in changing their mode of production, in changing their way of earning a living, they change all their social relations. The hand-mill gives you society with the feudal lord; the steam-mill, society with the industrial capitalist.[28]

Yet again mode of production is used here to refer to the manner of producing, the way in which men earn their living, and it is change in the production process which is the dynamic agent in historical change, both creating specific relations of production and then calling new relations into being:

> The relations in which productive forces are developed are anything but eternal laws, they correspond to a definite development of men and of their productive forces and ... a change in men's productive forces necessarily brings about a change in their relations of production.[29]

Marx develops his critique of Proudhon in a letter to Annenkov of December 1846 where he argues that although Proudhon identified progress in history, he could not explain this progress. Marx thus offered his own explanation of social progress:

> Assume a particular state of development in the productive forces of man and you will get a particular form of commerce and consumption. Assume a particular stage of development in production, commerce and consumption and you will have a corresponding social constitution, a corresponding organisation of the family, of orders or of classes, in a word a corresponding civil society.[30]

> A history of humanity takes shape which is all the more a history of humanity as the productive forces develop of man and therefore his social relations have developed.[31]

Marx anticipates modern productive force determinists in presenting the necessary correspondence of relations of production to the forces of production as a functional relationship, i.e. a relationship which explains the existence of particular production relations by their socially beneficial effects:

> Men never relinquish what they have won, but this does not mean that they never relinquish the social form in which they have acquired certain productive forces. On the contrary in order that they may not be deprived of the result attained and forfeit the fruit of civilization, they are obliged, from the moment when the form of their commerce no longer corresponds to the productive forces acquired, to change all their social forms. I am using the word commerce here in the widest sense, as we use *verkehr* in German (i.e. by 'commerce', Marx means form of social intercourse – S.R.).[32]

Marx criticises Proudhon for not recognising that as men live, they develop certain relations with one another and that 'the nature of these relations must necessarily change with the change and growth of the productive forces'. Proudhon falls into the trap of regarding economic categories as eternal when, in fact, they are only laws for specific historical epochs, i.e. 'for a definite stage of development of the productive forces'.[33] Marx here bases his productive force determinism on two claims which he himself was later to refute: firstly that we can conceive of 'men' who produce and then enter into social relations, when in fact production is itself a social act; and secondly, that a particular stage of historical development may be identified by the level of development of the productive forces.[34]

Yet although Marx was later to question these assumptions he continued, nevertheless, to offer a critique of Proudhon based on a productive force determinism. Thus in 1865 when J. B. Schweitzer wrote to him for his opinion of Proudhon, Marx reproduced his criticisms of 1846, i.e. that Proudhon: 'shares the illusions of speculative philosophy in his treatment of economic categories ... instead of conceiving them as the theoretical expression of historical relations of production corresponding to a particular stage of development of material production'.[35] At the end of 1847 Marx put his historical theory into popular form in a number of lectures to the German Workers Society in Brussels. Once more it was the productive forces which were identified as the fundamental and dynamic element in social change: 'The social relations of production change, are transformed with the change and development of the material means of production, the productive forces.'[36]

It is argued below that in the Grundrisse and Capital Marx offers an implicit critique of his own productive force determinism but, nevertheless, it would be quite wrong to present the evolution of Marx's thought as a unilinear development away from his earlier claims. On the contrary, Marx's works of the 1850s and 1860s continue to repeat his earlier claims for the importance of the productive forces. Even those Marxists who reject productive force determinism are prepared to concede that the 1859 'Preface' to A Contribution to the Critique of Political Economy is an avowedly productive force determinist text and this work is central to the interpretation of Marx offered by writers such as Cohen, Shaw and McMurtry. We will return to the 'Preface' later. Enough, for now, to note its explicit claim that: 'In the social production of their existence men invariably enter into definite relations of production which are independent of their will, namely relations *appropriate to a given stage in the development of their productive forces.*'[37] It is hardly surprising that Engels, in his review of this work, should stress Marx's 'revolutionary discovery' that 'the process of social, political and intellectual life is altogether necessitated by the mode of production of material life' – although it should be noted that Marx himself was in the fortunate position of being able to dictate the main points of this review.[38]

We have already seen that in Capital Marx approvingly cites Franklin's definition of man as the 'tool-making animal'. From this definition of man it follows that: 'Relics of bygone instruments of production possess

the same importance for the investigation of extinct economic formations of society as do fossil bones for the determination of extinct
species of animals. It is not what is made but how and by what instruments of labour that distinguishes different economic epochs.'[39] Marx
quite clearly compares instruments of production to the bones of animals which determine its specific structure. It may be objected that
when Marx claims that what distinguishes the different economic formations of society is 'how' they produce, this 'how' could include social
relations, i.e. that this phrase cannot be used to support a productive
force determinist reading of Marx. However, Marx makes it clear that by
'how' he is referring to the techique of production when he adds: 'The
least important commodities of all for the *technological* comparison of different epochs of production are articles of real luxury.'[40] Marx follows
the point to its logical empirical conclusion that:

> Writers of history have so far paid very little attention to the develop-
> ment of material production which is the basis of all social life, and
> therefore, of all real history. But prehistorical times at any rate have been
> classified on the basis of the investigations of natural science rather than
> so-called historical research. Pre-history has been divided, according to
> the materials used to make tools and weapons, into the Stone Age,
> Bronze Age and the Iron Age.[41]

Marx's point follows logically from his earlier claims; the problem is, as
we shall see, that historians (Marxist or otherwise) have been able to
make little use of Marx's advice.

Finally, it should be noted that Engels made a number of general
claims which repeat Marx's assertions of the primacy of the productive
forces in social development. Thus in 1884 when writing to Kautsky
Engels claimed that:

> Crop-rotation, artificial fertilizer, steam engine and power loom are insep-
> arable from capitalist production just as the tools of the savage or barbar-
> ian are inseparable from his production. The tools of the savage condition
> his society as much as the new ones condition capitalist society.[42]

In a letter of 1894 Engels clarified the nature of his and Marx's views on
historical materialism:

> By economic relations, which we regard as the determining basis of the
> history of society, we understand the manner in which men in a given
> society produce their means of subsistence and exchange the products
> (in so far as a division of labour exists). They comprise therefore the
> entire technique of production and transport. According to our
> conception this technique also determines the mode of exchange and,

furthermore, of the distribution of products and hence, after the dissolution of gentile society, also the division into classes, and consequently
of lordship and servitude and consequently the state, politics and law.[43]

Engels thus distinguishes between production on the one hand and the
distribution of society's product on the other. Production is the dominant element, the basis for the distribution of products and therefore of
classes. Engels makes the same distinction in his Prefaces to the later edi-
tions of the Communist Manifesto when he refers to 'economic production',
or the 'prevailing mode of production and exchange' on the one hand,
and 'the structure of society' or 'social organisation' on the other, the latter 'necessarily arising' or 'necessarily following' from the former.[44]
Recent critics of the French Marxist, Althusser, have berated him for
holding a 'Ricardian' conception of production and social relations, in
which production is seen purely in technical terms and social relations
are relegated to the sphere of distribution. He thus separates the 'economic' from the social, failing to realise that, for Marx, production is
simultaneously the production of things and of social relations. We are
not concerned here with the accuracy of this criticism of Althusser.[45]
What is interesting is that Marx and Engels's productive force determinism involves just such a 'Ricardian' view of production, a view where
individuals enter into production and then create corresponding social
relations. Neither should it be thought that the identification of social
organisation with 'distribution' can be shrugged off as a distortion
propagated by Engels after Marx's death. Not only is the distinction
between production and social relations the implicit basis of Marx's productive force determinism, it is specifically referred to in The German Ideology where industry, commerce, production and exchange 'determine
distribution, the structure of the different classes of society'.[46] It is
argued below that Marx did develop a critique of this Ricardian view of
production, in other words that Marx offers a critique of the productive
force determinism which he himself puts forward. Our aim once more,
should not be to attempt to identify the integrity or unity of Marx's
work, but rather to note 'the multiplicity and diversity of its possible
meanings, its incompleteness, the omissions which it displays but cannot describe, and above all its contradictions'.[47]

3.2 Marx not only makes the general claim that society's relations of production are determined by the level of development of its productive forces. He illustrates this claim with a number of historical examples.

As we have seen, Marx argued that the division of prehistory into the Stone, Bronze and Iron Ages should be seen as support for his belief in the determining role of the productive forces. *The German Ideology* offers a more detailed analysis of human history in terms of the growth of society's division of labour, i.e. of industry and agriculture, of town and country-side, within crafts, between nations. The division of labour is a crucial concept in tracing the evolution of society because it provides a measure of development of society's productive forces. 'Each new productive force ... causes a further development of the division of labour.' The stage of development reached by the productive forces and the division of labour in turn determines the 'whole internal structure of the nation'.[48] Marx goes on to illustrate his theory with specific historical examples.

I Primitive communism

Marx argues that the growth of society's productive forces leads to the emergence of specific forms of property or, in other words, specific forms of 'the power of disposing of the labour power of others'.[49] Thus

> The first form of property is tribal property. It corresponds to the undeveloped stage of production in which a people live by hunting and fishing, by cattle-raising or, at the most, by agriculture. In the latter case it presupposes a great mass of uncultivated stretches of land. The division of labour is at this stage very elementary – and is confined to a further extension of the natural division of labour existing in the family.[50]

It was of course Engels, not Marx, who presented the most detailed survey of human prehistory in *The Origin of the Family, Private Property and the State* (1884). Engels claimed that his book was 'the fulfilment of a bequest', the completion of Marx's intention to publicise the conclusions of Lewis Morgan's *Ancient Society* (1877) which had independently rediscovered the materialist conception of history discovered by Marx in the 1840s.[51] Morgan offered a much more complex picture of prehistory than that suggested by the division into Stone, Bronze and Iron Ages which Marx had accepted in volume I of *Capital*, but he retained a division based upon the prevailing technique of producing the necessities for human existence. Thus 'The great epochs of human progress have been identified, more or less directly, with the enlargement of the sources of subsistence.'[52] Morgan divided social evolution into three epochs, savagery, barbarism and civilisation, and subdivided the first two of these epochs into lower, middle and upper stages, 'according to the progress made in the production of the means of subsistence'. Under savagery, for instance, humanity lives by hunting and gathering whilst under barbarism the characteristic feature is domestication of animals and the cultivation of plants. Technology is also used to identify the subdivisions of savagery and barbarism. Thus the middle stage of savagery is distinguished by the use of fire, the lower stage of barbarism by the introduction of pottery, and so on. It was precisely the fact that these stages are based on the evolution of production which, for Engels, made Morgan's findings incontestable.[53]

II Ancient society

The second stage of social evolution identified in The German Ideology is that of ancient communal and state property. In this society several tribes merge to create a city, a city which possesses slaves as a form of communal property. Communal property does, however, gradually give way to private property. This historical epoch is, in a sense, contradictory. The productive forces have advanced and a division of labour emerges, which is reflected in the clash of interests between town and country, between states, between industry and maritime commerce, and between freeman and slaves.[54] On the other hand, although the productive forces have advanced beyond the earliest forms of tribal society, they are still at a relatively low level of development, so that each tribe 'had either to be a slave or possess slaves'.[55]

Engels later made the same link between the development of the productive forces and the appearance of slavery:

> In order to make use of a slave, a man must possess two kinds of things; first the instruments and materials for his slave's labour; and secondly the minimum necessities of life for him. Therefore before slavery becomes possible, a certain level of development of production must already have been reached and a certain inequality of distribution must already have appeared. And before slave labour could become the dominant mode of production in a whole social group, an even far higher increase in production, trade and accumulation of wealth was essential.[56]

Engels's The Origin of the Family, Private Property and the State develops The German Ideology's claim that human history is the history of the growth of the productive forces, hence of the division of labour and thus of social classes:

The increase of production in all branches (under barbarism – S.R.) – cattle breeding, agriculture, domestic handicrafts – enabled human labour power to produce more than was necessary for its maintenance. At the same time it increased the amount of work that daily fell to the lot of every member of the gens or household community or single family. The addition of more labour power became desirable. This was furnished by war; captives were made slaves. Under the given historical conditions, the first great social division of labour, by increasing the productivity of labour, that is wealth, and enlarging the field of production, necessarily carried slavery in its wake. Out of the first great social division of labour arose the first division of society into two classes: masters and slaves, exploiters and exploited.[57]

As productivity continued to increase, the division between master and slave became more general and was joined by the growing distinction between rich and poor:

The second great division of labour took place: handicrafts separated from agriculture. The continued increase of production and with it the increased productivity of labour enhanced the value of human labour power. Slavery which had been a nascent and sporadic factor in the preceding stage, now becomes an essential part of the system …

The division of production into two great branches, agriculture and handicrafts, gave rise to production for exchange, the production of commodities; and with it came trade … the distinction between rich and poor was added to that between freeman and slaves – with the new division of labour came a new division of society into classes.[58]

III Feudalism

If the slave labour of the Ancient World reflected the lack of development of the productive forces, then so too did the third form of property identified in *The German Ideology*, the feudal property of the medieval era. Feudal propery took two forms: landed property with serf labour attached to it and the small capital and personal labour of the urban craftsman who commands the labour of journeymen. Both varieties of feudal property corresponded to the undeveloped state of society's productive forces and the consequent limited extent of the division of labour: 'The organisation of both (forms of feudal property) was determined by the restricted conditions of production – the scanty and primitive cultivation of the land and the craft type of industry.' The strip system used in agriculture hindered the introduction of more productive techniques and a new division of labour, whilst in the towns a production based on crafts allowed for little division of labour within, or between, the branches of industry.[59] Marx repeats his association of feudal property with a lack of development of social productivity in his analysis of feudal rent in volume III of *Capital*. He argues that any mode of production requires regulation and order so that social stability may be maintained:

> Under backward conditions of the production process as well as the corresponding social relations, it achieves this form (i.e. regulation and order – S.R.) by mere repetition of their very reproduction. . . .

> . . . However since this form of surplus labour, enforced labour, is based upon the imperfect development of all social productive powers and the crudeness of the methods of labour itself, it will naturally absorb a relatively much smaller proportion of the direct producers' total labour than under-developed modes of production, particularly the capitalist mode of production.[60]

Yet again, Marx posits a pre-existing social productivity, upon which particular forms of surplus labour (in this case feudal rent) are 'based'.

IV The 'Asiatic' mode

In *The German Ideology* Marx distinguishes between the earliest form of tribal property, the communal state property of the ancient city, which evolved into a mode of production based on slavery, and the feudal form of property, based on an enserfed peasantry paying rent to the nobility. Each of these social forms corresponds to a specific stage in the evolution of the productive forces and the social division of labour.[61] However, nowhere in *The German Ideology* does Marx develop the concept of the Asiatic mode of production, the final form of property which we need to consider in our survey of pre-capitalist modes of production. Perry Anderson has shown that 'no wholly consistent or systematic account of "the Asiatic mode of production" can be derived' from Marx and Engels's writings on India and China since their interpretation of Asian society oscillated around a number of concepts.[62] Nevertheless, we can identify the central feature of this mode of production as a situation where the peasant producers are not confronted by a private landowner, but rather are subordinated directly to the state: 'then rent and taxes coincide, or rather there exists no tax which differs from . . . ground-rent'.[63] It is this identification of tax and rent which defines the Asiatic mode despite the problems associated with Marx's uncertainties about the prevalence of hydraulic agriculture, a state monopoly of land or tribal communal property.

Marx certainly claims in general that the Asiatic form of property relations is determined by a specific form of development of the productive forces and the division of labour:

> In the last instance the community (Marx is speaking in general terms here – S.R.) and the property resting upon it can be reduced to a specific stage in the development of the forces of production of the labouring subjects – to which correspond specific relations of these subjects with each other and with nature. ... Property – and this applies to its Asiatic, Slavonic, ancient classical and Germanic forms – therefore originally signifies a relation of the working (producing) subject (or a subject reproducing himself) to the conditions of production or reproduction as his own. *Hence according to the conditions of production, property will take different forms.*[64]

Marx repeats this claim in volume I of *Capital*, where he says that the Asiatic and ancient modes of production are 'the result of a low level of development of the productive power of labour'.[65] He also specifies the particular division of labour based upon this low level of development of the productive forces, which forms the basis for the Asiatic mode. The Ancient World had been marked by the development of a division of labour and of social interests between town and country.[66] The Asiatic mode of production, however, is based on a combination of manufacture and agriculture within the small community which thus becomes self-sustaining and contains within itself all conditions of production and surplus production.[67] As a result of its self-sustaining nature based upon the village community, the Asiatic mode 'necessarily survives longest and most stubbornly' of all the communal forms of property, its simplicity and undeveloped division of labour 'supplies the key to the riddle of the unchangeability of Asiatic societies'.[68]

V Capitalism

Marx's whole concern in *Capital* was to prove that capitalism was not an eternal social order which had always existed and which would endure indefinitely. His aim was to show that capitalism, like all earlier class societies, was historically transitory. It had arisen at a specific time, had its own distinct laws of development and would (Marx confidently predicted) eventually disappear in the same way that feudalism had been superseded by capitalism.[69] It will come as no surprise to the reader that Marx associated the existence of capitalism with a definite level of the development of the productive forces, just as the tribal, ancient, Asiatic and feudal modes had corresponded to specific stages in the development of material production. Thus the appearance of modern capitalist agriculture is based upon the introduction of new social relations, i.e. the relations between capital and wage labour. In turn this relationship:

'pre-supposes conditions which rest on a certain development of industry, of trade and of science, in short of the forces of production'.[70] This correspondence between the forces and relations of production is not confined to agriculture for 'in general, production resting on capital and wage labour differs from other modes of production not merely formally but equally pre-supposes a total revolution and development of the productive forces'.[71] Marx identifies capitalism as a particularly dynamic mode of production which dramatically accelerates the growth of society's productivity. However, capitalism does not only drive forwards the productive forces, it also 'pre-supposes a certain given historical development of the productive forces'.[72] The basis and premise for the formation of capital as a social relation is thus 'a particular stage in the development of the material forces of production'.[73] The association of capitalism with a specific level of development of the productive forces is discussed further under point 5.2 below.

4 The fourth main claim of productive force determinism is that the productive forces have an inherent tendency to develop throughout history (the 'development thesis').[74]

It is crucial for the case made by writers such as Cohen that the productive forces not only do develop throughout history, but also that they should have an *inherent* tendency to develop.[75] If this were not the case, if for instance the development of the productive forces was determined by the relations of production or by ideas from society's superstructure, then the whole case for the primacy of the productive forces in social evolution would collapse and some other factor would have to be recognised as the key determinant in human history.

McMurtry claims that Marx emphasises the accumulation of the productive forces throughout history more emphatically and more repeatedly than any other principle.[76] The claim is an exaggeration, but, even if it were true, it would still be wrong to say that Marx and Engels had a *theory* of why the productive forces should advance. Marx and Engels certainly assumed that the productive forces developed, they occasionally asserted as much, but they never *explained* why this should be the case. Thus in The Poverty of Philosophy Marx asserts that 'There is a continual movement of growth in productive forces, of destruction of social relations, of formation in ideas; the only immutable thing is the abstraction of movement.'[77] In volume III of Capital Marx again asserts the growth of the forces of production:

> To the extent that the labour-process is solely a process between man and nature, its simple elements remain common to all social forms of development. But each specific historical form of this process further develops its material foundations and social forms. Whenever a certain stage of maturity has been reached, the specific social form is discarded and makes way for a higher one.[78]

Elsewhere Marx does not so much assert the growth of productive forces, as simply assume it. In *The German Ideology*, for instance, Marx argues that society's relations of production correspond to the level of development of its productive forces. It thus follows that the history of social forms is 'the history of the *evolving* productive forces taken over by each new generation and is therefore the history of the development of the forces and of the individuals themselves'.[79] That the productive forces 'evolve' and so 'necessarily bring about a change in their relations of production',[80] is simply taken for granted. At most Marx only describes this evolution: 'this development takes place spontaneously, i.e. it is not subordinated to a general plan of freely combined individuals, it proceeds from various locations, tribes, nations, branches of labour etc., each of which, to start with, develops independently of the others and only gradually enters into relation with the others'.[81] The 1859 'Preface' claims that in production men enter into relations of production 'appropriate to a given stage in the development of their material forces of production', but why the productive forces should develop is not explained, it is simply assumed as a premise of the argument.[82] Marx tells us that society's relations of production must adapt to the evolving productive forces so that society is not 'deprived of the fruits of civilisation, of the acquired productive forces', because 'men' will 'never relinquish what they have won', but this still does not explain why the productive forces evolved in the first place.[83] That the productive forces have evolved is taken as an empirical fact which is expressed in society's tendency towards an increasing division of labour, but Marx and Engels never show why the productive forces must evolve. This problem is considered below in our discussion of Cohen's 'development thesis'.[84]

5.1 Society's relations of production correspond to the level of development of its productive forces (3). These productive forces, however, have an inherent tendency to develop and change (4). *Eventually a time is reached when society's relations of production lag behind the productive forces and become fetters on the growth of society's productivity.* Thus in order that the productive forces may continue to develop, these *antiquated relations of production are cast aside and new relations of production are called into being.*

That the relations of production lag behind the evolution of the productive forces is, of course, a central assumption of productive force determinism, as it is the productive forces which are held to be the dynamic and determining feature of historical development. This clash between the forces and relations of production is, for Marx, the key to understanding human history: 'All collisions in history have their origin, according to our view, in the contradiction between the productive forces and the form of intercourse.'[85] Human history is said to consist of a succession of forms of social intercourse (tribal, ancient, feudal, capitalist, etc.). The 'coherence' of this development consists in the fact that 'an earlier form of intercourse which has become a fetter, is replaced by a new one corresponding to the more developed productive forces and hence to the mode of the self-activity of individuals – a form which in turn becomes a fetter and is replaced by another'.[86] The contradiction between the productive forces and the relations of production is not merely an economic phenomenon. Its effects are felt through all the levels of the social structure since it 'necessarily on each occasion bursts out in a revolution, taking on at the same time various subsidiary forms, such as all embracing collisions, collisions of various classes, contradictions of consciousness, battle of ideas, political struggle etc.'[87] There can be no doubt that the 1859 'Preface', that key text of productive force determinism, assumes that the productive forces are the dynamic element in human history which periodically cast aside their social constraints: 'At a certain stage of their development, the material productive forces come into conflict with existing relations of production. ... From forms of development of the productive forces these relations turn into their fetters. Then begins an era of social revolution.'[88] Whenever social production has reached this contradictory level:

> The specific historical form is discarded and makes way for a higher one. The moment of arrival of such a crisis is disclosed by the depth and breadth attained by the contradictions and antagonisms between the distribution relations, and thus the specific historical form of their corresponding production relations on the one hand and the productive forces, the production powers and their development of their agencies on the other hand. A conflict then ensues between the material development of production and its social form.[89]

Social change and political revolution are thus based on the clash of the productive forces with the social form with which they are no longer in accord.[90] It follows from these claims that a particular social class may be revolutionary at one stage of history, as it embodies new relations of production which allow the continued development of the productive forces, and then become reactionary as those relations become fetters on the further development of productivity:

> The conditions under which definite productive forces can be applied are the conditions of rule of a definite class of society, whose social power, deriving from its property, has its practical-idealistic expression in each case in the form of the state, and therefore, every revolutionary struggle is directed against a class which till then has been in power.[91]

5.2 Marx and Engels not only make the general claim that a society's relations of production periodically become fetters on the development of its productive forces. They also give concrete historical examples of the conflict between the forces and relations of production and its resolution through social revolution.

In *The German Ideology*, Marx argues that the class society grew out of the earliest forms of tribal society with their community property 'with the development of the division of labour, i.e. with the growth of the productive forces'.[92] It was, however, Engels who gave most attention to this transition from primitive communisim to class society in *The Origin of the Family, Private Property and the State*. Engels argues that the reproduction of life has a twofold character: economic production and the propagation of the species. Therefore:

> The less the development of labour, and the more limited its volume of production and, therefore, the wealth of society, the more preponderatingly does the social order appear to be dominated by ties of sex. However within this structure of society based on ties of sex the productivity of labour develops more and more; with it private property

and exchange, differences in wealth, the possibility of utilizing the labour power of others and thereby the basic class antagonism: new social elements, which strive in the course of generations to adapt the old structure of society to the new conditions until finally the incompatibility of the two leads to a complete revolution.[93]

In its assumption that the productive forces inherently develop and that this development calls new social relations into being, this passage is a classic expression of productive force determinism. Again it must be stressed that this is no distortion of Marx to be laid at the door of Engels. On the contrary, Engels merely applies to this specific historical instance the general scheme outlined in Marx's 1859 'Preface'.

Interestingly, Marx and Engels did not attempt to explain the transition from the Ancient to the feudal mode of production in terms of the growth of the productive forces. Indeed, they argued that the end of the Roman Empire was marked by a *decline* of the productive forces and of society's division of labour.[94] Marx's classic example of society casting off production relations which had become fetters on the growth of the productive forces, is that of the transition from the feudal to the capitalist mode of production. According to the *Communist Manifesto*, the bourgeoisie arose from within feudal society whether as a class oppressed by the feudal nobility, a self-governing commune or a taxable third estate of the monarchy. In other words:

> the means of production and of exchange, on whose foundation the bourgeoisie built itself up, were generated in feudal society. At a certain stage in the development of these means of production and exchange, the conditions under which feudal society produced and exchanged, the feudal organisation of agriculture and manufacturing industry, in one word the feudal relations of production became no longer compatible with the already developed productive forces; *they became so many fetters. They had* to be burst asunder; they were burst asunder.[95]

The passage contains all the central ingredients of productive force determinism: the assumption that the productive forces develop, the eventual transformation of the production relations into fetters on production and the assertion that in their conflict with these fetters the dynamic productive forces *have* to win out.

In the *Grundrisse* Marx specifies the forms of development of wealth which led to the dissolution of the feudal mode of production:

> The feudal system, for its part, foundered on urban industry, trade, modern agriculture (even as a result of individual inventions like gunpowder and the printing press). With the development of wealth – and

45

hence also new powers and expanded intercourse on the part of individuals – the economic conditions on which the community rested were dissolved, along with the political relations of the various constituents of the community which corresponded to these conditions.[96]

As we have seen, the feudal mode of production was distinguished by two forms of property: a structure of landownership based on serfdom and urban industry based on the individual craftsmen united into the guild system.[97] Both provided obstacles to the development of capitalism: the serf is tied to the soil and did not provide a reservoir of free labour power; the guild system with its regulations and protection of the individual craftsman similarly restricted the development of a free labour market. The rise of industrial capitalism thus saw the conflict of the new industrial potentates with the feudal lords on the one hand and the guild masters on the other: 'in this respect their conquest of social power appears as the fruit of a victorious struggle both against feudal lordship and its revolting prerogatives, and against the guilds and the fetters they laid on the free development of production and the free exploitation of man by man'.[98] It is hardly surprising that Lenin should consider that Marx's great achievement was the creation of a harmonious historical theory which showed 'how, *in consequence of the growth of the productive forces*, out of one system of social life another and higher one develops – how capitalism, for instance, grows out of feudalism'.[99]

6 The primacy of the productive forces lies essentially in their determination of society's relations of production. *They are, however, fundamental in another sense, since if the productive forces are the basis for the relations of production then these relations, in turn, are the basis of society's political and ideological superstructure.*

There has been much discussion of Marx's famous metaphor of 'base' and 'superstructure'.[100] It is often thought that Marx's metaphor presents us with a two-storey model of society with an economic base (the mode of production consisting of the relations and forces of production), and the political and intellectual superstructure consisting of political institutions, ideas and culture.[101] In fact Marx repeatedly claims that we can distinguish three 'levels' of society. As so often it is the 1859 'Preface' which gives this idea its clearest expression:

> In the social production of their existence, men invariably enter into definite relations which are independent of their will, namely relations

of production appropriate to a given stage in the development of the material forces of production. The totality of these relations of production constitutes the economic structure of society, the real foundation on which arises a legal and political superstructure and to which correspond definite forms of social consciousness.[102]

This familiar litany has long been an obstacle to thought, but careful readers will note that Marx does not say that the relations of production are *society*'s foundation. Rather, they are the foundation for legal and political superstructures and definite forms of social consciousness. Marx has, however, become involved in a misleading metaphor, for this 'foundation' turns out to have a foundation of its own. Just as the state and ideas correspond to class relations, so these relations correspond to a definite level of development of the productive forces.

As this point follows quite logically from the primacy of the productive forces, it will not require copious quotation in order to establish its importance. As we have seen, relations of production are said to arise out of the productive forces. A particular class achieves social dominance because its rule is most suitable for particular stages of the development of production. The state is therefore 'the form in which the individuals of a ruling class assert their common interests and in which the whole of the civil society of an epoch is epitomised'.[103] The modern state is thus the 'form of organisation which the bourgeoisie are compelled to adopt, both for internal and external purposes, for the mutual guarantee of their property and interests'.[104]

Marx not only applies his argument to the state, but also to ideology. Thus modern society with its extensive division of labour, where producers relate to each other through commodities expressed as homogeneous human labour, finds its most fitting religion in Christianity, and particularly Protestantism, with its cult of abstract man. In less developed forms of production, relations between men do not take this abstract form and the narrowness of the relations between 'man' and 'man' and between 'man' and nature is 'reflected in the ancient worship of nature, and in the other elements of tribal religions'.[105] We are not concerned here with the accuracy of Marx's analysis but, rather, to establish that he proposed a three-tier model of society consisting of production, social relations and ideological and political forms.

That ideas and political institutions are rooted in the economic structure of society needs little elaboration, at this point, since we are concerned here with the relationship between the productive forces and the relations of production. The meaning and utility of Marx's claims for the social determination of the state and ideology are discussed in detail in Part III.

7 Finally, Marx claims that just as the feudal mode of production became a fetter on the growth of the productive forces, so *capitalism has become a barrier to the continued growth of the modern productive forces. The result is crisis for the capitalist mode of production and the creation of the basis for a higher stage of human development: the socialist mode of production.*

So far productive force determinism has been presented as a theory of historical evolution acceptable, in principle, to Marxists and non-Marxists alike. Marx's final claim leads us to the *political* implications of productive force determinism. It should, however, be noted that:

(1) It is possible to be a socialist even if one does not accept productive force determinism.

(2) It is possible to be a productive force determinist and yet reject Marx's prediction that the growth of the productive forces will lead to socialism. It could, for instance, be argued that the growth of industry leads to the continuation of exploitation, rather than its supersession.[106]

The political aspects of productive force determinism are more fully discussed below. Here we need only note why Marx believed that socialism would arise out of the development of capitalism itself. For Marx, capitalism and the rule of the bourgeoisie had become incompatible with the growth of the productive forces of society. The result would be crisis, revolution and the emergence of a new ruling class, the proletariat. Capitalism by its very nature propels the productive forces forwards and yet this very advance prepares the ground for new social relations. Thus 'the communist revolution will be guided not by the "social institutions of inventive socially-gifted persons" but by the productive forces'. It is the growth of the productive forces which capitalism itself brings about which makes possible the victory of socialism. In the past 'people won freedom for themselves each time to the extent that was dictated and permitted not by their ideal of man, but by their existing productive forces'.[107] In the past, however, the productive forces had been underdeveloped and so the abolition of private property: 'was impossible for the simple reason that the material conditions required were not present'.[108] It is the growth of the productive forces under capitalism which produces the 'material conditions of emancipation'. Capitalism by its very

48

nature 'strives towards the universal development of production and thus becomes the presupposition of a new mode of production … where the free, unobstructed, progressive and universal development of the forces of production is itself the presupposition of society'.[109]

Capitalism does not only create an abundance of wealth; this wealth appears in an increasingly socialised form, which makes the capitalist class superfluous to production. Money capital takes on a social character through banks; the supervisory tasks of the individual capitalist disappear with the growth of joint stock companies which employ their own managers.[110] Production is ever more based on social co-operation, as the productive forces grow and the division of labour increases. The capitalist class has become as unnecessary to society as the feudal lords were with the rise of capitalism.[111] In short, capitalism is marked by the increasing 'incompatibility of social production with capitalist appropriation'.[112]

That capitalism is a fetter on the growth of society's productive forces is one of Marx and Engels's recurring themes. As early as The German Ideology Marx argues that in the development of the productive forces of modern society 'there comes a stage when productive forces and means of intercourse are brought into being which, under the existing relations only cause mischief and are no longer productive but destructive forces'.[113] By 1848 Marx had optimistically decided that 'For many a decade past the history of industry and commerce is but the history of the revolt of the modern productive forces against modern conditions of production, against the property relations that are conditions for the existence of the bourgeoisie and its rule.'[114] The growth of the productive forces creates the commercial crises of capitalism, disorders created by the fetters on the growth of production, so that 'the weapons with which the bourgeoisie felled feudalism to the ground are now turned against the bourgeoisie itself'.[115] Engels later remarked that the state of economic development in 1848 was 'not, by a long way, ripe for the elimination of capitalist production' and that what he and Marx had seen as the death agony of capitalism was, in fact, its birth pangs.[116] Nevertheless, Marx and Engels never ceased to believe that the death agony of capitalism would come nor that it would be the result of the very forces which capitalism itself created.

It is in the Grundrisse and Capital that Marx first specifies the precise nature of the fetters which capitalist social relations impose on productive development. In particular, Marx came to see the tendency for the rate of profit to decline as the essential barrier to productive advance created by capitalism. The law of the tendency of the rate of profit to decline is thus 'in every respect the most important law of modern political economy'.[117] In what sense is the declining rate of profit the result of the growth of the productive forces? In what sense is capitalism a barrier to the growth of social productivity? Marx argues that the rate of profit should be calculated as the return of surplus value against the value of the capital invested on wages (variable capital) and on raw materials and machinery (constant capital), i.e. $\frac{S}{c+v}$ where 'S' is surplus value, 'C' is constant capital and 'V' is variable capital. Marx claims that as productivity advances, constant capital grows proportionately to variable capital, since such advances mean that more machinery and raw materials are employed by each worker. Only living labour, i.e. variable capital, produces surplus value. Constant capital merely passes on to the final product the labour power embodied within itself. The value of the final product consists of the value of the variable capital, the value of the constant capital passed on during production and the value of the surplus labour performed by the workers. The relative proportions of variable and constant capital thus have a key influence on the rate of profit, since the smaller the proportion of total capital expended on variable capital, the smaller becomes the rate of profit. 'The gradual growth of constant capital in relation to variable capital must necessarily lead to a gradual fall of the general rate of profit.'[118]

The truth of Marx's theory does not concern us for the moment and readers should not lose sleep if they have not understood the argument as to why the rate of profit declines. The important point, for our purposes, is that Marx claims that the growth of the productive forces, the increasing use of machinery and growing productivity of labour, which are inherent in capitalism, lead to a decline in the rate of profit.[119] The results are disastrous for capitalism as the rate of profit is 'the motive power of capitalist production'.[120] In other words, there is a contradiction between the capitalist relations of production, based on the production of profit, and the growth of the productive forces which leads to a decline in the rate of profit. The contradiction expresses itself in bitter spasms and crises. Thus 'the real barrier to capitalist development is capital itself'.[121]

Capitalism has thus become a fetter on production; it faces inevitable crises whilst at the same time creating the socialisation of production and abundance of wealth which makes possible a new form of society. However, capitalism does not only create the abstract possibility of socialism, it also creates the agents of its downfall who will make the possibility into a reality, the revolutionary class, the proletariat:

> With the development of industry the proletariat not only increases in number; it becomes more concentrated in greater masses, its strength grows and it feels that strength more.[122]

> Of all the classes that stand face to face with the bourgeoisie today the proletariat alone is a really revolutionary class. The other classes decay and finally disappear in the face of modern industry; the proletariat is its special and essential product.[123]

> What the bourgeoisie therefore produces, above all, is its own gravediggers. Its fall and the victory of the proletariat are equally inevitable.[124]

This point hardly needs elaborate supporting quotations. What is important to note is that Marx's theory of revolution arises from his productive force determinist reading of history: 'No social order is ever destroyed before all the productive forces for which it is sufficient have been developed, and new superior relations of production never replace old ones before the material conditions of production for their existence have matured within the framework of society.'[125] As Geoff Hodgson pointed out, Marx's claim has neither 'theoretical meaning nor practical consequence' since it is impossible to know *when* the productive forces are fully developed.[126] Presumably if capitalism is overthrown by a socialist revolution this would be a sign that the productive forces *had* developed to their full extent. The problem is that we could only know this *after* the revolution had taken place. The theory does not supply a guide to action before this date. Marx himself never grappled with this problem, and his faith in the inevitability of a socialist revolution continued on the basis of his productive force determinism. As he wrote in 1850:

> While this general prosperity lasts, enabling the productive forces of bourgeois society to develop to the full extent possible within the bourgeois system, there can be no question of a real revolution. Such a revolution is only possible when two factors come into conflict: the modern productive forces and bourgeois forms of production. ... A new revolution is only possible as a result of a new crisis; but it will come, just as surely as the crisis itself.[127]

Productive force determinism begins from a theory of human nature, it offers an explanation of social structure and of historical change. It culminates in a prediction of inevitable revolution. McMurtry is right to call technology the 'Marxian Providence'.[128] Just as Cromwell believed

51

that his victories were the result of necessity, of Divine Providence, so Marx offered a vision of communism which was not presented as an ideal to which reality had to be adjusted but rather as the result of the 'real movement' of present society.[129] In neither case did inevitabilism result in passively watching the flow of history. On the contrary, it gave both Cromwell's and Marx's striving for victory an even greater power and conviction.[130]

8 Was Marx really a productive force determinist?

It has been argued here that Marx offered a coherent productive force determinism. It has been necessary to buffet the reader with repeated quotations to this effect precisely because some commentators have denied this interpretation of Marx's writings. Even Rosenberg, one of the most informative and interesting of Marxists to write on technology, denies that Marx was a technological determinist (by technology Rosenberg means the productive forces, the means by which man acts on the world and thus realises his true nature). Rosenberg admits that there are 'certain passages' of Marx which could be cited to support a productive force determinist reading of Marx, a few 'aphoristic' assertions often tossed out in the heat of the debate, but denies that these passages represent Marx's 'real meaning'.[131] As any reader who has ploughed through this chapter will be more than ready to admit, Marx's productive force determinism was much more than a few aphoristic assertions or a temporary lapse in the 1859 'Preface'.[132] Why then is Rosenberg unwilling to believe that Marx was a productive force determinist? Firstly, because Marx stressed that technological innovation was a *social* process and that there was a mutual feedback between economy and society. In other words:

(1) Marx held views which are incompatible with productive force determinism; therefore

(3) Marx could not have been a productive force determinist.

The perceptive reader will have noted that this logic contains a missing middle clause:

(2) Marx was incapable of holding inconsistent and contradictory views.

It is precisely our argument here that Marx *did* hold contradictory views and that our task is not to decide what he really meant (assuming it is possible to decide such matters), but rather to decide which elements of his theory we wish to use. Rosenberg invokes the same argument on two further occasions. He correctly points out that Marx makes little use of productive force determinism in his study of specific historical episodes, and therefore argues that Marx could not really have held such a theory. The assumption once more, is that Marx could not have contradicted himself; again our argument here is just such a contradiction between Marx's explicit general claims and the implications of some of his specific historical analyses.[133] Rosenberg similarly claims that the *Communist Manifesto* is a 'definitive refutation' of the interpretation of Marx as a productive force determinist, since it offers an account of the rise of capitalism based not on the growth of the productive forces, but rather as a response to the growing markets and profit opportunities associated with the geographical explorations of the fifteenth century.[134] Even if this is a sufficient summary of Marx's account of the rise of capitalism (which is arguable), it again assumes that this account is incompatible with productive force determinism and therefore that Marx could not have been a productive force determinist since he was incapable of being inconsistent with himself. It may well be that Marx had the unique capacity never to contradict himself, but until this is proven it seems a little unwise to make it the hidden assumption underlying our interpretation of his works.

Anyway, it is not at all clear why an account of history based on the growth of wealth by the increase of trade, division of labour and the accumulation of capital should be incompatible with productive force determinism. Both Adam Smith and Karl Kautsky were undoubted productive force determinists, but both men managed to combine the two beliefs.[135] Those who are tempted to believe that the *Communist Manifesto* is a decisive refutation of productive force determinism may wish to reconsider Marx's claim in the *Manifesto* that:

> The means of production and of exchange on whose foundation the bourgeoisie built itself up were generated in feudal society. At a certain stage in the development of these means of production and of exchange, the conditions under which feudal society produced and exchanged, the feudal organization of agriculture and manufacturing industry, in one word, the feudal relations of property became no longer compatible with the already developed productive forces; they became so many fetters. They had to be burst asunder; they were burst asunder.[136]

The *Manifesto* argues that a similar movement arises in capitalist society, as the growing productive forces revolt against the property relations which contain them.[137] Finally, Rosenberg argues that when Marx says that: 'Relics of bygone instruments of labour possess the same importance for the investigation of extinct economic formations as do fossil bones for the determination of extinct species of animals',[138] this means only that instruments of labour are *indicators* of the prevailing social relations. Just as a thermometer indicates but does not determine temperature, so technology indicates but does not determine the level of development of social relations.[139] Similarly, McCarthy, in his otherwise excellent *Marx and the Proletariat*, argues that 'it seems unlikely that Marx held the view that technology determined the social relations of production'. Although Marx is 'unclear and imprecise' on the issue, he seems merely to mean that the productive forces are indicators of the nature of the relations of production.[140] There are two objections to Rosenberg and McCarthy's interpretation of this passage:

(1)   Although Marx says that instruments of labour are indicators of social relations, he stresses that he has in mind those instruments which are the 'bone and muscles of production', i.e. the elements which give an animal species a distinctive structure.

(2)   More importantly, whilst Marx says that instruments of labour are indicators of social relations, he does not say that they are *merely* indicators. He neither asserts, nor denies, their determining role. Thus whether Marx held that the productive forces are a determining factor in human history may only be discovered from other passages.

A final lengthy quotation from Marx will support the claim that a productive force reading of Marx is quite legitimate in terms of his considered explicit statements on the issue. The passage comes not from the heat of a polemic, but from the pages of the *New Rhenish Gazette* of 1849, and was in turn based on lectures of 1847 in which Marx outlined his views to the German Workers Society in Brussels:

> In production men not only act on nature but also on one another. They produce only by co-operating in a certain way and mutually exchanging their activities. In order to produce, they enter into definite connections and relations with one another and only within these social connections and relations does their action on nature, does their production, take place.
>
> These social relations into which the producers enter with one another, the conditions under which they exchange their activities and participate in the whole act of production, will naturally vary according to the character of the means of production. With the invention of new instruments of warfare, firearms, the whole internal organisation of the army necessarily changed: the relationships within which individuals can constitute an army and act as an army were transformed and the relations of different armies to one another also changed.

Thus the social relations within which individuals produce, *the social relations of production, change, are transformed with the change and development of the material means of production, the productive forces. The relations of production in their totality constitute what are called the social relations, society, and specifically, a society at a definite stage of historical development*, a society with a peculiar distinctive character. *Ancient society, feudal society, bourgeois society* are such totalities of production relations, each of which at the same time denotes a special stage of development in the history of mankind.[141]

That the productive forces develop, that these productive forces determine the nature of social relations and that social relations change as the productive forces advance are the explicit assertions of this passage, a productive force determinism which Marx repeats in *The German Ideology*, *The Poverty of Philosophy* and the 1859 'Preface'. It is not difficult to show that Marx was a productive force determinist, the problem is to show that he was *also* something much more.

Notes

1 G. A. Cohen, *Karl Marx's Theory of History: A Defence* (Oxford, 1978), p. 134.

2 E. P. Thompson, *The Poverty of Theory* (London, 1978), p. 346.

3 N. Bukharin, *Historical Materialism* (Michigan, 1969), pp. 120–9; Cohen, *Karl Marx's Theory of History*, Ch. 6; J. McMurtry, *The Structure of Marx's World View* (Princeton, 1978), p. 71.

4 E. J. Hobsbawn, 'Karl Marx's contribution to historiography', in R. Blackburn (ed.), *Ideology in Social Science* (London, 1973), pp. 278–9.

5 C. Bettelheim, *Class Struggles in the U.S.S.R. 1917–23* (Hassocks, 1976), p. 24; N. Rosenberg, 'Marx as a student of technology', in L. Levidow & B. Young (eds.), *Science, Technology and the Labour Process* (London, 1981), pp. 11–13; A. Levine & E. O. Wright, 'Rationality and class struggle', *New Left Review* 123 (September–October 1980), pp. 47–69; B. Hindess and P. Q. Hirst, *Pre-capitalist Modes of Production* (London, 1975), pp. 9–12.

6 W. H. Shaw, *Marx's Theory of History* (London, 1978), p. 139; Rosenberg, 'Marx as a student of technology', p. 12.

7 Ibid., p. 11; G. Lukacs, *Political Writings 1919–29* (London, 1972), p. 136.

8 K. Marx & F. Engels, *Collected Works*, vol. V (London, 1976), pp. 41–2 (*The German Ideology*).

9 K. Marx, *Capital*, vol. I (Harmondsworth, 1976, Pelican edn), p. 286, n. 6.

10 Marx & Engels, *Collected Works*, vol. V, p. 31 (*The German Ideology*).

11 Marx, *Capital*, vol. I, p. 286. See also Marx & Engels, *Collected Works*, vol. V, p. 82 (*The German Ideology*). For Marx on Franklin, see also *Capital*, vol. I, p. 444, n. 7.

12 Marx, *Capital*, vol. I, pp. 283–4. My emphasis.

13 K. Marx & F. Engels, *Selected Correspondence* (Moscow, 1975), p. 284 (letter of 12.11.1875).
14 Cohen, *Karl Marx's Theory of History*, p. 134.
15 Marx & Engels, *Collected Works*, vol. V, p. 35 (*The German Ideology*). Original emphasis.
16 K. Marx, *Grundrisse* (Harmondsworth, 1975), p. 85.
17 Marx and Engels, *Collected Works*, vol. V, p. 53 (*The German Ideology*). My emphasis.
18 Ibid., p. 43.
19 Ibid., pp. 81–2.
20 Ibid., p. 89.
21 Ibid., p. 231.
22 Ibid., p. 63.
23 K. Marx, *A Contribution to the Critique of Political Economy* (London, 1971), p. 20.
24 Marx & Engels, *Collected Works*, vol. V, p. 36 (*The German Ideology*).
25 Ibid., pp. 59–60.
26 D. McLellan, *Karl Marx* (London, 1976), p. 151.
27 F. Engels, *Ludwig Feuerbach and the End of Classical German Philosophy* (Moscow, 1969), p. 6. Engels was writing in 1888.
28 K. Marx, *The Poverty of Philosophy* (Moscow, 1973), p. 95.
29 Ibid., pp. 106–7.
30 Ibid., p. 156.
31 Ibid., p. 157. My emphasis.
32 Ibid. My emphasis.
33 Marx, *The Poverty of Philosophy*, p. 161.
34 Marx, *Grundrisse*, p. 85; Marx, *Capital*, vol. I, p. 325.
35 Marx, *The Poverty of Philosophy*, p. 171.
36 K. Marx, *Wage Labour and Capital* (Moscow, 1970), p. 28.
37 Marx, *A Contribution to the Critique of Political Economy*, p. 20, my emphasis; Levine & Wright, 'Rationality and class struggle', p. 48.
38 Marx, *A Contribution to the Critique of Political Economy*, p. 220; McLellan, *Karl Marx*, p. 310.
39 Marx, *Capital*, vol. I, p. 286.
40 Ibid., n. 5. My emphasis.
41 Ibid., n. 6.
42 Marx & Engels, *Selected Correspondence*, p. 356. (Letter of 26.6.1884.)
43 Ibid., p. 441. (Letter of 25.1.1894.)
44 K. Marx & F. Engels, *The Communist Manifesto* (Harmondsworth, 1970), pp. 57, 62. Marx makes the same point, ibid., p. 38.
45 S. Clark (ed.), *One Dimensional Marxism* (London, 1980), pp. 49–50, 160; E. Tomlinson, 'Althusser, Balibar and production', *Capital and Class* 4 (1978), pp. 127–9.
46 Marx & Engels, *Collected Works*, vol. V, p. 40. (*The German Ideology*). See also p. 44 below.
47 C. Belsey, *Critical Practice* (London, 1980), p. 109. See also ibid., p. 15.
48 Marx & Engels, *Collected Works*, vol. V, p. 32. (*The German Ideology*).
49 Ibid., p. 46.
50 Ibid., pp. 32–3.

51 F. Engels, *The Origin of the Family, Private Property and the State* (Moscow, 1968). See also Marx & Engels, *Selected Correspondence*, pp. 347, 442.
52 Morgan quoted by Engels, *The Origin of the Family*, p. 23.
53 Ibid., pp. 20–8.
54 Marx & Engels, *Collected Works*, vol. V, p. 33 (*The German Ideology*).
55 Ibid., p. 159.
56 F. Engels, *Herr Eugen Dühring's Revolution in Science* (London, Lawrence & Wishart, n.d.), pp. 182–3.
57 Engels, *The Origin of the Family*, p. 157.
58 Ibid., pp. 159–60.
59 Marx & Engels, *Collected Works*, vol. V, pp. 74–5 (*The German Ideology*).
60 K. Marx, *Capital*, vol. III, (London, 1979, Lawrence & Wishart edn), pp. 793–4.
61 Marx & Engels, *Collected Works*, vol. V, pp. 32–5 (*The German Ideology*).
62 P. Anderson, *Lineages of the Absolutist State* (London, 1979), p. 483.
63 Marx, *Capital*, vol. III, p. 791.
64 K. Marx, *Pre-capitalist Economic Formations* (London, 1975), p. 95. My emphasis.
65 Marx, *Capital*, vol. I, p. 173.
66 Marx, *Pre-capitalist Economic Formations*, p. 77; Marx & Engels, *Collected Works*, vol. V, p. 37 (*The German Ideology*).
67 K. Marx, *Surveys from Exile* (Harmondsworth, 1973), pp. 304–6.
68 Ibid., p. 83; Marx, *Capital*, vol. I, p. 479.
69 Marx & Engels, *The Communist Manifesto*, pp. 86–7.
70 Marx, *Grundrisse*, p. 277.
71 Ibid.
72 Ibid., p. 699.
73 K. Marx, *Theories of Surplus Value*, part I (London, 1969), p. 384.
74 Cohen, *Karl Marx's Theory of History*, p. 139.
75 Shaw, *Marx's Theory of History*, p. 65.
76 McMurtry, *The Structure of Marx's World View*, p. 65.
77 Marx, *The Poverty of Philosophy*, p. 96.
78 Marx, *Capital*, vol. III, pp. 883–4.
79 Marx & Engels, *Collected Works*, vol. V, p. 82 (*The German Ideology*).
80 Marx, *The Poverty of Philosophy*, p. 107.
81 Marx & Engels, *Collected Works*, vol. V, p. 83 (*The German Ideology*).
82 Marx, *A Contribution to the Critique of Political Economy*, pp. 20–1.
83 Marx, *The Poverty of Philosophy*, pp. 107, 157.
84 See below, pp. 115–25.
85 Marx & Engels, *Collected Works*, vol. V, p. 74 (*The German Ideology*).
86 Ibid., p. 82.
87 Ibid., p. 74.
88 Marx, *A Contribution to the Critique of Political Economy*, p. 21.
89 Marx, *Capital*, vol. III, pp. 883–4.
90 Engels, *Herr Eugen Dühring's Revolution in Science*, p. 300.
91 Marx & Engels, *Collected Works*, vol. V, p. 52 (*The German Ideology*).
92 Ibid., p. 33.
93 Engels, *The Origin of the Family*, p. 6.
94 Marx & Engels, *Collected Works*, vol. V, p. 34 (*The German Ideology*), and see below,

pp. 121–2, 129–32.

95 Marx & Engels, *The Communist Manifesto*, p. 85. My emphasis.

96 Marx, *Grundrisse*, p. 540: see also Marx, *Capital*, vol. III, p. 332; Marx, *The Poverty of Philosophy*, pp. 106–7.

97 Marx & Engels, *Collected Works*, vol. V, p. 34 (*The German Ideology*).

98 Marx, *Capital*, vol. I, p. 875.

99 V. I. Lenin, *The Three Sources and Three Component Parts of Marxism* (Moscow, 1969), p. 7. My emphasis.

100 See, for instance, E. P. Thompson, *The Poverty of Theory*, pp. 79–84; S. Hall, 'Re-thinking the "base and superstructure" metaphor', in J. Bloomfield (ed.), *Class, Hegemony and Party* (London, 1977), pp. 43–72; R. Williams, 'Base and super-structure in Marxist cultural theory', *New Left Review* 82 (November–December 1973), pp. 3–16.

101 C. Wright Mills, *The Marxists* (Harmondsworth, 1969), p. 82; R. Aron, *Main Currents in Sociological Thought*, vol. I (Harmondsworth, 1965), p. 121.

102 Marx & Engels, *A Contribution to the Critique of Political Economy*, p. 20.

103 Marx & Engels, *Collected Works*, vol. V, p. 90 (*The German Ideology*).

104 Ibid.

105 Marx, *Capital*, vol. I, p. 172: see also Marx & Engels, *Collected Works*, vol. V p. 36 (*The German Ideology*).

106 A. Giddens, *The Class Structure of the Advanced Societies* (London, 1978), pp. 59–63.

107 Marx & Engels, *Collected Works*, vol. V, pp. 431–2 (*The German Ideology*).

108 Ibid., p. 76.

109 Marx, *Grundrisse*, p. 540.

110 Marx, *Capital*, vol. III, pp. 388–436.

111 Marx, *Theories of Surplus Value*, part III (London, 1972), p. 315.

112 Engels, *Herr Eugen Dühring's Revolution in Science*, p. 304.

113 Marx & Engels, *Collected Works*, vol. V, p. 52 (*The German Ideology*).

114 Marx & Engels, *The Communist Manifesto*, p. 86.

115 Ibid., p. 87.

116 K. Marx, *The Class Struggles in France 1848 to 1850* (Moscow, 1972), p. 12. Engels's introduction was written in 1895.

117 Marx, *Grundrisse*, p. 748.

118 Ibid., pp. 745–58; Marx, *Capital*, vol. III, Chs. 13–15.

119 Marx, *Grundrisse*, p. 747; Marx, *Capital*, vol. III, p. 212.

120 Ibid., p. 259.

121 Ibid., p. 250.

122 Marx & Engels, *The Communist Manifesto*, p. 89.

123 Ibid., p. 91.

124 Ibid., p. 94.

125 Marx, *A Contribution to the Critique of Political Economy*, p. 21.

126 G. Hodgson, *Trotsky and Fatalistic Marxism* (Nottingham, 1975), p. 29.

127 Marx, *Surveys from Exile*, p. 131.

128 McMurtry, *The Structure of Marx's World View*, p. 71.

129 Marx & Engels, *Collected Works*, vol. V, pp. 49, 468 (*The German Ideology*).

130 G. V. Plekhanov, *Fundamental Problems of Marxism* (London, 1969), p. 141.

131 Rosenberg, 'Marx as a student of technology', p. 11. For Rosenberg on technology see N. Rosenberg's 'Factors affecting the diffusion of technology', *Explorations in Economic History* X (1972–3), pp. 3–33. F. Ferrarotti, 'Notes on Marx and the study of technical change', in D. McQuaire (ed.), *Marx: Sociology, Social Change, Capitalism* (London, 1978), pp. 109–11, also denies that Marx was a 'technological determinist'.

132 Hodgson, *Trotsky and Fatalistic Marxism*; see also n. 7, above.
133 Rosenberg, 'Marx as a student of technology', pp. 11–13.
134 Ibid., p. 12.
135 R. Meek, *Social Science and the Ignoble Savage* (Cambridge, 1976), pp. 221–2; K. Kautsky, *Ethics and the Materialistic Conception of History* (Chicago, 4th edn, n.d.), pp. 120–34; K. Kautsky, *Thomas More and his Utopia* (London, 1927), p. 29.
136 Marx & Engels, *The Communist Manifesto*, pp. 85–6.
137 Ibid., pp. 85–6.
138 Marx, *Capital*, vol. I, p. 286.
139 Rosenberg, 'Marx as a student of technology', p. 14.
140 T. McCarthy, *Marx and the Proletariat* (Westport, 1978), p. 24.
141 Marx, *Wage Labour and Capital*, p. 28. Original emphasis.

CHAPTER 4

Productive force determinism as Marxist orthodoxy

Marx's productive force determinism did not, as Lukács and Rosenberg have claimed, consist merely of occasional passages which 'it is possible' to interpret in this way.[1] Yet neither did this productive force determinism comprise a worked-out theory whose premises were clearly laid out and which anticipated and refuted possible objections to its claims. Marx's productive force determinism was much more than an occasional lapse, but much less than a theory of history. Rather it was a coherent set of assumptions which, as one of Marx's defenders has admitted, Marx made no attempt to justify.[2] It was the work of the next generation of Marxists, particularly Plekhanov and Kautsky, 'to *systematize* historical materialism as a comprehensive theory of man and nature, capable of replacing rival bourgeois disciplines and providing the workers' movement with a broad and coherent vision of the world that could be grasped by its militants'.[3] These thinkers did less than *defend* productive force determinism, but did more than assume it; rather they *asserted* it as the basis of Marxist historical and social history. Marx not only 'could' be interpreted as a productive force determinist; this was the dominant view of his theory of history until the Second World War. Indeed it is, in a sense, rather surprising that we should have to perform the rather tedious task of proving that Marx *was* a productive force determinist as, until recently, this was the orthodox interpretation of his historical materialism.

There were two main reasons why productive force determinism obtained such a hold over later interpreters of Marx. First, Marx himself made no lengthy statement of his historical method or theory. On those occasions when Marx did make explicit general historical claims, they were usually of a productive force determinist nature. The writers of the

Second and Third Internationals found in Marx's aphorisms (such as 'it is not what is made but how and by what instruments of labour that enables us to distinguish different economic epochs' and 'the hand mill gives you society with the feudal lord, the steam mill society with the industrial capitalist', and so on) the key to historical materialism.[4] Above all, it was the 1859 'Preface', where Marx consciously sets out the 'guiding principle' of his studies, which strengthened the productive force determinist reading of Marx. Later Marxists found it easy to pick up on the explicit claims of the 'Preface' that society's relations of production correspond to its productive forces and that these relations of production would necessarily be cast aside once they clashed with the needs of the expanding productive forces.[5] To the present day studies of Marx's theory of history frequently ignore the history which Marx actually wrote and prefer instead to give an extended gloss on the claims of the 'Preface'.[6]

Secondly, a productive force determinist reading of Marx was not only legitimate in terms of Marx's explicit statements. It was also well suited to the political practice of the Second International. For the Marxists of this generation the ruin of capitalist society and the advent of socialism were both equally inevitable. Marx's 'Preface' and Darwin's *Origin of Species* had both appeared in the same year. Their themes were united in the works of Kautsky, who argued that just as biological evolution was inevitable as species became extinct or adjusted to their environment, so capitalism, like feudalism, was doomed to extinction, not by the condemnations of moralists but by social development itself.[7] The Second International thus took from Marx an economism where political developments were seen as the expression of economic change which was, in turn, based on the growth of the productive forces.[8] Gramsci identified such inevitabilism and 'mechanical determinism' as a form of consolation during a time of defeat: 'I have been defeated for the moment but the tide of history is working for me in the long term.' In Kautsky's case, however, inevitabilism was not the last hope of the defeated, it was rather the result of the confidence drawn from the persistent growth of the workers' movement.[9] It was this faith in the growing social weight of the working class which went hand in hand with the productive force determinism of the theorists of the Second International.

The Third International represents, in many ways, a profound break with the political practice of the Second International. The belief that capitalism's own development assured the future victory of socialism could, as Gramsci recognised, lead to political passivity. The Bolsheviks replaced economism and passivity with initiative and the primacy of politics. It was for this reason that Gramsci hailed the Bolshevik revolution as the 'revolution against *Capital*'. The Second International's 'mechanistic' Marxism had left the movement unprepared for political crisis and had led to the collapse of the Second International in 1914; the Bolsheviks' 'voluntarist' Marxism forced the pace of historical change and led, as Kautsky warned, to dictatorship, bureaucracy and police control.[10]

Yet, although the political *practice* of the Bolsheviks implied a very different conception of Marxism from that of Kautsky and Plekhanov, this change was not accompanied by any innovation in the realm of historical theory. Lenin may have rejected Plekhanov's political position on the course of the Russian Revolution but he continued to recommend Plekhanov, an arch-productive force determinist, to young Communists 'because nothing better has been written on Marxism anywhere in the world'.[11] Indeed, the writings of the Second and Third Internationals are further proof that political stances cannot simply be read off from theoretical positions. Plekhanov and Kautsky rejected the Bolshevik revolution led by Lenin; Bukharin, Stalin and Trotsky disagreed on the way forward for the revolution in an age of international isolation, yet *all* were united by a conception of historical materialism as a form of productive force determinism.

Plekhanov and Kautsky

Productive force determinism appears in its most systematic form in the writings of the Russian Marxist G. V. Plekhanov. Indeed for Plekhanov the recognition of the primacy of the social role of the productive forces was one of the clearest signs of Marx's greatness and the answer to the riddle of social evolution which had perplexed earlier thinkers. The French materialists of the eighteenth century (such as Helvétius and Holbach) had realised that 'human nature' was not eternal, but was the product of the changing environment. However, they had seen this environment as governed by social 'opinion'. As a result, argued Plekhanov, they could explain neither the development of the social environment nor of 'opinion'. Similarly the French historians of the Restoration (Guizot, Thierry, Mignet) had anticipated Marx in explaining political events (such as the English and French Revolutions) in terms of the conflict of social classes based on particular property relations but were unable to identify the origin of property relations except by recourse to the notion of 'human nature', a failing shared by Saint-Simon and the Utopian socialists. Marx's greatness consisted for Plekhanov in his synthesis of the advances of the German idealists, the emphasis on conflict and change in human history, with a stress on the material origin of this change which had eluded earlier thinkers.[12]

Plekhanov's aim was to counter the Narodnik interpretation of historical materialism as a 'factoral' theory of history in which the economic was merely one, if the most important, of a number of factors in historical development. For Plekhanov such 'factors' were abstractions which distorted the complex movement of the real history of society. Humanity had only one single and indivisible history, the history of its own social relations 'which are determined by the state of the productive forces in each particular period'.[13] Marx's achievement was to show that property relations could not be explained by 'human nature' and that historical change was not the unfolding of the Idea, as it was for Hegel. Rather 'the principle cause of the social historical process is the development of the productive forces'.[14]

The idea that 'man' is fundamentally a 'tool-making animal' is central to Plekhanov's interpretation of historical materialism. He even claimed that the whole essence of Marx's historical theory was contained in Marx's comment that in 'acting on the external world man changes his own nature'.[15] In other words humanity's development consists of the perfection of its instruments of labour, its 'artificial organs', and from this development Plekhanov deduces the entire history of human society. The productive forces determine the lifestyle of each society. The whole existence of the Australian savage depends on his boomerang: 'if the savage became a tiller of the soil all of his habits, thinking and "nature" will change'. From the level of development of the productive forces we can predict corresponding class relations, and from the growth of the productive forces we can explain the rise and fall of particular property relations. From the development of the productive forces we can explain the history of the family, the evolution of private property, the emergence of the state, of particular habits, ideals and political theories and even the nature of relations between states and their forms of warfare.[16]

Plekhanov realised, however, that exactly the same sort of objection could be raised against his productive force determinism as he himself had raised against the pre-Marxist social theorists; i.e. if we are to explain social and political change by the development of the productive forces then what, in turn, is the explanation of this development?

Like Marx, Plekhanov simply assumed that the productive forces had an inherent tendency to advance, even if this advance took place 'extremely slowly' in certain social conditions. He was more concerned with the problem of why such productive advances were very uneven in time and place. Plekhanov refused to accept that such differences could be explained in terms of race as the capacity for toolmaking was a constant in human history and throughout the 'races'.[17] Marx had already addressed this problem and concluded that 'different communities find different means of production, and different means of subsistence in their natural environment'.[18] It was not race, but rather the geographical environment, which was the key variable, since it 'did not permit the various human tribes to make practical use to an equal extent of their capacity to "invent" '. Geographical environment thus had a 'decisive' effect on social development through its determining influence on the growth of the productive forces. Thus those areas lacking in suitable minerals could not independently develop beyond the Stone Age, and the development of the American Indians was restricted by the lack of animals suitable for domestication.[19]

Nevertheless, it would be wrong to accuse Plekhanov in particular of the heresy of 'geographical determinism'.[20] Firstly, Marx and Engels had already made very similar points.[21] Secondly, Plekhanov was well aware of Voltaire's critique of Montesquieu's geographical determinism, which had shown that a number of very different social systems could exist in the same geographical conditions. Plekhanov himself pointed out that British society in Caesar's time was very different from that of his own day, even though Britain's geography was much the same in both periods. It is thus irrelevant for a modern editor to object to Plekhanov's emphasis on geography on the grounds that eastern Europe has known four different social systems on the same geographical basis; Plekhanov himself had already made this point.[22] Plekhanov did not claim that the relatively unchanging geographical environment could explain the more rapid evolution of society. Rather, geography is invoked to explain the divergent paths and different rates of productive advance found in different areas. Geography gives the possibility of developing the productive forces, here in one way, there another, here faster, there slower. Geography thus acted as a sort of prime mover as once particular levels of the productive forces had come into existence they could then determine the influence of the relatively unchanging environment (as in the contrast between Caesar's Britain and modern Britain). A given level of the productive forces not only determines the influence of nature, but also creates specific relations of production which have their own laws of development. Plekhanov was explicitly *not* attempting to explain social change by change in the natural environment. He was attempting to explain why humanity had a changing relationship with this environment.[23] Even if one does not accept Plekhanov's point there seems little reason to label it a 'geographical determinism'.

Kautsky also adhered to the familiar tenets of productive force determinism whilst systematising the theory and refining its details. Thus the relations of production correspond to the level of the productive forces, the productive forces have an inherent tendency to develop which the relations of production can, at most, only temporarily hold back, private property arises with the growth of the productive forces and the division of labour, and the division of labour leads to the formation of distinct social classes.[24] As with Marx and Plekhanov, so Kautsky's productive force determinism was based on a definition of humanity's distinctive characteristics as a species. Humanity is not defined by production, since birds produce nests, or even by its use of tools, since animals use branches and stones as implements of defence or for cracking open nuts. However, whilst animals *find* and use instruments which are naturally available, humanity *invents* tools which are used to create products or even uses tools which will make other tools. Unlike the limbs of an animal, these implements are capable of rapid change, so that a new empire is opened to humanity, an empire whose development is based on the growth of the productive forces.[25]

Plekhanov had developed his productive force determinism to refute those who claimed that Marxism reduced the complexity of real human history to the passive reflection of the economic factor. Kautsky also wished to stress the complexity of human social organisation, but in so doing he tended to undermine his own productive force determinist claims. The recognition of the many-sidedness of historical causality tended to threaten Kautsky's ruling logic which was based on the primacy of the productive forces. At first Kautsky tells us, in *Ethics and the Materialist Conception of History*, that 'every society is modeled by the technical apparatus at its command'. But we are then told that this does not mean that social structure can be read off from the technical conditions of production, since the same tools are to be found in a number of different societies. A peasant economy, for instance, may lead to an Asiatic mode of production if it is found in an area needing a central authority to organise irrigation, to a feudal nobility in an area threatened by nomadic tribes, to slavery if near to the coast and so involved in commerce and the urban economy, or to a peasant economy if it is found in pastoral uplands. A Marxist historical study must not be content with working from the productive forces but must take into account specific geographical and historical conditions.[26] The determining role of the productive forces was even more weakened when Kautsky (like Plekhanov) noted that although society's relations of production are called into being by specific productive forces, these relations in turn influence the development of the productive forces and have their own laws of development.[27] If, as McMurtry claims, technology is the 'Marxist Providence', then in Kautsky and Plekhanov it threatened to become a Newtonian Prime Mover which activated the whole system, but in doing so created social systems with their own laws of motion. When Kautsky and Plekhanov recognised the complexity of social change and the interaction of geography, society and technology, their texts came to embarrass their own explicit claims and ruling assumptions.

Bukharin and Stalin

Bukharin regarded the Marxism of the Second International as a distortion of Marx's true meaning, a distortion which had led to the Social Democratic betrayal of 1914 and to patriotic tendencies in the working class. Nevertheless his *Historical Materialism* (1921), intended as a textbook or primer of Marxist theory, was quite happy to recommend Plekhanov's works on historical materialism and to outline a productive force determinism which added little to the systematic presentation of the theory to be found in Kautsky and Plekhanov.[28] Although Bukharin had little new to say his *Historical Materialism* is worth considering briefly, firstly because it emphasises that the political break between the Second and Third Internationals was not accompanied by any fundamental change in the interpretation of Marx's theory of history and, secondly, because the very nature of the work as a textbook means that the assumptions of productive force determinism appear in their clearest form.

The basis of Bukharin's interpretation of social change is the assumption that the productive forces have an inherent tendency to develop. This assumption is so self-evident for Bukharin that it needs no defending. It follows from this assumption that whenever the relations of production become fetters on the productive forces they must be cast aside in order to allow the inexorable growth of productivity.[29] If the 'development' thesis is simply assumed, Bukharin at least attempts some justification of the primacy thesis, that society's relations of production correspond to its productive forces. He argues that it would be quite impossible for a society to have a social technology based on machinery and yet have social relations based on hand tools. The economy is thus explained by its adaptation to the technology available to it, a claim which is as true for slavery in the Ancient World as for class relations under modern capitalism.[30] In fact Bukharin takes for granted the very hypothesis he sets out to prove, namely that certain social relations *are* 'based' on hand tools and so incompatible with machinery. Secondly, as a more sophisticated productive force determinist admits, if certain productive forces preclude the existence of certain relations of production then certain relations of production also rule out certain productive forces: if computers rule out the use of slavery then slavery also rules out the use of computers. In itself Bukharin's argument is not proof of the primacy of the productive force.[31]

Bukharin does little, then, to advance on the work of Plekhanov. He even adopts Plekhanov's use of geography as a prime mover of historical change which explains why countries embark on divergent social evolutions, whilst recognising that a static geography cannot explain the history of any one country and that geography's influence on society is mediated by the level of development of the productive forces. Bukharin's one advance was to anticipate Balibar in emphasising that society's productive forces do not consist of particular tools, or even of the whole aggregate of tools but, rather, are made up of 'the whole system of these tools' although this insight is rather diluted by the subsequent claim that 'of course a certain type of tool is always predominant'.[32] He concludes, quite logically, with advice which Marxist historians have spent most of the last sixty years ignoring: 'any investigation of society, of the conditions of its growth, its forms, its content etc. must begin with an analysis of the productive forces or of the technical base of society'.[33]

The political break between the Second and Third Internationals was not, as we have seen, marked by any break with the theory of productive force determinism. Neither was the theory threatened by the transformation of the Third International with the rise of Stalin and the doctrine of 'socialism in one country'. On the contrary, Stalin's *Dialectical and Historical Materialism* (1938) owed much to Bukharin's *Historical Materialism* and made very similar points about the role of geography and population in historical change. It may be doubted if Stalin was, at this time, over-concerned with accusations of plagiarism. Stalin's productive force determinism was based on the now familiar argument that the productive forces have an inherent tendency to develop and so must inevitably cast aside the production relations which have ceased to correspond with them. Capitalism is the final form of society to be marked by such antagonistic and contradictory relations between society and its productive forces, whereas in the Soviet Union the relations of production correspond harmoniously with the forces of production.[34] Stalin was more original when he attempted to specify the particular productive forces which had been responsible for historical change. Primitive communism, for instance, had corresponded to the age of stone implements and gave way to slavery as metal tools, agriculture and a social division of labour with handicrafts appeared. Feudalism arose on the basis of improved metalworking and agricultural techniques, capitalist social relations are associated with the emergence of machinery but capitalism itself only led to the crisis of the productive forces and hence to socialism. Thus changes in the productive forces and particularly in the instruments of labour 'sooner or later led to the corresponding changes and development of the relations of production'.[35] Whether the 'victory of socialism' in Russia *was* the result of the growth of the productive forces is a question that Stalin was unlikely to be tested with in the conditions of 1938.

Lenin and Trotsky

The one person who might have been expected to offer a critique of Stalin at this time was Trotsky, who roundly condemned Stalin's domestic and foreign policies throughout the 1930s. Yet although Trotsky had broken with Stalin politically, this did not entail any theoretical break with productive force determinism. On the contrary his *Marxism in our Time* (1939) follows Stalin's *Dialectical and Historical Materialism* of the previous year in explaining the evolution of society from primitive communism, through slavery, feudalism and capitalism 'by the growth of the productive forces i.e. of technique and the organization of labour'.[36] This is not to say that Trotsky had cribbed the point from his enemy. As early as 1906 he had argued that 'Marxism teaches that the development of the productive forces determines the social-historical process'.[37]

Given his admiration for Plekhanov it will come as no surprise to the reader to find Lenin espousing the cause of productive force determinism. In his *Karl Marx* (1918) Lenin summarises historical materialism with (inevitably) a long quotation from the 1859 'Preface', that key text of productive force determinism. So as to leave no doubt in the mind of the reader, Lenin emphasises that one of the two defects of pre-Marxist historiography was its failure to locate the roots of the system of social relations in the 'degree of development reached by material production'. The productive forces are the basis of society and so it follows that 'all ideas ... stem from the condition of the material forces of production'.[38] In an earlier essay, *The Three Sources and Component Parts of Marxism* (1914), Lenin argued that Marx had replaced the chaos of earlier interpretations of history with an integral theory which shows how 'in consequence of the growth of the productive forces, out of one system of social life another and higher system develops – how capitalism, for instance, grows out of feudalism'.[39] We are not concerned here with the argument that Lenin and Trotsky's political practice, or their analysis of specific historical conjunctures, would refute these general claims. All that interests us for the moment is that they were united in their explicit adherence to the principles of productive force determinism. Where the two men were divided was in their assessment of the orginality of this doctrine. For Lenin, as for Plekhanov, the tenets of productive force determinism were the sign of the greatness of Marx's intellectual achievement. In fact Trotsky was much nearer the truth when he argued that these 'fundamental propositions of social development were already clearly developed by Adam Smith'.[40] It is to the origins of productive force determinism that we must now turn.

Notes

1 N. Rosenberg, 'Marx as a student of technology', in L. Levidow & B. Young (eds.), *Science, Technology and the Labour Process* (London, 1981), p. 11; G. Lukács, *Political Writings 1919–1929* (London, 1972), p. 136.

2 W. H. Shaw, *Marx's Theory of History* (London, 1978), pp. 59-60. Hence also the need for G. A. Cohen's defence of *Karl Marx's Theory of History* (Oxford, 1978).

3 P. Anderson, *Considerations on Western Marxism* (London, 1977), p. 6.

4 G. V. Plekhanov, *Fundamental Problems of Marxism* (London, 1969), p. 51; G. V. Plekhanov, *The Development of the Monist Conception of History* (Moscow, 1972), p. 126; N. Bukharin, *Historical Materialism* (New York, 1969), p. 116; J. V. Stalin, 'Dialectical and Historical Materialism', in *Problems of Leninism* (Peking, 1976), p. 868.

5 K. Marx, *A Contribution to the Critique of Political Economy* (London, 1971), p. 20; Plekhanov, *Fundamental Problems of Marxism*, p. 62; Plekhanov, *The Development of the Monist Conception of History*, pp. 153 ff; Stalin, 'Dialectical and historical materialism', pp. 871–3; V. I. Lenin, *The Three Sources and Component Parts of Marxism* (Moscow,

1969), pp. 21-2.

6 Cohen, *Karl Marx's Theory of History*, pp. 136 ff; T. Carver, *Marx's Social Theory* (Oxford, 1982).

7 M. Salvadori, *Karl Kautsky and the Socialist Revolution 1880–1938* (London, 1979), pp. 24–5; K. Marx, *Collected Works*, Vol. V (London, 1976), pp. 381, 431–2 (*The German Ideology*).

8 R. Simon, *Gramsci's Political Thought* (London, 1982), pp. 11–13.

9 Q. Hoare & G. Nowell Smith (eds.), *Selections from the Prison Notebooks of Antonio Gramsci* (London, 1973), p. 336; Salvadori, *Karl Kautsky and the Socialist Revolution*, pp. 29–30.

10 Hoare & Nowell Smith, *Selections from the Prison Notebooks*, p. xxi; Simon, *Gramsci's Political Thought*, p. 12; Salvadori, *Karl Kautsky and the Socialist Revolution*, pp. 23, 218–19, 256–8.

11 Quoted in Plekhanov, *The Development of the Monist Conception of History*, p. 6.

12 Ibid., Chs. 1–3.

13 Plekhanov, *Fundamental Problems of Marxism*, pp. 106–7, 137–8.

14 Plekhanov, *The Development of the Monist Conception of History*, p. 169.

15 Ibid., p. 123.

16 Ibid., pp. 124, 133, 147, 159–60, 165, 171, 172.

17 Ibid., pp. 131, 133.

18 K. Marx, *Capital*, vol. I (Harmondsworth, 1976, Pelican edn), p. 472.

19 Plekhanov, *The Development of the Monist Conception of History*, pp. 129, 131, 216; Plekhanov, *Fundamental Problems of Marxism*, p. 49.

20 G. McLennan, *Marxism and the Methodologies of History* (London, 1981), p. 46.

21 See n. 18 above; F. Engels, *The Origin of the Family, Private Property and the State* (Moscow, 1968), p. 25; G. Cohen, *Karl Marx's Theory of History*, p. 23.

22 Plekhanov, *The Development of the Monist Conception of History*, pp. 129–30, 217.

23 Ibid., pp. 216–18, 262.

24 K. Kautsky, *Ethics and the Materialist Conception of History* (Chicago, 4th edn, n.d.), pp. 133–4, 144–5, 161, 171.

25 Ibid., pp. 120–37.

26 Ibid., pp. 133, 164–70.

27 Ibid., p. 169; Plekhanov, *Fundamental Problems of Marxism*, pp. 62, 64; Plekhanov, *The Development of the Monist Conception of History*, p. 217.

28 Bukharin, *Historical Materialism*, p. 256.

29 Ibid., pp. 249, 257.

30 Ibid., p. 140.

31 Cohen, *Karl Marx's Theory of History*, p. 158.

32 Bukharin, *Historical Materialism*, p. 134.

33 Ibid., p. 120.

34 Stalin, 'Dialectical and historical materialism', pp. 860–1.

35 Ibid., pp. 862–7.

36 L. Trotsky, *Marxism in our Time* (New York, 1970), p. 9.

37 L. Trotsky, *The Permanent Revolution and Results and Prospects* (London, 1971), p. 169.

38 V. I. Lenin, *The Three Sources and Component Parts of Marxism*, pp. 21–3.

39 Ibid., p. 7.

40 Trotsky, *The Permanent Revolution and Results and Prospects*, p. 170.

CHAPTER 5

The origins of productive force determinism

Our chief concern is to establish the main strands of Marx's theories of history and to assess the value of these theories for the study of specific societies. However, before we assess the value of productive force determinism we shall briefly consider the origins of this theory. There were a number of general intellectual influences which would make a productive force determinism attractive to Marx. The influence of Hegel gave Marx a view of history as more than a 'miscellany of mighty deeds and catastrophes', but rather as a coherent and progressive development which passes through distinct stages of evolution.[1] It was not only from Hegel that Marx obtained a stress on ordered historical development. Evolutionism, the stress on progress, the necessary development through stages and the acceptance of change as an inevitable part of reality, has been described as 'the intellectual arch model' of the nineteenth century, to be found in the works of Darwin, Spencer, Comte, Fourier and Saint-Simon. Marx was certainly not free from its influence.[2] Nevertheless, neither the influence of Hegel, nor a general stress on evolution as progress, will explain why Marx identified the source of change as the growth of society's productive forces. In order to understand the origins of productive force determinism we need a much more specific analysis of the intellectual and historical influences at work in the formation of Marx's historical materialism as it appears for the first time in its mature form in *The German Ideology*.

There is no doubt that Marx himself believed that he had discovered the real basis of history which earlier writers had ignored, i.e. the material production of life and the civil society created by it. French and English writers had stuck to the realm of politics whilst the Germans, even further removed from reality, had portrayed history in terms of 'pure spirit' and made 'the religious illusion the driving force of history'. At most French and English writers (in fact Marx means Scottish writers) had only made 'first attempts' to give history a materialist basis.[3] As we have seen, both Plekhanov and Lenin took Marx at his own word and found his intellectual greatness in his perception of the underlying causes of social development. Yet it was Marx himself who pointed out that 'one does not judge an individual by what he thinks about himself'.[4] How accurate were Marx's claims for his own originality? 'In every inquiry concerning the operations of men when united together in society, the first object of attention should be their mode of subsistence. According as that varies, their laws and polity must be different.' This recommendation to begin sociological enquiry with an investigation of society's productive base comes not from Bukharin but from William Robertson's *History of America* of 1777.[5] By this date the belief that human history consisted of a succession of modes of subsistence, the four stages of hunting, pastoralism, agriculture and commerce, was 'an integral part of the social thought of the Enlightenment . . . very few historical and social thinkers remained unaffected by it'.[6] Ronald Meek's exciting study of these French and Scottish thinkers of the eighteenth century should be compulsory reading for all those who believe that productive force determinism was an innovation of Marx's, for by 1780 the 'four stage theory' was a coherent theory of historical development and a central organising principle of the study of past societies. For instance, Adam Smith's lectures on jurisprudence (1762–3) sought to examine the origin and history of property rights in each of these four economic stages. Smith explains the evolution of society in terms of population pressure which creates the need for new resources. Each stage of development generates its own corresponding types of property, law and government. 'In a certain view of things all the arts, science, law, wisdom and even virtue itself tend all to this one thing, the provision of meat, drink, payment of lodging for men.'[7] The theory was used most ably and comprehensively in John Millar's *The Origin of Ranks* (1771) where the four modes of subsistence explain the evolution of lifestyles, social inequality, relations within the family and government.[8]

Marx could hardly fail to be aware of such theories given that classical political economy arose out of the four stage theory as a detailed account of the workings of the fourth stage.[9] Adam Smith's *The Wealth of Nations* (1776) takes the four stage theory as the background to its account of the contemporary economy. Smith distinguishes the nations of hunters ('the lowest and rudest state of society'), the nations of shepherds ('a more advanced state of society'), societies with husbandry ('yet more advanced') and finally a society with a marked progress of manufactures and advanced division of labour. Each society had its own type of warfare and size of army, each society had a different form of justice depending on their differing development of property and each had corresponding and distinctive forms of social inequality and political subordination. Each of the four stages had a varying level of expenditure on commerce, education and the maintenance of the dignity of the sovereign.[10] Marx was certainly familiar with Smith's work by 1844, well before The German Ideology.

By this date Marx was also familiar with the works of Malthus, who adopted the four stage theory to show that each of the stages could support a differing level of population according to its economic resources. In the lowest hunter-gatherer societies, for example, population must be thinly scattered. He argued, however, that in all four stages of society the population showed the same tendency to increase beyond the available means of subsistence and was kept in balance by means of the same checks.[11] Thus Marx's stress on the fundamental importance of society's production of the means of subsistence can hardly be claimed as an original contribution to historical theory. On the contrary works such as The German Ideology were, at most, merely the culmination of the materialism of the French and Scottish thinkers of the Enlightenment.[12]

Such writers did not only influence Marx through the primacy which they accorded to material production. Rather, their general historical and social assumptions were to colour Marx's productive force determinism of the 1840s onwards. Like Marx, writers such as Smith assumed that 'man is an active being disposed to improve the material conditions of life' and that there is 'in man a disposition and capacity for improving his condition by the exertion of which he is carried from one degree of advancement to another'. The chronology of social development was indicated by the degree of development of this capacity for improvement. Such a theory would allow the historian to see the real history of humanity, to penetrate 'beneath the common surface of events which occupies the detail of the vulgar historians'. Finally, as in Marx, the mode of subsistence was the fundamental basis of social and political organisation, of morals, manners and ideas.[13]

Marx not only felt the influence of eighteenth-century materialism through his studies of political economy which he had begun in the autumn of 1843, but also through his reading of Saint-Simon, whom he greatly respected.[14] Saint-Simon himself had expressed his admiration for the writers of the Scottish Enlightenment, such as Robertson and Ferguson, whose studies of civil society, based on the four stage theory, he saw as the beginning of a true history of human development, a history which went beneath the surface of political, religious and military facts.[15] For Saint-Simon, society is a workshop and 'man' is essentially a working animal who produces and consumes.[16] The history of medieval and modern Europe had a coherence based on the underlying trend of the emergence of 'industrial society', based on scientific knowledge and industrial progress. This society had replaced the earlier ecclesiastical-feudal society based on theology and a low level of productivity, a society where wealth was increased through conquest, not through trade and manufacture. The rise of self-governing medieval towns, the Reformation, and the English, French and American Revolutions were merely episodes of this history, part of a development which was, as yet, uncompleted.[17]

Saint-Simon inherited the eighteenth-century belief, evident in the four stage theory, that human history was essentially one of progress. It followed that social institutions would correspond to society's needs at certain times and would become anachronistic at others: 'Up to the fifteenth century lay authority was in the hands of the nobility, and this was useful because the nobles were then the most capable industrialists. They directed agricultural works, and agricultural works were then the only kind of important industrial occupation.'[18] The line of descent to Marx's claim that 'the conditions under which definite productive forces can be used are the conditions of the rule of a definite class of society' is obvious.[19] Eventually, said Saint-Simon, society would completely abandon the last vestiges of feudalism and the 'industrialists', the hard-working, peaceful and productive social class, would obtain political power.[20] Saint-Simon was thus an important influence on Marx's productive force determinism in his portrayal of production as the chief object of social organisation and in his conception of society containing the germ of its own destruction in the generation of forces which would make that social form superfluous.[21] This is not to say that there were not essential differences between the two thinkers. Marx would hardly have accepted Saint-Simon's emphasis on the growth of knowledge as the key determinant of economic change, or his claim that each social regime was the result of the application of a particular philosophical system.[22] Nevertheless, Saint-Simon's influence remains a real one. The origins of Marxism in German philosophy have received more than their fair share of attention. Those who wish to discover the roots of Marx's historical materialism should pay at least as much attention to 'English' political economy and to French socialism, as they would to the influence of Hegel and Feuerbach.

By the end of 1845 when Marx and Engels began *The German Ideology* they were intellectually prepared to adopt the theory of productive force determinism. Marx's critique of Hegel's theory of the state (1843), influenced by Feuerbach's materialism, had argued that (as Marx later put it) 'neither legal relations nor political forms could be comprehended whether by themselves or on the basis of a so-called general development of the human mind, but that on the contrary they originate in the material conditions of life'.[23] Marx's reading of political economy resulted in the *Economic and Philosophical Manuscripts* of 1844, where Marx adopted the view of the economists that 'man' was essentially a producer and consumer, and labour becomes the central category of his thought. For Marx (as for Hegel and the political economists), labour is the paradigmatic human activity, production is the means by which man creates his nature. Self-determined, free productive activity is what distinguishes 'man' from other animals. The centrality of production for human nature forms the basis of Marx's critique of the alienation endured by the worker in the capitalist mode of production with its compulsion, division of labour and inhuman conditions of labour, in a system which has been produced by 'man' but now appears as his master.[24] Yet, despite their materialism and their stress on the importance of production, neither Marx's critique of Hegel, nor the *Economic and Philosophical Manuscripts*, are productive force determinist texts. Civil society is shown to be the foundation of the state, but Marx did not go on to claim that civil society, in turn, corresponded to the level of the productive forces. The 1844 *Manuscripts* have much to tell us about production and, in particular, about alienation arising out of production, but neither here, nor in Engels's *Outlines of a Critique of Political Economy* (1843), are the productive forces described as the basis of society or as the motive force of historical change.

Engels had written his *Outlines of a Critique of Political Economy* during his first visit to England which lasted from November 1842 to August 1844. Over forty years later Engels recalled the impact which this visit had on him: 'While I was in Manchester it was tangibly brought home to me that the economic facts, which have so far played no role or only a contemptible one in the writing of history, are, at least in the modern world, a decisive historical fact.' These economic facts expressed themselves, above all, in the growth of modern industry, a development which gives rise to class antagonisms and political struggles.[25] In March 1844 Engels claimed that, far from being untouched by Europe's century of revolution, England had undergone a true social revolution and had changed more than any other country. By September he was claiming that the snowball growth of English industry was a revolution which formed the 'foundation of every aspect of modern English life, the driving force behind all social development'. The most important result of this Industrial Revolution was the creation of a proletariat, at first in the towns and then in agriculture, as small-scale farmers were ousted by tenant-farmers employing wage labour. This social revolution had not only created a proletariat but also increased the riches and influence of England's middle classes.[26]

These ideas were codified by Engels in The Condition of the Working Class in England, written on his return to Germany in 1844. Engels repeats here his claim that the English proletariat was a creation of the Industrial Revolution of the second half of the eighteenth century. Agriculture was then drawn into the process, with the creation of a rural proletariat following the introduction of the spinning jenny. Even this single clumsy machine was capable of transforming the social condition of the lower class, let alone the development of an interdependent system of finely adjusted machinery. In his discussion of the rise of factory production Engels claims that 'manufacture on a small scale created the middle class; on a large scale it created the working class and raised the elect of the middle class to the throne but only to overthrow them the more surely when the time comes'. This Industrial Revolution 'had altered the whole of civil society'; the 'chief product' of this revolution was the proletariat.[27] In this sense Engels's book was a product of Manchester in the 1840s, the epitome of the new industrial capitalism with its rapid economic change, polarisation of classes and intense social conflict.[28]

The first hints of the influence of Engels's English experiences appear in Marx and Engels's The Holy Family, written during the same period as Engels's The Condition of the Working Class in England. Marx and Engels write that the 'Critical Critics' wrongly leave out of the historical movement the relationship between 'man' and nature: 'does it (i.e. Critical Criticism – S.R.) think it actually knows any period without knowing, for example, the industry of that period, the immediate production of life itself?'[29] It was however in The German Ideology, written from November 1845 to August 1846, that 'the materialist conception of history was first formulated as an integral theory'.[30] The 1844 Manuscripts had invoked a philosophical concept of man's species – being his life-activity as a self-determining, free, creative producer – in order to argue that under capitalism 'man' was estranged, alienated in his relations with nature and with other men.[31] In *The German Ideology* this rather abstract concept of 'man' as a producer takes on an empirical meaning in the claim that history has a coherence in the growth of the productive forces and the creation of corresponding relations of production. The claims of *The German Ideology* for the role of the productive forces in determining social relations (or forms of intercourse, as Marx and Engels then referred to them) were merely generalisations from Engels's first hand experience of the social impact of technological change which had been outlined in *The Condition of the Working Class in England*. *The German Ideology* even repeats Engels's earlier claim that it was large-scale industry which had created the proletariat.[32]

Those such as Rosenberg, who wish to deny that Marx was a productive force determinist and claim that for Marx class struggle was the basic moving force of history, have to face the awkward fact that Marx himself denied this interpretation of his achievement. In a letter to Weydemeyer in 1852 Marx said that he deserved no credit for discovering the existence of class or class struggle in modern society since this had already been established by bourgeois historians and economists. Marx claimed simply to have discovered that: 'the existence of classes is merely linked to particular historical phases in the development of production'.[33] Although Marx claimed credit for this discovery Engels could have at least claimed as much. Productive force determinism can be added to the 'number of basic and enduring Marxist propositions (which) first surface in Engels' rather than Marx's early writings'.[34] Engels's 'empiricist' belief that 'the proof of the pudding is in the eating' has been blamed on Manchester; the city must also take its share of the blame for Marx and Engels's belief that society's relations of production are determined by the level of development of its productive forces.[35]

Notes

1 G. A. Cohen, *Karl Marx's Theory of History: A Defence* (Oxford, 1978). Ch. 1 is an excellent introduction to Hegel's philosophy of history.
2 T. Shanin (ed.), *Late Marx and the Russian Road* (London, 1983), p. 4.
3 K. Marx & F. Engels, *Collected Works*, vol. V (London, 1976), pp. 42, 55, 590

n. 16 (*The German Ideology*).

4 K. Marx, *A Contribution to the Critique of Political Economy* (London, 1971), p. 21; K. Marx, *Surveys from Exile* (Harmondsworth, 1973), p. 174.

5 Quoted in R. Meek, *Social Science and the Ignoble Savage* (Cambridge, 1976), p. 2.

6 Ibid., p. 174.

7 Ibid., p. 126.

8 Ibid., pp. 161–74.

9 Ibid., p. 219.

10 A. Smith, *The Wealth of Nations. An Inquiry into the Nature and Causes of the Wealth of Nations*, vol. II (Oxford, 1979), pp. 689, 690, 694, Book V, Ch. I *passim*.

11 T. Malthus, *An Essay on the Principle of Population* (London, 1973), pp. 6, 22. First published 1798.

12 G. Lichtheim, *From Marx to Hegel* (London, 1971), p. 69; Meek, *Social Science and the Ignoble Savage*, p. 229. The four stage theory could also be developed to an emphasis on class and property as well as on the mode of subsistence. See Meek, ibid., p. 229; J. Barnave, *Power, Property and History* (New York, 1971); K. Marx & F. Engels, *Selected Correspondence* (Moscow, 1975), pp. 63–4, 442.

13 A. Skinner, 'Introduction' to A. Smith, *The Wealth of Nations*, Books I–III (Harmondsworth, 1976), p. 30; Meek, *Social Science and the Ignoble Savage*, pp. 163, 164, 172. See also A. Skinner, 'A Scottish contribution to Marxist sociology', in I. Bradley & M. Howard (eds.), *Classical and Marxian Political Economy* (London, 1982), pp. 79–114.

14 G. Ionescu (ed.), *The Political Thought of St. Simon* (Oxford, 1976), pp. 24–5; D. McLellan, *Karl Marx* (London, 1976), p. 106.

15 F. E. Manuel, *The New World of Henri Saint-Simon* (Notre Dame, 1963), pp. 150–3, 224.

16 Ibid., p. 241; E. Wilson, *To the Finland Station* (London, 1966), p. 84.

17 Ionescu, *The Political Thought of St. Simon*, pp. 105, 143, 157.

18 Ibid., pp. 150, 156; G. D. H. Cole, *Socialist Thought: The Forerunners 1789–1850* (London, 1953), p. 40; G. V. Plekhanov, *The Development of the Monist Conception of History* (Moscow, 1972), p. 40.

19 Marx & Engels, *Collected Works*, vol. V, p. 52 (*The German Ideology*).

20 Ionescu, *The Political Thought of St. Simon*, p. 197.

21 Manuel, *The New World of Henri Saint-Simon*, p. 233; Cole, *Socialist Thought: The Forerunners*, p. 49.

22 Manuel, *The New World of Henri Saint-Simon*, p. 233; Plekhanov, *The Development of the Monist Conception of History*, p. 49.

23 Marx, *A Contribution to the Critique of Political Economy*, p. 20; K. Marx & F. Engels, *Collected Works*, vol. III (London, 1975), pp. 9, 75 (Contribution to the Critique of Hegel's Philosophy of Law).

24 K. Marx, *Early Writings* (Harmondsworth, 1975), pp. 322–34; T. McCarthy, *Marx and the Proletariat* (Westport, 1978), pp. 9–12.

25 K. Marx & F. Engels, *Selected Works*, vol. II (Moscow, 1962), p. 344 (On the History of the Communist League).

26 Marx & Engels, *Collected Works*, vol. III, pp. 485, 487 (The Condition of England, The Eighteenth Century).

27 K. Marx & F. Engels, *Collected Works*, vol. IV (London, 1975), pp. 307, 312–13, 318, 325 (The Condition of the Working Class in England).

28 A. Briggs, *Victorian Cities* (Harmondsworth, 1968), pp. 88–116, 184–7.

29 Marx & Engels, *Collected Works*, vol. IV, p. 150 (*The Holy Family*).

30 Marx & Engels, *Collected Works*, vol. V, pp. xiii, xviii.

31 Marx, *Early Writings*, pp. 52–4; McCarthy, *Marx and the Proletariat*, pp. 9–12.

32 Marx & Engels, *Collected Works*, vol. V, pp. 32–5, 41–3, 53–5, 63, 73, 81–2 (*The German Ideology*).

33 Marx & Engels, *Selected Correspondence*, p. 64. (Letter of 3.5.1852.)

34 G. S. Jones, 'Engels and the genesis of Marxism', *New Left Review* 106 (November–December 1977), p. 102.

35 L. Althusser & E. Balibar, *Reading Capital* (London, 1975), p. 56.

PART TWO

Productive force determinism: a critique and an alternative

Chapters 6 and 7 present a critique of the historical claims of productive force determinism as set out by Marx and elaborated by recent commentators such as Shaw and Cohen. Chapter 6 examines the claim that productive force determinism should be rejected because of its reliance on functional explanation and concludes that functional explanation is not, per se, invalid in the social sciences. Chapter 7 discusses the major theses of productive force determinism which were established in Chapter 3 and offers a logical and/or empirical critique of each. It is for these reasons that productive force determinism is rejected, rather than for its reliance on functional explanation.

Productive force determinism argues that:

(1) Society's relations of production are 'functional' for the development of its productive forces.

(2) Society's relations of production have a specific form because that form is suitable for the development of the productive forces in a given period.

(3) Although it is not possible to specify the mechanism through which the productive forces call forth specific relations of production there is empirical evidence to suggest that such a mechanism does exist.

Chapter 7 replies that:

(1) Society's relations of production are not necessarily functional for the development of the productive forces. On the contrary they have frequently led to the stagnation or even decline of social productivity.

(2) The validity of functional explanation is no longer an issue, in this context. As society's relations of production are not functional to the needs of the productive forces they can hardly be explained by such functionality.

(3) No empirical evidence has been given to suggest that a mechanism exists through which society's productive forces call forth functional relations of production. Given that the relations of production are not necessarily functional for the productive forces no such evidence could be provided.

In other words, productive force determinism is not rejected because of its reliance on functional explanation, but rather because it does not meet the requirements which make functional explanation valid in certain limited circumstances.

Chapter 7 thus rejects productive force determinism on logical and empirical grounds. Chapter 8 argues that Marx himself supplies an alternative theory of history, based not on the claim that the productive forces create specific social relations, but on the premise that production is itself a form of social activity. Marx's account of the transition from feudalism to capitalism, and recent debates about this transition, clarify the nature of this alternative approach and further suggest the explanatory redundancy of productive force determinism. This alternative approach rejects a 'philosophy' of history where Marxism is seen as a set of answers. Rather Marxism provides the concepts which allow us to ask specific historical questions. This alternative approach relies not on deduction from the axioms of productive force determinism, but on empirical investigation, to account for historically divergent paths of social evolution. This alternative is not a 'more correct' reading of Marx, but it is a more useful guide to historical change.

CHAPTER 6

Productive force determinism and functional explanation

Marx made no effort to outline his theory of history at length after *The German Ideology*. He thus made no attempt to justify his productive force determinism, or to defend it against possible objections. Marx regarded his theory as 'obviously and intuitively true', so the task of defending his claims has been left to modern commentators.[1] It is in the works of G. A. Cohen that productive force determination appears in its most sophisticated form and obtains its more impressive defence. For Cohen historical materialism may be defined by two 'functional' theses:

(1) the level of the productive forces explains the nature of a society's relations of production;

(2) the nature of a society's relations of production in turn determines the nature of that society's 'superstructure', e.g. its political institutions, legal code, and so on.[2]

It has been argued by writers such as Elster and Giddens that functional explanations are, in general, invalid in the social sciences.[3] If this were the case we could immediately reject productive force determinism for its reliance on such explanation. In fact, functional explanation cannot be rejected out of hand and it can legitimately be used in the social sciences in certain limited instances. Chapter 7 argues that productive force determinism is not one of these instances.

Productive force determinism assumes that society's relations of production are called into being by the functional requirements of the productive forces. There are thus two questions:

(1) *Are* the relations of production functional for the productive forces? (A question which has to be answered historically.)

(2) If the relations of production are functional for the productive forces does this *explain* the nature of the relations of production?

Chapter 7 argues that society's relations of production are not necessarily functional for the productive forces. Question (ii) is thus redundant. In other words a key objection to productive force determinism is *not* that it is a form of functional explanation, but rather that this theory does not show that the relations of production *are* functional in the first place, a failure not of logic but of historical evidence.

What is functional explanation? In what sense is productive force determinism a form of functional explanation? Is functional explanation invalid *per se* in the social sciences? In functional explanation specific forms of social behaviour are explained in terms of the effects which that behaviour brings about, effects which are beneficial for the existing social organisation. The classic instance of functional explanation is that of the Hopi rain-dance. The Hopi Indians periodically gather to perform a tribal rain-dance. This 'manifest' function of the dance appears to be a pure superstition, an irrational form of behaviour, since rain-dances do not (we are assured) have the effect which they seek to achieve. Only when we perceive the 'latent' function of the rain-dance, which is the reinforcement of the social cohesion of this scattered tribe, can we really appreciate its meaning and explain its existence. A social institution (the rain-dance) is thus explained in terms of its beneficial effects (social cohesion).[4]

How does functional explanation relate to productive force determinism? Cohen argues that in general society's productive forces explain the nature of its relations of production and that, in turn, the relations of production determine the nature of society's political and ideological superstructure. Yet Cohen is also very aware that relations of production have an important influence on the development of the productive forces and that political superstructures can affect class relations.[5] Why then does Cohen not adopt a theory of the mutual interaction of productive forces, class and superstructure? Why continue to emphasise the primacy of the productive forces? Cohen's answer is that the nature of society's relations of production and their influence on the productive forces are *functionally* explained by the requirements of the productive forces. He can therefore assert the fundamental primacy of the productive forces, whilst also recognising the interaction which takes place between the levels of the social formation. Only in this way, he adds, can the apparently conflicting claims of historical materialism be made 'consistent' – that historical materialism is not consistent seems a prospect too horrible to contemplate.[6] The relations of production are thus functionally explained by the needs of the productive forces since they have to be periodically changed 'in order that' humanity will not be deprived of the benefits of growing productivity.[7] It is precisely because the relations of production 'should' be functional for the productive forces that they have to be cast aside in those periods when they have become fetters on the further growth of productivity.

It should be stressed that to ascribe a function to an institution or form of behaviour is not necessarily to explain the existence of that institution or behaviour. For instance, the fact that conflict within bureaucracies has the effect of preventing them from ossifying does not mean that such conflicts exist in order to bring about this beneficial effect. In this case the beneficial effect is merely an unintended by-product of the conflict. Cohen merely argues that in some cases functional ascriptions (i.e. of beneficial effect) may also perform the task of explaining the institution or behaviour which produces that effect. Secondly, it should be emphasised that Cohen is not arguing that an event which comes later can explain an event which came earlier. The Hopi raindance is not explained by its subsequent consequences (social cohesion), its disposition to occur is explained by its tendency to produce certain consequences.[8]

The immediate problem, given that not all functional ascriptions are explanatory, is to distinguish those which are. Both the functionalists and their critics are agreed that for a functional explanation to be valid some form of 'feedback' mechanism must exist whereby the tendency to produce the benefit, 'f', guarantees the existence of 'e', the action, institution or organ which produces 'f'.[9] The long neck of the giraffe, for example, may be explained in terms of the benefits to its owner arising from the giraffe's acacia leaf diet. The mechanism linking the benefit and the organ in this example is Darwinian evolution, i.e. chance variation which explains the possibility of the development of the long neck, and natural selection, which explains the survival and proliferation of the favoured giraffes. In biology we do not need to specify the 'feedback mechanism' at work in each case, as the general theory of chance variation/natural selection provides a universal mechanism.[10]

The problem for social scientists (including historians) is that they have no equivalent general form of functional explanation. This absence is a great potential weakness for those who wish to explain social institutions in functional terms. The Polish Marxist, Sztompka, for instance, argues that merely to show that 'x' is beneficial for 'y' is not to explain the existence of 'x' by those benefits. 'The most precise determinism of a system's preferred states or functional requirements will be useless if one cannot point to the actual mechanism that achieves these states and fulfils these requirements.' Yet even Sztompka, who believes that functional explanations are vital to social science, has to admit that none of the four mechanisms, which he suggests may carry out this key task, is 'fully adequate or satisfactory'.[11] Elster also stresses the importance of specifying the causal mechanism at work which allows one not only to claim that society's relations of production are functional for the growth of the productive forces (in itself a controversial claim), but also that these relations exist *because* they are designed to meet the requirements of the productive forces.[12]

Elster gives an example where functional explanation does work in social science – the Chicago school's analysis of the market. According to these economists, the diffusion of a particular practice, such as the introduction of economies of scale, can be explained in terms of its beneficial future consequences (higher profits), a classic instance of functional explanation. In this model the feedback mechanism is not assumed to exist simply because we can witness certain beneficial effects. The mechanism is specified as competition on the market and survival of those enterprises adopting profit-maximising strategies. In this case the mechanism at work is very much like that of natural selection, although there is no assumption that this mechanism can be applied to society as a whole.

Why do these enterprises adopt beneficial policies such as the economies of large-scale production? There are two possible types of answer:

(1)   They adopt beneficial policies for 'irrational' reasons. For instance, the managers of firms could obtain social prestige through their association with large firms. Economies of scale are adopted for economically irrational reasons but, nevertheless, the market will tend to promote the survival and success of those firms which have, accidentally, adopted profit-maximising strategies. Similarly, in natural evolution, survival of the fittest operates without any guiding intelligence at work.

(2)   Enterprises could adopt economies of scale for rational reasons, i.e. their managers or owners consciously pursue profit-maximising policies. Those who reasoned correctly would come up with successful policies and so survive. This is a form of explanation unique to the social sciences, since biology and physics have no need of explanations based on *intention*.[13]

Elster argues that for functional explanation to be valid there must be a mechanism linking beneficial consequences to a functional event or institution. This mechanism cannot be taken for granted in the social sciences, as it can in biology, and so must be specified in each particular instance. He believes that the only legitimate uses of functional explanation in social science are those which

(1)   invoke a mechanism analogous to 'natural selection', as in the Chicago school's model of the market; or

(2)   involve human intention.[14]

There are two possible counters to Elster's position. The first is that of writers such as Stinchcombe and van Parijs, i.e. that there is such a general mechanism at work. The second counter is that of Cohen, who suggests that we do not actually have to specify the mechanism at work provided there are sound reasons to suppose its existence. Stinchcombe's argument is that we can see society as an 'absorbing Markov machine'. Just as a restless sleeper will toss and turn until she is comfortable, so we can see society as in a state of flux tending towards equilibrium. Non-equilibrium states are inherently unstable and produce pressure for change. Thus a rigid bureaucracy, which cannot adapt to a changing environment, will eventually disappear and give way to a more flexible organisation which can deal with the strains of change.[15] Relations of production which are not suitable for the existing productive forces will similarly be cast aside as society searches for equilibrium.

Elster's response is that this is not strictly a functional explanation, since it does not explain an institution by its beneficial consequences, but rather by its lack of destabilising consequences. Stinchcombe's argument would not explain the *origin* of society's relations of production nor why they should be optimal for the growth of the productive forces, but could be used to explain the *persistence* of particular relations of production in terms of their tendency to minimise crisis in the productive forces. This is hardly a key objection, since lack of dysfunction could itself be said to be socially functional. We still have the survival of the fit, even if not the survival of the fittest. Elster also asks if we can use the Markov model of tendency towards equilibrium in the study of entire societies, given their complexity and the rapidity of social change. Again we have to ask if this is a key objection, given that we are interested in functional explanations of *particular* social arrangements such as Hopi rain-dances or specific forms of class relations.[16]

A more important weakness of the Stinchcombe argument is that although we may wish to see society as an absorbing Markov machine this is, at best, a metaphor or analogy and that metaphors are *not* explanations. For example, a society faced by over-population can be seen as in an unstable state and will, eventually, tend to some new equilibrium. But at what point does a particular society reach over-population? How long will its problems last? What form of equilibrium will be found? A lower population through starvation or emigration? Annexation of neighbouring territories? Increased agricultural productivity? A growth in food imports? Why a society has particular problems, how long these problems last and which solutions are adopted cannot be explained by a metaphor.

Van Parijs also offers a mechanism which can link a particular social arrangement with its beneficial consequences: trial and error. At a given level of development of the productive forces people could try out different relations of production. They would soon realise which form of production relation was best for the growth of the productive forces and so adopt this optimal form until the productive forces had changed enough to require a further change in production relations.[17] Readers may find the idea that class relations are like a pullover of the wrong size, which may be easily exchanged for another, rather quaint, but nevertheless the point, in abstract, is a valid one. However, Elster should have little difficulty accepting this type of argument since it involves human awareness and intention. Given that this is a logically valid form of explanation 'all' that we have to do is to test the hypothesis empirically, to see if societies have gone about acquiring production relations in this manner.

Stinchcombe and van Parijs have attempted to specify the mechanism which would validate functional explanation by providing the feedback between an institution and its beneficial effects. Cohen agrees that such mechanisms must exist in those cases where functional explanations are applicable. Where he disagrees with Elster is his belief that social scientists do not necessarily have to specify what these mechanisms consist of. Naturally it would be preferable if we could identify such mechanisms, but our failure to do so does not make the use of functional explanation in social science illegitimate. Cohen uses the analogy of biology: the theory of evolution explains the structure of an organism, such as the long neck of the giraffe, in terms of its benefit to a species and its adaptation to its environment. Biologists can now specify the mechanism of this adaptation through chance variation, natural selection and reproductive maximisation, i.e. in terms of Darwinian theory. Yet, even before Darwin, natural scientists could see that animals' structures were functional and believed that they possessed these structures *because* they were functional. Many pre-Darwinian scientists could not specify any mechanism which produced the functional organ; others, such as Lamarck, offered incorrect explanatory mechanisms. Nevertheless these scientists were correct to adopt a functional explanation, even though they could not identify the mechanism behind it. For Cohen, social science is at a similar level of development to that of pre-Darwinian biology where it can observe functional links, such as that between the type of education provided by a society and that society's economic needs, but cannot specify the mechanism which produces them.[18]

The argument that there may be sufficient evidence to indicate the existence of a feedback mechanism, even where it cannot be identified, is a strong one, even allowing for Elster's reply that we must have some idea of the causal mechanism at work in order to distinguish a spurious correlation ('e' happens and is followed by 'f') from a real cause ('e' happens and results in 'f') or from a functional explanation ('e' happens because of its tendency to result in 'f').[19] Cohen's primacy thesis makes the functional claim that particular relations of production are explicable in terms of the requirements of the productive forces. Cohen admits that he does not have a good answer to the question of how productive forces select appropriate production relations.[20] It follows that the validity of the primacy thesis rests on the availability of suitable and sufficient evidence to make us accept its claims in advance of an elaboration of the mechanism at work.

Our aim is to assess the validity of the productive force determinist account of historical change. Our first conclusion is that this theory cannot be kicked firmly out of court by an anti-functionalist boot, without further hearing, since functional explanations can be legitimately invoked in certain circumstances. We must turn therefore from the abstract problem of the validity of functional explanation to the specific case of productive force determinism and ask:

(1) Are society's relations of production explained by their functionality for the productive forces? (The logical problem of the applicability of functional explanation to this case.)

(2) Are society's relations of production functional for the productive forces in the first place? (The empirical problem of functional ascription.)

Chapter 7 answers both questions in the negative and so rejects the social primacy of the productive forces. Chapter 8 offers an alternative explanation of long-term social change.

Notes

1 W. H. Shaw, *Marx's Theory of History* (London, 1978); G. A. Cohen, *Karl Marx's Theory of History: A Defence* (Oxford, 1978).

2 G. A. Cohen, 'Functional explanation: reply to Elster', *Political Studies* XXVIII (1980), p. 129.

3 A. Giddens, *A Contemporary Critique of Historical Materialism* (London, 1981), pp. 17, 215; A. Giddens, *Studies in Social and Political Theory* (London, 1979), Ch. 2; A. Giddens, *Central Problems in Social Theory* (London, 1979), pp. 7, 110–17, 211–14; J. Elster, *Ulysses and the Sirens* (Cambridge, 1979), Ch. 1.

4 Giddens, *Central Problems in Social Theory*, pp. 210–14. See also R. K. Merton, *Social Theory and Social Structure* (Glencoe, 1962), pp. 19–84.

5 Cohen, 'Functional explanation: reply to Elster', p. 130.

6 Ibid., p. 129; G. A. Cohen, 'Reply to Elster on "Marxism, functionalism and the game theory" ', *Theory and Society* XI (1982), p. 486; G. A. Cohen, 'Functional explanation, consequence explanation and Marxism', *Inquiry* XXV (1982), p. 30.

7 K. Marx, *The Poverty of Philosophy* (Moscow, 1973), p. 157.

8 Elster, *Ulysses and the Sirens*, p. 33; Cohen, *Karl Marx's Theory of History*, pp. 253, 261–2.

9 J. Elster, 'Cohen on Marx's theory of history', *Political Studies* XXVIII (1980), pp. 126–7; G. A. Cohen, 'Functional explanation: reply to Elster', p. 131.

10 Cohen, *Karl Marx's Theory of History*, pp. 269–70; J. Elster, *Sour Grapes* (Cambridge, 1983), p. 103. It should be stressed that chance variation assumes no director, purpose or goal, i.e. it does not occur 'in order' to produce the survival of the fittest.

11 P. Sztompka, *Systems and Function* (New York, 1974), pp. 140, 150, 151.

12 Elster, 'Cohen on Marx's theory of history', p. 126; Elster, *Sour Grapes*, p. 107; Elster, *Ulysses and the Sirens*, p. 34.

13 Ibid., pp. 31–2; J. Elster, *Explaining Technical Change* (Cambridge, 1983), pp. 57–8; Cohen, *Karl Marx's Theory of History*, pp. 287–8.

14 J. Elster, 'Marxism, functionalism and game theory: the case for methodological individualism', *Theory and Society* XI (1982), pp. 455, 463; Elster, *Sour Grapes*, p. 106; Elster, 'Cohen on Marx's theory of history', p. 126.

15 A. L. Stinchcombe, 'Merton's theory of social structure', in L. A. Coser (ed.), *The Idea of Social Structure* (New York, 1975), p. 29; J. Elster, 'Reply to comments', *Inquiry* XXIII (1980), pp. 226–8; Elster, *Explaining Technical Change*, pp. 61–4; Elster, 'Cohen on Marx's theory of history', p. 127.

16 Elster, *Explaining Technical Change*, pp. 61–4; P. van Parijs, 'Functionalist Marxism rehabilitated', *Theory and Society* XI (1982), p. 504.

17 Ibid., p. 503.

18 Elster, 'Cohen on Marx's theory of history', pp. 131–3; Cohen, *Karl Marx's Theory of History*, pp. 285–6; Cohen, 'Functional explanation, consequence explanation and Marxism', pp. 50–54; Cohen, 'Reply to Elster on "Marxism, functionalism, and game theory" ', pp. 490–2.

19 Elster, *Explaining Technical Change*, p. 67.

20 G. A. Cohen, 'Forces and relations of production', in B. Matthews (ed.), *Marx: A Hundred Years On* (London, 1983), pp. 119, 124.

CHAPTER 7

Productive force determinism: a critique

That Marx and Engels offered a coherent and explicit productive force determinist account of human history, and that this was the orthodox reading of historical materialism for later generations of Marxists, is, hopefully, no longer open to doubt. Our next task is to assess the validity of Marx's claims and of the defence of Marx's position offered by G. A. Cohen and W. H. Shaw.[1] We will review the seven main points of productive force determinism which were established in Chapter 3 and will consider modern refinements of Marx's theory, under these seven headings:

1 Human existence and human society are impossible without production. (See p. 28 above.)

Marx claimed that earlier writers had paid little attention to the development of production, which is the real basis of all social life and human history. As we have seen this is rather a strange claim, given the importance of the 'mode of subsistence' in eighteenth-century accounts of historical change;[2] the main issue is not, however, the originality of Marx's claim, but its role within the defence of productive force determinism. In practice even Marx's defenders admit that his claim that humanity must eat and have shelter before it can pursue politics and philosophy, 'hardly shows' the explanatory primacy of material production in social life and that Marx's logic is 'flimsy and perfunctory'.[3]

Even if we chose to see production as a 'moment' of human activity which precedes the existence of social relations this would not, in itself, tell us anything about the relative importance of production, class relations and society's superstructure once all of these social elements had

92

been called into existence. These levels of society could interact with one another or any one level could, in theory, have social dominance. If production is a *precondition* of social existence this tells us nothing about its role in *determining* social structure or historical change. Anyway, must we see production as distinct from and preceding social existence? An alternative view would be that production is itself a social activity. This alternative forms the basis for the reading of Marx offered below and for a quite different interpretation of historical change from that of productive force determinism.

2 Humans produce in a distinctive manner, in a way that distinguishes them from other animals. (See pp. 28–9 above.)

Two separate problems have to be distinguished about this claim. The first is whether we agree with those characteristics which Marx defines as uniquely human. The second is that if we agreed with Marx's definition would it provide the basis for a productive force determinist interpretation of historical change? Marx offers three ways in which human labour is unique. The first claim, that 'men' distinguish themselves from other animals only when they begin to produce, need not detain us as it would seem incapable of rational proof or disproof. The second claim, that 'man' is the toolmaking animal, may also be rejected since a number of animals may also be defined as toolmakers, although 'man' may be distinctive in creating tools which are used to make other tools.[4] Marx's third claim, that human labour is distinguished by its application of conscious ingenuity and intention, is more acceptable to modern anthropologists. It is the relationship between humans and their tools, not the use of tools *per se*, which distinguishes them from other animals.[5]

Even if we accept that humans do produce in a unique manner this does not compel us to accept that society's relations of production are determined by its productive forces. This second thesis seems to imply that because 'man' is essentially a toolmaking animal (or at least produces in some unique way), human history is essentially the history of the development of that unique form of production, and that other social elements correspond to this defining feature. Yet merely to define something does not allow us to make statements of causation about it. We may, for instance, define a bird as a feathered animal with two wings and two legs, but this definition tells us nothing about any particular bird's ability to fly, its habitat, mating patterns, migrations and so on. The argument that humans produce and so create social relations, assumes that production has social primacy and that we can conceive of production independently from and prior to social relations. It is exactly the truth of these assumptions which has to be *proved* if productive force determinism is to have any explanatory power. Recent writers have abandoned Marx's first two points in their defence of the primacy of the productive forces.

3.1 In general society's relations of production are determined by the level of development of its productive forces. (The 'primacy thesis'. See pp. 29–35 above.)

The critique of this major thesis of productive force determinism can be divided into six main points. It is argued here that:

(i)   Shaw's defence of this 'primacy thesis' depends on a circular logic.

(ii) Cohen's defence of this thesis is historically questionable.

(iii) Productive force determinism assumes that the productive forces are historical actors, yet it provides neither the mechanism whereby the productive forces produce their social effect nor the empirical evidence to suggest that such a mechanism exists. In other words the productive forces are 'fetishised' – endowed with powers which they do not really possess.

(iv) Productive force determinism is a deductive philosophy of history which gives us the answer to historical questions as soon as we have asked them. It is, therefore, a philosophy of history which rejects the historical method shared by Marxist and non-Marxist historians alike.

(v)   Productive force determinism involves a form of teleology in which the future needs of the productive forces determine the present structure of society's class relations. No mechanism is offered to show how the future determines the present.

(vi) Finally, much of the apparent credibility of productive force determinism rests on a confusion between work relations of production and social relations of production.

(i) Shaw's defence of the primacy of the productive forces

In his book *Marx's Theory of History* W. H. Shaw attempts to give a case for the determining role of the productive forces which, he admits, Marx and Engels never gave.[6] Shaw asks us to consider the three possible alternatives to the primacy of the productive forces. The first alternative is that the relations of production are determined by elements from society's superstructure, rather than by the productive forces. We can however discount this hypothesis, Shaw argues, because Marx claims that economic relations structure the social world in general. To accept this first alternative would undermine the whole thrust of Marx's theory.[7] In other words, Shaw is claiming that if Marx is true, this first alternative must be incorrect. It is, however, the truth of Marx's theory which we are attempting to assess. It is not, in this context, a premise which Marx, or Shaw, could use to exclude other alternatives. We are offered a circular logic where the truth of Marx is both the starting point and conclusion of the argument.

The second alternative to the primacy of the productive forces is that the relations of production are self-determining. 'If this is the case', asks Shaw, 'why should they (the production relations) develop at all?' It is, apparently, inconceivable that the relations of production should develop independently, yet it is quite possible for the productive forces to develop of their own accord.[8] In other words, Shaw has excluded the second alternative by reasserting the hypothesis which we are supposed to be testing, i.e. that society's relations of production cannot develop independently but that the productive forces can do so. In passing, it should be noted that, given that relations of production involve conflict between the producing class and the 'exploiting' class, it is quite possible that this conflict would give them the dynamic to change and develop. The historical truth of this claim does not concern us for the moment; simply the fact that Shaw has not disproved this second alternative, but instead merely reasserts the primacy of the productive forces.

The third alternative to the primacy of the productive forces is that the forces and relations of production are mutually determining. Shaw argues that we may reject this possibility because it has 'no textual support' from Marx.[9] There are two possible responses to Shaw. The first would be to show that this alternative *does* have textual support. Thus in *The German Ideology* Marx refers to civil society as 'the form of intercourse determined by the existing productive forces and *in its turn determining them*'.[10] Similarly he claims that 'industry and commerce, production and exchange of the necessities of life in their turn determine distribution, the structure of the different classes of society, *and are in turn, determined by it*'.[11] Therefore the state is based on society's 'mode of production and form of intercourse *which mutually determine* each other'.[12]

The second response to Shaw is that even if the mutual determination of the forces and relations of production had no textual support in Marx, this would only disqualify it as a reading of Marx. It would still be quite possible for the forces and relations of production to determine each other, even if Marx was totally oblivious of the fact. Yet again we cannot invoke Marx's authority, when it is this very authority which we are supposed to be testing. If we do not accept Shaw's reasoning (except as a reading of Marx), all three alternatives to the primacy of the productive forces remain as logical possibilities.

Shaw realises that even if he has excluded these three alternatives productive force determinism is still only a lesser evil, to be preferred to other inferior possibilities. He thus offers two *positive* reasons for accepting the primacy of the productive forces. The first is that as 'men never relinquish what they have won' they are forced to make their relations of production correspond to newly acquired productive forces. 'Men will or do change their social relations of production to accommodate existing or prospective productive forces', as otherwise the productive advance would be squandered. The 'second' positive justification for the primacy of the productive forces is that when a society's productive forces conflict with the existing relations of production, the fundamental economic equilibrium is disrupted. Since Marx believes that society will not sacrifice its acquired productive forces, it follows that only the adjustment of the production relations in order to accommodate the new productive forces will allow society to re-stabilize.[13] It is not clear why the second justification is different from the first. 'Both' of these positive reasons for believing in the primacy of the productive forces make two assumptions: the first is that the productive forces have an inherent tendency to develop and so outgrow the existing relations of production; the second assumption is that as these relations of production become fetters on the development of the productive forces they have to be cast aside and new relations of production are called into being. These are, of course, two central assumptions of productive force determinism. In short, Shaw's positive defence of the primacy of the productive forces rests on … the primacy of the productive forces. It is a reassertion of exactly the hypothesis which we are supposed to be testing.

(ii) Cohen's historical analysis

Cohen's primacy thesis is that 'the nature of a set of production relations is explained by the level of development of the productive forces embraced by it'.[14] In fact, Cohen later characterises his view more accurately, when he says that 'the relations which obtain at a given time are the relations most suitable for the forces to develop at that time'.[15] The relations of production do not only correspond to the level reached by the productive forces, they are also suitable for the *future* development of the productive forces except, of course, during those transitional periods when the relations of production have become fetters. Cohen specifies four stages in the development of the productive forces in terms of the level of surplus which they produce and suggests a corresponding form of economic structure or relations of production:[16]

Form of economic structure		Level of productive development
1. Pre-class society	Corresponding to	No surplus
2. Pre-capitalist class society	Corresponding to	Some surplus but less than
3. Capitalist society	Corresponding to	Moderately high surplus but less than
4. Post-class society	Corresponding to	Massive surplus

The primacy thesis posits a precise relationship between society's forces and relations of production. Cohen does, however, admit that in pre-capitalist class societies it may not be possible to specify a one-to-one relationship between the level of development of productive forces and the precise nature of the relations of production. A given level of social productivity may be able to support a variety of forms of class relations. Slavery, serfdom, free peasant, the Asiatic mode and so on are passed over as the 'endless nuances' of pre-capitalist modes of exploitation.[17] Social scientists may well find this argument disturbing, since it is precisely why certain societies have slavery, serfdom, free peasants, tax-rent etc., which is of interest to them. To have these differences passed off as 'nuances', and to describe the whole of world history between the end of primitive communism and the advent of capitalism as 'pre-capitalist class society', would seem to limit the utility of productive force determinism for historical research.

A theory of history which is not fruitful for historical research would seem to pose a number of problems but, for the moment, this is not our chief concern. The key point is that Cohen is no longer positing a precise relationship between a given level of development of the productive forces and the specific nature of a society's relations of production. In the case of 'pre-capitalist class societies', a case which takes up rather a large slice of human history, the determination by the productive forces takes the form of what they *rule out*, i.e. primitive communism, capitalism, and communism. The problem is that Cohen himself has already rejected this 'loose' formulation of productive force determinism. He argues that the fact that a certain level of technology rules out certain types of production relation (computers rule out slavery) is not in itself a defence of the primacy of the productive forces, since 'if high technology rules out slavery then slavery rules out high technology. Something must be added … to establish the primacy of the productive forces.' This 'something' must, in practice, be the identification of the mechanism through which the productive forces create specific relations of production, or strong empirical evidence to suggest the existence of such a mechanism (see Chapter 6).[18] As we shall see, Cohen supplies neither and so his argument leaves us with the 'mutual constraint' of the forces and relations of production. An alternative to mutual constraint is outlined in Chapter 8.

If the first problem with Cohen's defence of the primacy of the productive forces is that one level of development of the productive forces may result in very different forms of class relation, the second problem is that very different levels of development of the productive forces may 'produce' the same class relations. The classical example of this is the stages of capitalist development outlined by Marx in volume I of *Capital*. Marx divides the capitalist era into two periods, manufacture which prevailed from the mid-sixteenth century to the last third of the eighteenth century, and the age of large-scale industry and mechanisation following the Industrial Revolution.[19] Productive force determinism argues that as the productive forces develop so society's relations of production must alter. We should, at first sight, expect the Industrial Revolution to be a decisive instance of this theory since it represents the most massive increase ever seen in human productive capacity. As Marx said in 1848, the previous century had:

> created more massive and colossal productive forces than have all preceding generations together. Subjection of Nature's forces to man, machinery, application of chemistry to industry and agriculture, steam-navigation, railways, electric telegraphs, clearing of whole continents for cultivation, canalization of rivers, whole populations conjured out of the ground – what earlier century had even a presentiment that such productive forces slumbered in the lap of social labour?[20]

It is hardly surprising that Engels considered that this industrial revolution was the 'foundation of every aspect of modern English life, the driving force behind all social development'. As we have seen, Engels believed that England's modern class structure was the result of the Industrial Revolution; before 1780 England 'had few proletarians' and

was 'a country like any other'. The English proletariat arose with industrialisation and then spread to the countryside as large farms replaced
smallholdings.[21]

There can be no doubt that the Industrial Revolution was a turning
point in human history: 'some time in the 1780s, and for the first time
in human history, the shackles were taken off the productive power of
human societies, which henceforth became capable of the constant,
rapid and up to the present limitless multiplication of men, goods and
services'. The truth of this judgement remains, however, even though the
extent of industrialisation was rather limited before the railway age.[22]
Did this revolution in the nature of society's productive forces and productive potential lead to a revolution in its relations of production, as
Engels claimed? Did the social relations of production 'vary according to
the means of production' as Marx said they would? Were class relations
'transformed along with the change and development of the material
means of production'?[23] According to Marx himself, this was not the
case. Before the introduction of machinery industrial production took
the form of 'manufacture'. Marx outlines two distinct forms of the division of labour in this manufacturing system:

(a)   the assembling together in one workshop, under the control of a
      single capitalist, of workers belonging to various independent
      handicrafts through whose hands a given article must pass on its
      way to completion, such as the wheelwrights, tailors, harness
      makers, painters, etc., involved in the manufacture of carriages; or

(b)   a number of workmen who all do the same work and who each pro-
      duce an entire commodity under the control of a single capitalist.

In both cases the labour process remains dominated by skilled manual
labour, although there is a tendency for an increasing specialisation of
tasks and more systematic division of labour.[24]

Although manufacture is based on manual labour, it represents a
break with the guild system of the feudal mode of production. The producers are divorced from the means of production which now confront
them as capital. Manufacture is thus 'an entirely specific creation of the
capitalist mode of production'.[25] From the end of the eighteenth century
the manufacturing system declined. The nature of the labour process was
increasingly determined by machinery, by the instruments of production, rather than by labour power. Production is increasingly broken
down into its constituent parts and mechanised through the application
of the natural sciences.[26] In other words, the history of capitalism is
divided into two phases, divided by the greatest revolution in the

history of human technology. We may conceive of the capitalist mode of production as consisting of invariant relations of production, in which free wage labourers sell their labour power and produce profit for their employers; and variable forces of production, which can take the form of manufacture or mechanised industry.[27] There may be a revolutionary change in the nature of society's forces of production and yet no alteration in the nature of its relations of production. This would seem to be a problem for a theory of history which explains social change in terms of the development of the productive forces rather than vice versa.

Of course it might be argued that capitalist class relations are peculiarly elastic. They allow, indeed by their very nature must create, a 'constant revolutionizing of production' even if, in this case, this does not 'thereby' revolutionise the whole of society as Marx claimed it would.[28] But if this is the case, then it is the relations of production which are the dominant social element, and it is their nature which determines the impact of the productive forces. The case for the primacy of the productive forces could only be maintained by invoking the development thesis, i.e. that the productive forces have an inherent tendency to develop and so must eventually outgrow the relations of production to which they once corresponded. The primacy thesis comes to rely on the development thesis; if the development thesis falls then the primacy thesis falls with it.

(iii) The fetishism of the productive forces

In the *Economic and Philosophical Manuscripts* Marx argues that just as in religion 'man' creates God and yet perceives God as an alien power standing over him so, under capitalism, the products of labour are estranged from the producer so that they appear to exist 'independently of him and alien to him and begin to confront him as an autonomous power'.[29] Similarly, just as primitive peoples 'fetishise' material objects, endow them with powers which they do not, in fact, possess, so, under capitalism, commodities, human products, are fetishised and appear to have powers of their own.[30] In productive force determinism the productive forces take on a similar fetishistic power and are invoked as agents of historical change. It is the productive forces which inherently develop, cast aside class relations and call new relations into existence. History is thus the story of the development of the productive forces. Yet in fact 'the productive forces do nothing, they possess no immense wealth, they wage no battles. It is man, real living man who does all that, who possesses and fights. The productive forces are not, as it were, a person apart using humanity as a means to achieve its own aims.'[31] It is not the productive forces but real human beings who 'make their own history; but they do not make it just as they please; they do not make it under circumstances chosen by themselves, but under circumstances directly encountered, given and transmitted from the past'.[32] Humans are, of course, social beings who have entered into definite relations of production so that 'the history of all hitherto existing society is the history of class struggles'.[33]

As always the very familiarity of these quotations tends to prevent thought, so that it is easy to overlook their implied critique of productive force determinism. For writers such as Cohen, by implication if not by intent, humans do not make their own history, the productive forces do. The outcome of the class struggle, for example, becomes merely a reflex of the needs of the productive forces. Cohen would deny that he removes class struggle from the centre of history. Nevertheless, he does present the class struggle as only the means through which the productive forces achieve their ends. In the clash between the newly emergent bourgeoisie and the feudal ruling class, for instance, the bourgeoisie wins out and establishes capitalism. But why is the bourgeoisie victorious? Because, answers Cohen, it is 'the class most suited, most able and most disposed to preside over the development of the productive forces at a given time'.[34] His analysis thus attributes to the productive forces, needs (continued development) and agency (the power to select which class wins in the class struggle). The problem is, how can the productive forces have needs and by what mechanism can they determine the outcome of historical evolution? Of course it could be objected that the attribution of needs to the productive forces is merely a *façon de parler*, a shorthand term for the human needs which promote the growth of the productive forces. But in adopting this mode of expression we forget that humans have a variety of conflicting needs and that not all needs will be satisfied. We are then free to present the growth of the productive forces as an inevitable development.

Cohen is quite open in his admission that he can provide no satisfactory mechanism which would explain how the productive forces obtain their historical agency.[35] In the absence of the identification of such a mechanism, Cohen insists that the validity of functional explanation rests on the provision of sufficient empirical evidence to suggest the existence of such a mechanism even where, as in pre-Darwinian biology, the mechanism itself cannot be specified. At this point we should, then, expect an empirical discussion of specific historical relations of production and a demonstration of the fact that they were the form of relation 'most suitable for the forces to develop at that time'.[36] Yet this is the one task that Cohen does not undertake.

In two and a half pages he merely deals with the potentially difficult problem that Marx (correctly) regarded pre-capitalist modes of production as conservative, whereas capitalism revolutionised the productive forces. Did these conservative modes of production really correspond to the needs of development of the productive forces? Cohen's reply is that although feudalism gives a slower development of the productive forces than capitalism, it was most suited to the needs of the productive forces at the time when feudalism prevailed, i.e. 'sports cars are faster than jeeps but jeeps are faster on boggy land'.[37] The problem here is that in the vehicular analogy the conditions which the individual cars are suitable for are specified, e.g. boggy land, but Cohen does not tell us what it is about the conditions under which feudalism existed which made it best for the development of the productive forces. Of course, it may be answered, what made feudalism most suitable for this development was the nature of the existing productive forces – but this is to assume the truth of the hypothesis which we are trying to assess, i.e. that the relations of production are determined by the nature of the productive forces.

If Cohen's analysis of pre-capitalist modes of production is perfunctory, then his examination of the relationship between capitalism and its forces of production is little better. In itself this is not important, it is only significant in the light of Cohen's own (correct) stress on the crucial role of empirical evidence in the absence of a knowledge of the mechanisms which produce functional consequences. Productive force determinism suggests that capitalist social relations will emerge 'when and because productive power reaches a level beyond which it cannot rise within existing structures'.[38] To demonstrate the truth of this claim would entail:

(a)   the identification of the growing productive forces within feudalism;

(b)   specification of why feudalism was a fetter on the growth of these forces;

(c)   proof that the existence of feudal social relations was incompatible with further growth of the productive forces which therefore called into being new forms of relations of production.

In fact all that Cohen does is to show that feudalism was a fetter on the growth of the productive forces.[39] With this point there can be no disagreement, given the truth of Marx's claim that pre-capitalist modes of production were inherently conservative. It was precisely this inability to increase productivity which led to the crisis of feudalism of the fourteenth century.[40]

To show that the transition to capitalism was the result of the development of the productive forces would require a demonstration that the productive forces had reached a level incompatible with the continued existence of feudal class relations. Such an explanation would also have to account for the failure of capitalism to appear in the early fourteenth century, by which time feudal class relations were clearly a fetter on productive advance. In practice Cohen admits that he makes no attempt to demonstrate the truth of his claim that capitalism emerged out of feudalism as a result of the growth of the productive forces, but merely seeks to demonstrate its compatibility with Marx's general theory.[41] In other words he admits that he does not perform the one task which would demonstrate the historical validity of his theory of history.

In the absence of any mechanism through which the productive forces meet their needs, or the provision of empirical evidence to suggest the existence of such a mechanism, the primacy of the productive forces becomes a conditional statement, i.e. 'if the productive forces are to advance then specific relations of production must exist'. This formulation implies that certain types of relations of production allow, or promote, different forms of development of the productive forces. This is exactly the alternative to productive force determinism developed in Chapter 8. The determining role of the productive forces could only be salvaged if, in practice, there is no 'if' about the development so that eventually new class relations had to be created to meet their needs. Yet again, the truth of the primacy thesis comes to rest on acceptance of the development thesis.

The fetishism of the productive forces, their transformation into historical agents, can also be seen in Shaw's account of the transition from feudalism to capitalism. The historical detail of this account is considered below. For at the moment we need merely note that, for Shaw, capitalism emerged out of feudalism as a result of the 'needs' of the emerging productive forces. The new productive forces were 'begging for work relations which (could) appropriately manage them'.[42] If the productive forces do not have the power to 'beg', then it is difficult to see how they can create specific relations of production. How they do this, and why the productive forces persistently prove such successful beggars, remains a mystery.

(iv) A lever for constructing history

Productive force determinism may also be criticised for offering a theory of history which is based on a method which is unacceptable to both Marxist and non-Marxist historians. It offers *deductive* answers to historical questions irrespective of the *specific* situation being discussed. This is not to suggest that history does not need theory, that it deals with the unique, cannot generalise, etc., etc., etc. The choice is not whether to accept theory or not, but rather *which* theory to adopt. 'Hostility to theory usually means opposition to other people's theories and an oblivion of one's own.'[43] Marxist theory provides us with a number of concepts (mode of production, ideology, etc.) which allow us to ask questions and to construct hypotheses which can be tested against evidence. Marxist history differs from other interpretations of history not in its method of validation, but in its categories and characteristic hypotheses. What we need is not a 'theory of history', but a history which is theoretically informed and conscious.[44] As Engels said, 'our conception of history is above all a guide to study, not a lever for construction after the Hegelian manner'.[45]

That productive force determinism is such a 'lever' for constructing history can be seen from the tautologies of the 1859 'Preface'. The 'Preface' claims that 'no special order is ever destroyed before all the productive forces for which it is sufficient have been developed and new superior relations of production never replace older ones before the material conditions for their existence have matured within the old framework of society'.[46] If we ask then 'why did the transition from feudalism to capitalism take place?' the answer must be 'because of the growth of the productive forces'. If we ask 'what was the level of development of the productive forces needed to ensure this transition?' the answer must be 'whatever level the productive forces had reached when that transition took place'.

This sounds ridiculous. Indeed it is ridiculous, but it is exactly the logic that Shaw invokes to explain the transition to capitalism. What caused this transition? Shaw answers that it was the growth of commerce, commodities and an increasing throng of labourers divested of the means of their own subsistence. The role of the productive forces is not yet obvious and so, Shaw continues, 'there is a development of the productive forces sufficient to support capitalism'. What was specific about the nature of the productive forces in early modern Europe that allowed the development of capitalism? What were the vigorous productive forces breaking through the fetters of feudal property relations and calling new capitalist relations of production into being? We are never told, but, whatever they were, they were 'begging for work relations which could appropriately manage them' and relations of production which could accommodate these new work relations.[47] Cohen similarly claims that the transition to capitalism took place because of the needs of the productive forces, although he is not concerned to prove the point empirically.[48]

Cohen's analysis of the outcome of class struggle, like Shaw's, uses the primacy of the productive forces as a lever of historical explanation. Capitalism emerges because of the victory of the bourgeoisie, socialism because of the victory of the proletariat. 'But why does the successful class succeed? Marx finds the answer in the character of the productive forces.' That class most suitable for the development of the productive forces at a particular time is the class which will emerge victorious.[49] If we took another example and asked why the English peasantry of the later Middle Ages was able to use the shortage of tenants to obtain its freedom then the answer, presumably, is that the needs of the productive forces produced this result. If we ask why the Bohemian landlords of the seventeenth century responded to a similar shortage of tenants by successfully enserfing the peasantry than the answer, again, presumably lies in the needs of the productive forces. Our lever tends to produce rather banal results. Whether the class most suitable for the development of the productive forces *does* emerge as historically victorious is considered in our discussion of the development thesis. Our criticism here is that productive force determinism offers a historical short cut. It tells us the answer to questions as soon as we have asked them. As a result, the short cut turns out to be a historical dead end.

It should be noted that Marx and Engels themselves gave a number of warnings about such 'philosophies of history': 'The materialist method turns into its opposite if it is not taken as one's guiding principle of investigation but as a ready made pattern to which one shapes the facts of history to suit oneself.'[50] Marx criticised such master keys of history, 'the supreme virtue of which consists of being supra-historical', when he rejected the views of a critic who:

> insists on transforming my historical sketch of the genesis of capitalism in western Europe into an historico-philosophical theory of the general path prescribed by fate to all nations whatever the historical circumstances in which they find themselves in order that they may ultimately arrive at the economic system which ensures, together with the greatest expansion of the productive power of social labour, the most complete

development of man. But I beg his pardon. He is doing me too much honour and at the same time slandering me too much.[51]

(v) Teleology

A crucial objection to the general claim that society's relations of production correspond to the level of development of its productive forces is that the claim invokes a teleological explanation. History is seen as having a purpose and historical events are means to this end. The future goal, in this case the development of the productive forces, determines the prior path, i.e. the adoption of specific relations of production. Both Shaw and Cohen are quite open in their admission of the teleology involved in productive force determinism.[52] Cohen also implicitly invokes a preference for a teleological conception of history when he argues that any alternative to productive force determinism would have to show 'how the production relations tend to change in *some particular direction* throughout history and not because of the growth of the productive forces within them'.[53] But why should we assume that history and the relations of production move in a *particular* direction? Surely social scientists should explain a given situation in terms of previous trends rather than as a step towards some, as yet, non-existent future. For example, we know with hindsight that the Industrial Revolution occurred and this knowledge helps us to pick out significant trends in eighteenth-century history, such as the creation of new markets, new inventions and so on. The Industrial Revolution may be explained by new markets, new inventions or whatever, but it is not the explanation of those trends. The Industrial Revolution was not a goal which history flowed towards. If it was the goal then who set it? Similarly capitalism may lead to socialism but, despite Marx's claims, this does *not* mean that it is capitalism's 'destiny' or 'mission' to create socialism.[54] Marx was less poetic, but more accurate, when he explicitly rejected the 'distortion' where 'later history is made the goal of earlier history and the outcome of historical development is labelled the "destiny", "goal", "germ" or "idea" of earlier history'.[55] Capitalism has certain results but it has no mission.

Marx argued that 'human anatomy contains a key to the anatomy of the ape' not because human anatomy is the goal of earlier evolution, but because the final outcome allows us to identify significant trends in earlier developments.[56] He welcomed Darwin's *On the Origin of Species* precisely because it dealt 'the death blow to teleology in the natural sciences for the first time'.[57] Historians do not claim that history moves in a particular direction. It is precisely why paths of historical evolution diverge, such as the evolution of feudalism in western Europe whilst Byzantium remained dominated by the Ancient mode of production, or the evolution of capitalism in early modern England in a period when France was consolidating a free peasantry and eastern Europe was intensifying servile dues, which is of interest to them.

Cohen's teleology is most apparent in his discussion of the crucial point, made by Plamenatz, that in volume I of *Capital* Marx does not explain the end of feudalism in terms of the emergence of new productive forces. On the contrary, he claims that it was only *after* feudalism had ended and capitalist relations of property had been established, that new productive forces were introduced.[58] Cohen's reply is that Plamenatz fails to consider that 'not all fettering is of forces which already exist'; fettering not only limits the application of productive forces already in existence, but may also prevent the future development of productive forces which potentially exist.[59]

It is difficult to know where to begin with this argument. We have already been mystified by the fetishistic belief that the productive forces have historical agency and are able to beg or call into being new relations of production. Here our mystification goes even deeper. It is not the productive forces which do the begging but non-existent, future productive forces. How can we possibly assess such a claim? Cohen denies that he explains the present by a non-existent future, but merely explains 'e' in terms of its tendency to produce 'f'. But in such cases we must know that a feedback mechanism exists between 'e' and 'f', or have evidence to suggest that it exists. Otherwise how can we distinguish a mere correlation ('e' is followed by 'f') from a functional-causal link ('e' occurs because of its tendency to result in 'f')? In the absence of such a mechanism we are left with the very determination of the present by the future which Cohen explicitly wishes to avoid.[60]

If we reject the claim that capitalism emerged because of the needs of, as yet, non-existent productive forces, we are simply left with the view that as capitalism emerged, it created a particular form and pace of development of the productive forces. This is exactly the alternative reading of the relationship between the forces and relations of production offered below. Our problem is then to specify why capitalism emerged in the first place – but this is an empirical problem which can be answered only through research, not by setting in motion the deductive mechanism of a ready-made philosophy of history.

(vi) Confusion of work relations and relations of production?

Finally, it should be noted that much of the apparent weight of productive force determinism comes from a confusion of work relations and of the division of labour within society (e.g. work relations within productive units), with the social relations of production defined by a specific appropriation of surplus labour. Production necessarily involves social co-operation between individuals: 'in the social production of their existence men enter into definite relations, which are independent of their will ...'.[61] But are these definite relations work relations, class relations or both? It does, after all, seem convincing that a particular stage of production should create corresponding work relations:

> In production men not only act on nature but also on one another. They produce only by co-operating in a certain way and mutually exchanging their activities. In order to produce, they enter into definite connections and relations with one another and only within these social connections and relations does their action on nature, production, take place. These social relations into which the producers enter with one another, the conditions under which they exchange their activities and participate in the whole act of production, will naturally vary according to the character of the means of production.[62]

Marx seems here to be discussing work relations of production on the analogy of the introduction of firearms which, he says, 'necessarily changed' the whole internal organisation of the army. Yet he then goes on to say that 'The relations of production in their totality constitute what are called social relations, society and specifically society at a definite stage of historical development, a society with a peculiar, distinctive character. Ancient society, feudal society and bourgeois society are such totalities of production relations.'[63] In these passages Marx:

(a)   takes technical change for granted and then uses it as an explanation of social change. We have argued here that technical change is an *explanandum* rather than an explanation;

(b)   *confuses the division of labour involved in production* ('men' only produce by co-operation) *with the social division between classes in ancient, feudal and capitalist society;*

(c)   asserts that social relations correspond to the level of development of the productive forces and yet distinguishes between societies on the basis of the former, derivative feature not the latter, so-called fundamental one;

(d)   *assumes that the production process exists independently of social co-operation and determines the form of the latter. But this is only how production appears*

108

to the individual who enters into it. In a more general sense social co-operation is not the result of the production process, but is one of its vital constituents. Elsewhere Marx discusses four fundamental aspects of human existence: material production, the growth of new needs, the reproduction of human life and social co-operation. The first three of these have 'existed simultaneously since the dawn of history' and the fourth, social co-operation, is also as 'old as men themselves'.[64] If humanity only produces within certain work relations and if this social co-operation has existed for as long as humanity has, then *in what sense are the instruments of production prior to, and determinant of, work relations?* Of course the use of certain instruments of production may rule out certain work relations, but certain types of work relations would also rule out the use of certain tools.

Even if we accepted that work relations are determined by the instruments of production, *there is no reason to assume that changes in work relations lead to changes in the social relations of production.* Marx certainly seems to confuse work relations with class relations when he says both 'the hand-mill gives you society with the feudal lord; the steam-mill society with the industrial capitalist' and 'the hand-mill pre-supposes a different division of labour from the steam-mill'.[65] In these passages Marx fails once more to distinguish work relations in the production process from the social or class relations of production. It is possible however for there to be massive changes in the former, as in the transition from manufacture to large-scale industry, without any transformation of the latter.

Cohen offers three examples of how change in the work relations may lead to change in society's relations of production. One of these is a hypothetical story about canoes and need not detain us here.[66] The second example is Lynn White's claim that the introduction of the heavy plough into medieval Europe led to new field types and to more co-operative forms of agriculture. Cohen himself admits that this example is 'partly fanciful' and that it is subject to 'severe and convincing criticism' by Rodney Hilton. In fact Hilton firmly rejected the claim that the work relations of common field agriculture were based on the use of the heavy plough. He adds that such technical determinism has often proved attractive 'to those who like to have complex developments explained by simple causes'.[67] Another, more generous reviewer commented that White's whole argument was undermined by his own admission that 'some inventions change society because society is ready for change, and others do not because society is not ready for change. The context of the inquiry is immediately switched from technology to society.'[68]

Cohen's third example is that of the 1662 Act of Settlement, which tied poor relief to the pauper's parish of origin and so restricted the mobility of labour. He adopts Mantoux's argument that the Act had to be 'broken, ignored and finally scrapped' in order for large-scale industry to develop.[69] There are two problems with this example as a proof that change in the relations of production may be effected through the introduction of new work relations. The first problem is that it is difficult to see why the 1662 Act is defined as a work relation. It seems more logical to 'place' it in society's superstructure, i.e. its 'state and legal system'.[70] The second problem is that even if the Act was a work relation, its abolition did not result in the introduction of new class relations since England was already a capitalist country. In fact, neither the hypothetical example of the canoe, nor the fanciful example of the heavy plough nor the doubtful example of the 1662 Act illustrates Cohen's claim for a two stage determination whereby change in the productive forces requires new work relations, which in turn require new property relations. *Cohen has proved neither that the production process exists prior to work relations, nor that changes in the work relations lead to changes in class relations.*

3.2 The general claim that society's relations of production are determined by the level of development of its productive forces may be supported with a number of historical examples. (See pp. 36–41 above.)

Cohen's division of relations of production into pre-class societies, pre-capitalist class societies, capitalism, and post-class society, which correspond to specific levels of development of the productive forces (i.e. no surplus, some surplus, moderately high surplus and massive surplus respectively), is a systematic attempt to apply Marx's general claims to specific stages of historical evolution.[71] Consideration of this schema leads us to the conclusion that the primary thesis may be criticised on both logical and empirical grounds.

(i) Primitive communism

As we have seen, Marx welcomed the periodisation of prehistory in terms of technology, i.e. into the Stone, Bronze and Iron Ages. Engels, however, preferred Morgan's division into savagery (where hunting and gathering are dominant) and barbarism (characterised by cattle breeding and agriculture). Engels included both savagery and barbarism within the era of primitive communism. Only in the upper stage of barbarism, with the introduction of the use of iron, does the transition to class society begin, a transition completed in the stage of civilisation.[72] In other words, just as the Industrial Revolution of the eighteenth century did not put an end to the prevailing capitalist relations of production, so the agricultural revolution of the Neolithic period was quite compatible with the continued existence of primitive communism.[73] When a transformation of this order does not lead to a transformation of relations of production, it is difficult to see why the introduction of iron should be given such a 'revolutionary role' by Engels.[74]

A second, although less important problem, is Cohen's definition of primitive communism as a 'no surplus' society. He defines surplus as:

(a) production beyond what is necessary to satisfy the physical needs of the producers, now and in the future;

(b) production beyond what is necessary to satisfy the needs of the producers who have advanced to a level beyond physical subsistence;

(c) production appropriated by an exploiting, non-productive class.[75]

It may not, however, be useful to define primitive communism as a 'no surplus' society, except in the third of these senses. Hindess and Hirst have convincingly argued that all societies require the production of surplus labour, since 'the conditions of reproduction of the labourer are not equivalent to the conditions of the reproduction of the economy'. Communist society, even primitive communist society, is not defined by the absence of surplus labour but rather by a specific mode of appropriation of surplus labour, in this case a collective form of appropriation.[76]

The existence of surplus labour under primitive communism leads us on to a further problem with the first stage of Cohen's schema. Productive force determinism argues that new class relations emerge to meet the needs of the expanding productive forces. Cohen's schema, like Engels's The Origin of the Family, Private Property and the State, would require class societies to replace primitive communism as the productive forces develop sufficiently to generate a surplus or, more accurately, a larger surplus than was previously possible. With the emergence of classes came the origin of the state to guarantee the continued existence of class relations.[77] The problem with this seemingly plausible explanation of the emergence of classes and the state is that the direct opposite has been suggested with at least an equal plausibility. Primitive economies are marked by production at a level much below their potential. Whether agricultural or pre-agricultural their 'labor-power is underused, techological means are not fully engaged, natural resources are often untapped. This is not the simple point that the output of primitive societies is low: it is the complex problem that the production is low relative to existing possibilities.' In the course of the evolution of specific societies, control of the economy passes from the kin to the ruling chiefs. It is these rulers who transmit the impulses of organisation and of need which unleash the potential productivity of the existing forces of production. In other words, primitive societies produce a surplus and have the capacity to produce a larger one. It is not the development of the productive forces, and thus of surpluses, which leads to classes and the state, rather it is the emergence of political power which stimulates and organises surplus production.[78] For this reason the state itself may be the major appropriator of surplus, so that 'state' and 'class' are largely indistinguishable.[79]

The only possible answer to this argument is the functional-teleological one, i.e. that the political power must have developed within society in order to allow the future development of the productive forces. This answer faces two problems, one logical, the other historical:

(a)   Yet again we return to the lack of a feedback mechanism through which such functional effects are secured (see pp. 86–90 above).

(b)   The historical problem is why did the development of political power, and hence of surplus production, only take place in particular societies?[80] We return to the empirical question of why societies diverge, a problem which cannot be solved through the application of the unilinear 'lever' of productive force determinism.

(ii) Pre-capitalist class societies

Between the end of primitive communism and the transition to capitalism came a variety of pre-capitalist class modes of production. We may distinguish the appropriation of surplus labour produced by slaves; feudal modes of production with heavy labour services; feudal modes with free peasants and money rents; societies where the state has a monopoly of land so that rent and tax are indistinguishable; and societies where there is private ownership of land but the state is the major extractor of surplus labour.[81] To these differences in the dominant mode of extraction of surplus labour we may add the contrasts between specific social formations in their form of state, dominant ideologies (military, bureau-cratic, religious, etc.), extent of commodity production, urban indepen-dence and so on. If is difficult to see what is gained by claiming that societies as different as Ancient Athens, Imperial Rome, absolutist France, feudal Poland, Mughal India and Imperial China (to name only a few examples) all corresponded to a level of development of the productive forces which yields 'some surplus but less than capitalism'. Cohen him-self admits that it would be problematical to explain the transition from the Ancient to the feudal mode of production in terms of the develop-ment of the productive forces.[82] We have already stressed the logical prob-lem that the primacy of the productive forces is not established merely by the fact that they 'rule out' certain forms of social relations (in this case primitive communism, capitalism and post-class society), since cer-tain forms of class relations also rule out the use of certain types of pro-ductive force. Here we must stress that productive force determinism does not help us to understand the evolution of the wide variety of pre-capitalist societies. The relationship between the forces and relations of production in these societies is considered further in our discussion of relations of production as fetters on the productive forces.

(iii) Capitalism

The primacy thesis requires society's relations of production to corre-spond to the level of development of its productive forces. Marx cer-tainly claims as much when he says that 'capitalism presupposes a certain given historical development of the productive forces'.[83] Cohen follows in this tradition quite logically when he asserts that 'capitalism arose when and because the surplus became moderately high'.[84] The feudal fetters had to be cast aside in order to allow the continued growth of the productive forces. The problem is that Marx's whole analysis of the tran-sition to capitalism is based on the assumption that capitalist relations of production were introduced prior to, and indeed were the cause of, the new types of technology which allowed social productivity and the level of surplus to be increased. We shall emphasise the truth of Marx's claim below. Here we need only note that Cohen himself seems to concede this argument when he falls back to the claim that capitalism was not intro-duced in response to the growth of the productive forces but rather to allow the future growth of the productive forces.[85] We have already seen the problem with such teleological claims given the absence of any feed-back mechanism which ensures that 'e' occurs in order to bring about the future benefit 'f'.

113

(iv) 'Socialist' societies

Cohen's schema of social development passes from the third stage of capitalism to the fourth stage of 'post-class society' which corresponds to the production of a 'massive surplus'. An interesting omission from this schema are those societies such as the Soviet Union and China which proclaim themselves to be socialist and en route to communism. It is no accident that they are omitted from Cohen's schema as their existence presents it with a number of problems. Are such societies included in the scope of 'post-class society'? Even if we were to accept this generous assessment, we would still have to deal with the problem that these societies did not appear in response to the existence of productive forces which could create a massive surplus. It would be difficult to argue that they are, even now and despite their economic achievements, marked by a production of a more massive surplus than capitalism.

On the other hand we may wish to define these societies as a new form of class society with a new ruling class; the bureaucracy appropriating a distinct form of surplus labour in the form of 'revenue'.[86] One problem would be whether to define these societies as 'post-capitalist', given that many of them hardly knew capitalism in the first place. If we do so a problem emerges within Cohen's schema since 'post-capitalist' societies can emerge and can continue to exist with 'pre-capitalist' levels of productivity.

A more important point arises from an alternative, but non-Marxist, way of incorporating such 'socialist' societies into our schema. It could be argued that countries such as the Soviet Union are class societies with industrial productive forces of a similar type to those found in the capitalist world.[87] We could thus divide the stages of social evolution into pre-class society; pre-industrial class society; industrial class society; and post-class society. Just as pre-industrial productive forces were compatible with a number of types of class society (slavery, serfdom, etc.), so industrialisation could lead to a variety of class societies (the Soviet Union, USA, etc.). But in this perspective we would have to pass off the difference between the Soviet Union and the USA as a 'nuance' as we did the differences between pre-industrial class societies. In other words, we are not questioning the omission of the actually existing socialist countries from Cohen's schema per se. Rather we are arguing that they had to be omitted, because they pose a challenge to the schema's unilinear conception of social evolution.

(v) Post-class society

Assuming that the Soviet Union, etc., are not post-class societies, at least of the variety which produce a massive surplus, then the final stage of Cohen's schema has yet to come about. It thus calls for little comment in the context of a discussion of a theory of history. Presumably the massive surplus created in these societies would be the result of new types of relations of production, a democratically planned economy, production for social use not for private profit, and so on. The relations of production would once more appear to have social primacy. Of course it could be argued that post-class relations of production had been introduced in order to allow the future creation of a massive surplus. The needs of the productive forces would be met through the agency of a successful socialist revolution which would allow the future growth of social productivity. In order not to give class struggle primacy in our analysis we would then have to argue, as Cohen does, that the class which is victorious in the class struggle is the one whose rule is most suited to the future development of the productive forces. Whether such classes are necessarily victorious is considered in our discussion of the development thesis.

To summarise: the 'primacy thesis' argues that new class relations emerge in response to the development of society's productive forces so that society's economic structure corresponds to the needs of its productive forces. This is the outline of world history contained in Cohen's four stage schema. We have argued here that:

(a) It is society's relations of production which change prior to, and are the cause of, the growth of the productive forces as in the origins of class society, and in the transition to capitalism. There is no reason why we should explain such transformations of the relations of production by their functionality for the productive forces. They may result in the growth of the productive forces but this does not mean that they occurred in order to bring about such a growth.

(b) One level of development of the productive forces is compatible with a wide variety of class relations both in pre-industrial class societies and industrial societies.

(c) One type of class relation is compatible with very different stages in the growth of the productive forces under primitive communism and capitalism.

(d) The unilinear and necessary development of world history posited by productive force determinism is replaced by an interpretation

115

of history which stresses the divergent paths of historical evolution and the contingency of social development. The end of primitive communism in some societies but not in others; the variety of routes out of primitive communism; the range of pre-capitalist class societies; the development of capitalism in specific areas; the co-existence of capitalism and socialism in societies with similar types of productive forces; and the stagnation or even regression of society's productive forces in particular epochs, present a richness of historical experience which embarrasses the unilinear model of productive force determinism.

This final point brings us on to consideration of the development thesis.

4 The productive forces tend to develop throughout history. (See pp. 41–2.)

The development thesis, i.e. that the productive forces inherently tend to develop throughout history, is crucial for the defence of productive force determinism. This is so for five main reasons:

(a) If the advance of the productive forces were to be explained by some other factor (such as visitors from outer space), this factor would then have primacy in our explanation of social change.

(b) We have seen that certain relations of production are extremely elastic and are compatible with a range of productive forces. Only if we assume that the productive forces must eventually develop to a point where the relations of production can no longer contain them can the dynamic of the productive forces be maintained as the fundamental cause of social change. In this sense, the primacy thesis becomes a conclusion deduced from the premise of the development thesis, i.e. the forces of production inherently advance and so the relations of production must eventually change to come into correspondence with their needs.

(c) Productive force determinism is teleological. It gives history a goal, the maximum development of social productivity and the communist relations of production which would allow this development. The future is able to determine the present so that the bourgeoisie, for instance, must overthrow feudalism in order to continue the advance of the productive forces. Only if the productive forces do have an inevitable tendency to advance does this explanation have any credability.

116

(d) Productive force determinism is a form of functional explanation; certain relations of production exist in *order* to allow the development of the productive forces. Unfortunately, the defenders of productive force determinism are unable to specify the mechanism whereby the productive forces create appropriate relations of production. A minimum requirement for the defence of this functional argument is a demonstration of the fact that the productive forces *do* have an inherent tendency to develop, i.e. that society's relations of production are functional. If this were not the case then the whole issue of whether or how the needs of the productive forces functionally explain the existence of specific relations of production would become irrelevant. If we can show historically that the productive forces do *not* have an inherent tendency to develop then we need no longer wrestle with the *philosophical* legitimacy of functional explanation, at least in this context.

(e) 'If high technology rules out slavery then slavery rules out high technology. Something must be added to mutual constraint to establish the primacy of the productive forces. The development thesis provides the needed supplementation.'[88] The productive forces are said to have primacy because they are the *dynamic* element and the relations of production must adjust to their needs. In this way Cohen can allow for the interaction of forces and relations of production and yet still assert the primacy of the productive forces in the last instance.

The development thesis is criticised here (i) for its reliance on questionable assumptions about scarcity and reason which are said to promote the growth of the productive forces; (ii) because it is of little use in the analysis of pre-capitalist societies, where there is no inherent tendency for the productive forces to develop; and, finally, (iii) because it is redundant in the analysis of capitalism, where the growth of productivity may be explained in terms of the specific nature of the capitalist mode of production, rather than as the result of some trans-historical tendency for the productive forces to develop.

(i) Scarcity and reason

Marx, as we have seen, assumed that the productive forces do tend to develop throughout history, although he gave no explicit reason for this belief. He does suggest however that in social production 'the satisfaction of the first need, the action of satisfying and the instrument of production which has been acquired, leads to new needs; and this creation of new needs is the first historical act'.[89] If humans are constantly faced with new needs and if we assume that they are able to struggle success-fully to meet these needs, it follows that society's productive forces will develop over time. It is not just that the productive forces *have* developed but rather that they tend to develop throughout history. The develop-ment thesis thus 'asserts a universal *tendency* to develop'.[90]

Cohen's defence of the development thesis is also based on the strug-gle to meet human needs. He argues that:

(1)   humans are rational beings who know how to satisfy compelling wants;
(2)   the historical situation of humanity is one of scarcity;
(3)   humanity possesses intelligence of a kind and degree which enables it to improve its situation.[91]

It follows that where Nature is too lavish and 'man' is not faced with scarcity, there is no necessity for humanity to develop itself. In general, though, human need is rarely well catered for by unassisted nature and so humanity progressively overcomes the natural environment in order to meet its needs.[92]

There are two possible approaches in criticising the development the-sis. The first would question the ahistorical concept of 'need' which it rests upon. Sahlins, for instance, has distinguished two types of afflu-ence. In some modern societies there may be numerous needs, but also the material abundance and productivity to meet those needs. In others, technology may be at its most primitive pre-agricultural level, yet these societies may also be described as 'affluent' in the sense that they satisfy the needs of their members. These needs are not met by the development of productivity. Rather, because needs are few, the level of technology is adequate to meet them. Such hunter-gathering societies provide us with the model of 'uneconomic man, his wants are scarce and his means, in relation, plentiful'. The problem then is to identify the factors which in certain circumstances have led to intensification of production. Sahlins suggests the importance of the development of political apparatuses which both require and also help to organise a more efficient use of society's existing capacity to produce surplus.[93] In other words, it is ahis-torical to assume that the productive forces have an inherent tendency to develop because of the scarcity which confronts humanity since scarcity itself is a relative concept. The productive forces have developed (where they *have* developed) in different ways and at different speeds according to time and place. It is precisely why such differences and divergences exist which is of interest to the social scientist.

(ii) Pre-capitalist modes of production

The second problem for the development thesis is that even if we assume that humans are aware of scarcity and do have the capacity to apply reason to overcome it, then we are still left with the optimistic assumption that the social and institutional obstacles to the application of this individual reason are relatively weak. This is to assume that not only individuals but also societies will, in the long run, act rationally.[94] This is exactly the assumption which is questioned here.

Against this optimistic assumption we can counterpose the pessimistic Malthusian logic of the feudal mode of production. It has been argued that the feudal mode of production has an inherent tendency towards demographic crisis. A classic instance is England in the early fourteenth century. By 1300 England's population was at least double that of 1086 yet, despite the drainage of marshland and the clearing of forest, the area under cultivation could not have doubled. Given the failure to introduce significant improvements in productivity living standards amongst the bulk of the population declined as the size of holdings declined, rents and entry fines rose, food prices increased and a pool of cheap wage labour developed. The area under corn grew at the expense of pasture, a development that led to a shortage of manure, the main form of fertilizer in the medieval period. The lack of manure and the cultivation of marginal lands reduced grain yields. As living standards declined birth rates fell and death rates rose with large numbers of labourers and smallholders on the end of subsistence. England's population was 'disastersensitive'; a succession of bad harvests from 1315 caused an immediate and dramatic fall in population, although historians are divided on whether the famines were a turning point in population history, the beginning of a prolonged population decline; or merely a safety valve which allowed population to begin its climb back to former levels.[95]

In other words, the scarcity of the early fourteenth century was not resolved by improvements in productivity but rather by a reduction in population. We must assume either that the inhabitants of fourteenth-century England were less rational than Cohen's development thesis suggests, or that fourteenth-century society offered great obstacles to the application of individual reason to overcome scarcity. The latter seems a more plausible explanation of the feudal crisis, since potential agricultural improvements did exist.

The main restriction on the productivity of medieval agriculture was the lack of manure. This problem was overcome in the early modern period by the introduction of convertible husbandry, with its new rotations which abolished the rigid medieval distinction between arable and pasture and allowed more animals to be kept, thus producing more manure and creating increased arable productivity. In the Middle Ages arable production had increased at the expense of pasture; under convertible husbandry the two advanced hand-in-hand. Such improvements were known in the early fourteenth century and yet were not systematically adopted. The structure of medieval society prevented the introduction of new techniques. Feudal landlords had little incentive to invest. Their profits were already high with rising rents and entry fines, high prices for the produce of their demesnes which were cultivated with cheap wage labour. Their profits were spent on war and conspicuous consumption, rather than on productive investment, indeed it has been argued that convertible husbandry was eventually introduced under the pressure of a profit squeeze rather than in an era of landlord prosperity. Medieval landowners tended to increase their income through pressure on the peasantry, tallages, rents, fines and so on, rather than through increases in productivity.

If the lords would not, or did not need to, invest then the peasant could not. The unfree peasant had little surplus after the extraction of feudal rent and faced manorial and communal restrictions on the application of capital, the introduction of new techniques and the free movement of resources. Even the free peasant had few funds available for improvements whilst small plots and subsistence agriculture also reduced specialisation, productivity and innovation. Both lord and peasant tended to increase their production by purchasing new land, rather than investing in new techniques, a preference which did nothing, of course, to increase total output. The 'Malthusian' crisis of the early fourteenth century was thus a social, not a natural, phenomenon.[96]

This analysis of the crisis of the feudal mode of production assumes that feudal class relations were an obstacle to the growth of the productive forces. This recognition of the success of the feudal mode in fettering the development of social productivity is a challenge to Cohen's assertion that in the class struggle the class most suitable for the growth of the productive forces emerges victorious.[97] We have seen that in the case of the landlords of fourteenth-century England their aim was not to increase production, but to increase their income. The two did not necessarily go hand-in-hand. A useful distinction here is that between absolute and relative surplus labour developed from Marx's analysis of absolute and relative surplus value produced in the capitalist mode of production. Marx argues that under capitalism the labour performed by the wage labourer is divided into two parts. In the first the labourer produces the goods whose value goes to reproduce labour power in the form of the payment of wages; in the second the labourer works for the benefit of his employer in the production of surplus value, the value of the goods over and above that expended on the reproduction of the labourer. The employer may increase this surplus value in two ways. The first is to extend the working day and thus to increase the time spent on surplus rather than necessary labour. Marx calls this the production of absolute surplus value. The second way of increasing surplus value is to cheapen the commodities needed to maintain labour power, so that necessary labour may be performed in a shorter time. The working day is not lengthened, rather a larger proportion of it is available for the production of surplus value. Marx calls this the production of relative surplus value.[98]

Surplus value, for Marx, is merely the specific form of surplus labour produced in the capitalist mode of production. The distinction between absolute and relative surplus labour holds for pre-capitalist class societies, but in these societies absolute surplus labour was the dominant form. A classic instance is the serfdom of early modern Poland. In his discussion of the transition from feudalism to capitalism Shaw claims that 'it was inevitable that someone would start making money by hiring labour power given the climate of profit consciousness and the ripeness of the productive forces and other material pre-conditions'.[99] As we have already seen Shaw is unable to specify in what way the productive forces were 'ripe' for capitalism. Neither will 'profit consciousness' supply an explanation of the development of capitalism. In the case of Poland:

> its serf class structure ensured that existing means of production … remained locked away from potential capital accumulation. Precisely because free wage labour had failed to emerge, neither labour power nor means of production had emerged as commodities; as a result these use values could not constitute a field for capitalist investment and development, because they were not, could not be, combined as exchange values under the sway of capital.[100]

Prevented from capitalist investment by their own class dominance, the 'profit consciousness' of Poland's feudal landlords took the form of increasing the extraction of feudal rent by cutting down the size of peasant holdings and increasing the labour services owed on seigneurial regimes, i.e. they increased their income through absolute surplus labour. Far from Poland's relations of production existing because of their functional suitability for the development of productivity, the class relations of feudalism ensured declining productivity in basic food production: 'The ruling class sought to "use" the class relationship of serfdom to maximise its surplus for the market; this in fact led to the degeneration of the productive forces.'[101] Only with the relative surplus labour of the capitalist mode of production do surplus and productivity rise hand-in-hand. The class relations of Polish serfdom did not exist in order to maximise production. Indeed, 'serf peasant plots maintained significantly higher productivity than did the lords' demesnes'.[102] The victory of Poland's feudal lords and the enserfment of the peasantry had led not to the maximisation of the growth of the productive forces, but to the maximisation of the extraction of surplus from the peasantry. Once again the specific dynamic of a particular form of class relations contradicts the trans-historical claims of the development thesis.

A similar lack of persistent advance of the productive forces marked the Ancient World: the level of technology of the late Roman Empire was little different from that of the Greek city states. 'There were refinements and improvements in many spheres. But there were not many genuine innovations after the fourth or third century B.C.; and there were effective blocks.' A number of reasons for this stagnation of productivity have been suggested: the lack of incentives for slaves to master new techniques or to improve productivity, contempt for labour and for all forms of wealth except for large-scale ownership of land, chronic under-consumption from a population living largely at subsistence level, the consequent absence of a division of labour and commercial specialisation, the lack of economies of scale, the failure to develop joint stock companies and banks and the consequent high rates of interest due to the personal risk involved in credit. In short, the Ancient World was marked by a lack of incentives and opportunities to increase productivity. 'The strong drive to acquire wealth was not translated into a drive to create capital; stated differently, the prevailing mentality was acquisitive but not productive.'[103]

The under-consumption of the Ancient World meant that those inventions which did allow increases in productivity were not widely diffused. The water-mill is a famous example. A revolution in technology in its break with a reliance on human or animal energy, the water-mill was known to the Ancient World in the century before Christ, yet as late as 500 A.D. its use was 'still exceptional'. In other words, 'an invention rarely spreads until it is strongly felt to be a social necessity'. The invention of the water-mill was the work of an individual genius but its adoption 'only took place under the pressure of social forces'.[104] Once again our attention is drawn to the problem of why specific societies encourage the spread of innovation and the growth of productivity, whilst others present systematic obstacles to such developments. We are not denying that human history has seen a growth of productive power, but merely argue that such developments have been specific by time and place and so require a specific explanation. The growth of the productive forces ceases to be primarily an explanation and becomes, instead, something to be explained.

A final example which may be raised to counter the development thesis is that of the Asiatic mode of production. Cohen offers no analysis of those societies where the state is the main appropriator of surplus through tax-rent. Shaw adopts Marx's description of the stagnation of this mode of production, a failure of the productive forces to develop reflected in the self-sufficiency of the Asiatic village community and the underdevelopment of society's division of labour. For Shaw the Asiatic mode is 'stationary', 'petrified' and stagnant, the development of its productive forces is curtailed so that the development of both the forces and relations of production is 'paralysed'.[105] Once again our attention is drawn to the lack of development of the productive forces rather than to their inherent tendency to advance.

Perry Anderson has suggested that Marx's claims for the stationary and identical characters of the Oriental empires was largely the result of historical ignorance. It is the 'diversity and development' of these societies which now command the attention of the historian. As Cohen points out, Anderson provides a 'superb critique' of the concept of the Asiatic mode of production, although Anderson himself admits that he makes no attempt 'to pose the central question of defining the fundamental modes of production and their complex combination which constituted the successive social formations of Islamic or Chinese society'.[106] We are concerned for the moment with the validity of productive force determinism, not with the concept of the Asiatic mode of production. Here Anderson's analysis is of great interest, for in his discussion of Imperial China he concludes:

> Most of the purely technological pre-conditions for a capitalist industrialization were achieved far earlier in China then they were in Europe. China possessed a comprehensive technological lead over the Occident by the later middle ages, anticipating by centuries virtually every one of the key inventions in material production whose conjugation was to release the economic dynamism of Renaissance Europe. The whole

development of Sinic imperial civilization, indeed, can be seen as the most grandiose demonstration and profound experience of the power and of the importence of technique in history.

Anderson's explanation of the decisive brake on the Chinese economy is 'traced back to the whole structure of Chinese state and society itself', its specific urban structure, science, law, state and forms of class rule.[107] As in the Ancient World and the feudal mode of production we are presented with the blockage of the productive forces, a blockage which requires *social* explanation.

Paradoxically, Cohen agrees with Marx that 'constant revolutionizing of production ... distinguishes the bourgeois epoch from all earlier ones' so that 'all earlier modes of production were essentially conservative'. How is the admission compatible with the claim that 'the productive forces tend to develop throughout history'? Cohen's answer is that the rule of particular classes may be best for the development of the productive forces given the conditions of a particular historical epoch.[108] The logical problem is that we are never told why the class most suitable for the development of the productive forces should be victorious in the class struggle, nor what the conditions are which make the rule of a particular class suitable in a particular period. The historical problem is that specific class structures have persisted for centuries despite their failure to develop the productive forces, indeed despite an inbuilt tendency towards stagnation or even crisis and regression. The Ancient World, the entrenchment of serfdom in early modern Poland, and the recurrent Malthusian crises of French feudalism during a period when England was developing a productive agrarian capitalism, all pose a challenge to the development thesis.[109] We may ask why certain societies technically innovate, whilst in others the productive forces actually regress. At best the development thesis offers no help in this task, at worst it prevents us from asking such questions.

(iii) Capitalism

If the failure of the pre-capitalist modes of production to systematically develop productivity requires specific explanation, so does the huge impetus given to production by the advent of capitalism. 'Conservation of the old modes of production in unaltered forms was ... the first condition of existence for all earlier industrial classes. Constant revolutionizing of the means of production, uninterrupted disturbance of all social conditions, everlasting uncertainty and agitation distinguish the bourgeois epoch from all earlier ones.'[110] Why is it that 'the bourgeoisie

124

cannot exist without constantly revolutionizing the instruments of production'?[111]

The aim of capitalist production is the creation and accumulation of surplus value. Surplus value, as we have seen, may be increased through lengthening the working day (absolute surplus labour) or by reducing time spent on necessary labour by introducing a more efficient form of production (relative surplus labour). There are distinct limits to the extension of the working day, both physical (there are only so many hours in a day and a labourer can only work for so many of them) and social (the resistance of the working class to reductions in living standards). In the long run capitalism has increasingly relied on relative surplus labour. It has 'an immanent drive and constant tendency towards increasing the productivity of labour in order to cheapen commodities and by cheapening commodities to cheapen the worker himself'. The production of relative surplus value necessarily involves the introduction of new productive techniques and 'completely revolutionizes the technical process of labour'.[112]

Another incentive for innovation is the reduction of the value of those commodities produced by the innovating capitalist who then sells at the prevailing market price and so obtains an extra profit.[113] If competition and the drive to maximise surplus labour make technical innovation desirable, then the existence of wage labour, private property and the unrestricted application of capital to the production process make innovation a practical possibility. Thus even the example of capitalism, where the productive forces *have* massively developed, does not provide a defence of the primacy of the productive forces or of the development thesis. The innovation typical of the capitalist mode of production is not merely a speeded-up version of some trans-historical tendency. It is a dynamic specific to the capitalist epoch. Capitalist class relations do not 'correspond' to the needs of the productive forces. The direction and rate of advance of the productive forces is *determined by* these class relations rather than being their determinant.

(iv) The development thesis: conclusion

Cohen's development thesis is deduced from a concept of human nature based on humanity's tendency to apply reason to overcome scarcity.[114] Some writers would reject deductions from 'human nature' *per se*; if we are to work from this concept at all then we must do so in terms of human *potential*.[115] Whether this potential is realised and why, are precisely the questions which social scientists have to answer. To assert that the productive forces have an inherent tendency to develop and then to concede, as Cohen does, that pre-capitalist class relations 'afford no direct stimulus' to the growth of the productive forces is as unhelpful as to assert that there is an inherent tendency for rain to fall.[116] Those who live in the damper regions of Britain may feel some sympathy for this thesis, but meteorologists are more concerned to asky why particular regions have specific patterns of rainfall. The historian is similarly interested in why certain societies have been deserts of technological advance, whilst others are visited by periodic monsoons.

Cohen is more than aware that society's relations of production condition the particular path of development and the rate of growth of its productive forces.[117] His productive force determinism is rescued by the claim that the relations of production have a particular influence *because* of the needs of development of the productive forces. Once we reject both the primacy thesis and the development thesis as logically unproven and historically false, we are simply left with his recognition of the 'massive control' exerted by the relations of production over the evolution of the productive forces.[118] Such a recognition is the basis of the alternative to productive force determinism which is developed below, an alternative based on the specific forms of productive development generated by particular relations of production.

5.1 The productive forces have an inherent tendency to develop. It follows that eventually a time is reached when society's relations of production lag behind the productive forces and become unsuitable for the further development of productivity. In order that the productive forces may continue to advance the relations of production which have become fetters must be cast aside and new forms of class relations called into being.

5.2 This clash between the dynamic productive forces and the relations of production which fetter them may be illustrated with historical examples. (See pp. 43–6 above.)

If, as we have argued, the productive forces do *not* have an inherent tendency to develop it follows that we cannot allow that the productive forces must necessarily break through their fetters. On the contrary, (i) the relations of production have, historically, been very successful in restricting the development of the productive forces. As a result, (ii), productive force determinism cannot help us to understand the crises of the Ancient World or of feudal Europe. These crises were not caused by the development of the productive forces but were rather the result of their failure to develop. (iii) Neither does the growth of the productive forces explain the transition from the Ancient World to feudalism or from feudalism to capitalism. Marx's model of the transition from capitalism to socialism *is* based on the growth of the productive forces, but even if we wish to retain this model it implies no commitment to the general claims of productive force determinism.

(i) The success of the relations of production as fetters

We have disputed the claim that the forces of production *do* have an inherent tendency to develop. It follows that the claim that society's growing productive forces will eventually cast aside the relations of production which fetter them must be subject to a double qualification. It should now read: '*in those circumstances* where the productive forces are advancing they may reach a point where their future development would only be possible if new relations of production came into existence'. The claim that the relations of production will adjust to the needs of the productive forces ceases to be an iron law of history and becomes, instead, a conditional statement, i.e. 'if the productive forces are to advance then certain relations of production must obtain'. Whether these relations of production *do* develop is historically contingent and can only be established through empirical research, not by deduction from human nature.

There can be no objection to the claim that society's relations of production may fetter the growth of productivity. Indeed, it was the very success of pre-capitalist class relations in preventing the growth of the productive forces which led us to question the assumption that the productive forces have an inherent tendency to develop. But, if pre-capitalist modes of production are not marked by the presence of dynamic forces of production, it is unlikely that their history will be one in which the productive forces run up against the fetters of the production relations. Rather, as Perry Anderson said:

> Contrary to widely received beliefs amongst Marxists the characteristic 'figure' of a crisis in a mode of production is not one in which vigorous (economic) forces of production burst triumphantly through retrograde (social) relations and promptly establish a higher productivity and society on their ruins. On the contrary forces of production

typically stall and recede within the existing relations of production; these then must first themselves be radically changed and reordered *before* new forces of production can be created and combined for a globally new mode of production. In other words, the relations of production generally change *prior* to the forces of production in the epoch of transition and not vice versa.[119]

Only if we assume that the relations of production are re-ordered in order to allow the future growth of potential productive forces can such historical evidence be squared with the claims of productive force determinism. We have already argued that change in the relations of production cannot be explained by an, as yet, non-existent future. Our alternative reading of historical change explains such transitions *not* by the future but in terms of the prior development of specific social formations.

(ii) Three crises: the Ancient World; feudalism; capitalism

If every mode of production has its own laws of development according to the form of control exercised by its relations of production it follows that the economic crises experienced by each mode arise from specific historical circumstances and are not liable to explanation through the universal claims of productive force determinism. The classic instance where economic crisis is the result of dynamic productive forces coming up against the restrictive fetters of class relations is Marx's model of the crisis of capitalism. This is hardly surprising, since it is precisely the systematic encouragement to increases in productivity which Marx identifies as the unique dynamic of capitalist production. We need only summarise here the key points of Marx's model which we have already considered in some detail.[120] Marx's analysis of the crisis of capitalism was based on the tendency of rate of profit to decline. He argued that increases in productivity inherent to capitalism cheapened the commodities needed to reproduce labour power, i.e. the capitalists' expenditure on variable capital. The result was an increase in the rate of exploitation through the production of relative surplus value. However, whilst the rate of exploitation increases, the rate of profit, measured in terms of the value of total capital invested against the value of the goods produced by surplus labour, declines. The growth of productivity means an increase in the constant capital invested in machinery and raw materials. Only living labour produces surplus value, but living labour (variable capital) accounts for a declining proportion of total capital. The result is a decline in the rate of profit, which eventually leads to economic crisis, spasms and bitter contradictions. 'Thus the real barrier to capitalist production is capital itself.'[121]

It should be stressed that this model can be questioned on a number of grounds. Even if we accept the labour theory of value on which the model rests, there is the problem of the existence of those tendencies, identified by Marx, which counteract the tendency of the rate of profit to decline. Marx nowhere shows why these tendencies are necessarily weaker than the tendency to a decline in the rate of profit.[122] For the moment these problems do not concern us, since any alternative account of the crisis of capitalism, perhaps based on capitalism's tendency to over-production, would also have to take account of the tendency to productive advance characteristic of this mode of production. The key point is that Marx argues that capitalism will become a fetter on the growth of production, that its dynamic productive forces will clash with these fetters and that the result will be economic crisis.

The crisis of the capitalist mode of production is the result of the growth of the productive forces, but this example should give little comfort to productive force determinists since this growth is the product of the control of the productive forces by the relations of production. It is class structure which has primacy within our account. The crises experienced by pre-capitalist modes of production are even less amenable to explanation in terms of productive force determinism, since such crises were not the result of some inherent tendency for the productive forces to develop. On the contrary, the crises of the Ancient mode of production and of feudalism were the reflection of the failure to develop the productive forces, a failure typical of these forms of class relation.

In the crisis of feudalism the productive forces do not burst triumphantly through the fetters which have contained them. On the contrary, the feudal crisis is the result of the tendency of the productive forces to 'stall and recede', as in fourteenth-century England and seventeenth-century Poland. The result is a fall in agricultural productivity, a decline in living standards, the lack of a market for manufactured goods from a population living at subsistence level, and a lack of agricultural surpluses which would allow the continued growth of towns and industry. We have already argued that the feudal crisis was the result of the failure of feudalism to promote the development of the productive forces. The crisis of capitalism is, for Marx, the result of the growth of the productive forces which capital itself has produced. The feudal crisis, by contrast, is the result not of the growth but of the stagnation of the productive forces.

If the crisis of capitalism takes the form of a crisis of profits, and the crisis of feudalism is expressed in the decline of agricultural productivity, population and living standards, then the crisis of the Ancient World is expressed in terms of political collapse, a form of crisis appropriate to a society where taxation 'was the basis of the state and the key element in the whole economic system, the institution that determined the direction of the economy and defined the dominant mode of production'.[123] We have already examined the stagnation of the productive forces in the Ancient World as part of our rejection of the claim that the productive forces have an inherent tendency to develop. This inability to increase productivity was to have decisive political effects and lay at the heart of the downfall of the western empire. By the second century A.D. the limits of the empire had been reached and Rome was on the defensive, consolidating its frontiers along the Rhine and Danube with a consequent growth of expenditure on roads, arms, pay, garrisons, and so on. Once the empire ceased to expand the state could not longer live off the profits of conquest. The army was no longer a source of income, but became a financial burden which the empire had to maintain. The inevitable result of the *Pax Romana* was 'legalized extortion'. The third century saw a crisis in the empire with recurrent civil war, rival emperors and the invasions from the north and east. The crisis was overcome, temporarily at least, by the increased state control and regulation of all aspects of life established by the emperors in the years *c.* 270–340 and particularly by Diocletian (284–305). The provisioning of cities, public works, the bureaucracy and above all the army, whose paper strength doubled under Diocletian, all required an increase in imperial taxation and the empire began to feed off itself.[124]

Yet even this reorganised imperial state proved incapable of resisting the renewed pressure on its frontiers which was felt from the mid-fourth century. The imperial administration was increasingly unable to provide an effective defence of the far frontiers; its exactions made the loyalty of the provincial landowners and peasants a luxury they could not afford. It was not the strength of its enemies which led to the downfall of the western empire, but rather its own internal weaknesses and, in particular, the economic limits on the provision of manpower, food and transport:

> Taxes and compulsory services were increased, the burden falling largely on those least able to bear it. Men and means were shifted to the main danger points, sometimes benefiting frontier provinces at the expense of others. But nothing could be done to raise the productivity

of the empire as a whole or to redistribute the load. For that a complete structural transformation would have been required.[125]

The state was the main extractor of surplus in the late empire and was the unifying feature of late Roman history.[126] Its eventual collapse owed much to the economic structure of the empire, a structure which had proved incapable of developing the productive forces. The crisis of the Ancient World, like that of feudal Europe, *was* a result of the fettering of society's productive forces by its relations of production but, unlike Marx's model of the crisis of capitalism, these earlier crises were not the result of dynamic productive forces running up against the barriers imposed by class relations. On the contrary it was the very *success* of these modes of production in fettering the productive forces (despite the claims of the development thesis) which led to crisis when extra demands, such as imperial taxation or population growth, were made upon the economy.

(iii) Three transitions: to feudalism, to capitalism and to socialism

Productive force determinism is of little use in explaining the crises of pre-capitalist modes of production and is redundant in Marx's model of the crisis of capitalism. Neither is this theory of any use in explaining transitions from one mode of production to another, a central issue in Marxist historiography. Productive force determinism argues that society's relations of production are called into being by the needs of the productive forces. In fact there can be important changes in society's relations of production without prior changes in the level of the productive forces. When the productive forces do advance it is the *result* of the previous transformation of society's relations of production. That such transformations occur functionally, i.e. *in order* to produce the later development of the productive forces, is a claim which, as we have seen, the productive force determinists have not been able to logically or empirically demonstrate in terms of their own criteria of proof. Three transitions may be used to illustrate these claims: from the Ancient mode to feudalism, from feudalism to capitalism and Marx's model of the transition from capitalism to socialism. Are these transitions the result of the growth of the productive forces which call into being new class relations and require the existing relations of production to be cast aside as fetters?

Marx's model of the transition from capitalism to socialism *is* the result of the dynamic growth of the productive forces. The polarisation of society into bourgeoisie and proletariat, the concentration of production and growing organisation of the working class, the crises inherent to capitalism, the growing socialisation of production and the redundancy of the capitalist class, all flow from the growth of the productive forces which creates the material basis for socialism.[127] Once again we need to stress that the recognition of the importance of the growth of the productive forces in this model is not in itself a concession to productive force determinism, since this growth is itself the result of the capitalist class relations which exert a particular form of control over economic development. We also need to stress that this account of the transition to socialism is a hypothetical model. In fact where the transition to socialism has taken place it has been in areas where the productive forces were at a low stage of development, often a very low stage indeed. Whilst the growth of the productive forces has stabilised Western capitalism, socialism has developed in societies which had hardly begun to experience capitalist development. The reason for the success of socialist revolutions in such backward countries is certainly capable of a Marxist explanation, but it poses massive problems for the claims of productive force determinism.[128] Marxism provides us with the concepts which allow the empirical investigation of such revolutions, the deductive method of productive force determinism again provides a theory of history without historical application.

If Marx's account of the transition to socialism is based on the growth of the productive forces (even if reality has turned out differently from his expectations), the same cannot be said of the historical transitions from the Ancient mode to feudalism or from feudalism to capitalism. In neither case can it be demonstrated that the transition to a new mode of production was the result of a growth in the productive forces. It is argued below that Marx's recognition of this fact provides part of the basis for an alternative and more useful reading of historical materialism from that of productive force determinism. For the moment we need only note that Cohen himself admits that it is 'questionable' that the end of the Ancient mode was brought about by the incompatibility of the growing productive forces with the existing class relations.[129] He also admits that the transition to capitalism was not anticipated by any significant growth of the productive forces. On the contrary, this growth was the result of the introduction of capitalist class relations.[130] Shaw, as we have seen, is also unable to specify the new productive forces which could call forth capitalist relations of production.[131]

Productive force determinists claim that the inherent growth of the productive forces calls into being new forms of class relations which correspond to the needs of the productive forces. We have already questioned the claim that the productive forces have 'needs' or that they have an inherent tendency to develop. To these criticisms we have added:

(a)   that the crises of pre-capitalist modes of production are not the result of the growth of the productive forces. On the contrary they were caused by the failure of the productive forces to advance which is characteristic of these societies;

(b)   that transitions from one mode of production to another (i.e. from primitive communism to class society, from the Ancient to the feudal mode and from feudalism to capitalism) are not explicable in terms of the growth of the productive forces;[132]

(c)   that although Marx's model of the crisis of capitalism is based on the growth of the productive forces, this growth is itself the product of capitalist class relations;

(d)   that in the era of the transition from one mode of production to another, it is frequently the relations of production which change prior to any increase in productivity which may later occur;

(e)   it has not been shown that such prior transformations of class relations can be explained in terms of their future effects on productivity. Transformations of class relations are thus to be explained in terms of their historical pre-conditions, rather than through their results.

6 The productive forces are fundamental to social structure in the sense that they are the basis of society's relations of production which are, in turn, the basis of society's political and legal superstructure. (See pp. 46–7 above.)

We have denied the claim that the productive forces have an inherent tendency to develop, and that society's relations of production correspond to the level of development of the productive forces. It follows that we must also deny the primacy of the productive forces through their determination, in the last instance, of the state and ideology. The remaining central claim of Marx's theory of history, therefore, is that society's political structures, its laws and its forms of social consciousness, correspond to the nature of its relations of production. This claim is discussed, in detail, in Part III.

7 Just as feudalism gave way to capitalism because of the requirements of the productive forces, so socialism will replace capitalism which has become a fetter on the continued growth of the productive forces. (See pp. 48–52.)

The political conclusions which Marx drew from his productive force determinism can only be briefly considered in the context of a discussion of his philosophy of history. Marx's theory of revolution is obviously worthy of lengthy, separate treatment.[133] It should be stressed that the value of Marx's analysis of the *past* cannot be based on an assessment of his predictions about the *future*: it is easier to explain yesterday's weather than to forecast tomorrow's.

We have argued that the crises and demise of pre-capitalist modes of production cannot be explained in terms of the growth of the productive forces. It is more plausible that the end of capitalism will come about through the development of productivity, since this mode of production inherently creates technological advance. Why should this advance bring about the transition to socialism? Marx's first answer is that the productivity generated by capitalism makes *possible* an alternative form of society based on abundance and equality.[134] The problem is that the *possibility* of socialism does not, *per se*, guarantee its necessity. The labour movement could continue to prefer to make the best of capitalism, rather than risking a social transformation which could lead to the outcomes found in Chile or in the Soviet Union. Something else must be added to Marx's theory if it is to show the inevitability of socialism.

Marx's second argument is that capitalism increasingly socialises the production process, so that the capitalist class becomes economically superfluous.[135] The weakness of this argument is that the ruling classes of pre-capitalist modes of production were also often superfluous to production, they 'seldom have much direct effect on how peasants actually organize the farming of the land'.[136] Yet this economic superfluity did not prevent the continued social dominance of such classes for century after century. In other words, *class relations do not exist because of the needs of the production process*. The superfluity of the capitalist class does not, in itself, guarantee the end of capitalism, let alone the advent of socialism.

Marx also argues that because socialised production is increasingly incompatible with the existence of private property, capitalism has become a fetter on the continued growth of productivity. Marx believed this had been the case for 'many a decade' before 1848; thirty years later

Engels believed that the productive forces had then reached their limits under capitalism so that 'the imminent collapse of this mode of production is, so to speak, palpable'.[137] Over a century later this 'imminent collapse' is still to come about. Far from fettering the productive forces, capitalism has presided over the most massive and sustained era of productive advance and technological innovation in world history. As one Marxist pointed out in 1970, the capitalist system 'as a whole has never grown so fast for so long as since the war – twice as fast between 1950 and 1964 as between 1913 and 1950 and nearly half as fast again as during the generation before that'.[138] The expansion of production during this period dwarfs the achievements of the period before 1848 which Marx eulogised in The Communist Manifesto. This growth of the productive forces has led not to socialist revolution but, we argue below, has provided the basis for the enduring reformism of the labour movement in the advanced capitalist societies.

Marx also argued that the incompatibility of capitalist class relations with the increasing socialisation of production would lead to economic crisis, a crisis most evident in the declining rate of profit characteristic of the process of capital accumulation.[139] But why should economic crisis lead to socialism? After all, the crisis of feudalism did not necessarily lead to capitalism. One answer is that there must ultimately be a final catastrophic breakdown of the capitalist system.[140] Even if this were the case, it would not necessarily follow that the end of capitalism should mean the advent of socialism; capitalism could be replaced with a form of 'state capitalism' or even barbarism.[141] Anyway, must there be such a thing as the 'final' crisis of capitalism? Marx seems to think not. He describes the crisis of capitalism as not only the culmination of capitalism's own inherent trends but also as the means through which those trends are overcome: 'The crises are always but momentary and forcible solutions of the existing contradictions. They are violent eruptions which for a time restore the disturbed equilibrium.'[143] Just as a Malthusian demographic crisis both expresses and resolves a situation of over-population, so the capitalist crisis is the outcome, but also the safety-valve, of the system's contradictions.

It might be argued that although there is no automatic final crisis of capitalism, this crisis will eventually come about because of the active energy of the working class which is spurred on to struggle for socialism by the bankruptcy of capitalism. The weakness of this position is that economic crisis has produced some of the most conservative periods in the history of this century (e.g. Britain in the 1930s and 1980s). Where economic crises have led to 'radical' change it has more often been of fascist, rather than socialist, inspiration. That capitalism is prone to periodic crisis does not guarantee the end of that system; neither does it guarantee that it will be a socialist society which replaces it.

This brings us on to the central problem in Marx's theory of revolution: that the working class of the advanced capitalist countries has been markedly unwilling to adopt the historic mission which Marx assigned to it. Marx argued that whilst capitalist prosperity lasted the working class would not turn to socialism. He retained his faith in the inevitability of revolution because of his belief that capitalism could not guarantee more than a temporary prosperity. The cycle of capital accumulation, economic recession and the introduction of mechanisation means that the forest of arms applying for work 'becomes ever thicker, while the arms themselves become ever thinner'.[144] The whole aim of capitalist production is the accumulation of surplus value. Its result is that 'accumulation of wealth at one pole is, therefore, at the same time, accumulation of misery, the torment of labour, slavery, ignorance, brutalisation and moral degradation at the opposite pole, i.e. on the side of the class that produces its own product as capital'.[145] Whilst 'misery, oppression, slavery, degradation and exploitation' increase, 'with this there also grows the revolt of the working class, a class trained, united and organized by the very mechanism of the capitalist process of production'.[146] It was precisely because Marx did not expect the prosperity of capitalism to last that he 'had no theoretical space for the possibility of a workers' movement that is organized politically as a class and yet struggles for reforms within the capitalist system'.[147] Reformism has then to be explained away as an illusory consciousness produced by the deceptive appearances of capitalism, its commodity fetishism and opacity of exploitation in a mode of production where surplus labour takes the form of surplus value.[148]

Yet, Marx himself (or perhaps another 'Marx') offered an alternative explanation of reformism, an explanation which was based on the nature of capitalist production itself. He argued that as capitalism increased productivity, the value of those commodities needed to reproduce labour power would be reduced. He showed that it was possible that 'owing to an increase in the productivity of labour both the workers and the capitalists may simultaneously be able to appropriate a greater quantity of means of subsistence, without any change in the price of labour-power or in surplus value'.[149] Marx expected prices, in the long run, to adapt to values so that as the value of the commodities needed to reproduce labour power declined so would its price. In other words, wages would fall in money terms. Nevertheless: 'it is possible, given increasing productivity of labour, for the price of labour power to fall constantly and for this fall to be accompanied by a constant growth in the mass of the worker's subsistence'.[150] Whilst money wages might fall, *real wages would rise* in terms of the mass of use values consumed by the workers, even though they may be worse off, in relative terms, as the 'abyss' between them and the capitalist class widens.[151]

In short, the tendency towards growing production, which Marx sees as an inherent part of the capitalist system, creates the wealth which makes reforms possible. The unprecedented economic growth since 1945 has thus been accompanied by an equally unprecedented rise in living standards.[152] The growth of the productive forces produced by capitalism has led not to socialist revolution, but to working-class reformism. Socialists may disapprove of this reformism, but this does not mean that it can be dismissed as 'illusory', or the result of the 'dominion of bourgeois ideology'.[153] 'Trade union consciousness', in general, has not been based on an illusion, but has been a rational response to the possibility of real increases in living standards which have been opened up for the workers of the advanced capitalist nations. The renewed onset of capitalist recession, with its divisive and demoralising effects, has, as yet, shown no tendency to produce the revolutionary consciousness which Marx hoped for.

Notes

1 W. H. Shaw, Marx's Theory of History (London, 1978); G. A. Cohen, Karl Marx's Theory of History: A Defence (Oxford, 1978).
2 Above, pp. 72–3.
3 Shaw, Marx's Theory of History, p. 59.
4 J. Elster, Explaining Technical Change (Cambridge, 1983), p. 123.
5 M. Sahlins, Stone Age Economics (London, 1974), pp. 79–80.
6 Shaw, Marx's Theory of History, pp. 59–60.
7 Ibid., pp. 60–1.
8 Ibid., p. 61.
9 Ibid., pp. 61–2.
10 K. Marx & F. Engels, Collected Works, vol. V (London, 1976), p. 50 (The German Ideology).
11 Ibid., p. 40.

12 Ibid., p. 329. See also ibid., pp. 53, 437.
13 Shaw, Marx's Theory of History, pp. 62–3.
14 Cohen, Karl Marx's Theory of History, p. 134.
15 Ibid., p. 171.
16 Ibid., pp. 197–201.
17 Ibid., p. 200.
18 Ibid., p. 158. For the 'something' which Cohen wishes to add see p. 116 below.
19 K. Marx, Capital, vol. I (Harmondsworth, 1976, Pelican edn) Chs. 14, 15.
20 K. Marx & F. Engels, The Communist Manifesto (Harmondsworth, 1970), p. 85.
21 K. Marx & F. Engels, Collected Works, vol. III (London, 1975), pp. 485–7 (The Condition of England. The Eighteenth Century); K. Marx & F. Engels, Collected Works, vol. IV (London, 1976), pp. 307–25 (The Condition of the Working Class in England).
22 E. J. Hobsbawn, The Age of Revolution (London, 1969), p. 28; E. J. Hobsbawm, Industry and Empire (Harmondsworth, 1972), Chs. 3, 6.
23 K. Marx, Wage Labour and Capital (Moscow, 1970), p. 28.
24 Marx, Capital, vol. I, pp. 455–8.
25 Ibid., pp. 480–1.
26 Ibid., pp. 492, 590.
27 R. Mishra, 'Technology and social structure in Marx's theory: an exploratory analysis', Science and Society XLIII (1979), pp. 132–57.
28 Marx & Engels, The Communist Manifesto, p. 84.
29 K. Marx, Early Writings (Harmondsworth, 1975), p. 324.
30 Marx, Capital. vol. I, pp. 164–5.
31 A slight adaptation of Marx & Engels, Collected Works, vol. IV, p. 93 (The Holy Family).
32 K. Marx, The Eighteenth Brumaire of Louis Bonaparte (Moscow, 1972), p. 10.
33 Marx & Engels, The Communist Manifesto, p. 79.
34 Cohen, Karl Marx's Theory of History, pp. 148–9, 292; Marx & Engels, Collected Works, vol. V, p. 52 (The German Ideology).
35 G. A. Cohen, 'Forces and relations of production', in B. Matthews (ed.), Marx: A Hundred Years On (London, 1983), p. 119.
36 Cohen, Karl Marx's Theory of History, pp. 171, 285–6.
37 Ibid., pp. 169–71.
38 Ibid., p. 175.
39 Ibid., pp. 177–9.
40 R. Brenner, 'Agrarian class structure and economic development in pre-industrial Europe', Past and Present 70 (1976), pp. 47–50.
41 Cohen, Karl Marx's Theory of History, p. 175.
42 Shaw, Marx's Theory of History, p. 148.
43 T. Eagleton, Literary Theory (Oxford, 1983), p. viii.
44 E. P. Thompson, The Poverty of Theory (London, 1978), pp. 236, 303.
45 K. Marx & F. Engels, Selected Correspondence (Moscow, 1975), p. 393 (letter of 5.8.1890).
46 K. Marx, A Contribution to the Critique of Political Economy (London, 1971), p. 21.
47 Shaw, Marx's Theory of History, pp. 147–8, 151–3.
48 Cohen, Karl Marx's Theory of History, p. 175.
49 Ibid., pp. 148–9.

50 Marx & Engels, *Selected Correspondence*, pp. 390–1 (letter of 5.6.1890).
51 Ibid., pp. 293–4 (letter to the Editorial Board of *Otechestvenniye Zapiski*).
52 Shaw, *Marx's Theory of History*, p. 62; Cohen, *Karl Marx's Theory of History*, p. 177.
53 Cohen, ibid., p. 159.
54 Ibid., p. 201; K. Marx, *Grundrisse* (Harmondsworth, 1974), p. 325.
55 Marx & Engels, *Collected Works* vol. V, p. 50 (*The German Ideology*).
56 Marx, *Grundrisse*, p. 105.
57 Marx & Engels, *Selected Correspondence*, p. 115 (letter of 16.1.1861).
58 J. Plamenatz, *Man and Society*, vol. II (London, 1963), pp. 282–3.
59 Cohen, *Karl Marx's Theory of History*, pp. 176–7.
60 Ibid., pp. 261–2.
61 Marx, *A Contribution to the Critique of Political Economy*, p. 20. See also Marx & Engels, *Collected Works* vol. V, p. 45 (*The German Ideology*).
62 K. Marx, *Wage Labour and Capital* (Moscow, 1970), p. 28.
63 Ibid.
64 Marx & Engels, *Collected Works* vol. V, p. 43 (*The German Ideology*).
65 K. Marx, *The Poverty of Philosophy* (Moscow, 1973), pp. 95, 116.
66 Cohen, *Karl Marx's Theory of History*, pp. 168–9.
67 Ibid., pp. 166–7; L. White, *Medieval Technology and Social Change* (Oxford, 1971), pp. 41–57; R. H. Hilton & P. H. Sawyer, 'Technical determinism: the stirrup and the plough', *Past and Present* 24 (1963), especially pp. 95–100.
68 A. R. Bridbury, review of L. White, *Medieval Technology and Social Change*, in *Economic History Review* second series XV (1962–3), p. 371.
69 P. Mantoux, *The Industrial Revolution in the Eighteenth Century* (London, 1947), pp. 443–5; Cohen, *Karl Marx's Theory of History*, p. 167. In fact it has been argued that the Law of Settlement 'had little practical effect' in restricting labour mobility (D. Levine, *Family Formation in an Age of Nascent Capitalism* (New York, 1977), p. 36).
70 Cohen, *Karl Marx's Theory of History*, p. 216.
71 Ibid., pp. 197–201.
72 F. Engels, *The Origin of the Family, Private Property and the State* (Moscow, 1968), pp. 154–65.
73 B. Hindess & P. Q. Hirst, *Pre-capitalist Modes of Production* (London, 1975), pp. 48 ff.
74 Engels, *The Origins of the Family*, p. 159.
75 Cohen, *Karl Marx's Theory of History*, p. 61.
76 Hindess & Hirst, *Pre-capitalist Modes of Production*, pp. 23–8.
77 Engels, *The Origin of the Family*, pp. 161–5; Cohen, *Karl Marx's Theory of History*, p. 198.
78 Sahlins, *Stone Age Economics*, Chs. 2, 3.
79 E. M. Wood, 'The separation of the economic and political in capitalism', *New Left Review* 127 (May–June 1981), pp. 83–6.
80 Sahlins, *Stone Age Economics*, pp. 130–1.
81 See for instance G. E. M. De Ste-Croix, *The Class Struggle in the Ancient Greek World* (London, 1981); Hindess & Hirst, *Pre-capitalist Modes of Production*, Chs. 2–5; P. Anderson, *Lineages of the Absolutist State* (London, 1979), pp. 462 ff; R. Brenner, 'Agrarian class structure and economic development in pre-industrial Europe', pp. 68–71; C. Wickham, 'The other transition: from the Ancient world to feudalism', *Past and Present* 103 (1984), pp. 3–36.

82 Cohen, *Karl Marx's Theory of History*, p. 199.
83 Marx, *Grundrisse*, p. 699.
84 Cohen, *Karl Marx's Theory of History*, p. 201.
85 Ibid., p. 177.
86 A. Nove, 'Is there a ruling class in the U.S.S.R?', in *Political Economy and Soviet Socialism* (London, 1979), Ch. 12; M. Hirsowicz, 'Is there a ruling class in the U.S.S.R.? – a comment', *Soviet Studies* XXVIII (1976), pp. 262–73.
87 A. Giddens, *The Class Structure of the Advanced Societies* (London, 1978), pp. 59–63.
88 Cohen, *Karl Marx's Theory of History*, p. 158.
89 Marx & Engels, *Collected Works* vol. V, p. 42 (*The German Ideology*).
90 Cohen, *Karl Marx's Theory of History*, p. 135.
91 Ibid., pp. 150–5.
92 Ibid., p. 23; Marx, *Capital*, vol. I, p. 649.
93 Sahlins, *Stone Age Economics*, Chs. 1–3.
94 J. Cohen, review of G. A. Cohen, *Karl Marx's Theory of History: A Defence*, *Journal of Philosophy* LXXIX (1982), pp. 261–9.
95 J. Z. Titow, *English Rural Society 1200–1350* (London, 1969), Ch. 3; Z. Razi, *Life, Marriage and Death in a Medieval Parish* (Cambridge, 1980), Ch. 2.
96 Brenner, 'Agrarian class structure and economic development in pre-industrial Europe', pp. 47–51; R. Brenner, 'The agrarian roots of European capitalism', *Past and Present* 97 (1982), especially pp. 16–17, 24–41, 48–50; R. H. Hilton, *The English Peasantry in the Later Middle Ages* (Oxford, 1979), Ch. 10; E. Searle, *Lordship and Community: Battle Abbey and its Banlieu 1066–1538* (Toronto, 1974), pp. 268 ff; E. L. Jones, *Agriculture and the Industrial Revolution* (Oxford, 1974), Chs. 3–4; R. Davis, *The Rise of the Atlantic Economies* (London, 1977), Ch. 12.
97 Cohen, *Karl Marx's Theory of History*, pp. 149, 171.
98 Marx, *Capital*, vol. I, pp. 643–72.
99 Shaw, *Marx's Theory of History*, p. 148.
100 R. Brenner, 'The origins of capitalist development: a critique of neo-Smithian Marxism', *New Left Review* 104 (July–August 1977), p. 71.
101 Ibid., p. 60. See also J. Topolski, 'Economic decline in Poland from the sixteenth to the eighteenth centuries', in P. Earle (ed.), *Essays in European Economic History 1500–1800* (Oxford, 1974).
102 Brenner, 'The origins of capitalist development', p. 69.
103 M. I. Finley, *The Ancient Economy* (London, 1979), Ch. 5. Quotations from pp. 144, 146–7. See also A. W. Walbank, *The Awful Revolution* (Liverpool, 1969), pp. 40–57, 109–10.
104 M. Bloch, *Land and Work in Medieval Europe* (London, 1967), pp. 143–7. See also M. I. Finley, 'Technical innovation and economic progress in the Ancient world', *Economic History Review* second series XVIII (1965), pp. 29–45.
105 Shaw, *Marx's Theory of History*, pp. 129–30. For Marx see S. Avineri (ed.), *Karl Marx on Colonialism and Modernization* (New York, 1969).
106 P. Anderson, *Lineages of the Absolutist State*, p. 495; Cohen, *Marx's Theory of History*, p. 199.
107 Anderson, *Lineages of the Absolutist State*, pp. 540–6.
108 Marx, *Capital*, vol. I, p. 617; Cohen, *Karl Marx's Theory of History*, pp. 169–71.
109 Cohen, *Karl Marx's Theory of History*, p. 173. See nn. 100–1, 106–8, above and

Davis, *The Rise of the Atlantic Economies*, Chs. 12, 13.
110 Marx & Engels, *The Communist Manifesto*, p. 83.
111 *Ibid.*
112 Marx, *Capital*, vol. I, pp. 436–7, 645.
113 K. Marx, *Capital*, vol. III (London, 1974, Lawrence & Wishart edn), pp. 258–9.
114 Cohen, *Karl Marx's Theory of History*, pp. 151–4.
115 N. Geras, *Marx and Human Nature: Refutation of a Legend* (London, 1983); S. Sayers, 'Marxism and the dialectial method: a critique of G. A. Cohen', *Radical Philosophy* (spring 1984), pp. 11–12.
116 Cohen, *Karl Marx's Theory of History*, p. 171.
117 *Ibid.*, pp. 165, 278.
118 G. A. Cohen, 'Functional explanation: reply to Elster', *Political Studies* XXVIII (1980), pp. 129–30.
119 P. Anderson, *Passages from Antiquity to Feudalism* (London, 1977), p. 204.
120 See above, pp. 48–51.
121 Marx, *Capital*, vol. III, Chs. 13, 15. (Quotation from p. 250.)
122 *Ibid.*, Ch. 14; G. Hodgson, *Trotsky and Fatalistic Marxism* (Nottingham, 1975), pp. 65–86; I Steedman, *Marx After Sraffa* (London, 1977), pp. 116–36, 205.
123 Wickham, 'The other transition', p. 6.
124 *Ibid.*, pp. 13–14; Walbank, *The Awful Revolution*, pp. 61–8, 70–80; De Ste-Croix, *The Class Struggle in the Ancient Greek World*, especially pp. 502–3.
125 Finley, *The Ancient Economy*, p. 149.
126 Wickham, 'The other transition', p. 14; Hindess and Hirst, *Pre-capitalist Modes of Production*, pp. 82–91.
127 See above, pp. 48–51.
128 See for instance F. Halliday & M. Molyneux, *The Ethiopian Revolution* (London, 1981), especially Chs. 1, 2.
129 Cohen, *Karl Marx's Theory of History*, p. 199. In this context Oliva's unsubstantiated claim, that the crisis of the Roman Empire was the result of the growth of technical efficiency in agriculture which clashed with the fetters of slave relations of production, can only be regarded as eccentric. P. Oliva, *Pannonia and the Onset of Crisis in the Roman Empire* (Prague, 1962), pp. 171 ff.
130 Cohen, *Karl Marx's Theory of History*, p. 177.
131 Shaw, *Marx's Theory of History*, p. 148. See also above, pp. 103–5, 120–1.
132 For the transition from the primitive communist mode of production see Sahlins, *Stone Age Economics*, Chs. 2, 3, and pp. 49–50 above.
133 The assessment of Marx's theory of revolution offered here is based on an unpublished paper by Jon Dyson.
134 See Ch. 3 above, nn. 107–9.
135 *Ibid.*, nn. 110–11.
136 Wickham, 'The other transition', p. 14.
137 Marx & Engels, *The Communist Manifesto*, p. 86; F. Engels, *Herr Eugen Dühring's Revolution in Science* (London, Lawrence & Wishart, n.d.), p. 299.
138 M. Kidron, *Western Capitalism Since the War* (Harmondsworth, 1970), p. 11.
139 See Ch. 3 above, nn. 111–21.
140 Luxemburg, for instance, believed in the final impasse and collapse of capitalism. See R. Luxemburg, *Social Reform or Revolution* (Colombo, 1969), pp. 12–13.

See also L. Trotsky, *Marxism in our Time* (New York, 1970), p. 34.

141 For the latter see L. Trotsky, *The Death Agony of Capitalism and the Tasks of the Fourth International* (London, 1970), p. 12.

142 Marx, *Capital*, vol. III, p. 249.

143 K. Marx, *Surveys from Exile* (Harmondsworth, 1973), p. 131.

144 Marx, *Wage Labour and Capital*, p. 44.

145 Marx, *Capital*, vol. I, p. 799.

146 Ibid., p. 929.

147 The quotation comes from Fernbach's introduction to K. Marx, *The First International and After* (Harmondsworth, 1974), p. 59.

148 C. Johnson, 'The problem of reformism and Marx's theory of fetishism', *New Left Review* 119 (January–February 1980), pp. 70–96.

149 Marx, *Capital*, vol. I, p. 659; K. Marx, *Wages, Price and Profit* (Moscow, 1970), p. 50.

150 Marx, *Capital*, vol. I, p. 659.

151 Ibid.

152 Kidron, *Western Capitalism Since the War*, p. 12. Kidron emphasises that this trend is a real one, despite the persistence of real poverty in some areas and despite the failure to achieve a re-distribution of wealth. See also N. Harris, *Of Bread and Guns* (Harmondsworth, 1983), Ch. 2.

153 V. I. Lenin, *What Is To Be Done?* (Moscow, 1973), p. 42.

CHAPTER 8

Productive force determinism: an alternative

Part A: Marx's alternative to productive force determinism

Productive force determinism may be summarised by Marx's claim that the productive forces are the 'material basis of all social organisation'.[1] For Cohen, Marx's historical theory therefore involves a 'systematic opposition' between the material and the social.[2] In this chapter we argue that Marx himself offered an alternative to his own productive force determinism. We begin by analysing the distinction between the material and the social and argue that this distinction does not provide the basis for the primacy of the productive forces (Section 1). On the contrary, Marx argues that social relations are one of the fundamental elements which constitute the production process (Section 2) and so uses this fundamental element to distinguish between modes of production (Section 3). In this alternative approach to social structure Marx gives primacy to the relations of production (Section 4) and argues that each form of social production has its own laws of development (Section 5). As a result Marx rejects the claims of the development thesis and argues that the productive forces may advance, regress or stagnate (Section 6). Finally Marx can be shown to have rejected productive force determinist explanations of the transition from feudalism to capitalism, a central issue in Marxist historiography (Section 7). Marx did not, however, offer his own alternative explanation of this transition. Part B of this chapter argues that in the modern debate on the transition to capitalism it is the approach based on the primacy of class relations which has been of most value. In other words, we argue not only that Marx held and made analytical use of a view which contradicts his own productive

143

force determinism, but also that this alternative does not suffer from the logical and empirical difficulties of historical explanations based on the primacy of the productive forces.

(1) A distinction between the material and the 'social'?

Cohen draws a distinction between the material *content* of the production process, i.e. people and productive forces, and the social *form* which material production takes on. The social properties consist, on the one hand, of the purpose of production and, on the other, of the form of exploitation and the means of enforcing that exploitation. By the purpose of production Cohen means the distinction between consumption by the producer, consumption by others (e.g. rent in kind consumed by a feudal lord) and production for exchange.[3]

An immediate problem is one of definition. It is not clear why the productive forces are labelled as material since, as Cohen rightly insists, they can include scientific and technological *ideas*.[4] The implication seems to be that the productive forces are 'material' because they are explanatory – but, in turn, they are explanatory because they are material. The 'material' is here defined not by what it is but by its antonym, i.e. that it is not 'social'. This is not, however, the main problem with Cohen's case. Even if we accept his categories of the material and the social there is still the problem of determination, i.e. how does the material determine the social? Unfortunately Cohen does not specify how the material production process creates a corresponding social form. Indeed he goes as far as to admit that just as the shape of a statue cannot be deduced from the material it is made of, so the form taken by social relations cannot be *deduced* from their material content. As Marx put it: 'A Negro is a Negro. He only becomes a slave in certain relations.'[5] Cohen does believe, however, that although we cannot deduce social relations from a material description 'we can *infer* them more or less confidently, by dint of general or theoretical knowledge'.[6]

It is not clear why this should be the case. After all, if we cannot *deduce* a statue's form from its material composition then neither can we infer it. We can infer what form a statue will *not* have, e.g. a statue made of old sardine tins will probably not have the same form as the Venus de Milo, but Cohen himself denies that the productive forces merely *rule out* certain social forms in this way. Rather, they directly *determine* social form.[7] Thus, for Cohen, the material content of society is able to determine social form in a way that the content of a statue cannot determine the statue's form. Why this is the case we are never told.

Neither do Cohen's empirical examples show how the material determines the social. Indeed they seem to prove the very opposite. He argues that 'we may envisage a complete material description of society, a description which is "socio-neutral"'. Thus 'The Soviet collective farm and the American "agribusiness", despite their difference of social form, display the same material mode of production of grain if they plough, sow and reap using similar methods and instruments of production.'[8] Similarly, when capitalist relations of production replaced feudal guild relations, the new social form was, at first, accompanied by the persistence of the pre-capitalist production process.[9] Both examples are historically accurate but, unfortunately for Cohen, they disprove the claim that we may infer the social mode of production from the material production process since, in these cases, we may 'infer' quite different social forms from the same material content.

Nevertheless, Cohen continues to claim that Marxist theory allows us to make 'ambitious inferences' about social form, from social content. As an example of such inferences Cohen gives us Marx's claim that from the hand mill we can infer feudal society and from the steam mill we can infer capitalist society. What Marx actually says is that the hand mill gives you society with the feudal lord and the steam mill gives you society with the industrial capitalist, i.e. steam mills did not give us capitalism per se.[10] Marx's aphorism sums up all that is wrong with productive force determinism. Firstly, as Marx was well aware, there were hand mills long before there were feudal lords and so it is not clear in what sense hand mills 'give us' feudalism.[11] Secondly, it is a tautology to say that there is no industrial capitalism without industry. For productive force determinism to be applicable, steam mills (or industry in general) would have had to create capitalism. In fact, as Marx was at great pains to point out, capitalist social relations existed long before the advent of the steam mill. Finally, Marx and Engels confidently expected socialist revolution in their own lifetime and the subsequent social ownership of industry (including steam mills). In other words:

(a) the hand mill is compatible with a number of class relations. Its material content does not allow us to infer social form;

(b) capitalism is compatible with both industrial and pre-industrial productive forces. We are thus asked to infer the same social form from different material contents;

(c) steam mills (or large-scale industry) are compatible with both capitalism and socialism. Again we cannot infer social form from material content.

Cohen then goes on to claim that: 'if productive forces are at the handmill stage they are relatively undeveloped. Most labour will be agricultural in which case capitalist relations are unlikely'.[12] But, historically, this is not the case. Indeed, the key problem in the debate about the transition from feudalism to capitalism is to explain why England was the first country to develop a form of *agrarian* capitalism.[13] Even if it were the case that agriculture excludes capitalism, this would only allow us to infer which social form did *not* prevail. It is precisely this form of constraint which Cohen himself admits is not a proof of productive force determinism.[14]

Cohen, in short, provides us with no logical reason or empirical example to persuade us that those factors which he labels as 'material' determine the form taken by society's relations of production. This is not to deny the usefulness of distinguishing between the production process on the one hand and the social relations and purposes of production on the other:

> It is important to remember that, apart from the slave mode, all exploitative pre-capitalist modes were based on peasant agriculture: the work process of the peasantry, and even their productive forces, are not necessarily affected by changes in the appropriation of surplus ... landlords and the state seldom have much direct effect on how peasants actually organize the farming of the land, until the onset of agrarian capitalism.[15]

The material content of the production process of peasant agriculture can be conceived of separately from its social form. This does not mean that the production process has explanatory primacy. On the contrary the fact that peasant agriculture is compatible with a variety of pre-capitalist social forms suggests that we cannot infer social form from material content.

The example of capitalism also illustrates the difficulties of inferring the social from the material, since the capitalist social form is compatible with two very different forms of the production process, manufacture and large-scale industry. The fact that we can distinguish the different stages of the production process of capitalism from the social form, class relations and the purposes of production, does not, in itself, mean that one exists independently from the other, historically antedates the other or determines the nature of the other.

(2) Production as social production

So far we have accepted that, in a sense, we can analyse the material and the social modes of production as separate, if related, categories. Marx, however, laid great stress on the fact that 'whenever we speak of production then what is meant is always production at a definite stage of social development – production by social individuals'.[16] If we take 'social' in the broadest sense to mean relations between humans then Marx could be referring to co-operation in the production process, i.e. to work relations.[17] But Marx also makes it clear that by social production he is referring to property, to the social relations of production as well as to the work relations. Thus in the *Grundrisse* he argues that 'All production is appropriation of nature on the part of the individual within and through a specific form of society. In this sense it is a tautology to say that property (appropriation) is a pre-condition of production. ... That there can be no production and hence no society where some form of property does not exist is a tautology.'[18] Marx thus accepts that property is a precondition of production and that production takes place through a specific social form. His target is those writers who confuse the general precondition of property with a defence of the specific form of property characteristic of bourgeois society.

Marx criticises the shallow conception held by economists that in production humans appropriate nature and that the distribution process apportions products to the individual: 'distribution thus appears as the distribution of products, and hence as further removed from and quasi-independent of production'. He argues instead for a more sophisticated view in which this distribution of products is itself the result of another form of distribution, i.e.: '(1) the distribution of the instruments of production, and (2) which is a further specification of the same relation, the distribution of the members of society among the different kinds of production. (Subsumption of the individuals under specific relations of production.)' These two forms of distribution cannot be seen as independent from the production process since they are 'comprised within the production itself and determine the structure of production'. To examine production without examining these social relations can only lead to 'empty abstraction'.[19] Marx's conclusion is that production, distribution, exchange and consumption are 'members of a totality, distinctions within a unity'. Although these different 'moments' interact it is production which predominates, but production must be seen as including the social distribution of the instruments of production and the subsumption of individuals within specific relations of production.[20] In other words: 'human life has since time immemorial rested on production, and in one way or another, on social production, whose relations we call, precisely, economic relations'.[21] For this reason, 'political economy is not technology'.[22]

The foundations of Marx's two theories of history should now be clear. In the first, based on the primacy of the productive forces, material production gives us social relations. In the second theory, production itself is seen as a social activity, structured by the distribution of the instruments of labour through specific relations of production such as the possession of tools by the medieval artisan, or the divorce of the wage labourer from the means of production under capitalism. This is not to say that in the *Grundrisse* Marx was carrying out a conscious 'auto-critique'. Nevertheless, his recognition that production is itself a social activity does open up the theoretical space for a very different account of historical change from that of productive force determinism. Marx's position remained inconsistent and ambiguous. He continued to assert the claims of productive force determinism even after formulating a concept of production as social production which provided an implicit critique of those claims. The implications of these two contrasting conceptions of historical materialism are immediately apparent in Marx's categorisation of economic epochs and it is to this issue that we now turn.

(3) How societies are distinguished

The most convincing demonstration that Marx did hold two theories of history is provided by the contrasting ways in which he distinguishes the stages of the economic development of society. If the productive forces determine the nature of society's relations of production it follows that:

> It is not what is made, but how, and by what instruments of labour, that distinguishes different economic epochs. ... The writers of history have so far paid little attention to the development of material production, which is the basis of all social life, and therefore of all real history. But prehistoric times at any rate have been classified on the basis of the investigations of natural science, rather than so-called historical research. Prehistory has been divided, according to the materials used to make tools and weapons, into the Stone Age, the Bronze Age and the Iron Age.[23]

If material production is the basis of all social life it seems logical to categorise societies according to their stage of development of their productive forces. Yet, in practice, Marx did not follow his own advice. In the 1859 'Preface' Marx argues that 'In broad outline the Asiatic, Ancient, feudal and modern bourgeois modes of production may be designated as epochs marking progress in the economic development of society.'[24]

These epochs are not defined by their material mode of production. On the contrary the capitalist epoch has been divided by the Industrial Revolution into two distinct stages of material production. Capitalism is not defined by a specific type of productive force, but rather by a specific mode of appropriation of surplus labour.[25] This categorisation of economic formations flows logically from the conception of production as social production and the distribution of the instruments of production as production's 'precondition', 'presupposition' and 'determinant'.[26] Social production is a union of labourers and means of production. It follows that 'the specific manner in which this union is accomplished distinguishes the different economic epochs of the structure of society from one another'.[27] In other words, 'what distinguishes the various economic formations of society – the distinction between a society based on slave labour and a society based on wage labour – is the form in which surplus labour is in each case extorted from the immediate producer, the worker'.[28] It is precisely because society's relations of production do not correspond to its productive forces that Marxist historians classify societies not by *how* they produce, but rather by their dominant form of surplus labour. Their classification is an implicit criticism of the claim that we can infer social form from the material content of the production process.

(4) The primacy of class relations: historical illustrations

Marx's productive force determinism makes the claim that social relations correspond to the level of development of the productive forces and he illustrates this claim with a number of historical examples. His rather different claim that it is the social relations of production which determine the structure of production so that 'production corresponds to class antagonism' was also illustrated with specific examples.

In the chapter on co-operation in volume I of *Capital*, for instance, Marx argues that co-operation between individuals in the labour process is rooted in the class relations of each form of society. Thus co-operation amongst primitive hunting peoples or in the Indian village community 'is based on the common ownership of production, and on the other hand on the fact that in those cases the individual has as little torn himself from the umbilical cord of his tribe as a bee from his hive'. In the Ancient World, in the Middle Ages and in the modern colonies the labour process, in contrast, 'rests on direct relations of domination and servitude, and in most cases on slavery'. Under capitalism, however, such co-operation 'pre-supposes from the outset the free wage labourer who sells his labour power to capital'.[29] For McMurtry society's work relations are part of the productive forces which determine class relations; for Cohen they are part of the 'substratum' of the relations of production.[30] Yet in these quotations Marx claims that work relations are 'based on', 'rest on' and 'presuppose' certain forms of social relations of production. No longer does the production process give us particular relations of production. Instead, specific social relations become the condition of certain forms of production. It is no longer the productive forces but the relations of production which have social primacy.

The primacy of society's relations of production is repeatedly emphasised in those passages where Marx refers to class relations as the basis or the foundation of the Ancient, medieval and modern worlds and of their respective modes of production. Thus in referring to the Ancient World Marx says that 'Direct forced labour is the *foundation* of the Ancient world, the community rests on this as its foundation.'[31] The Ancient mode of production 'depended on slavery' and as a result its producers provided only a limited market, restricted more or less to necessities. The plebeians of the Ancient World did not form a proletariat, even after their expropriation from their peasant holdings, but became, instead, a 'mob of do-nothings'. The evolution of large-scale property which followed their expropriation thus led to 'a mode of production which was not capitalist but based on slavery'.[32] Similarly, in the modern world, slavery can be seen as the basis for a material mode of production: 'To steal a slave is to steal the instrument of production directly. But then the production of the country for which the slave is stolen must be structured to allow of slave labour, or (as in the southern part of America, etc.) a mode of production *corresponding to the slave* must be created.'[33]

Marx makes the same point about the feudal mode of production. He argues that labour which was not yet generally producing exchange values, i.e. labour with a particular purpose or social form, was 'the *basis* of the world of the middle ages'.[34] In the guild system the basis of production was a particular form of distribution of the instruments of labour, the close unity of the labourer and the means of production. The guild system thus differed from manufacture, the 'basis' of which is the separation of the labourer from the means of production.[35]

It is, however, in his discussion of the capitalist mode of production where Marx most clearly claims that the social relations of production are the basis and precondition of the production process: 'It is the *elementary pre-condition* of bourgeois society that labour should directly produce exchange value, i.e. money; and similarly that money should directly purchase labour, and therefore the labourer, but only so far as he alienates his activity in exchange.'[36] In other words the two aspects of the social form of production, its purpose (the production of exchange value) and its class relations (capital and wage labour) are the elementary preconditions of capitalism. The 'basis for capitalist production' is thus the separation of the producers from the means of production and their conversion into wage labourers.[37] It follows that the creation of the capitalist mode of production, 'and of the conditions of production and distribution which correspond to it',[38] 'can be nothing other than the process which divorces the worker from the ownership of the conditions of production'.[39] At first capitalism may employ artisans who work in their own homes. The material mode of production in this case 'is not yet determined by capital but rather found on hand by it'. Only with the concentration of labour in one workshop does capital create a 'mode of production corresponding to itself'.[40] Large-scale industry is the other form of production which 'corresponds' to capital.[41] Indeed, Marx claims that the full development of capital is only reached with the introduction of machinery, a form of production 'posited by capital and corresponding to it'.[42] In other words, new productive forces do not create the capitalist mode of production; they were, on the contrary, the creation of capitalism. It is class, not technology, which must have the central and active role in any analysis of the transition to capitalism.

(5) Each form of social production has its own laws of development

Productive force determinism is based on the development thesis, the inherent tendency for the productive forces to advance. An alternative reading of Marx would question his reliance on such trans-historical laws. If, as Marx claims, class relations are an important determinant of the form of the production process it follows that we need to specify the 'laws', or tendencies, of development of each mode of production. Our attention turns away from deductions from trans-historical laws and towards the empirical investigation of particular societies. The growth of the productive forces is no longer assumed as the explanation of social change, but requires its own explanation. First, however, we need to establish that Marx did believe that each mode of production had its own laws of development.

One of Marx's main criticisms of earlier political economy was precisely its tendency to present the laws of the capitalist mode of production as eternal and natural when, in fact, these laws are transitory and historically specific. Marx therefore criticises those economists who base their work on a discussion of the 'general pre-conditions of all production'. In fact these preconditions turn out to be a few very simple characteristics, which the economists hammer out into 'flat tautologies':[43] 'There are characteristics which all stages of production have in common and which are established by the mind; but the so-called general pre-conditions of all production are nothing more than these abstract moments *with which no real historical stage of production can be grasped.*'[44]

The real starting point of production is not production but rather 'individuals producing in society, hence socially determined production':[45] 'Production by an isolated individual outside society is as much of an absurdity as is the development of language without individuals living together and talking to each other.'[46] Yet again production is not distinguished from social relations, but is itself a social activity. The varying forms taken by this social activity have their own laws of development. The English and the Patagonians, for instance, have very different economic systems so that:

> anyone who attempted to bring Patagonia's political economy under the same laws as are operative in present day England would obviously produce only the most banal commonplace. Political economy is therefore essentially a *historical* science. It deals with the material which is historical, that is, constantly changing; it must first investigate the special laws of each separate stage in the evolution of production and exchange, and only when it has completed this investigation will it be able to establish the few quite general laws which hold good for production and exchange considered as a whole.[47]

Marx himself approvingly quoted a Russian reviewer of volume I of *Capital* who summarised Marx's method thus: 'It will be said that the general laws of economic life are one and the same, no matter whether they are applied to the present or the past. This Marx directly denies. According to him such abstract laws do not exist. On the contrary every historical period has laws of its own.'[48] As an example we may cite Marx's refutation of the claim, made by Malthus, that population has a constant tendency to increase beyond the means of subsistence irrespective of the social relations of the time. Marx argues that the surplus population to be found in capitalist societies is a distinct product of the process of capital accumulation: 'This is a law of population peculiar to the capitalist mode of production; and in fact every special historic mode of production has its own special laws of population, historically valid within its limits alone.'[49]

(6) The productive forces: regression, stagnation and advance

Each mode of production has its own laws of development. There are, however, a 'few quite general laws which hold good for production and exchange considered as a whole'.[50] Is the inherent tendency for the productive forces to advance, proposed by the development thesis, one such general law? Marx's answer is that it is *not*. His analysis of specific historical situations emphasises that the productive forces may stagnate for centuries or even regress. Where the productive forces do advance, it is for specific reasons, rather than as part of a trans-historical tendency.

The classic instance of the regression of the productive forces is that of the transition from the Ancient mode of production, which Marx believed was based on slavery, to feudal forms of property. In *The German Ideology* Marx claims that 'The last centuries of the Roman Empire and its conquests by the barbarians destroyed a considerable part of the productive forces; agriculture had declined, industry had decayed for want of a market, trade had died out or been violently interrupted, the rural and urban population had decreased.'[51] It was these conditions of decline in the productive forces, together with the nature of the conquest of the Empire, which formed the basis for the development of feudalism. The emergence of a new mode of production was based not on the development, but on the regression, of the productive forces. Cohen notes the example but argues that this regression may have been caused by the 'external' factor of the barbarian invasions. Yet he admits that the Empire's degeneration 'had "internal" causes too'. The 'real problem' is thus 'to define the difficult notions of "internal" and "external" factor in a suitably rigorous way'.[52] It is difficult to follow Cohen's argument at this point as:

(a)   he does not rigorously define internal and external factors nor decide whether the decline of Rome was due to either. The possibility remains that the Empire's decline and the regression of the productive forces *were* the result of 'internal factors'. The decline of Rome would thus refute the development thesis, the essential basis of productive force determinism;

(b)   even if we decided that the conquests were an 'external factor' and that the regression of the productive forces was 'socially abnormal', we would still be left with the task of explaining the decline of Rome. This, *not* the rigorous definition of 'internal' and 'external', is the 'real problem'. We would, in this case, have to admit that a major social transition was not explicable in terms of the growth of the productive forces.

These problems only arise when we assume, before we begin, that we already know that society's relations of production change because of the growth of the productive forces. If we drop this assumption then we need no longer search for definitions of internal and external, normal and abnormal. Our attention is drawn away from definition and towards historical investigation and explanation.

Engels also argued that the later years of the Roman Empire saw an economic decline. He explained this decline in terms of the 'internal' factor of fiscal exploitation by the imperial administration rather than the destruction of the Germanic invasions: 'Universal impoverishment; decline of commerce, handicrafts, the arts and of the population; decay of the towns; retrogression of agriculture to a lower stage – this was the final result of Roman supremacy.'[53] The decline in the market for the products of the slave plantations meant the replacement of the slave with the *colonus*, the forerunner of the medieval serf. By the time of Charlemagne (768–814), 400 years later, the free Germanic peasantry had been forced into the same feudal servitude as the *coloni* of the late Empire:

> this proved only two things: firstly that the social stratification and distribution of property in the declining Roman Empire correspond entirely to the then prevailing stage of production in agriculture and industry and hence was unavoidable; secondly that this stage of agriculture had not sunk or risen to any material extent in the course of the following four hundred years.[54]

In one sense Engels's claim, that social stratification corresponds to the stage of development of production, is a classic statement of productive force determinism. Yet, in another sense, his analysis poses two challenges to the primacy of the productive forces. Firstly, it questions the assumption that social change is the result of *growth* in the productive forces since Engels argues that the economy was in decline. Secondly, the stagnation of the productive forces poses a challenge to the development thesis: if the productive forces can stagnate for four centuries then their advance in other periods can no longer be assumed but requires specific explanation.

That the productive forces can stagnate for century after century and that pre-capitalist modes of production have no systematic tendency to develop social productivity is one of Marx's most recurrent themes. In pre-capitalist modes of production 'the development of the forces of production is not the basis of appropriation' whereas, under capitalism, the compulsion to produce surplus labour is exercised 'in a manner far more favourable to production'.[55] In the Ancient World, for instance, production based on slavery did not yield a surplus in the form of capital which was systematically applied in order to expand production. Production was not 'directed to the release and development of the material productive forces'. Ancient society thus lacked the unconditional development of the productive forces which is characteristic of capitalist society.[56]

It was not only the Ancient World which lacked persistent development of the productive forces which 'distinguishes capital from all earlier modes of production'.[57] In both the Asiatic system and the peasant agriculture of feudalism the social structure was 'unfitted to develop labour as social labour and the productive power of social labour'.[58] Marx inherited a view of the Orient as socially static and technologically conservative. India's social condition, for instance, had 'remained unaltered since its remotest antiquity until the first decennium of the nineteenth century'. There was no inherent tendency for the productive forces to develop. On the contrary, 'we are quite accustomed to see agriculture deteriorating under one government and reviving again under some other government'.[59] The self-sufficiency of the Asiatic village community with its under-developed division of labour provided the basis for the 'unchangeableness of Asiatic societies, an unchangeableness in such striking contrast with the constant dissolution and refounding of Asiatic states'.[60] The fact that all pre-capitalist modes of production 'were essentially conservative' is a major problem for the 'development thesis', the central prop in the defence of productive force determinism.[61] As we have seen, it is a problem to which Cohen fails to provide an answer.[62]

In contrast to pre-capitalist modes of production, capitalism is 'compelled by its own immanent laws' to develop the productive capacity of society. It is the capitalist mode of production which is the 'most advantageous for production in general' and for the creation of wealth since the universal development of the productive forces is the pre-supposition of capital's own reproduction.[63] Marx gives a number of reasons why capitalism should possess this unique ability to develop society's productive power. In *The Poverty of Philosophy* Marx explains this development of the productive forces as the result of the growth of the market which stimulated production. After 1825 mechanisation had been used by the capitalists to reduce working-class militancy, to de-skill labour and to reduce wages.[64] *The Communist Manifesto* and *Wage Labour and Capital* stress the importance of competition amongst capitalists to sell at the lowest price in order to capture the mass market as the force impelling capitalism to innovate and to mechanise.[65]

Finally, in his mature economic theory, Marx argues that capitalism has a particularly effective control over the labour process which allows it to innovate and to increase relative surplus value through the reduction of the time spent on necessary labour. The increase in the time available for surplus labour produces the wealth which allows a further extension of the scale of production. The growth of production itself then becomes a further stimulus to productivity as the capitalists obtain the benefits of large-scale production.[66]

The 'development thesis' is redundant in pre-capitalist modes of production, where the productive forces have no inherent tendency to develop. Neither is it needed in the analysis of the capitalist mode of production, where the growth of the productive forces can be explained in terms of the market and class structures peculiar to this mode of production. If the development thesis is abandoned, then we must also reject the primacy thesis which, as we have seen, takes the development thesis as its starting point. Marx's analysis of specific societies lead us to question the trans-historical claims of both the primacy and the development theses. The implications of Marx's analysis thus undermine the claims of his own productive force determinism.

(7) Marx on the transition to capitalism

Marx's analysis of the transition from the Ancient World to feudalism is, in effect, a critique of productive force determinism since it challenges the assumption made by the development thesis that the productive forces have an inherent tendency to develop throughout history. His analysis of the transition from feudalism to capitalism also offers the basis for a rejection of productive force determinism in its implicit rejection of the primacy thesis. Marx argues that it was not change in the productive forces which led to the emergence of capitalism. Rather, it was the development of capitalism which later brought about a new stage of the growth of the productive forces. Only if we assume that this change in the relations of production was called into being by the needs of the productive forces which were to appear in the future can the claims of productive force determinism be salvaged. Chapter 7 argued that there was no need to explain the emergence of new class relations in terms of the functional requirements of non-existent productive forces. Below, we offer an alternative explanation of the emergence of capitalism. Here we are concerned merely to establish that Marx eventually claimed that capitalism was not the result of the growth of the productive forces. On the contrary, capitalism was the *cause* of that growth.

It is in *The German Ideology* that Marx's analysis of the transition to capitalism *does* owe most to his productive force determinism. Marx argues that the extent of society's division of labour is an indication of the stage of development of its productive forces. In practice, his analysis takes the form of a *description* of the growth of society's division of labour: the separation of town and country, the division of commerce and production with the development of a class of merchants, the growth of the division of labour between towns and the rise of manufactures with new capitalist social relations and, finally, the Industrial Revolution.[67] Marx's analysis is remarkable given the date at which it was written but, nevertheless, it does not offer an explanation of the rise of capitalism. Rather, it offers 'a description which wishes to be self-explanatory'.[68] In so far as an explanation is offered, it is based on the growth of trade as the 'prime mover' of the decay of feudalism.

The Communist Manisfesto offers a similar analysis in which the growth of the bourgeoisie is traced from its origins in the medieval town, through the various stages of its development called forth by the evolution of the world market. Why trade should develop, and why it should lead to capitalism, is never specified. In general, Marx claims that the division of labour is the measure of the growth of the productive forces but, in practice, it is the division of labour, as determined by the extent of demand, which is the active agent in creating capitalism. Marx adopts Adam Smith's belief that economic development can be seen in terms of the growth of the division of labour and continued Smith's emphasis on the importance of towns, trade and industry in the emergence of capitalism.[69]

In the *Grundrisse* and *Capital* Marx offers an implicit critique of his own earlier views. Again and again Marx stresses that the mere development of monetary wealth and of trade are not enough to bring about capitalism 'or else ancient Rome, Byzantium etc. would have ended their history with free labour and capital'. The extent of the dissolving influence of trade is determined by the nature of the society it reacts with. 'In the ancient world the effect of commerce and the development of merchant's capital always resulted in a slave economy.' The commercial revolutions of the early modern period doubtless helped to dissolve feudal class relations but, nevertheless, in itself commerce could not bring about capitalism which 'developed only where the conditions for it had taken shape within the middle ages'.[70] Unfortunately Marx nowhere specifies what these conditions were.

Marx gives an emphasis to the emergence of agrarian capitalism as the basis of the transition process which was absent in his earlier writings: 'Although capital can develop itself completely as commercial capital without this transformation of landed property it cannot do so as industrial capital. Even the development of manufactures presupposes the beginning of a dissolution of the old economic relations of landed property.'[71] Any society with exchange can *circulate* commodities by means of merchant capital, but for capital to take hold of *production* assumes the transformation of agrarian class relations. The period of primitive accumulation in which the capitalist mode of production emerged is thus the era of the creation of a class of free wage labourers: 'so called primitive accumulation is nothing else than the historical process of divorcing the producer from the means of production'.[72] The bulk of producers in the feudal mode of production are, of course, peasants who possess the means of their own subsistence. It follows therefore that 'the expropriation of the peasant, of the agricultural producer, from the soil is the basis of the whole process (of primitive accumulation – S.R.)'.[73] Marx explores three aspects of the emergence of capitalism: the expropriation of the agricultural population, the genesis of the capitalist farmer and the emergence of the industrial capitalist. His analysis is full of insights but, nevertheless, it is still essentially a *description* of the rise of capitalism. The reasons why feudalism gave way to capitalism are never specified.[74]

Marx does, however, refute various rival explanations of the growth of capitalism, even if he does not supply his own. Firstly, as we have seen, he rejects the idea that the growth of trade was the prime mover of the transition. The growth of commerce was a necessary but not a sufficient cause of the appearance of capitalist relations in the sphere of production. More importantly, for our discussion, in his detailed analysis of the rise of capitalism Marx makes no use of his own productive force determinist claims that feudalism's fetters were burst asunder by the growth of the productive forces.[75] Still less does he make use of the idea that the rise of capitalist relations of production was the result of the needs of the *future* productive forces. Lenin may have accurately summarised Marx's productive force determinism when he claimed that Marx had shown how capitalism grew out of feudalism 'in consequence of the growth of the productive forces'; but in volume I of *Capital*, Marx shows the opposite, i.e. that the productive forces grew in consequence of the introduction of capitalism.[76]

Marx argues that the growth of the productive forces was an effect of the introduction of new relations of production in both agriculture and industry. He believed that the modern system of agriculture dated from the parliamentary enclosures of the mid-eighteenth century but 'the revolution in property relations on the land *which is the basis of the altered mode of production* occurred much earlier'.[77] Similarly, in the development of capitalist industry, capital at first adapts itself to the existing forms of the labour process. Only later does it develop distinctively capitalist forms of production with manufacture and later large-scale industry.[78] In other words, 'if changes occur in these traditional labour processes after their takeover by capital, these are nothing but the gradual consequences of that subsumption'.[79] Even under manufacture: 'technologically speaking the labour process goes on as before, with the proviso that it is now subordinated to capital'.[80]

If capitalism did not emerge as a result of the growth of trade, or of the rise of new productive forces, then why did it develop? In so far as he gives an answer Marx looks at the development of a free proletariat in England in terms of the dissolution of bands of feudal retainers, the substitution of the agricultural population with sheep pastures (which he wrongly attributes to the growth of wool exports to Flanders) and the opportunities given to capitalist landowners by the Reformation. He also stresses the role of the state, particularly after the Glorious Revolution of 1688, which consolidated the power of the bourgeoisie.[81] In other words, Marx's analysis:

(1)   is historically specific – the transition to capitalism is the result of circumstances in England in the early modern period;
(2)   centres on the role of class and political power;
(3)   ignores the role of new productive forces since they are not the starting point but rather the result of the process of primitive accumulation.

Marx's productive force determinism answers the question 'why did capitalism replace feudalism?' as soon as we have asked it: capitalism emerged as a result of the past or future growth of the productive forces. Marx's analysis of the rise of capitalism in volume I of *Capital* suggests a different approach in which his concepts are used to formulate questions which require specific historical investigation. The latter approach, based on the assumption that we do not know the answer to every question as soon as (or even before) we have asked it, would seem to be the preferable one. Certainly, as the remainder of this chapter argues, it has turned out to be the most historically productive.

It is impossible to weigh up Marx's conflicting claims about the relationship between society's productive forces and its class relations and then decide which is the 'most Marxist'. Marx himself had no clear view on the issue, because he was never challenged and so forced to clarify his position. In the course of one page of volume III of *Capital*, for instance, Marx claims that, under feudalism, society's mode of material production 'corresponds' to its social relations of production, and then says that these social relations 'correspond' to the backward conditions of feudalism's production process.[82] Elsewhere in the same chapter he claims that class relations grow out of production but that, in turn, class relations react upon production 'as a determining element'.[83] In other words social primacy is granted to class, then to the productive forces and then it is claimed that the two interact. Marx's works can thus be used to justify the conflicting interpretations of modern commentators for whom Marx either definitely was or, on the other hand, obviously was not, a productive force determinist. The key question is not which interpretation is the more Marxist but which is the most analytically productive. It is to this issue that we now turn.

Part B: The transition debate

Whilst Marx put forward his own philosophy of history based on the determining role of the productive forces he also, paradoxically, rejected the idea that historical trends could be summarised by the 'master key of a general historico-philosophical theory' whose supreme virtue 'consists in being supra-historical'.[1] In doing so he opened up the way for an interpretation of historical materialism based on its characteristic questions and concepts rather than as a distinct method of historical validation or as a set of pre-existing answers to the question of how social change comes about.[2] The weaknesses of productive force determinism and the value of Marx's alternative approach can be seen in the long-running debate on the transition from feudalism to capitalism, a central issue in Marxist historiography. Can the transition to capitalism be explained in terms of the growth of the productive forces as Lenin and Marx (sometimes) claimed? We are not concerned here with the historical detail of the debate, but rather with what the debate reveals about the relative merits of Marx's conflicting theories of history. We argue that, in practice, writers such as Dobb and Sweezy have been able to make little use of productive force determinism in explaining the transition to capitalism. Wallerstein has attempted to explain the existence of specific class relations in terms of the requirements of production but his analysis presents a number of problems. The method offered by Robert Brenner, based on the primacy of class and of class struggle, shows the strengths of the Marxist tradition which rejects productive force determinism even though his historical account is open to empirical question.

1 Dobb and Sweezy

The fact that Marx's analysis of the process of primitive accumulation was descriptive rather than explanatory led to attempts by Dobb and Sweezy to identify the 'prime mover' behind the transition to capitalism. Dobb argued that, although capitalism consists of the production of commodities, the rise of commodity production could not, in itself, explain the emergence of capitalism. Examples such as the economy of early modern eastern Europe suggested that 'there seems to be as much evidence that the growth of a money economy *per se* led to an intensification of serfdom as there is evidence that it was the cause of feudal decline'.[3] Dobb identified the main cause of the decline of the feudal system as its inherent tendency towards crisis, rather than the impact of 'external factors' such as merchant capital. His analysis was based on the inefficiency of feudalism as a system of production, the growing demand of the ruling class for revenue and a tendency for population to grow. The inefficiency of feudal production meant that the rising demands placed on it by rising population and the exactions of the ruling class meant a tendency towards falling living standards and declining agricultural productivity. The feudal system, by its very nature, was bound for crisis.[4]

Despite its insights Dobb's interpretation presents a number of problems. In particular, the reasons why capitalism should emerge from the crisis of feudalism are never specified. Such a tendency is simply assumed as a natural result of the crisis.[5] This failure to specify why capitalism emerged is particularly paradoxical in the light of Dobb's own recognition of the divergent economic paths taken by different areas of Europe in the early modern period: the establishment of agrarian capitalism in England with its landlords, capitalist tenant farmers and wage labourers; the consolidation of peasant agriculture in France where the peasants obtained, in effect, freehold rights over their holdings; and the eastern European path of the 'Second Serfdom' with oppressive labour services and strict control of the unfree peasants by feudal landlords.[6]

At one point Dobb touches on the importance of class struggle in determining these different outcomes, when he suggests that it was the varying reactions of the nobility in the different areas of Europe to the feudal crisis which determined the economic history of the ensuing centuries. He concludes, however, that 'political factors ... can hardly be regarded as sufficient to account for the differences in the course of events in various parts of Europe ... all the indications suggest that ... economic factors must have exercised the outstanding influence'.[7] There are two problems with Dobb's claim. The first is that he never shows why economic factors 'must' have had the greatest influence. The second is that he does not show why class struggle should be considered as a 'political' rather than as a social or economic factor. This is particularly a problem in a society such as feudalism where the mode of production was, Dobb claims, based on the extra-economic coercion of surplus labour from the producers by legal and political means.

Besides these theoretical problems, there are a number of empirical weaknesses in Dobb's analysis. His search for 'economic factors' to explain the transition to capitalism led him to the relative scarcities of land and labour as an explanation of social change: where labour is scarce the landlords will tend to tie the peasant to the soil and use labour services to produce surplus. The labour scarcity of eastern Europe explains its serfdom. In England it was the population *growth* of the mid-fifteenth century onwards which led to the commutation of labour services and the end of serfdom.[8] The difficulty with this analysis is that:

(1) Population growth which made good the effects of the Black Death of 1348 did not recommence until the early sixteenth century.[9] It can hardly explain the decline of serfdom before this date.

(2) As Marx realised, serfdom had begun to disappear by the end of the fourteenth century. In other words serfdom disappeared not in an era of rising population, as Dobb claimed, but in the era of labour scarcity which followed the Black Death. Indeed, the current orthodoxy is to explain the end of serfdom as a result of the scarcity of labour (and the consequent strong bargaining position of the peasantry), exactly the conditions which Dobb thought would strengthen serfdom.[10]

Dobb's 'internal' account of the decay of feudalism was countered by Paul Sweezy, who emphasised the importance of the 'external' factor of long-distance trade in undermining feudalism, which he conceived of as a system of production for use. Since 'trade can in no sense be regarded as a form of feudal economy', it follows that the growth of trade was the key element in the decay of feudalism. The result was the rise of a new system of commodity production which at first coexisted with the older system, but which increasingly revealed its inefficiency.[11] The problem with Sweezy's analysis is that it is difficult to draw from it a coherent account of the decay of feudal class relations, since he himself admits that 'the triumph of exchange economy does not necessarily imply the end of either serfdom or demesne farming'.[12] Secondly, even if trade did lead to the end of the classic manor with its unfree serfs and labour services, Sweezy gives no reason why the subsequent system of free tenants paying money rents should give way to capitalism based on wage labour.[13]

Sweezy's analysis owes much to *The Communist Manifesto*, where the emergence of capitalism was presented in terms of the development of an urban bourgeoisie under the impact of the growth of the market. Eventually the new productive forces associated with this class expand beyond the capacities of feudal class relations. The fetters of feudalism are swept aside and a new mode of production develops. Certainly Sweezy (and Pirenne, whose analysis Sweezy had adopted) saw trade as increasing productivity through the growth of the division of labour, specialisation and competition on the market.[14] Yet Sweezy himself argued that 'one cannot say that feudalism had created productive forces which could be maintained and developed only under capitalism – as, for example, one can say that capitalism has created productive forces that can only be maintained and further developed under socialism'.[15] In practice Sweezy went no further than Marx in describing the growth of trade as a necessary, but hardly a sufficient, cause of the growth of capitalism.[16] He made no attempt to develop a productive force determinist account of the transition even though his stress on the importance of trade brought him nearest to it.

The Dobb–Sweezy debate was marked by a rather sterile concern with the 'internality' or 'externality' of the prime movers, such as trade, which explain the transition from one model of production to another. Yet the definition of feudalism by its dominant form of surplus labour, feudal ground rent, necessarily leads to a view where trade is 'external', i.e. to this definition. The definition of feudalism is, however, only an abstraction; a useful abstraction, but an abstraction nevertheless. It was not the feudal mode of production which underwent the transition to capitalism but rather particular social formations with distinct economic structures, state forms, cultures and so on. The key question of the transition debate is not 'why did capitalism replace feudalism?' but (for instance) 'why did capitalism emerge in England in a particular period and in a specific form?' Trade may be external to the definition of the feudal mode of production but, nevertheless, it was an integral part of the societies in which it was found.[17] Indeed, it is the compatibility of trade with the continuance of feudal class relations which makes historians doubt the claim that it was trade which caused the transition to capitalism.[18] It is not because of trade's theoretical status as an 'external' factor that we reject it as the main explanation of the decay of feudalism, but because of the historical evidence which shows that trade can intensify feudalism as well as undermine it.[19]

2 Wallerstein

Immanuel Wallerstein offers an alternative solution to the problem that the growth of trade in early modern eastern Europe did not undermine but, on the contrary, intensified feudalism. For Wallerstein, the essential feature of a capitalist 'world economy' is production for sale in a market, where the aim is to realise the maximum profit. Innovation is a natural result of this system, as the producers seek to expand their profit margin. It is the world system which is capitalist. It follows that any region within it is also capitalist, even if its production process is not carried out on the basis of free wage labour. The wage system is only one of the possible forms of rewarding labour in the capitalist system. Serfdom and slavery may also form part of the capitalist world system. The essential theme of the creation of the capitalist world system is not, therefore, the process by which the producer was turned into a proletarian but is rather the growth of a capitalist world market.[20]

There are a number of problems with Wallerstein's analysis, in particular its reliance on a form of productive force determinism. Wallerstein argues that the differing class relations of the regions of the world economy result from the technical requirements of particular production processes: 'Why different modes of organizing labour – slavery, 'feudalism', wage labour, self employment? ... Because each mode of labour control is best suited for particular types of production.'[21] Yet, as we have already seen, eastern European serfdom did not maximise agricultural productivity. On the contrary the plots held by the peasants produced and marketed more grain per acre. The lords' own demesnes were subject to a declining productivity and exported only a small percentage of their total grain production: 'the main reason for the emergence of this system (demesne farming) was not that it produced more food, but that it enabled the ruling class to increase its revenue'.[22] The serfdom of early modern eastern Europe was not introduced because it was the form of class relation most suited to grain production. On the contrary, it was the wage labour-based agriculture of England which managed to avoid the declining productivity of Poland and the Malthusian crises of early modern France. Serfdom was not introduced in reponse to the 'needs' of a particular production process. The form of production adopted in eastern Europe was the result of the ability of the landlords to assert their class power. Why they were able to assert this power and why other paths of economic development were opened up elsewhere cannot be deduced from the nature of the productive forces or the requirements of 'agricultural production'.[23]

3 Brenner

In a sense it was unfortunate that Dobb's *Studies in the Development of Capitalism* appeared when it did (1946), as economic history was about to be revolutionised by the school of historians who based their analysis of the pre-industrial economy on the theories of Malthus and Ricardo. This school created a new chronology of economic change based on alternating cycles of rising population, associated with higher rents, rising food prices, declining real wages and the extension of arable cultivation, and of declining population in which these trends were reversed.[24] The achievements of this school are so great that it may seem churlish to criticise it but, nevertheless, the use of population as a prime mover of social change does have a number of weaknesses when it is seen in the light of comparative analysis. It is these problems which Robert Brenner was to raise in his critique of the 'Malthusian' school, a critique which forms the basis for an alternative explanation of long-term social and economic change in which class struggle plays a central part.[25]

The weakness of population change as an explanation of social change is apparent in the divergent economic paths of England, Languedoc and Poland in the sixteenth century. In Languedoc the growth of population led, as Malthus would have expected, to a growing demand for land, increasing rents, fragmented holdings, declining living standards, diminishing returns and, eventually, to demographic crisis as population outstripped resources.[26] Yet in England, according to Bowden, the growth of population did not lead to smaller farms and declining productivity. On the contrary, the growing demand for food led to the development of increased production through more efficient agriculture based on larger units of production.[27] In Poland, according to Pounds, the sixteenth century was a time of rising population. The land:labour ratio gave an advantage to the landlords in their relations with the peasantry who were obliged to accept growing seigneurial controls and increased rents and labour services.[28] In other words growing population is the 'explanation' of smaller free peasant farms in Languedoc, larger capitalist enterprises in England and the development of serf production in Poland.

Another contrast which provides problems for the Malthusian school is that between eleventh- and fifteenth-century England. In the fifteenth century the low level of population due to the recurrent outbreaks of plague gave the peasantry the upper hand in their relations with the landlords. Land was in little demand. The result was a decline in rents and the weakening of manorial controls over the peasantry.[29] Yet, it has been argued, eleventh-century England was also a time when labour was in demand and land was abundant. In order to maintain a high level of income the landlords had to use manorial powers to ensure a level of rent above that which the market for land would have produced.[30] In other words the abundance of land 'explains' peasant freedom in the fifteenth century – and serfdom in the eleventh century. Clearly there are two logics at work: the peasant logic which will attempt to use the abundance of land to ensure low rents; and the landlords' logic which will attempt to overcome the effects of this low labour:land ratio in order to maintain their levels of income. In *itself* the land:labour ratio will not determine which of these logics will prevail.

In 1953 Rodney Hilton suggested that the struggle for rent was the prime mover of the feudal economy. His later study of the decline of serfdom in England showed that it was not merely the declining population of the later Middle Ages that led to peasant freedom. The struggles of the peasants themselves also helped to prevent the victory of a seigneurial reaction and the imposition of the landlords' logic.[31] Brenner has extended this type of analysis to the entire history of Europe in the late medieval and early modern periods. It was not population, or the growth of trade, or the requirements of particular types of production which led to particular forms of social relations. Rather the outcome of particular class conflicts opened up specific paths of economic and social development.

He offers three case studies: in eastern Europe the logic of the feudal landlords prevailed and the peasantry was enserfed; in France the peasants' logic was victorious and the peasants achieved, in effect, the security of freehold tenure; in England the landlords were unable to impose the strict serfdom of eastern Europe but neither did the peasantry win the security of tenure enjoyed in France, with the result that the eventual victory of the landlords opened up a new path of economic development based on large capitalist farms employing wage labour. The growth of population or of trade may well give an impetus for economic change but, as Marx said of the growth of commerce, where this change leads to depends not on trade or on population *per se* but on the nature of the society which feels their impact.[32]

Brenner's first task is to explain the victory of the landlords in eastern Europe. His account centres on the weakness of the eastern European peasant community. Although originally free, these communities were ill-equipped to resist the seigneurial offensive that developed from the fifteenth century onwards. Eastern European society was the result of colonisation and immigration from the west. Lordship had played a key part in organising this colonisation so that, despite peasant freedom, the landlords' *potential* power was particularly strong. Villages tended to be small and under the control of a single lord unlike the large villages of the west which often benefited from divided lordship. The lack of common lands, individualistic agriculture and the inability to develop peasant institutions at a village level all help to explain the weakness of the peasantry and their defeats at the hands of the landlords. The result was a classic manorial system with large demesnes, heavy labour services and numerous restrictions on peasant freedom.[33]

In France, by contrast, the peasantry managed to obtain fixed rents, hereditary succession and guaranteed use of the commons, in short, a secure free tenure held for a money rent. The security of the peasantry thus short-circuited the English path whereby the producer was divorced from the means of production and the peasantry gave way to a rural proletariat. For Brenner this development was associated with the rise of the absolutist state which confirmed the peasantry's free and hereditary tenure and restricted the powers of the landlord class. Yet, ironically, this 'protection' was to rebound on the peasant. The restriction of the demands of the landlords opened up the way for the exactions of the state. By the seventeenth century the main appropriator of the peasant surplus was not the landlord, through feudal rent, but rather the absolutist state, through its taxation. As a result peasant revolts tended to be directed against taxation and the state rather than against the landlords.[34]

If feudalism was strengthened in eastern Europe and restructured in France, then in England it disappeared altogether. The English landlords proved incapable of defending their manorial rights in the later Middle Ages but, nevertheless, were eventually able to develop a new system of agriculture based on large consolidated holdings employing wage labour. Co-operation between landlord and capitalist tenant, holding by lease-hold tenure, replaced the exploitation of peasant by lord. This co-opera-tion, along with regional specialisation based on production for the market, economies of scale and competition, promoted the development of more efficient forms of agricultural production. The conflict between increased output and increased surplus, inherent in the feudal relation-ship of lord and peasant, gave way to a new system whose productivity supported the population and helped create the demand necessary for industrialisation. Whilst eastern Europe was unable to break out of the trend to declining productivity and France continued to suffer from demographic crises, England was, by the end of the seventeenth century, a grain exporter. The contrast with the fourteenth century when, with similar levels of population, England had been hit by economic and demographic crisis, is obvious. It was its new class relations which had allowed England to escape the Malthusian cycle of the feudal economy.[35]

Empirically Brenner's analysis is open to a whole number of ques-tions. Can the success of the eastern European landlords in enserfing the peasantry be explained in terms of the weakness of peasant protest and village institutions?[36] Can the differences between England and France be drawn in such clear-cut national terms, given that northern France did possess large consolidated farms?[37] If the growth of the absolutist state explains the security of the French peasant then what explains that growth? After all in England, Brenner suggests that it was the absence of an independent peasantry as a fiscal base which *prevented* the development of absolutism. In other words, is absolutism the cause or the effect of an independent peasantry?[38]

These are all important issues but here we are interested in the *method-ological* implications of Brenner's approach and, in particular, its rejection of productive force determinism. Take for instance Brenner's explanation of the development of serfdom in eastern Europe based on its distinct form of village organisation. It has been argued that there was no essen-tial difference between the village structure of west Germany, which developed peasant freedom, and east Germany, which saw the rise of serfdom. Yet the fact remains that the east German peasantry was enserfed. How is the contrast with the west to be explained? A number of other explanations have been offered for the rise of the 'second serf-dom' such as the growth of the grain exports to western Europe or the lack of towns as refuges for escaped serfs or as allies in peasant revolts.[39] Whichever explanation we adopt, village organisation, the grain trade, the minor role of towns, cannot, in itself, be deduced from the concept of feudal mode of production since other feudal societies possessed different forms of trade, town life and village structure, and had different courses of economic development. In that sense the search for the 'prime mover' of the feudal economy had to end in the identification of those factors which would account for historical *difference* as models based on the growth of trade, on population or on the needs of the productive forces, tend to break down under comparative analysis.

The advantage of Brenner's approach is that it allows for empirical complexity and diversity. In this sense Marx was quite right when he argued that, although it was possible to define production in general, it is precisely those elements which are not common to all forms of production which explain the development of specific epochs.[40] Any suggested prime mover of feudalism must be able to deal with the divergent paths taken by particular feudal economies such as England, France and Poland.

The second conclusion to be drawn from Brenner's analysis is that the relations of production cannot be explained in terms of the needs of society's productive forces. On the contrary:

(1) from a given level of the productive forces societies may evolve in divergent ways (England, France);

(2) prevailing relations of production are not a response to the needs of society's productive forces, they are the result of the outcome of earlier class struggles. Far from being forms of development of the productive forces, class relations can have an inbuilt tendency towards declining productivity and demographic crisis (Poland, France, medieval England);

(3) the development of the capitalist mode of production was not a response to the needs of the productive forces which had been fettered by the class relations of feudalism. It is true that feudal class relations were fetters on the growth of productivity but this, in itself, does not explain their demise, since in France and Poland they continued to restrict productive advance. When new productive forces did develop it was not as the cause but as the result of changes in the relations of production (England);

(4) productive forces could only be salvaged as the explanation of the rise of capitalism if we assumed that new class relations emerged in order to allow the future development of the productive forces. We would then have to specify the mechanism, or at least have

169

reason to believe in the existence of a mechanism, which would allow the as yet non-existent productive forces to produce historical change.

An approach based on the contingent outcome of class struggles deals a 'death blow' to teleological explanations of historical change. This approach may be compared with the scientific account of biological evolution. In the latter evolution does not take place in order to ensure the survival of the fittest. This outcome is the result of the evolutionary process (chance variation and natural selection), not its cause. Similarly the growth of the productive forces under capitalism is the result of the evolution of these new class relations. This does not mean that capitalism emerged in order to ensure the future growth of the productive forces. Neither the evolution of animal species nor of class relations can be explained in terms of their future effects. In that sense it is Cohen's analysis of social change, not, as he claims, historical materialism in general, which is still at the pre-Darwinian level.[41]

Notes (Part A)

1 K. Marx, *Capital*, vol. I (London, 1977, Lawrence & Wishart edn), p. 352. This translation is preferred here to the Pelican edition (Harmondsworth, 1976), p. 493.

2 G. A. Cohen, *Karl Marx's Theory of History: A Defence* (Oxford, 1978), pp. 30, 88–114.

3 Ibid., pp. 79–80, 89.

4 Ibid., p. 47.

5 Ibid., p. 90; K. Marx, *Wage Labour and Capital* (Moscow, 1970), p. 28.

6 Cohen, *Karl Marx's Theory of History*, p. 95.

7 Ibid., p. 158.

8 Ibid., pp. 80, 94.

9 Ibid., p. 80.

10 Ibid., p. 96; K. Marx, *The Poverty of Philosophy* (Moscow, 1973), p. 95.

11 K. Marx, *Grundrisse* (Hardmondsworth, 1974), p. 835.

12 Cohen, *Karl Marx's Theory of History*, p. 96.

13 R. Brenner, 'Agrarian class structure and economic development in pre-industrial Europe', *Past and Present* 70 (1976), pp. 63–80; E. L. Jones, *Agriculture and the Industrial Revolution* (Oxford, 1974), Chs. 4, 5.

14 Cohen, *Karl Marx's Theory of History*, p. 158.

15 C. Wickham, 'The other transition: from the ancient world to feudalism', *Past and Present* 103 (1984), pp. 12–13.

16 Marx, *Grundrisse*, p. 85.
17 K. Marx & F. Engels, *Collected Works*, vol. V (London, 1976), p. 43 (*The German Ideology*).
18 Marx, *Grundrisse*, pp. 87–8.
19 Ibid., p. 96.
20 Ibid., pp. 99–100.
21 Ibid., p. 489.
22 Ibid., p. 86.
23 Marx, *Capital*, vol. I (Pelican edn), p. 286.
24 K. Marx, *A Contribution to the Critique of Political Economy* (London, 1971), p. 21.
25 K. Marx, *Capital*, vol. III (London, 1974, Lawrence & Wishart edn), pp. 879–80.
26 Marx, *Grundrisse*, pp. 87, 97.
27 K. Marx, *Capital*, vol. II (London, 1976, Lawrence & Wishart edn), pp. 36–7.
28 Marx, *Capital*, vol. I (Pelican edn), p. 325.
29 Ibid., p. 452. My emphasis.
30 J. McMurtry, *The Structure of Marx's World View* (Princeton, 1978), p. 72; Cohen, *Karl Marx's Theory of History*, p. 113.
31 Marx, *Grundrisse*, p. 245. My emphasis.
32 K. Marx, *Theories of Surplus Value*, part II (London, 1969), p. 528; K. Marx & F. Engels, *Selected Correspondence* (Moscow, 1975), p. 294 (letter of November 1877 to the editorial board of *Otechestvenniye Zapiski*). My emphases. We are concerned here with the theoretical implications of Marx's claims, rather than their historical accuracy.
33 Marx, *Grundrisse*, p. 298. My emphasis.
34 Ibid., p. 245. As Cohen points out, the purpose of production (such as production for direct consumption or for exchange) is part of the social form of production (Cohen, *Karl Marx's Theory of History*, pp. 80–1).
35 Marx, *Capital*, vol. I (Lawrence & Wishart edn), p. 339. See pp. 479–80 of the Pelican edition.
36 Marx, *Grundrisse*, p. 225. My emphasis.
37 K. Marx, *Theories of Surplus Value*, part III (London, 1972), p. 315.
38 Ibid., p. 429.
39 Marx, *Capital*, vol. I (Pelican edn), p. 874.
40 Marx, *Grundrisse*, pp. 586–7.
41 Ibid., pp. 585, 749.
42 Ibid., pp. 692–9. The quotation comes from p. 692.
43 Ibid., p. 86.
44 Ibid., p. 88. My emphasis.
45 Ibid., p. 83.
46 Ibid., p. 84.
47 F. Engels, *Herr Eugen Dühring's Revolution in Science* (London, Lawrence & Wishart, n.d.), pp. 167–8. Original emphasis.
48 Marx, *Capital*, vol. I (Lawrence & Wishart edn), p. 28. See Pelican edition, p. 101.
49 T. Malthus, *An Essay on the Principle of Population* (London, 1973), pp. 6–7; Marx, *Capital*, vol. I (Lawrence & Wishart edn), p. 592. See also Marx, *Grundrisse*, pp. 605 ff.

50 Engels, *Herr Eugen Dühring's Revolution in Science*, pp. 167–8. See also Marx, *Grundrisse*, pp. 85, 88.

51 Marx & Engels, *Collected Works*, vol. V, p. 34 (*The German Ideology*).

52 Cohen, *Karl Marx's Theory of History*, pp. 156–7.

53 F. Engels, *The Origin of the Family, Private Property and the State* (Moscow, 1968), pp. 145–6.

54 Ibid., p. 151.

55 Marx, *Grundrisse*, p. 605; K. Marx, *Theories of Surplus Value*, part I (London, 1969), p. 390.

56 Marx, *Theories of Surplus Value*, part II, p. 528.

57 Marx, *Grundrisse*, p. 540.

58 Marx, *Theories of Surplus Value*, part III, p. 423. Again we are concerned at this point with Marx's theoretical assumptions rather than the historical accuracy of his analysis.

59 K. Marx, *Surveys from Exile* (Harmondsworth, 1973), pp. 303–4. See also P. Anderson, *Lineages of the Absolutist State* (London, 1979), pp. 462–72.

60 Marx, *Capital*, vol. I (Lawrence & Wishart edn), p. 338. See Pelican edition, p. 479. See also Marx & Engels, *Selected Correspondence*, p. 79 (letter of 14 June 1853).

61 Marx, *Capital*, vol. I (Lawrence & Wishart edn), p. 457. See Pelican edition, p. 617. See also K. Marx & F. Engels, *The Communist Manifesto* (Harmondsworth, 1970), p. 83.

62 Cohen, *Karl Marx's Theory of History*, pp. 169–71. See above, pp. 118–24, 152–5.

63 Marx, *Theories of Surplus Value*, part III, p. 84; Marx, *Theories of Surplus Value*, part II, p. 117; Marx, *Grundrisse*, p. 541; Marx, *Capital*, vol. I (Lawrence & Wishart edn), p. 457. See Pelican edition, p. 617.

64 Marx, *The Poverty of Philosophy*, p. 122.

65 Marx & Engels, *The Communist Manifesto*, pp. 83–4; Marx, *Wage Labour and Capital*, pp. 40–1.

66 Marx, *Theories of Surplus Value*, part I, p. 390; Marx, *Grundrisse*, pp. 769–70.

67 Marx & Engels, *Collected Works*, vol. V, pp. 64–74 (*The German Ideology*).

68 J. Baechler, *The Origins of Capitalism* (Oxford, 1975), p. 12.

69 Marx & Engels, *Collected Works*, vol. V, pp. 32, 64–74; Marx & Engels, *The Communist Manifesto*, pp. 80–5; G. E. Mumy, 'Town and country in Adam Smith's *The Wealth of Nations*', *Science and Society* XLII (no. 4, winter 1978–9), pp. 458–77; R. Brenner, 'The origins of capitalist development: a critique of neo-Smithian Marxism', *New Left Review* 104 (July–August 1977), especially pp. 27, 33–8.

70 Marx, *Grundrisse*, pp. 506, 508–12, 859; Marx, *Capital*, vol. III, pp. 327–33.

71 Marx, *Grundrisse*, p. 277.

72 Marx, *Capital*, vol. I (Pelican edn), pp. 874–5.

73 Ibid., p. 876.

74 Ibid., part VIII (so-called primitive accumulation). For rather different assessments of the historical value of Marx's analysis see K. Collins, 'Marx on the English Agricultural Revolution: theory and evidence', *History and Theory* VI (1966), pp. 351–81; J. Saville, 'Primitive accumulation and early industrialization in Britain', *The Socialist Register*, 1969, pp. 247–71.

75 See, for instance, Marx & Engels, *The Communist Manifesto*, p. 85; Marx, *Grundrisse*, pp. 277, 699.

76 V. I. Lenin, The Three Sources and Three Component Parts of Marxism (Moscow, 1969), p. 7.
77 Marx, Capital, vol. I (Pelican edn), p. 828.
78 Marx, Grundrisse, p. 586.
79 Marx, Capital, vol. I (Pelican edn), p. 1021.
80 Ibid., p. 1026. See also ibid., p. 1031.
81 Ibid., Chs. 26–9.
82 Marx, Capital, vol. III, p. 793.
83 Ibid., p. 791.

Notes (Part B)

1 Marx & Engels, Selected Correspondence, pp. 225 (letter of 27.6.1870), 294 (letter to the editorial board of Otechestvenniye Zapiski, November 1877).
2 E. P. Thompson, The Poverty of Theory (London, 1978), pp. 229–42.
3 M. Dobb, Studies in the Development of Capitalism (London, 1975; 1st edn 1946), p. 40.
4 Ibid., pp. 42 ff.
5 See R. Brenner, 'Dobb on the transition from feudalism to capitalism', Cambridge Journal of Economics II (1978), pp. 121–40.
6 Dobb, Studies in the Development of Capitalism, pp. 39–42, 51–3, 124–6.
7 Ibid., pp. 52–3.
8 Ibid., pp. 54–67.
9 I. Blanchard, 'Population growth, enclosure and the early Tudor economy', Economic History Review, second series XXIII (1970), pp. 427–45; J. Cornwall, 'English population in the early sixteenth century', ibid., pp. 32–44; J. Hatcher, Plague, Population and the English Economy 1348–1530 (London, 1977), p. 69.
10 Marx, Capital, vol. I (Pelican edn), pp. 876–7; M. M. Postan, The Medieval Economy and Society (London, 1972), pp. 151–2.
11 P. Sweezy, 'A critique' (1950), in R. H. Hilton et al., The Transition from Feudalism to Capitalism (London, 1976), pp. 35, 40.
12 Ibid., p. 44.
13 P. Sweezy, 'A rejoinder' (1953), ibid., pp. 106–8.
14 H. Pirenne, Economic and Social History of Medieval Europe (London, 1965; first French edn 1933), especially pp. 79–86; Sweezy, 'A critique', pp. 43–6, 49–52.
15 Sweezy, 'A rejoinder', p. 106.
16 Ibid., pp. 106–7.
17 Ibid., p. 105.
18 R. H. Hilton, 'Introduction', in Hilton et al., The Transition from Feudalism to Capitalism, pp. 22–6; J. Merrington, 'Town and country in the transition from feudalism to capitalism', ibid., pp. 170–95.
19 Brenner, 'Agragrian class structure', pp. 42–6.
20 I. Wallerstein, The Modern World System (London, 1974), especially pp. 346–51.
21 Ibid., p. 87.
22 R. Brenner, 'The origins of capitalist development', pp. 69–70.
23 Ibid., pp. 69–77. For an empirical critique of Wallerstein's approach see P. O'Brien, 'European economic development: the contribution of the periphery', Economic History Review second series volume XXXV (1982), pp. 4–18.

24 M. M. Postan, *Essays on Medieval Agriculture and General Problems of the Medieval Economy* (Cambridge, 1973); Postan, *The Medieval Economy and Society*; E. Le Roy Ladurie, *The Peasants of Languedoc* (Illinois, 1976); H. J. Habakkuk, 'The economic history of modern Britain', *Journal of Economic History* XVIII (1958), pp. 486–8.
25 Brenner, 'Agrarian class structure', pp. 32–42; R. Brenner, 'The agrarian roots of European capitalism', *Past and Present* 97 (1982), pp. 20–8.
26 Ladurie, *The Peasants of Languedoc*, pp. 289–96.
27 P. Bowden, 'Agricultural prices, farm profits and rents', in H. P. R. Finberg (ed.), *The Agrarian History of England and Wales*, IV 1500–1640 (Cambridge, 1967), p. 593.
28 N. J. G. Pounds, *An Economic History of Medieval Europe* (London, 1974), p. 475.
29 Hatcher, *Plague, Population and the English Economy*, pp. 36–44; Postan, *The Medieval Economy and Society*, p. 152.
30 J. Hatcher, 'English serfdom and villeinage: towards a re-assessment', *Past and Present* 90 (1981), pp. 26–33, 37–9.
31 R. H. Hilton, 'A comment', in Hilton et al., *The Transition from Feudalism to Capitalism*, p. 115; R. H. Hilton, *The Decline of Serfdom in Medieval England* (London, 1969), pp. 32–43, 57.
32 Brenner, 'Agrarian class structure'; Brenner, 'The agrarian roots of European capitalism'. For a similar emphasis on class struggle see J. E. Martin, *Feudalism to Capitalism: Peasant and Landlord in English Agrarian Development* (London, 1983).
33 Brenner, 'Agrarian class structure', pp. 52–60; Brenner, 'The agrarian roots of European capitalism', pp. 66–76.
34 Brenner, 'Agrarian class structure,' pp. 69–75; Brenner, 'The agrarian roots of European capitalism', pp. 76–83.
35 Brenner, 'Agrarian class structure', pp. 61–68; Brenner, 'The agrarian roots of European capitalism', pp. 83–110.
36 H. Wunder, 'Peasant organisation and class conflict in east and west Germany', *Past and Present* 78 (1978), pp. 47–55.
37 J. P. Cooper, 'In search of agrarian capitalism', *Past and Present* 80 (1978), pp. 20–65.
38 Brenner, 'Agrarian class structure', pp. 71–2; Brenner, 'The agrarian roots of European capitalism', pp. 50–60, 77–89.
39 Wunder, 'Peasant organisation and class conflict in east and west Germany', p. 52; Wallerstein, *The Modern World System*, pp. 87, 90–99; P. Anderson, *Passages from Antiquity to Feudalism* (London, 1973), pp. 252–4.
40 Marx, *Grundrisse*, p. 85.
41 G. A. Cohen, 'Reply to Elster on "Marxism, functionalism and game theory"', *Theory and Society* XI (1982), p. 488.

PART THREE

'Base and superstructure' in historical materialism

We have rejected Marx's claim that the nature of society's relations of production corresponds to the level of development of its productive forces. How persuasive is the second central thesis of classical historical materialism, the claim that the relations of production constitute a 'base' which determines the nature of society's 'superstructure' of politics, law and ideology? Here we examine alternative interpretations of Marx's 'base and superstructure' metaphor and argue that the 'base' should be defined in terms of all those elements (including law, politics or ideology) which function as relations of production, rather than in narrowly 'economic' terms (Chapter 9). This definition is then used as the starting point of a discussion of the succession of economic formations of society oulined by Marx and Engels and developed by later Marxists (Chapter 10). Having established the nature of the 'economic foundation' of society, we are then in a position to assess the value of Marx's approaches to the state (Chapter 11) and to social consciousness (Chapter 12), before offering a final assessment of the worth of Marx's contribution to historiography.

Throughout these chapters a number of themes recur and intersect:

(1) Can 'base' and 'superstructure' be distinguished in practice?
(2) How are variant forms of the 'base' distinguished?
(3) Does the 'base' have the determining role which Marx claims for it? If so, how does it achieve this role?
(4) Is the nature of society's political and ideological superstructure functionally explained by the requirements of its relations of production?

CHAPTER 9

'Base and superstructure': definition and determination

Marx's historical materialism is often seen as consisting of little more than the claim that society's relations of production are the 'base', upon which is built a 'superstructure' of law, politics and ideology. In this chapter we establish the implications of this metaphor for Marx's social theory and note analogous metaphors which Marx used to express the relationship between economics, politics and forms of social consciouness. We then discuss variant interpretations of the base and superstructure metaphor (the 'fundamentalist' and the 'dialectical' versions) and consider Marx's alternative metaphor of society as an organic totality. The difficulty of the metaphor of base and superstructure is that it is impossible to define the 'base' without invoking elements of politics and ideology which are often seen as part of the 'superstructure'. The problem with the organicist interpretation of Marx is that its recognition of the interaction and interpretation of base and superstructure tends to undermine Marx's claims for the determining role of society's mode of production.

It is argued here that the 'base' must be seen in a broad sense to consist of all those elements which function as relations of production; Marx's theory is thus not a claim for the primacy of some pure 'economic' level. This definition of society's so-called 'economic foundation' is then used as the basis for a rejection of Althusser's 'determination by the economic in the last instance'. Finally, we note the dangers of an organicist model of social structure, where the social system itself is turned into an agent which uses individuals as the bearers of its relations. The functional definition of the base in terms of the elements which constitute the relations of production is then used as the starting point for the taxonomy of social relations offered in Chapter 10.

The metaphor of 'base' and 'superstructure'

All assessments of Marx's theories of history must consider the bold claims of his 1859 'Preface' to *A Contribution to the Critique of Political Economy*, a text to which commentators on Marx must compulsively return. We have already discussed, at length, the claim made in the 'Preface', that society's relations of production correspond to the level of development or future needs of its productive forces. Here we are concerned with the second major claim made in the 'Preface':

> In the social production of their existence, men inevitably enter into definite relations, which are independent of their will, namely relations of production appropriate to a given stage in the development of their material forces of production. The totality of these relations of production constitutes the economic structure of society, the real foundation, on which arises a legal and political superstructure and to which correspond definite forms of social consciousness.[1]

It must immediately be emphasised that class relations are not literally a 'base' nor the state a 'superstructure'. Base and superstructure is an architectural metaphor which Marx uses in order to persuade the reader that a certain perspective is useful. Unfortunately it has become a dead metaphor, so that Marxists sometimes ask which elements are included in each, as if the two actually existed. In fact, the superstructure does not exist. It is an analogy which draws our attention to a particular relationship, the determination of 'x' (the 'superstructure') by 'y' (society's relations of production). It is thus of little significance that the passage quoted from the 'Preface' does not include social consciousness within the superstructure. The important point is that both the state and consciousness correspond to the economic structure of society in a similar manner: 'From the specific form of material production arises in the first place a specific structure of society, in the second place a specific relation of men to nature. Their state and their spiritual outlook is determined by both.'[2] Indeed, elsewhere, Marx refers to social organisation as, in all ages, 'the basis of the state and the rest of the idealistic superstructure' whilst later, in the 'Preface' itself, Marx seems to include social consciousness in the 'whole immense superstructure' of society which is transformed under the impact of change in the economic base.[3] The state and forms of social consciousness are not part of the superstructure *and so* dependent on class relations; on the contrary, the state is referred to (analogously) as part of the superstructure *because* is is determined by class relations.[4]

178

Another immediate problem with the metaphor of base and super-structure is that the 'base' is not society's most 'basic' element. Marx refers to the totality of the relations of production, the economic struc-ture, as society's 'foundation'.[5] Many writers have taken this to mean that the economy in general, comprising both the relations and the forces of production, is included in the 'base'.[6] Whatever the validity of this approach it is not the one adopted by Marx in the 'Preface'. Here the relations of production are referred to as society's 'foundation', but this foundation is, in turn, grounded in a certain stage of the development of the productive forces.[7] As a productive force determinist text, the 'Preface' distinguishes three tiers of society: material production, rela-tions of production, and the social superstructure. We have rejected the claim that the productive forces determine the nature of the relations of production; it is the relationship between the latter and the superstruc-ture which is at issue here.

The 'Preface' offers not only a synchronic snapshot of social structure, but also a diachronic analysis of historical change. Just as the develop-ment of the productive forces requires the relations of production to be periodically cast aside as fetters on productive advance so, since politics and consciousness correspond to class relations, changes in the relations of production will 'lead sooner or later to the transformation of the whole immense superstructure'.[8] Eras of social revolution occur, the 'Preface' claims, when the relations of production have become fetters on the productive forces, but these social transformations are fought out in 'ideological forms' – legal, political, religious and philosophical. Such forms of consciousness must be explained from the conflict of the forces and the relations of production, but it is not only in such eras of social revolution that ideas are rooted in social reality. In more general terms, 'it is not the consciousness of men that determines their existence, but their social existence that determines their consciousness'.[9]

'Base and superstructure' is thus an analogy which illustrates Marx's synchronic claims about social structure and his diachronic claims con-cerning historical change. In a given social formation, it is the relations of production which have causal primacy over politics and ideology. The 'real basis of the state', the relations 'upon which the state rests', are thus society's productive forces and its forms of social intercourse. 'These actual relations are in no way created by the state power, on the contrary they are the power creating it.'[10] Similarly, Marx's historical method asserts the primacy of social existence over ideas and consciousness.[11] This does not mean that Marx denies any causal role or historical influence to society's superstructure. The 'Preface' itself does not affirm such an interaction of base and superstructure, but elsewhere Marx is quite explicit that the relationship between the productive forces, relations of production, the state and ideology can 'be depicted in its totality (and therefore too, the *reciprocal action* of these various sides on one another)'.[12] The problem is not that Marx and Engels failed to recognise the interaction of base and superstructure, but rather why the superstructure should be seen as more determined than determining.

The social primacy of the relations of production is most apparent in Marx's account of political and ideological change. A building's foundations must be constructed before its superstructure can arise; similarly change in the economic base must occur as the precondition for the emergence of new political and ideological forms. The chronological precedence of social change over political change is most apparent in Marx's explanation of bourgeois revolutions as the political recognition of prior changes in society's relations of production: 'The new bourgeois society which rests on entirely different foundations (i.e. from feudalism — S.R.) and on a new mode of production, had to seize power for itself; it had to snatch this power from the hands of those who represented the foundering society. ... Hence the revolution.'[13] The French Revolution of 1789, which marked the victory of bourgeois over feudal forms of property, was thus a political revolution 'in which the social transformation had also an official expression in the form of constitutional struggles'.[14] Just as the productive forces changed prior to the relations of production, so capitalist relations of production emerged within feudal society and came into conflict with the existing political superstructure. The social basis of absolutism, feudal landed property, was eroded by historical development and the state no longer corresponded to the emergent class relations: 'It had become a fetter and a hindrance to the new bourgeois society with its changed mode of production and its changed needs.'[15] Marx similarly argues that ideological change is the result of social change. 'A definite consciousness is appropriate to definite people and definite circumstances'; it follows that only changed empirical conditions will lead to different forms of consciousness. Religion, for instance, is a 'celestialised form' which 'corresponds' to existing social relations. In capitalist society where human relations and labour appear in the form of abstract labour expressed in commodities and values, Protestantism, with its cult of the abstract individual, is the most suitable form of religion.[16] The classic example of Marx and Engels's approach to consciousness is the apparent contrast between their account of the Protestant Reformation and that offered by Max Weber. For the latter, Calvinist theology developed autonomously out of Lutheran theology and then had the unintended consequence of encouraging capital accumulation, given the conditions of early modern Europe. For Marx and Engels, the doctrines of Calvin were ideological representations of class relationships which had arisen prior to the emergence of the new theology.[17]

The exception to this chronological precedence of change in society's economic foundation over change in its superstructure, is the functional explanation of ideological change in terms of the future needs of the relations of production. Cohen, for instance, argues that just as society's relations of production may alter in order to allow the future development of, as yet, non-existent productive forces, so political institutions or forms of social consciousness may be transformed in order to allow the future development of the relations of production: 'When Marx says that "Protestantism, by changing almost all the traditional holidays into workdays, plays an important role in the genesis of capital" he is not just assigning a certain effect to the new religion, but proposing a (partial explanation) of its rise in terms of that effect.'[18] Unfortunately Cohen does not develop this argument at length. The validity of this approach is discussed in Chapter 12.

Alternative metaphors

Marx and Engels frequently refer to the relations of production as society's 'base' or 'foundation', but elsewhere they use other metaphors to illustrate the relationship between class, politics and ideology. At times they employ a vegetative analogy where states and political economy have their 'root' in, 'stand on the ground' or 'spring from the soil' of capitalist society.[19] The determining role of the relations of production within society as a whole is also emphasised by the metaphor of 'expression': 'Assume a particular society and you will get particular political conditions which are only the official expression of civil society.'[20] The *Code Napoléon*, for example, did not create bourgeois society; on the contrary, it is bourgeois society 'which finds its merely legal expression in the Code'. As soon as such laws cease to 'correspond' to social relations they are worth no more than a bundle of paper.[21] Unfortunately the metaphor of 'expression' tends to render law and politics totally passive, as does the equally unhappy metaphor of 'reflection', where human

181

thoughts are described as the 'ideological reflexes and echoes' of real life, even if this reflection is not always accurate and may present the world in inverted form. Kant's philosophy is said to 'reflect' the state of affairs in late eighteenth-century Germany; legal principles are similarly a reflection of economic relations. Unfortunately the metaphor of reflection obscures more than it reveals, for if the superstructure is not to be rendered totally passive, it has to be presented as an impossibility, as an 'active reflection' which is not only determined by but which, in turn, influences and modifies the ecomomic base. Nevertheless, the choice of this unfortunate metaphor is significant. Marx and Engels were searching for an analogy which gave primacy to the base and yet also allowed for the interaction of social relations with ideas and politics. Perhaps no metaphor is adequate for this task, but there is no doubt about the central idea which they sought to emphasise, even if it is expressed in a regrettable form.[22] The metaphor of society as an 'organic totality' as an alternative to 'base and superstructure' is discussed in more detail below.

'Base and superstructure': the fundamentalist version

Marx's theory of history is usually associated with, indeed, is often seen as consisting of little more than, his metaphor of economic base and political and ideological superstructure. Melvin Rader, however, has argued that Marx not only uses the model of base and superstructure (which itself may be expressed in 'fundamentalist' or 'dialectical' versions) but also sees society as an organism, as an 'organic totality'. Althusserian Marxism also prefers to envisage society as an 'organic hierarchized whole' rather than as a 'base' and 'superstructure'. How useful is the distinction between these two metaphors for an understanding of Marx's historical method?

In the fundamentalist reading of Marx the economy, state and ideology are seen as 'distinct and externally related'. Through these 'external relations', society is composed of an association of separate elements, rather than as a system of 'internal relations' where the nature of any one thing taken by itself is incomplete, and can only be fully comprehended in terms of the whole system on which it depends. In this fundamentalist version, the economy is the dynamic stratum of society which produces corresponding changes in the superstructure. As a result causal determinism is seen as almost exclusively one-way and there is very little reaction of the superstructure upon the base. The fundamentalist interpretation of Marx's metaphor 'implies that the base is already there before the superstructure is erected. Drawing this conclusion would be inconsistent with the mutual determinism of base and superstructure by dialectical interaction.'[23]

Rader seems unclear as to whether there was a fundamentalist Marx, or whether this interpretation has simply been foisted on him by later readers. He agrees that there is 'no want of quotations' to support such a reading and that Marx has been interpreted in this way by friend and foe, philosopher and revolutionary. He even entertains the possibility that there was no single, coherent Marx and that the greatness of his thought 'is based precisely on this brilliant lack of coherence'. He concludes, however, that Marx did not adhere to a reductionist, or fundamentalist, view of politics and ideology except 'temporarily and in isolated passages', which are not really faithful to his mature insights. The fundamentalist reading of base and superstructure is thus a 'misinterpretation' which has to be corrected.[24]

The problem for Rader is why the fundamentalist version of base and superstructure should have become 'the common interpretation' of Marx, shared by Marxists and non-Marxists, if it is confined to isolated and unrepresentative passages. It is not difficult, in fact, to show that there was a fundamentalist Marx who offered a reductionist version of base and superstructure. The claim that 'the base is already there before the superstructure' is not a fundamentalist misinterpretation of Marx. On the contrary it is the whole basis of Marx's account of the bourgeois revolution which, he claimed, gives political recognition or expression to the economic and social emergence of capitalism from within the feudal mode of production. Each step in the economic advance of the bourgeoisie is accompanied by a 'corresponding political advance'.[25] Political change is presented here as merely the political expression of a prior social transformation. Similarly Marx refers to bourgeois ideas as no more than the outgrowth of capitalist production, modern law as no more than the expression of class will or of economic relations and the works of philosophers as merely the 'reflection' of their age.[26] It is not with this easily refuted economic determinism that Marx's critics must grapple, but rather with the strongest elements of Marx's legacy. Engels and Rader have offered alternative readings of Marx's theory, those of 'dialectical interaction', and of 'organic totality'. Both readings overcome the deficiencies of the fundamentalist reading of Marx, but both, however, present problems of their own.

'Base and superstructure': the dialectical version

Those who believe that they have identified the real, non-determinist Marx are obliged to find a scapegoat for later 'vulgar' readings of his works. Engels is the victim usually chosen for this role. Yet it was Engels who first warned of the dangers of the 'fundamentalist' version of base and superstructure and who offered the alternative model of 'dialectical interaction'. In this reading of Marx, the various strata in the social order are still seen as 'distinct and externally related' but, unlike the funamentalist model, the superstructure is now seen as an active historical agent in its own right, even if the economic base prevails 'in the last instance'.[27]

Engels argued that the fundamentalist interpretation of historical materialism was a 'misunderstanding' and a 'distortion', whilst conceding that he and Marx were 'partly to blame for the fact that the younger people sometimes lay more stress on the economic side than is due to it'. They had not intended to make the 'meaningless, abstract and absurd' claim that the economic factor was the only determining one. Those who made such allegations were simply tilting at windmills. It would be 'fatuous' for critics to claim that they had denied ideas any effect upon history simply because they had denied that ideology had an 'independent historical development'. Thinkers do not merely passively reflect economic conditions. On the contrary, they inherit an existing body of ideas which they take as a starting point. Thus there is a dialectical interaction of ideas and the economy. The material mode of existence is the primary agent in society but 'this does not prevent the ideological spheres from reacting upon it and influencing it in their turn'.[28]

Engels similarly denied that politics could be seen as a purely passive expression of the economic base. The class struggle, politics, constitutions, juridical forms, all 'exercise their influence upon the course of the historical struggles and in many cases determine their form in particular'. The state's active role can be seen in its ability to prevent economic development from proceeding along certain lines and its ability to prescribe other paths. Law too has a certain independence of economics: 'in a modern state, law must not only correspond to the general economic development and be its expression, but must also be an internally coherent expression which does not, owing to internal conflicts, contradict itself. And in order to achieve this, the faithful reflection of economic conditions suffers increasingly.' It would be pedantic to explain every detail of political and legal history, such as the existence of every small German state or the varying degrees of liberty enjoyed by testators in

France and England, in terms only of economic necessity. Yet such details, which cannot be accounted for purely by economics, 'exert a very considerable effect on the economic sphere'.[29]

Engels emphasised the need to look at Marx's application of his materialist method in *Capital* and particularly in *The Eighteenth Brumaire of Louis Bonaparte*. Certainly Marx's analysis in *Capital* of the state in the era of the transition to capitalism would support a 'dialectical' interpretation of base and superstructure. The victories of the English bourgeoisie in the revolutions of the 1640s and 1688 may well have depended on the prior development of capitalism. But in turn the development of capitalism was promoted by the political victory of the bourgeoisie through new financial and tariff arrangements: the colonies, the national debts, new forms of taxation and the protectionist system. Marx similarly emphasised the active role played by the state in regimes such as Prussia and Russia, where military defeat revealed the need for social reform. Government policy thus caused 'great social changes' and altered the economic basis of the old society. Modern commentators have shared Engels's enthusiasm for *The Eighteenth Brumaire*. Williams, for instance, contrasts this work with Marx's earlier *The Class Struggles in France 1848 to 1850*. In the earlier work, Marx employs a direct equation between classes, individuals, political ideas and political parties. In *The Eighteenth Brumaire*, however, 'the autonomy of politics comes into its own'. The direct connection between class and politics is replaced by a conception of the political as a realm where class interest is not merely reflected, but is actively mediated.[30] In practice then, Marx and Engels had no difficulty in allowing politics and ideas a certain autonomy from economic determination and in accepting that both had an active causal role in historical change.

Engels was thus obliged to deny, at the end of his life, a reductionist version of historical materialism and to establish what he and Marx had 'intended' to say. Whether this was Marx's 'intent' is largely irrelevant. The point is that Engels offered a legitimate reading of Marx as a proponent of 'dialectical interaction'. He recognised that politics and ideas interacted with the economy but argued that this interaction is of 'very unequal forces, the economic being by far the strongest, the primary and the most decisive'. It is the economic factor which is 'ultimately determining', 'ultimately decisive' and 'finally bound to assert itself'. The economy is thus the 'primary agent' and ideology is only a 'secondary effect', an effect whose roots in economic development become more apparent, the longer the period under consideration.[31]

Engels's meaning is clear enough. Less clear is why, if historical development is the result of a number of interacting forces, economic necessity should be held to enjoy an 'ultimate supremacy'. Engels's answer to this problem is not particularly convincing. He argues that the productive forces and relations of production are a precondition of law, politics and ideology.[32] But in what sense is the economy a precondition of politics and social consciousness? Engels gives an answer in his funeral oration for Marx who, Engels argued, had made the startling discovery that:

> mankind must first of all eat, drink, have shelter and clothing, before it can pursue politics, science, art, religion etc.; that therefore the production of the immediate means of subsistence and consequently the degree of economic development attained by a given epoch form the foundation upon which the state institutions, the legal conceptions, art and even the ideas on religion, of the people concerned have evolved, and in the light of which they must therefore be explained, instead of vice versa, as had hitherto been the case.[33]

Marx made a similar point when he said that 'the middle ages could not live on Catholicism, nor the ancient world on politics'.[34] But to say that production is a precondition of human existence does not mean that the character of production 'therefore' determines the character of the rest of social life, any more than the fact that biological reproduction is a precondition of human existence determines that society will therefore adopt a particular form of family organisation.[35] Engels's dialectical reading of Marx has the advantage of allowing the superstructure an active historical role, but leaves us with the problem of why the superstructure should be considered 'secondary' and the base primary, i.e., why the 'superstructure' should be regarded as merely the superstructure in the first place.

Base and superstructure versus organic totality

Rader argues that besides the fundamentalist and dialectical versions of base and superstructure, Marx also employed the metaphor of society as an 'organic totality', where society is seen not as a heap of disparate elements but as a whole in which all the parts function for the others and can only be understood as part of the whole. This does not mean, however, that society is merely a constellation of equally important factors. Just as in the human body some organs are more vital than others, so Marx saw the social organism as a hierarchical structure in which some elements have more importance than others. In particular, it is society's mode of production which is the most vital element within the whole. Indeed, it is precisely this emphasis on the determining role of the mode of production which helps to distinguish Marxism from structural-functional sociology, which it superficially resembles. Organic totality thus retains the hierarchical image of base and superstructure, but employs it in a 'more subtle and coherent form'. The two metaphors or models should thus be distinguished because of the key differences between them.[36]

Certainly Marx did employ the metaphor of society as an organism when he refers to production, law and forms of government as 'organically related', although it is not clear that Marx's metaphor will always bear the theoretical weight which Rader wishes to assign to it. At times Marx employs the metaphor only to emphasise that all social forms are transient, that society 'is no solid crystal but an organism capable of change' and is constantly changing.[37] It should also be stressed that on many of the occasions where Marx invokes the metaphor of organic totality, he is concerned not with society as a whole, but rather with the realm of the economic. It is, for instance, the economic relations of capitalism which form an 'organic system', in which all the elements presuppose one another; it is production, distribution, exchange and consumption which form 'distinctions within a unity' and it is the economic relations of modern society (value, the division of labour, competition and so on) which 'coexist simultaneously and support each other'.[38] Such passages are not concerned with the relationship between class, the state and ideology and cannot be used to support an organicist reading of Marx's view of the social formation as a whole, as some commentators have been tempted to do.[39] Neither can such passages be used to argue that the organic metaphor is more faithful to Marx's 'mature insights'.[40] As early as The German Ideology, Marx had referred to the 'reciprocal action' of production, class, the state and ideology, but he continued to employ the metaphor of base and superstructure in his later works.[41]

The most important point, however, is not the 'correct' interpretation of certain passages in Marx, but whether the metaphor of organic totality adds anything to the more familiar metaphor of base and superstructure. The difference between the fundamentalist model of base and superstructure and the organic analogy is obvious. But, is there any significant difference between the latter and the dialectical version of base and superstructure? The two are, in many respects, similar, since both allow the superstructure an active causal role whilst retaining a primacy for the economic base. Why should we prefer the organic analogy? Rader argues that the metaphor of base and superstructure 'connotes stability and not change', unlike the inherent development implied by the organic analogy. But why should this be the case?[42] The model of base and superstructure possesses a number of causes of social change: the alleged inherent tendency of the productive forces to develop; the consequent clash between the productive forces and the relations of production; the periodic lack of fit between new relations of production and the political and ideological superstructures; the class struggle inherent in specific relations of production and the active causal role which the dialectical version of base and superstructure allows to ideas and politics. The difference between the dialectical version of base and superstructure and that of organic totality is still not clear.[43]

The interpenetration of base and superstructure: the problem

Another reason why Rader prefers the organic metaphor to that of base and superstructure is that only the model of organic totality allows us to understand the 'internal relations' between society's elements, relations through which the social levels interdepend and interpenetrate. Base and superstructure are not separate structures; neither is the superstructure a mere reflection of the base. Law, for instance, establishes a specific system of rights, expectations and obligations without which 'the modern economic system could not exist'. Law is not merely a superstructure to the economy but is also one of the economy's constitutive parts. Science, education and politics all break down any sharp distinction between base and superstructure since they are in certain respects superstructural and in certain respects belong to the base. Only the model of organic totality allows us to appreciate this interdependence and interpretation.[44]

The interpenetration of base and superstructure is most apparent in classical Marxist accounts of pre-capitalist modes of production where peasants, the direct producers, have effective possession of land and tools, the means, in effect, of producing their own subsistence. As a result, the producers are under no economic compulsion to produce surplus labour which must therefore be extorted through extra-economic coercion, for example, the power of the manor.[45] Under capitalism, by contrast, the producers have been stripped of the means of producing their own subsistence and are obliged to sell their labour power in order to survive, and so produce the commodities which yield a profit to the employer. Pre-capitalist modes of production thus ensure the production of surplus labour through non-economic sanctions, whether legal, political or ideological: 'the "superstructures" of kinship, religion, law or the state necessarily enter into the constitutive structure of the mode of production in pre-capitalist social formations'. Capitalist social relations merely require legally guaranteed property rights as their precondition; in pre-capitalist modes the mechanism of exploitation is itself 'superstructural': 'in consequence pre-capitalist modes of production cannot be defined except via their political and ideological superstructures since these are what determines the type of extra-economic coercion that defines them'.[46] In pre-capitalist societies, then, the mode of production cannot be seen as a purely 'economic' core separate from ideology and politics. In these societies, access to the authoritative resources of politics are as fundamental to social relations as the control over allocative resources enjoyed by the dominant class in capitalist society.[47] The problem is not that Marx was unaware of this fact, since it was Marx himself who stressed the centrality of extra-economic coercion in pre-capitalist societies.[48] The problem is the implication of this recognition of the interpenetration of base and superstructure for Marx's general theoretical claims for the primacy of the economic base. How is it possible to give explanatory primacy to the economic foundation of society if it is impossible to define that foundation independently from the so-called superstructure? If we cannot characterise the economic base of society without introducing elements from the superstructure then the whole mode of historical explanation offered by Marx in the 1859 'Preface' is called into doubt. The implications of this interpenetration of base and superstructure can then be used to reject the explanatory primacy of the relations of production, which the interpenetrative model of organic totality was explicitly intended to retain.[49]

It is precisely this apparent inability to define the base independently from the superstructure which writers such as Acton and Plamenatz see as the fatal flaw in Marx's system. The economic base of society is not 'something which can be clearly conceived, still less observed, apart from the legal, moral and political relationships of men'. The distinction between base and superstructure is untenable, so it is illegitimate to derive the latter from the former. Law and morality cannot be confined to the superstructure, but are constitutive aspects of all forms of social activity. Property relations involve morals, customs, rules of conduct and the recognition of rights. They thus involve a set of mental attitudes to

189

which the people involved in those relations conform. Law, morality and consciousness are not simply derived from social relations but rather from an inherent part of those relations.[50]

Rader claims that the analogy of organic totality retains the strength of the base and superstructure metaphor (its emphasis on the primacy of the mode of production) whilst rejecting the latter's reductionist tendency. In fact, the analogy of organic totality, like that of base and superstructure, is open to two readings. The first of these can scarcely be distinguished from the dialectical version of base and superstructure; both allow the superstructure an active historical role whilst assigning causal primacy to the base. In the second reading of organic totality, however, the analogy comes to function as a critique of the primacy of the economic base, since if base and superstructure interpenetrate, and if all the elements of society depend on each other, there is no reason why the economic base should retain the 'strongest emphasis' within the organic hierarchy. The analogy of organic totality thus explicitly retains the determining primacy of the base, whilst implicitly opening the way for objections of the type made by Acton and Plamenatz which call that primacy into doubt.[51]

The interpenetration of base and superstructure: possible solutions

There are two possible replies to the objections made by Acton and Plamenatz. The first, by G. A. Cohen, is the traditionalist response that it is possible to conceive of the economic base independently from superstructural elements; the second form of reply is Godelier's revisionist solution which involves the redefinition of base and superstructure. Cohen argues that it is possible to distinguish base and superstructure by distinguishing between *de facto* powers and *de jure* rights. Relations of production may exist in *de facto* form before they are expressed in *de jure* property rights. Thus a squatter and the legal tenant of a piece of land may have similar powers to use and enjoy a piece of land, even if the squatter's possession is maintained by force and the tenant's by legal right. The economic position of the two, their power to use the land, may be distinguished from what sustains that power. Property rights may well help to sustain basic *de facto* relations of production, but this is merely a confirmation that the nature of the legal superstructure is functionally explained in terms of its benefits for the economic base; it does not mean that legal property rights actually constitute part of the base.[52]

190

There are, however, a number of possible objections to Cohen's defence of the separation of base and superstructure and his derivation of the latter from the former. The first objection is that although it is theoretically possible to distinguish certain relations of production from their legal form as property rights, and whilst it is even possible to cite historical examples of the shift from de facto power to de jure rights, the question is whether the programme can be carried out in all cases, 'since in many cases there is no independently existing control that is stabilised by legal relations'.[53] More important is the objection that even if we can conceive of relations of production separately from law, this does not mean that the relations of production may be defined separately from all superstructural elements, in particular from forms of consciousness. Cohen argues that social positions involve fulfilling a role within specific relations, a form of behaviour which may be defined independently from ideas.[54] Yet most social roles involve the internalisation of norms and customs, i.e. they involve forms of social consciousness. If we define the base in terms of those relations which do not involve ideas, then we would reduce the base to those relations of production which are non-normative, for instance to those relations which depend purely on violence and coercion for their maintenance. This would mean that the base would only contain a very narrow range of social relations and so would lose the general explanatory primacy which is claimed for it. Cohen has not shown that the economic base may always be defined independently of law and forms of consciousness. His reading of base and superstructure thus remains open to the kind of objections made by Acton and Plamenatz.[55]

The weakness of Cohen's approach is that it sees law as an institution which has to be located either in the base or in the superstructure, an assumption which Acton and Plamenatz use to call the model of base and superstructure into question. In practice, it seems impossible to characterise society's economic base, its relations of production, without invoking elements which are often seen as superstructural. In Australian aboriginal society, for instance, a precondition for the appropriation of nature is membership of a kinship group. Kinship, in other words, functions as a relation of production. Notions of kinship are not reflections of existing biological relations, rather kinship determines which biological relations are to be taken as significant for filiation. Kinship is thus constructed through thought; thought organises social practice. Does this mean then, that ideas have primacy within the aboriginal social structure? A similar problem emerges in ancient Sumerian society

191

where the peasant producers rendered surplus labour, in the form of tribute, to the temple and to the priests of the god who nominally owned the land of the city-state. Was religion, an institution or ideology usually seen as part of the superstructure, dominant in Sumerian society? Does the apparent dominance of politics in Ancient Greece, where the institution of citizenship determined access to land, the key productive resource, refute the determining role of the economic foundation of society? In all of these examples base and superstructure interpenetrate. The problem for historical materialism is that it is the so-called superstructural elements which appear to have the more basic and determining role.[56]

Godelier's solution to the problems which the interpenetration of base and superstructure pose for historical materialism, is to reconceptualise the meaning of base and superstructure through a reconsideration of the meaning of the apparent primacy of religion, kinship or politics in Sumerian, aboriginal and Ancient Greek society. Many societies, after all, have a religion which provides a morality, explains the nature of the universe, legitimates the rule of particular classes, and so on. Yet religion is not held to be dominant in all of these societies. On the contrary, politics or kinship may provide the key to understanding social relations. In other words, *to say that religion was socially dominant in ancient Sumeria means precisely that it functioned as a relation of production*. One institution, such as a religion, may thus perform a number of social functions. Religion may function both as a relation of production and as an ideology. In certain societies, there is a tendency for institutions to specialise in one function. Elsewhere, as in Sumerian society, one institution may carry out functions which are both 'economic' and superstructural.[57]

We have seen that certain ideas may form part of the productive forces because of their technological-productive function. Similarly, certain forms of ideology may form a constitutive part of the relations of production, as in the case of aboriginal kinship, whilst others, such as the doctrine of the divine right of kings, may form part of the ideological superstructure. If we conceive of the base and superstructure as separate *institutions*, then the apparent interpenetration of the two poses a problem for the primacy of the economic base, even when seen as part of a complex organic totality. If we define base and superstructure in terms of their *functions*, then the institutional interpenetration of the two no longer provides the grounds of objections of the type made by Acton and Plamenatz. This functional definition would allow us to include those aspects of politics or ideology which functioned as relations of production within the 'economic' foundation of society. The superstructure would not then consist of law or social consciousness in their entirety, but only those legal and political institutions and forms of ideology 'that cannot be usefully regarded as constituents of production relations even if they help to sustain the system of production'.[58]

So far we have stressed the interpenetration of base and superstructure in pre-capitalist societies where, because of the appropriation of surplus through non-economic mechanisms, this interpenetration is most apparent. Yet if we define economic roles normatively, so-called 'superstructural' elements will also help to constitute the relations of production of capitalist societies.[59] If certain forms of law and private property are a precondition of capitalism, it follows that judicial relations and legal forms are also essential constitutive elements of capitalist relations of production. The difference between capitalist and pre-capitalist societies is not that in the former base and superstructure are separate whilst in the latter they interpenetrate. The difference is rather that under capitalism, political and legal elements form the general preconditions of the production of surplus, whilst in pre-capitalist societies, the mechanism of exploitation may itself be political or ideological, as opposed to the economic purchase of labour power and the sale of commodities which define the capitalist mode.[60]

Base and superstructure: the primacy of the 'economic'?

Traditional accounts of Marxism assert the primacy of a pre-existing economic level which determines the relationship between ruler and ruled; political power is separate and derived from economic and social superiority rather than constituting an inherent part of that superiority. De Ste Croix, for example, argues that the claim that relations of dominance and subjection are an integral component of pre-capitalist class relations is 'clearly contrary to the views of Marx', for whom political power merely reinforces a dominant economic position.[61] In fact it would be possible to quote Marx to the effect that relationships of domination, the appropriation of another's will, enter into the formation of relations of production, but this is not the central issue.[62] Our main concern is not with which interpretation of the relations of production is most 'Marxist', but which is most useful. The relations of production are defined by their function, their determination of access to society's productive forces and to the products of labour. Ideology and power may form an inherent part of these functions and so are a constitutive part of, not merely a secondary derivation from, the relations of production. This is not to say that the interpenetration of base and superstructure would have been made clear if Marx had written his intended work on the state;[63] rather a recognition of the interpenetration of base and superstructure is the only means of making Marx's claims at all plausible in the face of the criticisms made by Acton and Plamenatz.[64]

It is important, however, to emphasise the implications of this functional distinction between base and superstructure, a distinction which allows for the institutional interpenetration of the two. If we include law, politics and social consciousness as possible constitutive elements of the relations of production, is is impossible to retain any notion of a pure 'economic' level upon which the political rests. In ancient Sumeria, for instance, the state was not merely derived from a pre-existing economic level, but was itself an inherent part of the 'economic' foundation through its function as an appropriator of surplus labour. But if this is the case, we can no longer continue to maintain the dominance of the 'economic' in however distant a final analysis or last instance. The 1859 'Preface' is no longer to be seen as a claim for the primacy of the 'economic foundation' except in the broad sense that this foundation is composed of the relations of production. For Marx's claim to make sense, it must be seen as implying the primacy of the relations of production, not the primacy of a narrowly-defined economic level. Of course we may still object to Marx's hypothesis, but at least it has the advantage of not falling at the first hurdle, the recognition of the institutional interpenetration of base and superstructure. Once more it is the strongest interpretation of Marx's works with which we must come to terms; once more it is Marx's claims for the primacy of the relations of production which constitute the least vulnerable aspect of his thought.

'Determination by the economic': the Althusserian solution

One of the most influential of recent interpretations of Marx's historical materialism is that of Althusser who, like Rader, prefers the analogy of society as an organic totality to that of base and superstructure. Althusser's works offer an original, but ultimately unsuccessful, attempt to offer a non-reductionist reading of the 'primacy of the economic' in which determination by the economic 'in the last instance' takes on a more precise meaning than the formulation offered by Engels's famous letters. For Althusser, reductionist readings of Marx regard society as an 'expressive totality' rather than as an 'organic hierarchized whole'.[65] In an expressive totality, all the economic, social, political, legal and ideological relations and events which constitute the concrete life of an historical epoch are reduced 'to one principle of internal unity'.[66] As parts of a unity, each of these elements contains the expression of some central contradiction whose effects are ultimately felt at all levels of the social totality. In the 1859 'Preface', for instance, it is the contradiction between the expanding productive forces and the restrictive relations of production which is expressed in the other levels of society in the form of political revolution and ideological struggle.[67] It is ironic that Althusser has been accused of acting as the Stalinist Pied Piper, seducing the innocent young into the ways of economic reductionism, since it was precisely the reductionism of the expressive totality which Althusser took as his main target.[68] The point is not that Althusser was unaware of the problem of reductionism, but rather that he failed to resolve it.

Althusser's alternative to the concept of expressive totality is that of society as a 'complex structural unity'. In this conception the levels of society do not merely reflect some central contradiction. A social formation is thus 'constituted by a certain form of complexity, the unity of a structural whole containing what can be called levels or instances which are distinct and "relatively autonomous", and co-exist within this complex structural unity, articulated with one another according to specific determinations'.[69] There is no simple determination by the economic of the rest of society since each of the social levels has its own chronology of development, and its own internal conflicts, which cannot be reduced to an expression of a single central contradiction. Any given historical moment is thus 'over-determined' by the effects of each level of the totality. In a revolutionary period, for example, it is the general contradiction between the productive forces and the relations of production which defines the revolutionary situation but a specific revolutionary moment is also the product of a mass of circumstances which cannot be reduced to a mere expression of this general contradiction. The political and ideological levels have an effectivity of their own, each level is both determined and determining, each is necessary for the reproduction of the social formation. Politics and ideology are thus not mere reflections of a pre-existent economic base, since specific relations of production 'pre-suppose the existence of a legal-political and ideological superstructure as a condition of their peculiar existence'.[70] The economic level is thus never active in a pure state. The social superstructures 'are never seen to step respectfully aside when their work is done or when the Time comes, as his pure phenomena, to scatter before His Majesty, the Economy as he strides along the royal road of the dialectic. From the first moment to the last, the lonely hour of the last instance never comes.'[71] For Althusser, a mode of production consists not only of the economic level (made up of the productive forces and the relations of production) but also of the political and ideological levels.[72] Each of these levels, as we have seen, has its own effectivity and chronology of development. What then is specifically Marxist about this complex organic whole? Althusser argues that although each level of the whole is 'relatively autonomous', it is the economic level which is, 'in the last instance', the region which determines the specific articulations of all the levels within the complex structured whole.[73] This determination by the economic level can be seen in two ways: the determination of which levels of society are called into existence, and the determination of the degree of effectivity of each level within the social whole. Firstly, the economic level determines which of the possible instances or levels will be called into existence. In classless societies, for example, the existence of specific relations of production means that there is no requirement for the existence of a political instance, the state, which is a form of social organisation only required where society is divided into classes.[74]

Secondly, it is the economic instance which determines which of the social levels will be dominant within the whole.[75] As Marx said, it is clear 'that the middle ages could not live on Catholicism, nor the ancient world on politics. On the contrary it is the mode in which they gained a livelihood that explains why here politics, and there Catholicism, played the chief part.'[76] The nature of this determinism is clear if we consider the example of serfdom, where the producers effectively possess the means of their own subsistence so that surplus labour, in the form of feudal rent, can only be obtained through the legal and political powers of lordship.[77] In this example it is the political level which is socially *dominant* in ensuring the reproduction of feudal class relations, but it is the economy, in the form of a specific relation of production, which *determines* that the political level should be dominant. In capitalist society the extraction of surplus labour through economic means, by the purchase of labour power and the sale of commodities, means that the economy is both determinant and dominant. Such a coincidence cannot be taken for granted in pre-capitalist societies where, as we have seen, other levels of the mode of production may have the dominant role.

Althusser's conception of the social totality allows each level its own 'relative autonomy', whilst denying that each is independent. The effectivity of each level is based on its articulation within the whole, on certain forms of dependence within the whole, forms which are fixed, in the last instance, by the economic level. Together these levels form an organic hierarchy in which the effectivity of base and superstructure takes on a different meaning from that of a reductionist expressive totality.[78]

There are two main objections which may be raised against Althusser's claim for a 'structural causality' through which the economic level determines which of the levels of the whole is to enjoy dominance. The first objection is that structural causality is not, in practice, a form of determination, so it cannot, therefore, be used to show that the economic level is 'determinant' in the last instance. This problem is clear in Balibar's analysis of serfdom. In this example, the dominance of the political level is a precondition of the appropriation of surplus labour in the form of rent. In what sense does this mean that the economic instance is 'determinant'? It is determinant only in the sense that the definition of the relations of production allows us to specify the preconditions necessary for the reproduction of these relations of production, in this case the legal-political powers of the landlord. In other words, if feudal rent is to be extracted, certain political conditions must obtain. However, to specify the conditions which are needed for the existence of 'x' does not mean than these conditions will be met in practice. This would only be a form of determinism if we argued that these preconditions of feudal rent were a need of the relations of production which had to be met. But, if the existence of specific relations of production entailed the reproduction of the conditions of their own existence, those relations would be eternal. The relations of production cannot, in practice, automatically produce the ideological and political conditions of their own existence.[79] Social relations have no 'needs' except in the counter-factual sense that if certain conditions did not obtain, those relations would not exist in the first place. Even these 'needs' often turn out to be tautologous: for 'x' to exist it requires 'y', but 'y' often turns out to be the very thing which defined 'x'.[80] Thus, if we take non-economic coercion to be a defining feature of feudal exploitation, it is a tautology to say that a 'need' of feudal relations of production is the existence of institutions of non-economic coercion. The first problem with determination by the economic level in the last instance is that, in effect, it is not a form of determination but merely a specification of the preconditions 'needed' for the existence of the economic level.

The second weakness of determination in the last instance by the economic is that it maintains a distinction between the economic and the political/ideological of the type which we have already rejected, which is not to say that we should reject all distinctions between the two. If we return to the examples of Australian aboriginal or ancient Sumerian society, it is apparent that ideology and politics are not merely assigned a certain degree of effectivity by the economic level; rather, politics and ideology, in these examples, are constitutive parts of the relations of production and thus of the economic level. At times Althusser does, in practice, break down the distinction between the economic and the other levels, as in his analysis of the need for certain legal relations and specific ideological and political practices in order to reproduce the capitalist economy. Here the whole superstructure is 'implicit and present in a specific way in the relations of production'. If this is the case, however, there is no reason to continue to insist on a clear distinction between the economic relations of production and the legal-property relations of the superstructure, as Althusser does in his broad theoretical claims.[81] To repeat, once more, the words of Perry Anderson: 'The "superstructures" of kinship, religion, law or the state necessarily enter into the constitutive structure of the modes of production in pre-capitalist social formations.'[82] It follows that the so-called economic level cannot have the qualities of a given. 'The concept of the economic must be constructed for each mode of production'[83] precisely because the relations of production are not purely economic phenomena, but may include ideological and political elements which enable them to carry out their functions.

Where we would disagree with Anderson's formulation is firstly in extending the interpenetration of base and superstructure to all modes of production, not just those of the pre-capitalist era, and secondly in arguing that in so far as they operate as constitutive parts of the relation of production, ideology and politics cease to be part of the 'superstructure' and may be functionally defined as part of the 'base'.

Paul Hirst has described Anderson's concept of a mode of production as 'amazing' but, significantly, Hirst himself could not avoid invoking 'superstructural' elements in his own definitions of pre-capitalist modes of production. The Ancient mode of production, for instance, is characterised by the appropriation of surplus labour through right of citizenship, a definition which, as Hirst later admitted, conceptualised Ancient relations of production as 'extra-economic, basically political, in form'. Similarly, in primitive communist societies the relations of production are 'constituted on the basis of ideological relations between individuals' and the social produce is redistributed through relations which 'are the product of determinate ideological practices'.[84] In both cases, so-called 'superstructural' elements (the state, ideology) form central features of the social relations of production. It is only when we redefine base and superstructure in terms of their functions that this interpretation ceases to be a problem. Our task is then to assess the claim for the primacy of these broadly defined relations of production over those elements of the state and ideology which do not form a constitutive part of the 'base'.

Superstructural variation and the typology of modes of production

Where Anderson's analysis of the nature of modes of production is more problematic is in his claim that because legal and political forms are central aspects of the relations of production, it follows that 'a scrupulous and exact taxonomy of these legal and political configurations is ... a pre-condition of establishing any comprehensive typology of pre-capitalist modes of production'. Feudalism, for example, cannot merely be defined as a mode of production where private landlords extract rent from peasant producers, but is to be identified with a particular super-structural form of the state, involving parcellised sovereignty, vassals and the system of fiefs. It follows that societies which lack this form of superstructure are not genuinely feudal, even though they possess land-lords and peasants who produce surplus labour under the sanction of extra-economic coercion.[85]

From the correct premise that political and ideological elements may constitute part of society's relations of production, and thus of its mode of production, Anderson draws the problematical conclusion that modes of production may be distinguished by superstructural variation *per se*. However, the presence of a particular form of superstructure is not needed for us to identify a particular mode of production. Under capitalism, for example, the superstructure may take the form of fascist dictatorships, democratic republics, military juntas and so on. All of these political forms are compatible with capitalism because they leave the fundamental relations of production untouched.[86] Variation in 'super-structual' form can only be used to distinguish modes of production in so far as it leads to variation in the form taken by surplus labour or in

199

the mechanism through which surplus labour is produced. But in this case, such variation ceases, by definition, to be merely 'superstructural'. It is precisely because these so-called 'superstructural' elements are a constitutive part of the social relations of production that they allow us to distinguish between specific modes of production.

Whilst disagreeing with Anderson's identification of particular modes of production with the presence of particular superstructural forms, we share his original motivation for emphasising this point which was to provide a precise typology of pre-capitalist social forms. For if societies as different as, for instance, Ming China, Mughal India, Ummayad Syria and Norman England are all to be labelled as 'feudal', does the concept retain any explanatory weight? If any number of European, Asian and African societies were 'feudal', why did an indigenous capitalism emerge within only one of these continents? Is the concept of the feudal mode of production able to deal with the facts of variation in social form and uniqueness of historical development?[87]

In practice, it is possible to retain broad categories of mode of production whilst allowing for the peculiarities of structure and evolution of each historical society. Firstly, the variant social forms may be accounted for as specific sub-forms of the mode of production. Feudalism, for instance, may appear with rent in the form of money, produce or labour services. It may be found in association with a greater or lesser degree of commodity production in which either peasants or landlords may play the greater part. It may take freer, or more servile forms. Secondly, the peculiarities of social forms may be accounted for by the fact that particular modes of production are compatible with a variety of superstructural forms. From the definition of a society's class relations as capitalist, for instance, we cannot deduce that its political constitution will be republican or monarchical, democratic or dictatorial. Why a specific society is fascist rather than democratic can only be explained in terms of its own particular economic, social, political and ideological history. To assume otherwise is to lapse back into an economic reductionism, in which concrete historical explanation is replaced by the deduction of specific political forms from the broadest of economic categories.

The existence of sub-forms of each mode of production, the fact that a specific social formation may include a number of modes of production and the variety of superstructural forms with which a particular mode of production may be associated, means that even societies which share a common dominant mode of production will not exhibit shared paths of historical evolution. Particular routes of social development can no more be deduced from specific modes of production than particular political superstructures can. Anderson is thus mistaken to question whether African or Asian societies may be labelled as 'feudal', merely because these societies did not undergo an indigenous transition to capitalism. On the contrary, there is no inherent, teleological necessity for a feudal society to progress towards capitalism. Even within Anderson's 'genuine' western feudalism, each country underwent the transition to capitalism in its own unique way and with its own specific chronology.

'Organic totality' and Marxist structuralism

We have now offered a more precise formulation of the 'interpenetration' of base and superstructure, which Rader saw as one of the advantages of the analogy of 'organic totality' over that of 'base and superstructure'. The fact that law and politics are 'in some respects superstructural and in other respects basic' does not mean that base and superstructure 'overlap'.[88] It would be more precise to say not that base and superstructure interpenetrate, but rather that specific institutions, such as law or religion, are themselves interpenetrated by functions which may be either those of the 'base' or those of the 'superstructure'. This formulation has the advantage of allowing us to see the alleged primacy of the base as a claim not for a determination by the 'economic', but for the primacy of the social relations of production. The second advantage of the analogy of 'organic totality' is that it allows us to retain the dialectical interaction between base and superstructure. The organic analogy reminds us of the active historical role of the superstructure, a role ignored in the fundamental reading of determining base and 'reflected' superstructure.

The metaphor of society as an 'organism' has the advantage of avoiding a simple economic determinism, but is not without dangers of its own, in particular the problems of structuralism and of human agency. The dangers of the organic analogy are apparent in the 'Preface' to *Capital*, where Marx refers to capitalist society as an 'organic whole' whose 'economic cell form' is the commodity. This social organism is ascribed its own 'natural laws' which work 'with iron necessity towards inevitable results'. The economic evolution of society is thus 'viewed as a process of natural history' where individuals are only dealt with 'in so far as they are personifications of economic categories, embodiments of particular class relations and class interests'. Thus the individual is not held responsible

for the social relations 'whose creature he socially remains'. There seems
no reason to believe that Marx wrote this passage 'with his tongue firmly
in his cheek', as Thompson suggests, since Marx later approvingly quoted
a Russian reviewer of *Capital* who summarised Marx's work as one which
saw social change as 'a process of natural history, governed by laws not
only independent of human will, consciousness and intelligence, but
rather, on the contrary determining that will, consciousness and intelligence. … Economic life offers us a phenomenon analogous to the history
of evolution in other branches of philosophy.'[89] It is from such passages
that Althusser draws the conclusion that:

> the structure of the relations of production determines the place and
> functions occupied and adopted by the agents of production, who are
> never anything more than the occupants of these places, in so far as they
> are the 'supports' (*Träger*) of these functions. The true 'subjects' (in the
> case of the constitutive subjects of the process) are therefore not these
> occupants or functionaries, are not … 'concrete individuals', 'real men'
> – but the definition and distribution of these places and functions. *The*
> *true subjects are these definers and distributors: the relations of production* (and politi-
> cal and ideological social relations).[90]

Far from Darwin's *The Origin of the Species* helping to spring the structuralist trap of Political Economy (which presents society as an organic system which is its own subject, 'working out its self-fulfilment with its
own inexorable idealist logic'), it is precisely Marx's desire to present
economic evolution as 'a process of natural history' which forms the
basis for the structuralist reading of *Capital*, where the relations of production, rather than concrete men and women, are the agents of their
own history.[91]

The problem with the conception that social change is analogous to
organic evolution is that it leads to the misapprehension that individuals have no effect upon history when, in fact, 'the citizen must simultaneously conceive of himself as one whose will is a factor in social
evolution and yet as one whose will is a product of all antecedent
influences'.[92] An organicist or structuralist Marxism is open to the same
criticisms as Parsonian sociology; in both schools of thought social systems are reified and transformed into social actors, rather than being
explained as the outcome of social action. In both approaches, social
wholes are attributed characteristics such as the possession of goals or
aims, which are properly only the property of individuals or groups of
individuals. Human beings then become mere agents fulfilling the needs

of the system. Society is perceived as a subject, an extra-human entity with its own inner laws, independent of human action.[93]

It is important, however, for accounts of society and of historical change to take account of human actions and intentions. This is not because of any pragmatic need to think that we are free[94] but because societies, social determination and human agency may best be under-stood as very complex games:

> If four people sit around a table and play cards together, they form a configuration. In this case it is still possible to bow to tradition and to speak of the game as if it had an existence of its own. ... But despite all the expressions which tend to objectify it the course of the game will obviously be the outcome of the actions of a group of interdependent individuals.[95]

This is not to claim that history or social structure merely consists of the direct outcome of the conscious desires and intentions of individual agents. Both history and social structure will also be affected by uncon-scious desires and motivations, by the structural conditions of actions, by the unintended consequences of actions and by the intersection of individual actions.[96]

There is no doubt that a structuralist reading of Marx is a legitimate one, given his repeated references to economic relations as the agents of a process of which the individual is only the 'representative' or 'personification'. Such economic relations are presented as subjects with 'requirements' of their own and the ability to bring into being the economic forms which correspond to those requirements.[97] These metaphors are useful when they remind us that society is not merely an aggregate of individuals, but rather is the sum of 'the relations in which these individuals stand', that a negro is a negro, 'he only becomes a slave in certain relations'.[98] Nevertheless, they tend to obscure the fact that social relations are not Platonic ideas which adopt concrete individuals as their material forms; a system of social relations is a recurrent set of actions carried out by interdepedent subjects. It is this 'personal, indi-vidual behaviour' which creates social relations and 'daily produces them anew'.[99] Society is not 'one single subject' or an 'abstraction con-fronting the individual'. Society, capital or a mode of production are not subjects with their own ends which they use 'men' to achieve. Like 'his-tory', society is 'nothing but the activity of men in pursuit of their ends'. In society, as in a game, people make their own history, 'but not of their own free will, not under circumstances they themselves have chosen, but under given and inherited circumstances with which they are directly confronted'.[100] Players have roles within games but this does not mean they are merely the 'bearers' of the game or are being 'gamed'. Neither society nor games are subjects with their own needs and agency as structuralist theories would lead us to believe. To see society in terms of the alternative analogy of a game allows us to allot a role to both structural regularity and to human agency. The view of society as an organic structure with agency of its own is a valid reading of Marx, but it is the metaphor of society as a 'game' which is more useful in explaining social structure and historical change.[101]

Notes

1 K. Marx, *A Contribution to the Critique of Political Economy* (London, 1971), pp. 20–1. My emphasis.
2 K. Marx, *Theories of Surplus Value*, part I (London, 1969), p. 285.
3 K. Marx & F. Engels, *Collected Works*, vol. V (London, 1976), p. 89 (*The German Ideology*); Marx, *A Contribution to the Critique of Political Economy*, p. 21.
4 G. A. Cohen, *Karl Marx's Theory of History: A Defence* (Oxford, 1978), pp. 216–17; J. Elster, *Making Sense of Marx* (Cambridge, 1965), pp. 31–2.
5 Marx, *A Contribution to the Critique of Political Economy*, p. 20.
6 See, for example, S. Hall, 'Re-thinking the "base and superstructure" metaphor', in J. Bloomfield (ed.), *Class, Hegemony and Party* (London, 1977); J. Larrain, *The Concept of Ideology* (London, 1979), p. 66; M. Rader, *Marx's Interpretation of History* (New York, 1979), p. 57.
7 Marx, *A Contribution to the Critique of Political Economy*, p. 20.
8 Ibid., p. 21.
9 Ibid.
10 Marx & Engels, *Collected Works*, vol. V, p. 57 (*The German Ideology*).
11 Ibid., p. 239.
12 Ibid., p. 53. My emphasis.
13 K. Marx, *The Revolutions of 1848* (London, 1973), p. 250.
14 Marx & Engels, *Collected Works*, vol. V, p. 380 (*The German Ideology*).
15 Marx, *The Revolutions of 1848*, p. 189; see also ibid., pp. 250, 259–60.
16 Marx & Engels, *Collected Works*, vol. V, pp. 154, 159, 250 (*The German Ideology*); K. Marx, *Capital*, vol. I (London, 1977), pp. 83, 353; K. Marx, *Theories of Surplus Value*, part III (London, 1977), p. 448.
17 G. Marshall, *In Search of the Spirit of Capitalism* (London, 1982), pp. 142–3.
18 Cohen, *Karl Marx's Theory of History*, pp. 176–7, 278–9.
19 Marx, *Capital*, vol. I, p. 23; K. Marx, *The First International and After* (London, 1974), p. 335 (*Critique of the Gotha Programme*).
20 K. Marx, *The Poverty of Philosophy* (Moscow, 1973), p. 156.
21 Marx, *The Revolutions of 1848*, p. 250.

22 Marx & Engels, *Collected Works*, vol. V, pp. 36, 193 (*The German Ideology*); K. Marx & F. Engels, *Selected Correspondence* (Moscow, 1975), p. 400 (letter of Engels to Schmidt, 27.10.1890); M. Dobb, 'Historical materialism and the role of the economic factor', *History* XXXVI (1951), p. 4; E. John, 'Some questions on the materialist interpretation of history', *History* XXXVIII (1953), p. 4; E. P. Thompson, *The Poverty of Theory* (London, 1978), p. 79.

23 Rader, *Marx's Interpretation of History*, pp. xx, 3, 70.

24 Ibid., pp. 4–5, 8, 9, 56, 97, 184–5.

25 K. Marx & F. Engels, *The Communist Manifesto* (Harmondsworth, 1970), pp. 81–2; Marx, *The Revolutions of 1848*, pp. 92, 97, 250; Marx & Engels, *Collected Works*, vol. V, p. 32 (*The German Ideology*).

26 Marx & Engels, *Collected Works*, vol. V, p. 193; Marx & Engels, *The Communist Manifesto*, pp. 99–100; K. Marx, *The Poverty of Philosophy* (Moscow, 1973), p. 72.

27 Rader, *Marx's Interpretation of History*, pp. xx, 3–4, 10.

28 Marx & Engels, *Selected Correspondence*, pp. 393–6 (Engels to Bloch, 21/2.9.1890), 400 (Engels to Schmidt, 27.10.1890), 433–4 (Engels to Mehring, 14.7.1893).

29 Ibid., p. 395 (Engels to Bloch, 21/2.9.1890), 399 (Engels to Schmidt, 27.10.1890).

30 Ibid., pp. 396, 402 (Engels to Schmidt, 27.10.1890), 443 (Engels to Turati, 26.1.1894); Marx & Engels, *Collected Works*, vol. V, p. 409 (*The German Ideology*); Marx, *The Revolutions of 1848*, p. 192; K. Marx, *Surveys From Exile* (Harmondsworth, 1973), p. 251; Marx, *Capital*, vol. I, p. 703; K. Marx, *Grundrisse* (Harmondsworth, 1974), p. 507; K. Marx, *The Civil War in France* (Peking, 1970), p. 135; G. Williams, '18 Brumaire: Karl Marx and defeat', in B. Matthews (ed.), *Marx: A Hundred Years On* (London, 1983), especially pp. 12–13, 32–3.

31 Marx & Engels, *Selected Correspondence*, pp. 393–5, 410–12, 443 (full references to letters in n. 30 above).

32 Ibid., p. 393.

33 O. Henderson, *The Life of Friedrich Engels* (London, 1976), p. 509. My emphasis.

34 Marx, *Capital*, vol. I, p. 86.

35 J. Plamenatz, *Man and Society*, vol. II (London, 1963), p. 278.

36 Rader, *Marx's Interpretation of History*, pp. xx, 70, 75–6, 78, 181, 186, 204.

37 Ibid., p. 57; Marx, *Capital*, vol. I, p. 29; Marx, *Grundrisse*, p. 88.

38 Marx, *Grundrisse*, pp. 99–100, 278; Marx, *The Poverty of Philosophy*, pp. 96, 183–4.

39 T. B. Bottomore & M. Rubel (eds.), *K. Marx: Selected Writings in Sociology and Social Philosophy* (Harmondsworth, 1970), pp. 33–4; Rader, *Marx's Interpretation of History*, pp. 58, 60.

40 Ibid., pp. 56, 58–60, 119.

41 Marx & Engels, *Collected Works*, vol. V, p. 53 (*The German Ideology*); K. Marx, *Capital*, vol. III (London, 1974), pp. 791–2.

42 Rader, *Marx's Interpretation of History*, p. 82.

43 Marx, *A Contribution to the Critique of Political Economy*, pp. 20–1. Marx's desire to avoid the attentions of the Prussian censor may have led him to underplay the role of class struggle in his 1859 'Preface'; see A. M. Prinz, 'Background and ulterior motive of Marx's Preface of 1859', *Journal of the History of Ideas* XXX (1969), pp. 437–50.

44 Rader, *Marx's Interpretation of History*, pp. 3, 10, 27–8, 35–6, 38–9, 40–1, 70, 72.
45 Marx, *Capital*, vol. III, p. 791.
46 P. Anderson, *Lineages of the Absolutist State*, pp. 403–4.
47 R. S. Gottlieb, 'Feudalism and historical materialism: a critique and a synthesis', *Science and Society* XLVIII (1984), pp. 3–4; A. Giddens, *A Contemporary Critique of Historical Materialism* (London, 1981), pp. 4, 7, 212–14; E. M. Wood, 'The separation of the economic and the political in capitalism', *New Left Review* 127 (May–June 1981), pp. 66–95.
48 Marx, *Capital*, vol. III, pp. 790–1.
49 Rader, *Marx's Interpretation of History*, pp. 28, 181; S. Lukes, 'Can the base be distinguished from the superstructure?', in D. Miller & L. Siedentop, *The Nature of Political Theory* (Oxford, 1983), pp. 104, 111.
50 H. B. Acton, *The Illusion of the Epoch* (London, 1955), pp. 164–8, 177, 258; Plamenatz, *Man and Society*, vol. II, pp. 283–9, 345.
51 Rader, *Marx's Interpretation of History*, pp. 40–1, 56, 70, 84–6, 97, 181.
52 G. A. Cohen, 'Being, consciousness and roles: on the foundation of historical materialism', in C. Abramsky & B. J. Williams, *Essays in Honour of E. H. Carr* (London, 1974), p. 88; idem, 'On some criticisms of historical materialism', *Proceedings of the Aritotelian Society* xliv (supplement, 1970), pp. 121–4; idem, *Karl Marx's Theory of History*, pp. 223–4.
53 Elster, *Making Sense of Marx*, p. 403.
54 Cohen, 'Being, consciousness and roles', pp. 91–2.
55 Lukes, 'Can the base be distinguished from the superstructure?', pp. 103–19.
56 M. Godelier, 'Infrastructures, societies and history', *New Left Review* (November–December 1978), pp. 83, 87–8.
57 Ibid., pp. 88–90.
58 Wood, 'The separation of the economic and political in capitalism', p. 79.
59 Lukes, 'Can the base be distinguished from the superstructure?', pp. 11–16.
60 Rader, *Marx's Interpretation of History*, pp. 40–1; Wood, 'The separation of the economic and political in capitalism', pp. 68, 77–9.
61 G. E. M. de Ste Croix, *The Class Struggle in the Ancient Greek World* (London, 1981), pp. 43–4, 49, 98; E. Gellner, 'The Soviet and the savage', *The Times Literary Supplement* 3789 (18 October 1974).
62 Marx, *Capital*, vol. III, p. 881; K. Marx, *Pre-capitalist Economic Formations* (London, 1975), p. 102.
63 Rader, *Marx's Interpretation of History*, p. 41.
64 See n. 50 above.
65 L. Althusser & E. Balibar, *Reading Capital* (London, 1975), p. 98.
66 Ibid., p. 17; L. Althusser, *For Marx* (London, 1977), p. 103. My emphasis.
67 Marx, *A Contribution to the Critique of Political Economy*, pp. 20–1; L. Althusser, *Lenin and Philosophy and Other Essays* (London, 1971), p. 201.
68 Thompson, *The Poverty of Theory*, pp. 254, 355, 360.
69 Althusser & Balibar, *Reading Capital*, p. 97.
70 Ibid., p. 177; Althusser, *For Marx*, pp. 96–101.
71 Ibid., p. 113.
72 Althusser & Balibar, *Reading Capital*, p. 183.

73 Ibid., p. 97.
74 Ibid., p. 177.
75 Ibid., pp. 177–8.
76 Marx, Capital, vol. I, p. 86.
77 Althusser & Balibar, Reading Capital, pp. 220–4.
78 Ibid., pp. 100, 187, 223–4.
79 Ibid.; B. Hindess & P. Q. Hirst, Pre-capitalist Modes of Production (London, 1975), pp. 13–15; B. Hindess & P. Q. Hirst, Mode of Production and Social Formation (London, 1977), pp. 55–6; Giddens, A Contemporary Critique of Historical Materialism, p. 19; idem, Central Problems in Social Theory (London, 1979), p. 113.
80 A. Giddens, Studies in Social and Political Theory (London, 1979), pp. 111–12.
81 Althusser & Balibar, Reading Capital, pp. 177–8.
82 Anderson, Lineages of the Absolutist State, p. 403.
83 Althusser & Balibar, Reading Capital, p. 183.
84 P. Q. Hirst, Marxism and Historical Writing (London, 1985), p. 100; Hindess & Hirst, Pre-capitalist Modes of Production, pp. 18–19, 44, 82, 229–30; Hindess & Hirst, Mode of Production and Social Formation, pp. 33, 51.
85 Anderson, Lineages of the Absolutist State, pp. 401–4, 408.
86 Hirst, Marxism and Historical Writing, p. 113.
87 Anderson, Lineages of the Absolutist State, pp. 402–3.
88 Rader, Marx's Interpretation of History, pp. 27–8, 36.
89 Marx, Capital, vol. I, pp. 19–21, 27–8; Thompson, The Poverty of Theory, p. 340.
90 Althusser & Balibar, Reading Capital, p. 180.
91 Thompson, The Poverty of Theory, pp. 252–6.
92 H. Spencer, 'The study of sociology', in K. Thompson & J. Tunstall, Sociological Perspectives (Harmondsworth, 1971), p. 38.
93 N. Elias, What is Sociology? (London, 1978), p. 20; Thompson, The Poverty of Theory, p. 271.
94 Ibid., p. 344; P. Anderson, Arguments Within English Marxism (London, 1980), p. 18.
95 Elias, What is Sociology?, p. 130.
96 Giddens, Studies in Social and Political Theory, pp. 123–34; Elster, Making Sense of Marx, Ch. 1. See also the debate between Elster, Cohen, Roemer, Berger and Offe, van Parijs and Giddens in Theory and Society XI (1982), pp. 457–539.
97 See, for instance, Marx, Capital, vol. I, pp. 151, 555; idem, Capital, vol. III, pp. 617, 818–19, 824.
98 Marx, Grundrisse, p. 265; K. Marx, Wage Labour and Capital (Moscow, 1970), p. 28.
99 Marx & Engels, Collected Works, vol. V, p. 437 (The German Ideology).
100 K. Marx, Early Writings (Harmondsworth, 1975), p. 350; Bottomore & Rubel, Karl Marx: Selected Writings in Sociology and Social Philosophy, pp. 78, 91–2; Marx, Surveys From Exile, p. 146 (The 18th Brumaire of Louis Bonaparte); Marx, Grundrisse, p. 94.
101 Thompson, The Poverty of Theory, p. 345.

CHAPTER 10

Modes of production: variant forms of the 'base'

The concepts of specific modes of production are defined by theory and do not immediately correspond with any particular society. A particular society may, for instance, contain a number of modes of production and will contain 'superstructural' forms which cannot be reduced to the mere epiphenomena of the economic 'base'.[1] Nevertheless, the concept of a mode of production does refer to concrete historical relations and, for Marxists, has a crucial role in explaining social structure and historical change. It is this centrality of the concept of mode of production which, 'for better or for worse, gives Marxism distinctiveness as a theory of the social world' and which explains the 'truly obsessional preoccupation' which Marxists have with this concept.[2]

As we have seen, Marx himself used the term 'mode of production' in a number of ways but, as argued above, the concept may most profitably be defined as a combination of specific relations of production (which identify the mode of production) with a variable form of productive forces; primitive communism may be found in association with agricultural or pre-agricultural forms of the labour process, capitalism with industrial or pre-industrial technologies.[3] For Marx, it is society's relations of production, the specific form in which surplus labour is extracted from the producers, which distinguish the different economic formations of society.[4] These relations of production, as we have seen, are not an 'economic' concept in the narrow sense of the term, but include also those political and ideological elements which function as part of the productive relations. Societies may thus be distinguished by their class structures, by their specific forms and mechanisms of appropriation of surplus labour and by their particular modes of social 'exploitation'. In this chapter we discuss the concepts of 'exploitation', 'class' and 'surplus labour' in more detail and then examine how Marxists have attempted to define specific historical modes of production, in order to establish the advantages and disadvantages of this taxonomy of societies.

'Exploitation' and 'surplus' labour

Exploitation and surplus labour would appear to be central terms of Marxist historiography. All societies, it is claimed, produce surplus labour, a level of production over and above that which is needed to satisfy the immediate (historically specific) needs of the producers. Even primitive communism is distinguished not by the absence of surplus labour but by its communal appropriation. A society is said to be exploitative where there is a mechanism whereby the producers are made to perform surplus labour for a class of non-producers.[5] The elements of coercion (the producer is made to produce) and of surplus labour are thus central to the concept of exploitation. Exploitation is not merely an 'economic' relationship, it is also a relationship of power.

Marx's main aim in *Capital* was to show that the capitalist mode of production was based on exploitation, that the control over production enjoyed by the capitalist class was not merely part of a technical division of labour, but was a class division through which the capitalist appropriated the surplus value produced by the working class. The capitalists' control of the labour process is not just a neutral managerial role, it is a 'function of the exploitation of a social-labour process, and is consequently rooted in the unavoidable antagonism between the exploiter and the living and labouring raw material he exploits'.[6] Other writers, however, have not been convinced of the centrality of the concepts of 'exploitation' and 'surplus labour' to describe class societies. Dalton, for instance, sees these terms as merely 'prejudicial words' for something of which we morally or politically disapprove, rather than as technical concepts of social science.[7] It is argued below that it is possible to classify societies in terms of modes of production without the use of the concepts of exploitation and surplus labour. Modes of production may be described in terms of their relations of production and the specific forms taken by the income of the ruling class without resort to concepts which ultimately rely on subjective moral criteria.

Why should the income drawn by the ruling class be seen as a form of exploitation? Why does Marx regard this income as an embodiment of surplus labour? The answer is most clear in the case of feudalism, where the peasant producers hand over a portion of their labour time to the landlords in the form of actual labour services, in the form of labour expressed as produce (rent in kind) or as produce which has been sold on the market (money rent). For Marx, rent in this case is a form of exploitative surplus labour because the peasants' labour produces benefits for others for which the peasants themselves receive no equivalent.[8] Similarly, under capitalism Marx believed that the working class provided labour for the capitalists for which it received no equivalent in the form of wages, that labour-power was bought by the capitalist at its value but was, in turn, capable of producing an extra value which was appropriated by the capitalists.[9] In each case, there appears to be a relationship of exploitation, a relation where 'I derive benefit for myself by doing harm to someone else'.[10] In this case, the benefit takes the form of the income derived by the ruling class; the harm is the excess labour which the producers are obliged to perform.

There are, however, obvious objections to Marx's claims that feudal rent or capitalist profit are forms of exploitation. Neoclassical economists, for instance, could argue that the transfer of labour/wealth to the capitalist class is not necessarily exploitative since the production process, from which the producers benefit, is only possible through the combination of certain factors of production. The capitalists are rewarded for their contribution of certain factors such as capital or co-ordination.[11] Similarly it could be argued that the rent paid by peasants is not necessarily 'surplus' to their requirements since in return for rent, the peasants may receive protection from bandits, justice in the lord's court[12] or, most obviously, access to land, a factor of production from which the landlords draw their return.

Roemer has provided a more exact formulation of why Marxists would consider these relationships to be one of unequal exchange, of exploitation. For social inequalities to be regarded as exploitative, we must imagine a society ('N') made up of a coalition of agents ('S') and the members of 'N' who are not in 'S', who are labelled 'T'. The coalition of agents 'S' is said to be exploited if 'there is an alternative which we can conceive of as hypothetically feasible, in which "S" would be better off than in its present situation' and where 'T' would be worse off than at present. Furthermore, for this situation to be defined as exploitative, 'T' must be in a position of power over 'S' in order to prevent the realisation of the alternative where 'S' would be better off and 'T' worse off than at present.[13]

The example of feudalism should clarify Roemer's meaning. For feu-

dal relations of production to be considered exploitative, then the peasant producers ('S') who exist in a specific society ('N') would be better
off in a hypothetically feasible alternative, whilst the feudal lords ('T')
would be worse off. The peasants would gain through this alternative by
not having to pay rents and by gaining a greater control of their own
affairs with the ending of their domination by the landlords; the landlords would be worse off in terms of their wealth, status and power. In
this hypothetical alternative, the peasants would obtain land, provide
their own defence and administer their own justice and yet still be better off than by 'paying' their lords to provide these services. It is precisely
because this was the situation in medieval Europe that serfdom has been
seen as exploitative, rather than as a simple exchange of services.[14]

Similarly, to say that wage labourers under capitalism are exploited is
to imply an alternative where the functions now performed by the capitalist class (the provision of resources, management and so on) could
be carried out without the capitalist class and where the labourers would
be better off than at present.

Roemer's emphasis is on the benefits enjoyed by 'T' at the expense of
'S', but it should be stressed that the *power* of 'T' over 'S' is an integral part
of this exploitative relationship. If we imagine a relationship between
those not able to work (the old or the sick) and the producers we may
at first appear to have a situation of exploitation since the producers ('S')
would be better off, and the non-producers ('T'), worse off, if they
withdrew from their relationship. It is the fact that the non-producers in
this example do not enjoy a coercive dominance over the producers
which prevents us from describing it as one of exploitation.[15] Nevertheless, although all forms of exploitation involve a relationship of power,
not all power relationships are necessarily one of exploitation. It would
be possible to imagine a situation (as in Kurosawa's *The Seven Samurai*)
where peasant producers were in need of, and so were willing to pay for,
military protection from the raids of bandits. It would be in the interest
of any individual villager to avoid paying for protection and yet to share
in the protection offered to all. In this case it would be in the general
interest to coerce individuals to pay their share. Coercion would only
constitute exploitation where the coerced were not maximising their
benefits, i.e., not receiving protection, of if they were able to provide
their own protection more cheaply. Similarly, oppression may be defined
as a restriction which does not maximise benefits: everyone being
forced to drive on the left-hand side of the road is thus a restriction but
not an oppression.

Roemer's theory is a great advance on previous attempts to define exploitation but, nevertheless, contains two main weaknesses which lead us to question the use of the term 'exploitation' in the social sciences. These difficulties relate to Roemer's claim that for 'S' to be exploited there must be a 'hypothetically feasible' alternative in which 'S' would be 'better off'.[16] The concepts of both a 'hypothetically feasible' alternative and being 'better off' unfortunately introduce subjective moral criteria into the definition of exploitation. Unless these criteria are shared by observers, exploitation and surplus labour do indeed become 'prejudicial words' rather than social scientific descriptions.

The problems of the hypothetically feasible alternative where 'S' would not be exploited are apparent in Roemer's concept of 'socially necessary exploitation' where 'S' (peasants, workers, etc.) would be worse off, in the shorter or longer term, by withdrawing from their relationship with 'T'. If peasants, for instance, were worse off without their landlords, through a lack of military protection, then their relationship with their lords is one of 'socially necessary exploitation'. There may be a *hypothetical* alternative where the peasants would be better off without 'T' but *in practice* this would not be the case.[17] But in what sense does this so-called socially necessary exploitation actually constitute exploitation, since through this arrangement the peasants maximise their benefits? The fact that there is a 'hypothetical' alternative is less important in defining a situation as exploitative than the existence of a practical alternative.

Thus, under capitalism we can only define the situation of the proletariat as one of exploitation if there is the practical possibility of an alternative where the working class would be better off, and the capitalist class would be worse off. Otherwise, the workers under capitalism would be maximising their benefits and the capitalists' profits would not constitute exploitation but, as in neoclassical economics, would merely be an incentive/reward for the contribution of certain factors of production. Profits could then only be described as 'exploitative' if they were above the level required to obtain the employment of the factor of production of capital. This is precisely the socialist case: the employment of capital, in the general sense of 'resources', does not require the existence of capitalism in the sense of a specific social relation; *any* rewards which go to the capitalists are socially unnecessary and so constitute an exploitative surplus. But in this case profits do not constitute a 'surplus' unless we consider socialism to be a practical alternative. We may thus reformulate Roemer's definition of exploitation from one where 'S' would be better off in a *hypothetically alternative* situation, to one where 'S' would be better off (and 'T' worse off) in a *practically possible* alternative situation.

The problem with this definition of exploitation is that it assumes agreement on what is a practical alternative. Whether, for instance, socialism is a practical alternative to capitalism, is a rather controversial issue, involving assessments about the possibilities of 'human nature' and the desirability of certain economic, social and political policies; an assessment which will be based on the moral and political standards of the observer. That socialism is a desirable and practical alternative is self-evident to socialists, but not always to others. In the absence of such agreements about the practicality of alternatives, 'exploitation' would not be a description of real social relations (as, for instance, is the concept of wage labour), but would merely be the subjective perception of the observer. It would seem problematical, to say the least, to make such perceptions of surplus labour and exploitation the basis of a taxonomy of modes of production.

The second, but less important, problem with Roemer's definition of exploitation is that it requires us to identify a situation where 'S' would be 'better off'.[18] He seems to regard the definition of 'better off' as unproblematical, but in practice the assessment of whether 'S' is better off under one situation or another is based, once more, on the subjective perceptions of the observer. Many modern writers, for example, would agree that 'it is not hard to tell' if a peasant community is exploited and that medieval peasants did not maximise their benefits through feudal relations of production.[19] It could be argued, however, that medieval peasants gained, in the long term, through their lack of wealth, status and power: 'The poor may claim their place in heaven by right, whilst the rich can only gain it, if at all, by the grace and mercy of God.'[20] It is only because the modern mind does not usually value poverty or meekness that the definition of the peasants' situation as one of exploitation does not appear to be based on subjective criteria. The fact that a number of writers agree that benefits may be measured in terms of material rewards and political self-determination, does not make this any less of a subjective moral assessment. The definition of 'better off', like that of the 'practical alternative to exploitation', comes again to rely on the observer's own moral and political values.

Another approach would be to define a situation as exploitative if there is a practical alternative where the members of 'S' would be better off according to their own criteria of good and bad. The advantage of this approach is that it avoids the subjective perceptions of the observer but only at the cost of invoking the subjective assessments of the observed. Do the members of 'S' cease to be exploited if they do not believe themselves to be exploited? Do they cease to be exploited if they do not perceive the existence of a practical alternative? Is capitalism only exploitative where the producers perceive the possibility of socialism? Relying on the perceptions of 'S' causes as many problems as it solves.

At first sight, Roemer's theory seems to offer a definition of exploitation which would function as a descriptive concept in social science. In fact, the theory involves the use of moral and political assessments of 'alternatives' where the producers are 'better off'; these are subjective and, in terms of the theory, arbitrary. To say that medieval social relations consisted of peasants who paid rents to landlords is a conceptual description of reality. To say that this situation was one of exploitation is a moral assessment dependent on subjective criteria. Personally, it may be an assessment with which we agree, but it will hardly function as the basis of a classification of social forms.

Class and the relations of production

If 'surplus labour' and 'exploitation' are problematical terms, then it may seem that Marx's classification of societies, based on the form in which 'surplus labour' is extracted from the producer, has little to offer the historian or the social scientist. However, it is possible to separate the descriptive basis of Marx's classification of social forms from its subjective moral superstructure. The claim that societies should be distinguished by their specific form of 'surplus' labour can be rephrased in terms of a descriptive typology which would draw agreement from writers who may have conflicting moral and political outlooks:

> Whatever the social form of production, labourers and means of production always remain factors of it. But in a state of separation from each other either of these factors can be such only potentially. For production to go on at all they must unite. The specific manner in which this union is accomplished distinguishes the different economic epochs of the structure of society from one another.[21]

Balibar offers a more precise definition of the elements whose connections go to make up a specific mode of production. These elements consist of:
(1)   labourers;
(2)   means of production (the object of labour and the means of labouring);

214

(3)   the non-labourer who appropriates 'surplus labour'.

Between these elements there are the relationships which identify particular forms of property. Finally, we must consider the extent to which
the direct producer is able to set to work the means of production, i.e.
the process of appropriation of the means of production by the direct
producer in the labour process.[22]

These elements and relationships allow us to contrast the inability of
the proletarian to set to work the means of production independently
from the capitalist class, with the productive autonomy enjoyed by the
artisan. Similarly, they allow us to distinguish the slave and the proletarian, who share a similar lack of independent access to the means of production, but who are separated by property relations where the
wage-labourer owns and is able to sell the commodity labour-power,
whilst slaves have no control of their own labour-power and are themselves commodities. Far from the Marxist theory of class implying that
the slave and the free wage-labourer are members of the same class, as
Finley has claimed, it is precisely the aim of Marxist theory to distinguish these classes on the basis of the factors with which they are
endowed; the producers under capitalism own and sell their own
labour-power, those under slavery do not.[23] We may thus define a class,
for the purpose of establishing a typology of social forms, as 'a group of
people who by virtue of what they possess are compelled to engage in
the same activities if they want to make the best use of their endowments'. An individual's class is thus established by 'nothing but his
objective place in the network of ownership relations', a situation which
exists irrespective of the subjective perceptions of that person.[24]

Marx distinguishes this objective definition of a class 'in itself', from
the subjective class-consciousness achieved by the class 'for itself'. A class
in itself is defined by a common situation and common interests, by the
objective conditions of life which predetermine the individual's position
in life. A class for itself exists only in so far as it carries on a battle against
another class to defend its own interests, a struggle which takes a political form.[25] The objective definition of class appears, at first sight, to be
very different from the definition made familiar by E. P. Thompson:
'Classes arise because men and women, in determinate productive relations, identify their antagonistic relations and come to struggle, to think
and to value in class ways; thus the process of class formation is a process
of self-making although under conditions which are "given".' For
Thompson, the criterion of a true class is class-consciousness. A class is
not merely 'so many men who stand in a certain relation to the means

of production', but also involves the articulation of common interests by the class for itself.[26] The issue, however, is largely a semantic one. If we wish to reserve the label of 'class' only for a class which exists 'for itself' then we must find some other term for the concept of a group of people who 'stand in a certain relation to the means of production'.[27] It is this latter concept, the objective definition of 'class', which Marx invokes when he claims that we may distinguish between societies in terms of the different combinations of labourers and means of production. More specifically we may distinguish between the economic structures of societies on the basis of:

(1) the nature of the class of producers defined in terms of their endowments: slaves, peasants, proletarians, and so on;

(2) the nature of the non-producing class: slave-owners, feudal landlords, employers of wage labour, and so on;

(3) the form taken by the income of the non-producers and the means through which this income is appropriated.

We may continue to follow convention and refer to this income as 'surplus labour', provided that we emphasise that the use of the term implies no reliance on a subjective-moral definition of exploitation of the kind rejected above.

How successfully have Marx, Engels and later Marxists used these concepts in order to analyse the nature of specific historical societies?

Marx's history or Marx's method?

One approach to Marx's theory of history would be to provide a lengthy commentary on his analysis of each of the historical modes of production and to examine, in detail, how Marxist historians have attempted to refine this analysis. Here, however, we offer no detailed survey of Marx's writings on past societies. Firstly, because Marx was writing at a time when the scientific study of the past had hardly begun, which means that many of his specific comments have been refuted by later research. Secondly, because, despite all appearances to the contrary, many of Marx's comments about pre-capitalist modes of production were not intended as historical analyses in their own right, but were made in order to emphasise the historical specifity of the capitaist mode of production. Marx's main concern in these passages is not with the past, but the present. In the *Grundrisse*, for instance, Marx's real priority is not to analyse the nature of Ancient or feudal society, but rather to establish that the various forms of unity of the labourer and the means of production which characterised such societies are in marked contrast with the separation of the labourer from the means of production which characterises the capitalist mode. His point is that the social relations of capital are not natural, inevitable or eternal, but are themselves the product of specific and transitory circumstances. Similarly, Marx's discussion of pre-capitalist forms of rent in volume III of *Capital* is actually designed to emphasise the nature of *capitalist* social relations and to show that surplus labour under capitalism does not directly take the form of rent. The true test of Marx's theory of history is thus not the accuracy of his scattered comments on historical societies, but, rather, to what extent his method and general concepts allow us to understand past societies.[28] This is not the place for a detailed study of the entire corpus of Marxist historiography. Rather, we will attempt to define the forms of property and relations to production which distinguish the modes of production referred to by Marx and Engels and examine some of the major theoretical and empirical problems involved in some representative Marxist attempts to employ these concepts in historical analysis.

Primitive communism

The analysis of the relations of production of 'primitive' societies poses a number of problems for Marxist analysis, not least of which is the heritage of Engels's admiration for the 'simple moral grandeur' of the 'noble savage'. Engels portrayed primitive societies as free of poverty and need; all were free and equal, 'everything ran smoothly' despite the absence of a coercive state, society produced individuals endowed with bravery, dignity and straightforwardness. Whether prehistoric society did constitute a communist Golden Age, which was brought to an end by greed, avarice, theft, rape and deceit, can only be judged according to our individual moral criteria.[29] Our real task is to establish the relations of production found in these societies. A subjective like, or dislike, of such forms of social organisation is neither here nor there for the purpose of this analysis. Bloch has argued that in characterising primitive societies as classless Marx and Engels were unable to offer an adequate analysis of them, since 'class' is the central descriptive and explanatory concept of Marxist social theory.[30] However, Marx and Engels did not merely classify societies in terms of class or explain social change and forms of ideology only in terms of class and class conflict. Their social theory was based upon the concept of the social relations of production, of which class relations are merely one sub-category. How, then, can we characterise the relations of production found in primitive societies?

That the concept of 'primitive communism' need not be a term of moral like or dislike is apparent from the analysis of the earliest forms of human-society offered in *The German Ideology* and the *Grundrisse*. Marx and Engels distinguish societies here in terms of their forms of property and the producers' access to the means of production and the social product. The earliest human societies, they claimed, were characterised by the existence of tribal property where the means of production, whether for hunting, pastoralism or early agriculture, are the common property of the tribe. Only through membership of the tribe does the individual have access to the productive forces and the results of the process of production. Nevertheless, although property is communal, this does not mean that social relations within the tribe are necessarily egalitarian. On the contrary, the tribe may be divided between chieftains, the mass of the tribe and the slaves, who are the common property of the tribe. Tribal relations develop as an extension of family relations which are, to begin with, the only social relations, but even within the family there may be an inequality and the development of the latent slavery of the wife and children.[31]

The most familiar of Marx and Engels's analyses of primitive society is, of course, Engels's *The Origin of the Family, Private Property and the State*, a work which, disappointingly, devotes most of its attention to kinship (the aspect of Engels's analysis which is now considered most obsolete by anthropologists), rather than to property relations and the state.[32] Engels divides primitive society into two phases: savagery, where hunting and gathering form the basis of subsistence, and barbarism, the epoch during which animals were domesticated and agriculture was introduced. Engels claims that kinship had a 'decisive role' in the social order of all societies in the stages of both savagery and barbarism but, following Morgan (his chief source), Engels concentrates on the higher stages of barbarism. Here society is organised on the basis of lineage groups ('gentes') which form the basis for the entire social organisation of *phatries* and tribes. The Iroquois Indians, for example, organise their social relations through multifunctional kinship relations, which not only determine inheritance, but also provide mutual support and carry out political and ideological tasks. The tribe has no separate state authority and between members of the tribe there is no social inequality. There is a division of labour between the sexes, but this division has not yet become an inequality, and each sex is dominant within its own sphere. There is individual ownership of tools and utensils, but resources used in common by large communistic households (such as a house, garden or boat) form common property; hunting grounds are the common property of the tribe as a whole. Engels pays surprisingly little attention to the relations of production or forms of property of primitive society, but emphasises the lack of class and gender inequality, the absence of private property and the consequent lack of a state authority to guarantee such property.[33]

In itself, the presence of common property is not enough to characterise a specific mode of production, any more than it is adequate to characterise slave, feudal and capitalist societies as sharing a common 'private property' mode of production. Marx himself argued that common property could be found in a number of forms, including not only tribal property, but also the communal property of the Ancient city-state (where at first private property is subordinate and slaves belong to the community of citizens) and the Asiatic village (which is also based on 'tribal or common property'), where possession of land is dependent on membership of a wider community.[34]

Marx and Engels argued that 'tribal' property was the earliest form of property and that kinship played a decisive role in primitive social relations but, in practice, this does not seem to have been the case. An example of a society where kinship is of only secondary importance is that of the Mbuti pygmies, hunter-gatherers of the Zaïre rain forest. Mbuti social organisation is based on the band of around seven to thirty male hunters with their families. The men hunt with nets, whilst the women and children act as drivers on the hunt. Women also collect mushrooms and other plants, which account for over half of the band's food resources. Each band has its own territory within which it is itinerant. The individual can only survive through membership of this community, expulsion from which is equivalent to death. There is no separate state authority and little social inequality within the band, although men, in particular older men, do enjoy a higher status. The relations of production of the band are based on the daily division of the product of hunting and gathering amongst the band members. It is the band which possesses a specific area as its common territory whilst work tasks are allotted according to age and sex. As a result kinship relations are of only secondary importance in Mbuti society. Hindess and Hirst characterise such societies as possessing a 'simple' mechanism of redistribution of the social product, where all those involved in the production process enjoy an immediate share of the product of the hunt or of gathering.[35]

In other societies, kinship may play a more central role in the organisation of production and of the redistribution of the social product and may overlap with other forms of collective organisation such as the household, village and tribe. An example of this 'complex redistribution' of the product is the Gouru hunt. The hunting of large animals by the Gouru involves small bands of men under the leadership of the hunter who found the animal. This leader receives specific parts of the animal, such as the tusks, the trunk and the feet or the heart and liver. The elders of the village also receive certain parts of the animal and the remainder is left for the other inhabitants of the village and neighbouring tribesmen. Access to the product here is not merely dependent on a direct input into the labour process, it is also the result of an individual's position within a permanent social order of lineage and rank. This 'complex' redistribution of the social product through social relations which exist prior to the particular labour process, is even more apparent in the sphere of agriculture where the Gouru produce rice, maize, yams and so forth. Here there is a division of labour between work teams which carry out the complementary tasks of clearing the earth, sowing, tending the crops and harvesting. These teams are composed on the basis of gender, kinship and neighbourhood under the supervision of the elders of the lineages within the village. The harvest is then divided, part of the product being retained by individual households and the remainder being communally stored and then redistributed, through communal means, according to the individual's age, sex and status.[36]

There is thus no reason why the existence of forms of common property should involve a social equality between all members of the community. Amongst the Baruya of New Guinea, for example, land ownership is collective: 'the descendants of a common ancestor are co-owners of the lands which he first cultivated'. Nevertheless, there is a marked inequality between the sexes, an inequality which is fundamental to all other forms of inequality amongst the tribe, such as the higher status of the great warrior or shaman.[37] Other societies, such as the Tiv of Nigeria, have developed greater inequalities of wealth with the emergence of the 'big man', distinguished by his accumulation of wealth and temporary network of supporters. Such power, prestige and wealth is, however, only individual and temporary and does not form the basis for the emergence of a permanent and hereditary aristocratic caste, as is the case in the Polynesian chiefdoms, where there is a stable hierarchy of rank irrespective of the personal capabilities of the holder – unlike the Baruya 'great man', or the Tiv 'big man'.[38]

The example of the Gouru emphasises the conclusion of other anthropological studies: 'production and its relations do not constitute an autonomous economic level dominating the totality of social relations, since the relations of production are relations of kinship'.[39] Nevertheless, this centrality of kinship in the social relations of production is to be found only in specific primitive societies. Elsewhere it is the band, rather than the tribe, village, lineage or household, which is the collective property owner and the basis for the redistribution of the social product. Whether we consider these variants to be separate modes of production or merely sub-forms of a 'primitive communist' mode, is immaterial. The central point is that the concept of the relations of production allows us to describe and to distinguish between these societies. In practice, however, it may be best to drop the label of 'primitive communism', because of its implication that there is a single collective form of property ownership common to all primitive societies, and because of its egalitarian and approbatory overtones.

The 'Asiatic' mode of production

In the 1859 'Preface' Marx includes the 'Asiatic' mode of production in his list of the forms of the economic structure of society, but nowhere does he provide a detailed or consistent analysis of this mode. In the *Grundrisse*, Marx emphasises that the foundation of Asiatic society is 'tribal or common property', even where there is a state which appropriates surplus labour. In this analysis the Asiatic despot 'represents the community' and the relations of production are a variety of the primitive communist mode of production, where the producer has access to the means of production as the member of a community.[40] Yet these relations of production are not those of an archetypal primitive communism, since they involve the appropriation of surplus labour by the state, a separate public authority of the kind usually regarded as absent in primitive communism. Marxists such as Godelier have thus seen the Asiatic mode of production as the form of social production which characterises the transition from classless to class society, with the state acting in a classlike fashion. Marx himself also used the term to apply to the complex society of Mughal India, a society which Godelier would see as a variety of feudalism.[41] Marx's views are further complicated by the red herring of 'hydraulic agriculture', the claim that in the climatic conditions of the Orient agriculture required extensive irrigation and that these irrigation works could only be provided by a centralised state. In fact, there is no necessary theoretical or historical correspondence between major irriga-tion works, despotism and a lack of private property in land. Early modern Persia, Turkey and India lacked private property in land, but did not possess major public irrigation schemes. China had such public works, but was characterised by the existence of private feudal property, whilst early modern Russia possessed a despotism which was based nei-ther on the absence of private property in land nor on extensive public works.[42]

The defining feature of the 'Asiatic' mode of production is not, of course, that it is to be found in Asia. On the contrary, modern defenders of the concept are quite prepared to locate it in Africa or pre-Columbian America.[43] Neither can the 'Asiatic' mode be defined by the presence of a specific form of productive forces: irrigated agriculture. The so-called 'Asiatic' mode must be defined by a specific form of property and by its relations of production. The clearest indication of the nature of these relations appears in volume III of *Capital*:

> Should the direct producers not be confronted by a private landowner, but rather, as in Asia, under direct subordination to a state which stands over them as their landlord and simultaneously as sovereign, then rent and tax co-incide, or rather there exists no tax which differs from this form of ground-rent. Under such circumstances, there need exist no stronger political or economic pressure than that common to all sub-jection to the state. ... No private ownership of land exists although there is both common and private possession and use of the land.[44]

Anderson is surely right to reject the idea that all pre-industrial Asian societies can be described in terms of a single mode of production but, despite his claims, it does not follow that the notion of the 'Asiatic' mode of production, where rent and tax coincide, need be abandoned alto-gether. Indeed, Anderson's description of Mughal India before European penetration would seem to present us with just such a society. Under the Mughals, agricultural land was 'subject to the sole economic and politi-cal power of the Emperor', a subjection which resulted not from the state's provision of irrigation, but from the Islamic law that all land was the property of the sovereign. Land was not communally owned, as Marx claimed, but was tilled by peasants who enjoyed hereditary pos-session so long as they paid tax-rent (in the form of money or produce), which could account for a half or more of the peasant's output. These revenues went largely to support a military elite, the mansabdars, 8,000 officers responsible for raising the state's cavalry army. In 1647, for instance, 445 mansabdars received over sixty per cent of the total income of the state. Yet, unlike the feudal landlords of western Europe, this military elite did not enjoy private and hereditary possession of property. They were appointed at the discretion of the emperor, received only temporary grants of revenue and were periodically shifted around the country in order to prevent them developing a regional power base. Other state revenues were granted to the *zamindars*, lesser potentates in command of infantry and of castles.[45] The existence of peasant producers rendering tax-rent to a landlord-state allows us to define the 'Asiatic' mode of production in theory; Mughal India would seem to provide an empirical example of the existence of this form of property.

However, in *Pre-capitalist Modes of Production* Hindess and Hirst reject the validity of the concept of the 'Asiatic' mode. For Hindess and Hirst, a mode of production may be defined as 'an articulated combination of a specific mode of appropriation of the product with a specific mode of appropriation of nature', in other words a combination of specific relations of production with a specific set of productive forces. The tax-rent form of surplus labour does not, it is claimed, form the basis for the concept of a mode of production, since it corresponds to at least two sets of productive forces: independent peasant cultivation and communal cultivation. These combinations of relations of production and forces of production are arbitrary, since both sets of productive forces are 'equally deducible' from the concept of tax-rent. The substitution of one set of productive forces for the other would thus have no transforming effect on the relations of production. Furthermore, the productive forces of the 'Asiatic' mode are quite compatible with the relations of production of other modes. Independent peasant cultivation, for instance, is quite compatible with the existence of feudal rent.[46] Given this definition of a mode of production, the concept of the 'Asiatic' mode would seem to lack any theoretical coherence and would thus be incapable of empirical application.

Here, however, we do not accept Hindess and Hirst's definition of a mode of production or their consequent rejection of the concept of the Asiatic mode. We can agree that a mode of production is characterised by specific relations of production, since it is precisely the variation in the forms of property which is the basis for any classification of modes of production. But there is no reason why a mode of production should be characterised by the existence of specific productive forces. The Asiatic mode is thus quite compatible with independent or communal forms of cultivation, just as primitive communism is compatible with agricultural or pre-agricultural forms of the productive forces and just as capitalism may be found in either industrial or pre-industrial forms. A mode of production is best defined as the combination of a specific set of relations of production with a potentially variable set of productive forces. The variable forms of the labour process in the Asiatic mode allow us to define sub-forms of this mode of production rather than providing, as Hindess and Hirst claim, a refutation of the validity of this concept.

An 'Ancient' mode of production?

Marx provides us with no detailed account of class relations in the Ancient World, but his occasional comments on the subject have two main emphases. The first is the centrality of slavery as the dominant form of the production of surplus labour; the second is the importance of citizenship and of the urban community within Greek and Roman society. Marxist studies of the Ancient World tend to be divided between these two traditions, with writers such as Walbank, Anderson and De Ste Croix emphasising the importance of slavery in the social relations of Antiquity, whilst Wickham and Hindess and Hirst stress the importance of citizenship and of the state.[47]

In *The German Ideology* Marx outlines the emergence of slavery from earlier communal forms of property. The earliest tribal form of property gives way to the communal property of the city-state, in which the citizen has access to wealth, including slaves, only as a member of the urban community. This form of communal property is, in turn, undermined by the growth of private property, first in movable and then in landed wealth. Property becomes concentrated into fewer hands and class relations between citizens and slaves achieve a complete form, a development hastened, Marx later added, by warfare, conquest, commerce and the growth of commodity production. The Ancient state and society were thus based on slavery since slaves, at least in Roman Italy, formed 'the great productive mass of the population'. This did not mean, however, that Ancient politics took the form of a confrontation between master and slave. On the contrary: 'The class struggle took place only within the privileged minority, between the free rich and the free poor ... the slaves formed the passive pedestal for these combatants.'[48] Despite Finley's claims to the contrary, Marx was concerned to emphasise the contrast between the slave of Antiquity and the modern free wage-labourer. The labourer is separated from the means of production and can be united with them only through the workings of the capitalist labour market. Under slavery, however, there is no such separation: 'It is rather labour itself, which is placed among the other living things as inorganic conditions of production, alongside the cattle.'[49] That one of the most theoretically aware historians of the Ancient economy can claim that Marx's analysis would include slaves and proletarians in the same class, only goes to emphasise the lack of impact which Marxism has had on the study of the Ancient World, a lack which G. E. M. De Ste Croix's *The Class Struggle in the Ancient Greek World* ambitiously sets out to repair. De Ste Croix's employment of Marxist concepts allows him to perceive and to emphasise many aspects of Antiquity to which other historians have turned a blind eye, but ultimately his central claim that 'the Greek and Roman world always remained what we may loosely call a "slave society" ' fails to convince.[50] By a 'slave society' De Ste Croix does not mean that the bulk of the population were slaves. On the contrary, the majority of the work-force (before *c.* 300 AD) were free peasants and independent artisans. Unlike Ellen Wood, De Ste Croix does not make this fact the basis of his analysis of the social relations of Antiquity. A mode of production is defined not by the occupations of the bulk of its members but by its relations of production and, in particular, by the form in which the propertied class derives its income. For De Ste Croix the ruling class of Antiquity 'derived its surplus mainly from unfree labour (especially that of slaves)'.[51]

De Ste Croix's analysis poses a number of problems; problems which arise not from his objective-structural definition of class and of a mode of production, but rather from his failure to follow through the logic of that definition. Firstly, it is not clear in what sense slavery was 'in the forefront' of the forms of unfree labour found in Antiquity. At times it seems that this pre-eminence is meant in a quantitative sense – the ruling class derived the bulk of its income from slavery. De Ste Croix never actually shows, however, that chattel slaves were the predominant producers of surplus labour in Antiquity. Elsewhere slavery is said to be the 'dominant form' of unfree labour in the sense that slavery, along with the very similar relations of debt bondage, was 'the archetypal form of unfree labour' throughout Graeco-Roman Antiquity, 'omnipresent in the psychology of all classes ... even if it is serfdom which provides the propertied class with much of its surplus'. Slavery was thus the model for Ancient perceptions of all forms of unfree labour. De Ste Croix's original objective definition of the centrality of slavery gives way, here, to the subjective perceptions of the inhabitants of the Ancient World. De Ste Croix even adopts the argument put forward by Perry Anderson that 'slavery was the most important form of unfree labour *at the highest periods of Greek and Roman civilization*', a thesis which replaces the subjective perception of the Ancients with the subjective assessment of the modern historian. That chattel slavery was in fact, if not in the mind of Ancient authors, the dominant form of exploitation throughout Antiquity (rather than the 'exploitation' of peasant producers by the state or by landlords), is never proved by De Ste Croix's analysis.[52]

The second major difficulty of De Ste Croix's analysis is his blurring of the distinction between slavery and other forms of unfree labour: 'the Greek and Roman world always remained what we may loosely call a "*slave* society" with *unfree* labour continuing to be a main source of exploitation'. But the definition of unfree labour as the main form of 'surplus labour' does not allow us to specify the social relations of Antiquity, as the broad concept of 'unfree labour' can include the very different relations of production of slavery and of serfdom, where production is carried out not by slaves, but by peasant producers. The claim that 'unfree labour' was dominant in the Ancient World allows us to contrast Antiquity with the free labour of the capitalist mode of production, but this contrast reveals more about the unique and specific nature of capitalism than it does of Antiquity.[53]

The difficulties of defining the Ancient mode of production by the dominance of 'unfree labour' are apparent in De Ste Croix's analysis of the peasantry. If the peasantry is a class, and if this class excludes slaves, as De Ste Croix rightly claims, it follows that societies where slavery is the main form of surplus labour (such as Athens in the fifth century BC or Italy in the first century BC) possess different class relations from societies where the bulk of surplus labour is performed by unfree peasants (such as the Spartan helots or the late Roman colonate). The form of surplus labour, and hence the character of the dominant mode of production, is markedly different in these societies.[54] De Ste Croix's problem arises from his initial acceptance of the unity of the Ancient Greek world, a unity which can only be defined in cultural terms. In fact there is no more reason to treat 'Antiquity' as a social formation or a mode of production 'than there is to treat Africa since da Gama as one'.[55] There is no reason why Antiquity should be perceived as a social unity, let alone a unity characterised by the dominance of slavery as the main form of surplus labour.

In the *Grundrisse* Marx argues that 'classical history is the history of the cities'. It is this emphasis on the urban community of Antiquity which forms the basis of Hindess and Hirst's definition of the 'Ancient mode

of production'. Like De Ste Croix, Hindess and Hirst accept that the predominant form of the labour process in the Ancient World was that of
the peasant and the artisan and they agree that, in itself, the presence of
independent producers does not characterise a specific mode of production. For Hindess and Hirst, the dominant social relation of production of Antiquity was 'appropriation of surplus labour by right of
citizenship'. The state acts as the collective appropriator of surplus
labour which is then redistributed amongst the citizens by virtue of
their political rights. Citizenship gave access to land and to resources, to
tribute, booty, taxation and state doles. The advantage of this definition
is that it can allow for the prominence in Antiquity of the legally defined
orders, or status groups, which pose a problem for De Ste Croix's analysis, where such orders have to be grafted on to, or reduced down to, pre-
existing class relations. For Hindess and Hirst, the status system creates
a set of differential political rights which determine access to surplus
labour: 'relations between classes are realised at the political level in a
system of legally defined statuses'.[56]

The disadvantage of this analysis, as Hindess and Hirst's 'auto-critique'
acknowledged, is the continued assumption of a single dominant
Ancient mode of production, a concept which has to be stretched to
breaking point when applied to societies as different as those of Sparta,
Athens and Rome. The example of Sparta does provide a classic instance
of Hindess and Hirst's 'Ancient mode'. Spartan society cannot usefully be
'loosely labelled' as a 'slave society'. In Sparta, the direct producers (the
helots) were excluded from citizenship and formed a subject population,
with no political rights. The Spartan citizens constituted a military elite,
whose income came primarily from grants of land from the state. Neither the land itself nor the serf-helots belonged to individual citizens, but
citizens could claim an assignment from the state's land through their
political rights.[57]

If Sparta does provide an example of an 'Ancient' mode of production
where surplus labour is appropriated by right of citizenship, then we
need to distinguish these social relations from those of Athens or Rome,
where the citizens did not form a unified class of non-producing appro-
priators of surplus labour. On the contrary, in these societies the citizen
body was socially divided between artisans, peasants, landowners and
merchants. In such cases the citizens themselves could be 'exploited',
either by the state (in the form of taxation or forced labour), or by other
citizens (through rent or debt-bondage). At Sparta the dominant form
of 'surplus labour' was the rent in kind paid by the state serfs; at Athens

in the fifth century BC, or at Rome in the first century BC, the dominant form of income for the propertied class came from slavery. Indeed, at Athens the existence of 'democracy' and the political rights of the poorer citizens tended to increase the propertied citizens' reliance on slavery.[58] We need to distinguish the relations of production of the Spartan state-serfdom, where surplus labour is appropriated by right of citizenship, from those of slavery, where surplus labour is extracted by ownership of a certain form of property, not from citizenship *per se*. Hindess and Hirst's 'Ancient mode' did exist in Antiquity, but by no means characterised all of the city-states, let alone the later history of the Roman Empire. The 'Ancient' mode was no more universal in Antiquity, than the 'Asiatic' mode was in Asia.

The late Roman Empire saw a shift away from slavery to a system of serfdom, where the agricultural population was tied to the land. Such measures may have found favour amongst the propertied classes, but their primary function was to raise taxation, soldiers and labour services for the state. The Empire's response to the economic and political crisis of the third century was to extend state regulation and to increase fiscal demands in order to support the growing state apparatus and, in particular, the army. Society's surplus was thus increasingly appropriated directly by the state. It is this growing appropriation of surplus by the state which forms the basis for Wickham's definition of the 'Ancient mode', where taxation was 'the institution that determined the direction of the economy and defined the dominant mode of production'. The period from *c*. 300 to *c*. 700 AD saw the coexistence of two modes of production articulated within one social formation: the Ancient mode based on the state appropriation of surplus, and the feudal mode based on private rents. It was the latter which was, eventually, to emerge triumphant. This does not mean that society became 'feudal' the moment that feudal rent accounted for fifty-one per cent of the surplus labour. Rather, the form taken by surplus labour had *qualitative* social effects on the ideology of the upper classes, on the role of towns (which ceased, under feudalism, to be foci of taxation and administration) and on the nature of political power, which became increasingly privatised in the hands of the rural aristocracy of the Germanic kingdoms which replaced the Empire.[59]

Wickham's 'Ancient mode' is a variety of the 'tributary mode of production' outlined by Amin. The 'tributary mode' is one of five modes of production distinguished by Amin: the primitive communal mode; the slave-owning mode; capitalism; the simple petty-commodity mode, which is usually found in subordination to some other dominant mode (for instance, the subordination of handicraft production to feudal social relations in medieval Europe); and the tributary mode. The latter is defined by relations of production where the village community pays surplus labour in the form of tribute to a ruling class which monopolises political power.[60] The concept is a useful one, provided that we emphasise the sub-forms of this mode: the 'Asiatic' variety where the state monopolises land and appropriates surplus as tax-rent; the Spartan version, where surplus is appropriated by right of citizenship; and the late Roman variant, where there is private ownership of land and yet the state takes a growing percentage of the social product in the form of taxation. It is not really important whether we see all of these forms of social relations as distinct modes of production, or as sub-forms of the 'tributary' mode, although it would seem useful to distinguish between the state's appropriation of surplus in these societies and the private appropriation of rent characteristic of the feudal mode. The labelling of these societies is largely an issue of semantics. We are concerned here to describe and to distinguish societies in terms of the nature of their producers, the nature of the class which draws its income from these producers and the forms and mechanisms through which this income is obtained. It is these differences between the varieties of the so-called 'tributary mode' which we must emphasise if the whole of human history between tribal and industrial society is not to be dissolved into a single, amorphous 'peasant' mode of production, with little classificatory or explanatory value.[61]

The feudal mode of production

The problems involved in deriving a 'Marxist' analysis of pre-capitalist modes of production from Marx's own comments about past societies are clearly illustrated by the example of feudalism. Marx was concerned to show that under capitalism rent takes a special form, which distinguishes it from rent in previous societies. In a capitalist society the producers are separated from the means of production, and 'exploitation' takes place through the exchange of capital for labour-power and through the production of surplus value, the specifically capitalist form of surplus labour, embodied in the commodity. Rent, under these circumstances, is not itself the fundamental form of surplus labour obtained from the producers. Rather, surplus value is produced by the capitalist enterprise and shared between the capitalist and the landlord, in the form of profits and rents. Rent does not directly constitute surplus labour, but is rather a redistribution of the surplus labour created in the production process. It would thus be possible to nationalise land, and to abolish rent, and yet leave the fundamental relations of capitalism untouched. Marx contrasts this situation with that of pre-capitalist societies, where the producers have not yet been divorced from the means of production. Here the labourer remains 'in possession of his own means of production, the necessary material labour conditions required for the realisation of his labour and the production of his means of subsistence'. Since the producers possess the means of their own subsistence, they are under no economic compulsion to provide the landlord with surplus labour. It follows that 'under such conditions the surplus labour for the nominal owner of the land can only be extorted ... by other than economic pressure' and property relations must 'appear as a direct relationship of lordship and servitude'.[62]

It is this view of the peasant as 'united to the means of production' which has dominated many Marxist accounts of the feudal mode of production. Hilton, whose works are a model of the empirical value of the Marxist approach, repeats Marx's claim that 'Given the effective possession of the subsistence-producing holding by the peasant family, the transfer of surplus labour must be forced, since the peasant, as contrasted with the wage labourer, does not need to alienate his labour power in order to live.' In medieval England this extra-economic coercion was carried out by the manor, an institution which, despite all its variety of empirical form, had the common function of providing the landlords with a decentralised political power, which allowed them to appropriate surplus labour from the peasant producers.[63] Yet, despite the value of this analysis as an empirical description, it fails to specify the exact meaning of the 'possession' of the means of production which the producers are said to enjoy.

Although Marx emphasised that the peasants under feudalism were the *possessors* of the subsistence holding, he also stressed that the producers were not the *owners* of the means of production. Their possession was merely conditional upon the payment of surplus labour, a payment which could be ensured through legal enactment or even 'fixed by contract'. Feudal landed property, like that of the capitalist mode, is thus 'based on the monopoly of certain persons over definite parts of the globe'. The possession enjoyed by the peasant producers is thus a conditional possession: 'all rent is based upon the title to land as a right of exclusion'. The landlords' right to control peasant access to land is thus best understood in terms of the separation of the producers from the means of production, rather than a unity or a simple possession.[64]

If the payment of rent is determined by the landlords' rights of exclusion of the producers from the means of subsistence, it follows that 'there is no reason why the direct producer should be the legal subordinate and bondsman of the landlord'.[65] All that feudal relations of production require is some form of political power, which will guarantee the landlords the right to enforce their property rights, just as under capitalism the production of profit merely requires the state to guarantee the sanctity of certain forms of property and contract, rather than intervening directly to appropriate surplus labour.

If serfdom and bondage are not inherent parts of feudal social relations, then we need some specific historical explanation of why, in practice, feudalism has sometimes appeared in this form. One possible explanation may be illustrated by the case of seventeenth-century Bohemia, where the Thirty Years' War led to a population decline of over forty per cent. The result was a fall in grain prices and an increase in wages, due to a falling demand for food and a shortage of labour. The 'predictable' results of this situation were that the landlords introduced labour services, in order to produce grain, for the home and foreign market, without resort to expensive wage labour. Labour services were thus increased considerably from the mid-seventeenth century, backed by the lords' political and legal means of non-economic coercion. That the shortage of labour in late medieval England had the equally 'predictable' result of peasant freedom need not concern us for the moment. The important point is that the Bohemian landlords resorted to extra-economic means of obtaining feudal rent at a time of falling demand for land, in other words to obtain a level of rent above that which the market would have produced.[66]

We can see the opposite trend at work in late thirteenth-century England where the growth of population and the demand for land offered the landlords the possibility of increased rents. In practice, however, this possibility was not always fully realised, since the level of rents drawn from villein tenants was, on occasion, kept down by the power of custom, a force which, as Marx noted, could act in the interest of the peasant producers by limiting the extent of surplus extraction. The customary tenures of the unfree, which had once raised the level of rents above that which would have been set by market demand, became, in an age of land-hunger, a potential defence for the unfree tenant, compared with the terms which the landlord could obtain from contractual leasehold tenants.[67] However, both the unfree customary tenant and the free lease-hold tenant were paying feudal rents. Thus feudalism does not, *per se*, require serfdom, but may be conceived of in the broader sense of a mode of production where peasant producers pay rent (in the form of money, produce or labour services) to the landlords who enjoy a private monopoly of land. The specific form of rent and the degree of peasant freedom have to be established by empirical investigation, but do not themselves constitute defining features of this mode of production.

The capitalist mode of production

'Capital is money; capital is commodities': this is the beginning of Marx's analysis of capitalism, an analysis which begins in the realm of circulation and ends in the world of production and class relations. Marx distinguishes the circulation of capital from simple circulation. Under simple circulation the owner of a commodity (C) sells the commodity (e.g. a coat) for money (M), in order to buy another commodity (C) of the same value (e.g. a table). The circuit of simple circulation thus takes the form C–M–C, where the aim of the process is the consumption of a commodity, the enjoyment of its use-value, in this case of the table. In the circuit of capital it is not the enjoyment of use-values, but the accumulation of exchange-values, which is the aim of the whole process. Capital can thus be expressed by the formula M–C–M', where the initial capital (M) is used to buy commodities (C), which are then sold at a profit (M'), thus creating for the capitalist an augmented sum which provides the basis for a new and expanded round of accumulation.[68]

Buying in order to sell dear is most apparent in the form of merchant's capital, where the merchant buys a commodity in one place and, without changing its form, sells at a profit elsewhere. In this case capital remains penned within the sphere of circulation. As such it requires no other conditions of existence than the presence of trade, commodities and money. It is thus quite compatible with the existence of primitive communism, slavery or independent artisan and peasant production. In this sense Marx's definition of capital is very similar to that of Weber: a capitalist action is one which rests on the expectation of profit by the utilisation of the opportunities for exchange. Marx distinguishes the existence of capital from the existence of capitalism, i.e. a distinct mode of production with its own specific class relations, which emerge only when capital has established its sway over production. Capital may have existed 'in all forms of societies but the modern world has developed 'a

very different form of capitalism which appeared nowhere else: the rational capitalistic organization of (formally) free labour'.[69]

Thus, the fact that capitalism produces commodities does not, per se,
distinguish it from other modes of production. The important point is
that under capitalism 'being a commodity is the dominant and determinant characteristic' of the product. Under the feudal mode of production, by contrast, much of production is aimed not at the production of
commodities, to be sold for exchange-value, but at the production of
use-values, for direct consumption by peasant and feudal households.
There is thus a relative stability of grain consumption, with the result
that fluctuations in the harvest tend to be reflected mainly in the amount
of grain offered for sale. 'The extent to which products enter trade and
go through the merchants' hands depends on the mode of production
and reaches its maximum in the ultimate development of capitalist production where the product is produced solely as a commodity and not
as a direct means of subsistence.' Marx divides this product into two
departments: department one, which produces the means of production
which are productively consumed; and department two, which produces articles of consumption, luxury and subsistence goods, individu-
ally consumed by capitalists and workers.[70]

If articles of consumption, the necessities of life, are commodities it
follows that the producers have no independent means of subsistence.
They have no access to land (unlike peasants) to grow their own food.
Neither, under capitalism, do the producers own the tools and raw materials which would allow them to produce and sell on the market for
their own benefit (unlike the artisan). The formula of capital means that
'living labour stands in the relation of non-property to raw material,
instrument and means of subsistence required during the period of production'. The creation of capitalism can thus be 'nothing else than the
historical process of divorcing the producer from the means of production'. This separation of the producer from the means of subsistence
takes a specific form which requires the labourers to sell their labour-
power on the market. Labour under capitalism is thus 'free', but free in
a double sense: firstly in the sense that the producers are legally free, sellers of the commodity of labour-power, unlike slaves who are themselves
commodities; but secondly it means that they are 'unencumbered by any
means of production of their own'. Capitalism is not only the production of commodities, it is the production of commodities by the means
of the commodity of labour-power. Marx's conclusion is that we should
not see capital merely as money or as specific commodities, even though

capital may be embodied in these forms. Capital is not a thing, it is a social relation; it is this specific social relation which turns money, or commodities, into capital. The capitalist mode of production may thus be defined in terms of its objective-structural relations of production, relations between the capitalists, who buy commodities in order to accumulate more exchange-value, and the proletarians, the sellers of the commodity labour-power.[71]

All large-scale co-operative labour processes require a directing authority. Under capitalism, management is, initially, one of the functions of the owner of capital. Nevertheless, this managerial function is not merely part of a technical division of labour, it is itself the outcome of capital's existence as a specific social relation of production. 'It is not because he is a leader of industry that a man is a capitalist; on the contrary, he is a leader of industry because he is a capitalist. The leadership of industry is an attribute of capital, just as in feudal times the functions of general and judge were attributes of landed property.'[72] Capital is thus not merely an economic relation, but is also a relation of coercion through which the labourer is subordinated to the capitalist. Marx usefully distinguishes two forms of subordination of the producer: the formal and the real subsumption of labour to capital. The formal subsumption of labour is the first genuine subordination of the labourer to capital, although there may be prior relations between capital and labour. In India, for example, the usurer may lend money to the artisan with which to buy raw materials and tools. The interest paid by the artisan is a form of surplus value, representing in money form the surplus labour of the producer; but, nevertheless, usurer's capital does not, as yet, intervene in the process of production itself.[73]

Under the formal subsumption of labour the capitalist does directly intervene in the production process, but creates no real modification to the existing modes of labour. Capital merely takes over existing forms of the labour process. The only initial change for the producer is that work tends to become longer, and more continuous, than that of the independent artisan dependent on individual customers. The relation between capital and wage labour is established but, as yet, the capital involved is of a limited scale and the capitalists differ little from the workers 'in their education and their activities'. Since capital here is only small-scale, and merely takes over existing forms of production, it follows that there is only limited potential for making production more efficient. The capitalist thus has few opportunities to reduce the portion of the working day spent on producing the goods equivalent in value to the wages of the worker, i.e the time spent on 'necessary labour'. As a result, if the capitalist wishes to increase the amount of labour time over and above that spent on necessary labour, he can only do so by extending the working day. Marx refers to this as the production of absolute surplus labour.[74]

Marx distinguishes the production of absolute surplus labour from that of relative surplus labour. Under relative surplus labour the amount of surplus is increased not by lengthening the working day, but by reducing the proportion of labour time expended on necessary labour. In order to do this it is necessary for the capitalist to make production more efficient, by introducing more productive forms of the labour process or by increasing the intensity of the existing forms of labour. Naturally, there are limits on the extent to which the working day can be extended, or the intensity of labour increased. It is through productive innovation, with the application of science and technology to large-scale production, that surplus labour can most consistently be produced. Mechanisation is the most obvious example of this. Hand-spinners could only work one spindle at a time; the earliest spinning jenny was able to work twelve to eighteen spindles at a time. Increases in production thus cease to be dependent on human labour-power. Large-scale industry therefore converts the worker into a 'living appendage of the machine'.[75]

However, even before the mechanisation of the work process, the capitalist may be able to produce relative surplus labour, through an increase in the division of labour within the workshop which makes production more efficient. Marx refers to this stage of capitalism as 'manufacture', to distinguish it from industrial capitalism. At first, manufacture may simply take the shape of a formal subsumption of labour, with a number of workers in one workshop, all performing the same task under the supervision of the capitalist. Eventually, this will develop into a more complex division of labour, the classic example of which is Adam Smith's pin-making workshop, where the eighteen tasks involved in making a pin could be divided between ten or more labourers. Even with a limited division of labour these ten workers could make 48,000 pins a day, whereas individual or untrained labourers could not have produced twenty pins. The creation of relative surplus labour is thus the result of an increase in the productivity of labour effected by the application of science, the introduction of machinery, the use of economies of scale, or an increased division of labour. Through these means capital not only takes over, but also transforms, the nature of the labour process.

Marx refers to this as the real subsumption of labour to capital. The real subsumption of labour is both dependent upon, and in turn results in, the accumulation of capital and so creates a growing social division between employer and worker. Eventually, the capital required for production can no longer be provided by a single individual, but is supplied through the mechanism of the joint-stock company. As a result the functions of management and of the ownership of capital are divorced, so that the capitalist's profit becomes a mere reward for owning capital, 'entirely divorced from the function of direction of the labour process'.[76]

Marx thus offers an extremely useful objective-structural definition of capitalism in terms of its specific relations of production, a definition which has much in common with that of Weber. He draws a fruitful distinction between capital *per se* and capitalism as a mode of production, establishes the stages of capitalist development and emphasises the shift from the formal to real subsumption of labour, a shift which is the result of capitalism's inherent tendency to growing productivity, and which leads to a growing scale of capital and the eventual formation of joint-stock companies. However, in addition to this structural definition of capitalism Marx also offers a further definition: 'the second distinctive feature of the capitalist mode of production is the production of *surplus value* as the direct aim and determining motive of production'.[77] The capitalist mode of production is thus 'essentially the production of surplus value'.[78] Capitalism cannot merely be defined by the production of surplus labour, since the existence of surplus labour is common to all modes of production. For Marx, capitalism is distinguished by the production of surplus labour in specific form: surplus value. Marx's account of the creation of surplus value is an extension of his labour theory of value; it is this aspect of his account of capitalism which has drawn most criticism from later commentators.

Marx's analysis of the creation of surplus value begins with an account of commodity exchange, and a search for the common element which allows the diverse goods which come onto the market to be compared with each other. Marx finds the answer to this problem in the claim that all commodities are the product of human labour-power. He thus assumes, in volume I of *Capital*, that commodities are exchanged in proportion to the labour which they contain. This does not mean, however, that goods exchange at a value which is a direct reflection of the concrete labour time which they embody; a product containing five hours of skilled labour, for instance, will not be exchanged for a commodity which is the product of five hours of unskilled labour. Rather, the value of a commodity is to be measured in terms of the units of 'abstract, socially necessary labour' which it contains, so that the product of five hours of concrete skilled labour may be exchanged for the product of (perhaps) ten hours of unskilled labour. If the capitalist buys labour-power, tools and raw materials at their values, and then sells his product at its value, the problem is how to explain the existence of profit, i.e. how does the capitalist augment his values in the course of the production process? Marx's theory of surplus value is an attempt to answer this question.[79]

Marx assumes that the capitalist buys the commodities needed for the production process at their values. The value of these commodities is then passed on to the final product. The value of the commodity labour-power is the value of the goods needed for the reproduction of labour-power, for the maintenance of living labour. The value of labour-power is thus transferred to the final product along with the value of the instruments of labour and raw materials used up in the production process. How does profit arise from this process? Marx argues that the capitalist is lucky enough to find a commodity on the market which can be bought at its value, but which can then be used to create extra value; this commodity is human labour-power. The labourer's work is thus divided into two parts: in the first he or she creates the goods equivalent to the value of labour-power, i.e. equivalent to the cost of the wages bill. Marx calls this necessary labour time. In the second part, the worker creates commodities over and above the value of labour-power. It is this 'surplus labour' which is the origin of the capitalist's profit, a surplus labour embodied in the value of the commodities produced during this period. Marx thus distinguished between the capital which is spent on raw materials and instruments of labour on the one hand, and the capital which is spent on labour-power on the other. The former merely buys commodities whose value is fixed and is embodied in the value of the final product; the latter not only passes on value but also creates new value. Marx thus labels the former 'constant capital', and the latter 'variable capital'.

The rate of 'exploitation' (or the rate of surplus value) may thus be expressed as the ratio of necessary to surplus labour or, in value terms:

$$\frac{\text{Surplus value } (s)}{\text{Value of variable capital } (v)}$$

Marx claims that as capitalism becomes more efficient, there is a change in the composition of capital and constant capital (c) becomes more important, relative to the investment in human labour-power. The mass of employed labour declines as a proportion of the total capital invested. Yet only living labour-power can create surplus value during the production process. Thus a declining percentage of the total capital invested is capable of producing new value. Marx believed that there must, therefore, be a tendency for the overall rate of profit to decline, despite the existence of various counter-tendencies which slow down the rate of decline.[80]

Finally, it should be stressed that in volume III of *Capital* Marx abandons the assumption that commodities exchange at their value, an assumption which sufficed for his purposes in volume I. Marx argues that, in practice, commodities do not tend to be exchanged at their values, but rather at their prices of production, i.e. at their cost price plus the average rate of profit. With a given rate of suplus value, capitals which vary in their composition will have different rates of profit, e.g.

Capital A
$$60c + 40v + 40s = 140$$

Rate of surplus value = 100%: $\dfrac{40s}{40v}$

Rate of profit = 40%: $\dfrac{40s}{60c\ 40v}$

Capital B
$$40c + 60v + 60s = 160$$

Rate of surplus value = 100%: $\dfrac{60s}{60v}$

Rate of profit = 60%: $\dfrac{60s}{40v + 60c}$

Overall the average rate of profit is fifty per cent but in order to receive this average, capital A would have to receive a price of production of 150, i.e. obtain more value than it created, whilst capital B would only receive the average rate of profit by selling below its value:

Capital A
Price of production $(60c + 40v) =$ 100
Average rate of profit =   50%
Total price of production =   150

Capital B
Cost of production $(40c + 60v) =$ 100
Average rate of profit =   50%
Total price of production =   150

Nevertheless, within the two capitals total value (140 plus 160) is equal to total price (150 plus 150), and total profits (50 plus 50) are equal to total surplus value (40 plus 60). If total price is equal to total value, it follows that average price is equal to average value, even though individual commodities do not exchange at their value.[81]

Marx's theory thus explains the existence of surplus value through his labour theory of value, a theory which assumes that commodities can only be compared because they are the products of human labour-power, of which they embody a greater or lesser amount. It is the assumption that human-power is the source of all value which is the basis of his claim that only variable capital can create surplus value. It follows that if production were to be totally automated there would be no variable capital, no surplus value and hence no profits.[82]

Unfortunately almost every step of Marx's argument is open to damning criticism. Firstly, it cannot be assumed that being the product of labour is the only common property of commodities and the basis of their comparison. One could equally say that all commodities are scarce in proportion to demand, or that they are all subject to supply and demand in the market place.[83] Secondly, Marx's analysis of the transformation of values into prices hinges on his definition of the rate of profit, $\frac{s}{c+v}$. However, the actual rate of profit received by any individual capitalist is dependent on the price of the inputs purchased by the capitalist compared with the price of the outputs of the production process. If prices diverge from values, as Marx insists that they do, it follows that $\frac{s}{c+v}$ is not the rate of profit. This definition of the rate of profit in value terms is, in practice, 'of no concern to capitalists, it is unknown to capitalists and there is no force acting to make it equal between industries'. It is thus redundant in the analysis of the capitalist production process, where the rate of profit cannot be established prior to the existence of prices.[84] Even if $\frac{s}{c+v}$ was the rate of profit, Marx nowhere shows that it will eventually decline, i.e. that this tendency will outweigh its counter-tendencies.[85] Far from profits being dependent on the presence of variable capital (living labour-power), it is possible to show that positive profits are quite compatible with a situation of full automation, i.e. of zero labour costs.[86]

Finally, whilst it is possible to express a given economy in terms of the labour values of its inputs and outputs, it is not possible to deduce prices or profits from such values. Total value does not equal total price, total profits do not equal total surplus value and the value rate of profit does not equal the price rate of profit. The measurement of an economy in value terms is thus possible but not particularly fruitful, given that it is money prices and profits which form the basis for the functioning of the capitalist economy.[87] Thus, far from the labour theory of value being the essential aspect of Marx's analysis of capitalism[88] it is, in practice, the most redundant part of his system. It is, however, possible to retain Marx's definition of capitalism in terms of its specific relations of production, whilst rejecting his labour theory of value and the conclusions which he draws from it.

'Post-capitalist' societies

The problems involved in attempting to define the class relations of a mode of production in purely 'economic' terms, free of any political or ideological elements, are apparent in Marxist characterisations of 'post-capitalist' societies such as the Soviet Union or China. How can we define the social relations of a country such as the Soviet Union? As a variety of capitalism? As socialism? Or in terms of some other mode of production?

Marx himself had little to say about the nature of future socialist society but, in general, he presented a two stage scheme. The first, or lower, stage of communism, usually labelled as 'socialism' or the 'dictatorship of the proletariat', is marked by the abolition of private property in the means of production, and their socialisation through their ownership by the proletarian state. The nature of the state thus becomes crucial for an understanding of the social relations of the socialist mode of production. For Marx a 'true' state is one which defends the interests of a minority ruling class at the expense of the bulk of the population. In this sense even a democratic republic constitutes the dictatorship of the bourgeoisie, i.e. the political rule of a particular class. The dictatorship of the proletariat would be more, not less, democratic than the bourgeois republic, through its encouragement of popular participation in political affairs. The state would cease to be a separate body imposed on society from without. Government would be by elected representatives, serving for short periods and under the right of recall. Government members would be proletarian in origin, whilst public servants would only receive workers' wages, judges would be elected and the professional standing army would be replaced by a people's militia. Political power would still be needed to establish the socialisation of the means of production against the resistance of the capitalists but, since this power would no longer impose the interests of a minority upon the rest of society, it would cease to be a 'true' state and would become the state's dissolving form. The permanent divide of ruler and ruled would be overcome by the social ownership of the economy and popular control of the government.

Once the resistance of the capitalists had finally been defeated, and the economy reorganised to produce for social need, there would no longer be any need for a political power set over the population and the state would wither away. The stage would be set for the higher stage of social production ('communism'), where the individual was no longer rewarded according to work done, but according to social need. Naturally, this would involve the redistribution of society's wealth to those with the greatest need. Society would still need a surplus over and above the immediate needs of the producers in order to provide insurance against disaster, to maintain and expand the level of output and to support an administration and social services. Socialism is thus defined not by the absence of surplus labour, but by its social appropriation.[89]

How does this analysis help us to understand the social relations of the Soviet Union? Are Soviet relations of production those of capitalism, of socialism, of the transitional stage between the two, or of some other mode of production? The Soviet Union does not claim, of course, to have reached the higher stage of communism, and we may agree that in the Soviet Union the state has not withered away, scarcity has not been abolished and individuals are not rewarded according to personal need, so this possibility may be discounted. Neither does it seem very useful to describe the Soviet Union as 'capitalist', given its lack of private property in the means of production, its absence of a hereditary capitalist class, shareholders and so on. The official Soviet position is that 'a developed socialist society has been built in the Soviet Union' and that this 'victorious socialism' is now building the base for the higher stage of communism.[90] However, many socialists have been unwilling to accept at face value the pronouncements of the Soviet Union's ruling elite. Since the time of Kautsky, Marxists have argued that the lack of democracy and the persistent social inequalities of such 'post-capitalist' societies disqualify them from the label of 'socialism'.[91] In itself the name we give to these societies is not particularly important; what is significant is how we conceive of their relations of production and dominant mode of production.

241

The classic attempt to characterise the Soviet Union from a Marxist position is that offered by Trotsky in *The Revolution Betrayed*. Trotsky offers two main reasons why the Soviet Union should not be seen as a socialist society. The first is based on the productive force determinist claim that a society's relations of production correspond to the level of its productive forces. Socialism corresponds to a level of social productivity higher than that of capitalism; the Soviet economy has not yet caught up with that of the more advanced capitalist world; it follows that the Soviet Union does not have the level of productive forces required for socialism, but is rather a preparatory regime, transitional from capitalism to socialism.[92] We have already rejected this form of productive force determinism. If we are to characterise the Soviet Union's mode of production, we must do so not in terms of its level of productivity, but rather by its dominant relations of production. This brings us on to Trotsky's second reason for rejecting the claim that the Soviet Union is socialist.

Trotsky defines the social relations of the Soviet Union as those of a 'workers' state' which is defined by the state monopoly of industry, agri-culture and trade. However, the backward conditions of Russia at the time of the Bolshevik Revolution (its lack of industrial development, the predominance of peasant production), the subsequent dispersal of the working-class vanguard in the Civil War, the bureaucratisation of the party and the international isolation of the Revolution, had all led to the degeneration of the workers' state and the transformation of the state bureaucracy into an 'all powerful ruling caste'. That the Soviet Union is a 'degenerate' workers' state implies that it was once healthy, which is in itself a controversial claim. It is less problematical to see Trotsky's definition of the Soviet Union as that of a 'deformed workers' state', 'a social formation characterised by the institutional exclusion of the working class from the administration of its own state, an administrative monopoly for the party-state bureaucracy itself'. The ruling class of the Soviet Union is the proletariat, just as under capitalism it is the capital-ist ruling class which defends its property through the state. In the same way that the French bourgeoisie under Napoleon III was excluded from political power whilst the state continued to guarantee bourgeois prop-erty, so, under 'Soviet Bonapartism', the proletariat is the ruling class and yet is denied direct political power.[93]

Trotsky rejected alternative characterisations of the Soviet Union as 'state capitalist', where the bureaucracy constitutes a new ruling class through its monopoly of state power. The bureaucracy does not depend for its power on the rise of a new form of social property, but is obliged to defend the form of property of the workers' state established by the proletarian revolution. The bureaucrats cannot be described as 'state capitalists', since they possess no hereditary privilege, no private property and own no stocks and bonds. The bureaucracy enjoys its privileges as an abuse of power, and is obliged to pretend that it has no real social existence.[94]

This analysis presents a number of problems. Firstly, it is not legitimate to compare the position of the proletariat in the Soviet Union with that of the capitalist ruling class under Napoleon III. Under capitalism the bourgeoisie is guaranteed wealth, influence and power by its class position and consequent control of society's means of production. It does not have to possess government office in order for it to be perceived as the main interest group in society, an interest group whose decisions will have a massive effect on government policies and finances. The social and economic power of the bourgeoisie provides a counter-weight to the political power of the state apparatus but, as Trotsky himself admitted, the proletariat have no such counter-weight against the political power of the bureaucracy. As a result the bureaucracy forms the sole privileged and commanding stratum of Soviet society, a monopoly of power which cannot be compared with that of the capitalist Bonapartist state.[95]

The second weakness of Trotsky's rejection of the characterisation of the Soviet Union as 'state capitalist' is his emphasis on the legal expression of property relations. The bureaucracy has no private property and its privileges have no validation of law. Only if the bureaucracy's position was legalised would the liquidation of the gains of the proletarian revolution be secured.[96] But this is to overemphasise the importance of law and of private property as the basis for class rule. Trotsky argues that the bureaucracy's lack of private property means that it cannot be characterised as a class. Yet similarly whilst the Spartan citizens, Mughal mansabdars and medieval ecclesiastical landlords did not enjoy absolute private property rights, it would be reasonable to see their societies as class societies. Property rights may take the form of effective control, rather than total private ownership. It is this effective control which the Soviet bureaucracy obtains by virtue of its monopoly of political power. Lack of private property does not, in itself, make the Soviet Union into a workers' state, either deformed or healthy.

Finally, Trotsky saw the appropriation of power by the bureaucracy as a transitional, rather than as an enduring, form of social organisation. The Soviet Union would either move forward to 'true' socalism, or revert to capitalism and private property in the means of production.[97] Yet at the moment neither the revolutionary seizure of power by the proletariat, nor the restoration of capitalism, seems a very likely option for the Soviet Union. On the contrary, even dissidents find Soviet society depressingly stable.[98] The Soviet Union is thus not a transitional but a new form of society. If this is the case how are we to define its relations of production?

The Soviet Union is best conceptualised as a new form of class society. State ownership of the means of production is not, in itself, sufficient to define a society as socialist. Where political power is monopolised by the state's own functionaries and administrators, these bureaucrats become, in effect, the proprietors of the means of production. The Soviet Union is thus characterised by many writers as a 'state capitalist' society ruled over by a new class, the 'state bourgeoisie', which controls the entire economic, political and social life of the nation. Naturally there are differences between the branches of this elite (the party, state, military, industry, the security services), just as there are differences between the fractions of the bourgeoisie under capitalism; but, nevertheless, this elite can be seen as a new ruling class, controlled by no one and subject to no appeal.[99]

Thus, in the Soviet Union, the state and political power are not merely 'superstructural', but constitute an integral part of social relations of production. Power is a vital constituent of class relations in a society where privilege is based not on the ownership of private property, but on the allocation of resources by administrative decision. It is this political power which allows the administrative elite its privileges: flats; country cottages; holidays; cars; better schools; consumer goods; special shops; and so on. We may thus characterise the specific form of 'surplus labour', or form of income, of the Soviet ruling class as that of 'surplus revenue', i.e. a share of society's wealth which accrues to the bureaucracy through its political power, over and above the share which would have to be allocated as socially necessary to maintain administrators, managers and generals. The label which we give to this society is not particularly important, although it may be misleading to describe the Soviet elite as a 'bourgeoisie', given that it owes its privileges to a position in a graded hierarchy of power and to its administrative resources. Once more this mode of production must be defined in terms of its class of producers, the nature of its ruling class and the form taken by the income of that class.[100]

Conclusion

The concept of a mode of production is extremely useful in allowing us to distinguish between societies, provided that we do not attempt to force all societies into the categories listed by Marx in the 1859 'Preface'. It is not Marx's specific historical analyses, but rather his structural definition of class through the concept of the relations of production, which provides the tools which allow us to investigate particular societies in terms of their dominant mode of production. Marx's theory thus provides us with the concepts which would allow us to construct the concepts of modes of production of which Marx himself was unaware.

The concept of a specific mode of production is not the direct product of generalisation from a particular historical society, but this does not mean that the concepts of modes of production can 'only be evaluated in theoretical terms'.[101] Certainly it is preferable to define modes of production with theoretical coherence but, in the final analysis, such concepts will not prove right or wrong in the abstract, but as more or less useful in the practice of describing specific social formations and explaining their transformation. The examples given in this chapter show that the concept of mode of production does offer a coherent classification of social forms; the analysis of the transition from feudalism to capitalism offered in Chapter 8 shows that the emphasis on class and on class struggle, inherent to a mode of production analysis, functions not merely descriptively, but also as a vital explanation of long-term historical change.

Finally, it must be stressed that the empirical examples discussed in this chapter support the theoretical conclusions of Chapter 9, i.e. that the social relations of production cannot be conceptualised merely as economic phenomena, but are also constituted by politics and by ideology. The concept of class involves relations of domination and subordination. Political power, the law and ideology are not merely derivative from the relations of production, but may form integral elements of those relations. For Marx's claims for the determination of the social 'superstructure' by its 'base' to have any plausibility the base cannot be defined in narrow, economic terms. The Marxist model, in its strongest version, claims that the relations of production in a broad sense determine those aspects of the state and ideology which are not a constitutive part of the relations of production. It is to these claims that we must now turn.

Notes

1 L. Althusser & E. Balibar, *Reading Capital* (London, 1975), pp. 97, 207.
2 T. Lovell, *Pictures of Reality* (London, 1980), pp. 27–8; R. Mishra, 'Technology and social structure in Marx's theory: an exploratory analysis, *Science and Society* XLIII (1979), p. 134; E. P. Thompson, *The Poverty of Theory* (London, 1978), p. 346.
3 See above, pp. 98–9, 110.
4 K. Marx, *Capital*, vol. I (London, 1977), p. 209.
5 B. Hindess & P. Q. Hirst, *Pre-capitalist Modes of Production* (London, 1975), p. 22; G. A. Cohen, *Karl Marx's Theory of History: A Defence* (London, 1978), pp. 82–3.
6 Marx, *Capital*, vol. I, p. 313.
7 G. Dalton, 'How exactly are peasants "exploited"?', *American Anthropologist* LXXVI (1974), pp. 553–61. See the ensuing debate, ibid., LXXVII (1975), pp. 337–8; LXXVIII (1976), pp. 639–42; LXXIX (1977), pp. 115–19.
8 Marx, *Capital*, vol. I, pp. 227–9.
9 Ibid., pp. 208–9.
10 K. Marx & F. Engels, *Collected Works*, vol. V (1976), p. 409 (*The German Ideology*).
11 P. Sloan, *Marx and the Orthodox Economists* (Oxford, 1973), pp. 44–5.
12 D. C. North & R. P. Thomas, 'The rise and fall of the manorial system: a theoretical model', *Journal of Economic History* XXXI (1971), pp. 777–803.
13 J. E. Roemer, *A General Theory of Exploitation and Class* (Cambridge, Mass., 1982), especially Chapter 7.
14 S. Fenoaltea, 'The rise and fall of a theoretical model: the manorial system', *Journal of Economic History* XXXV (1975), pp. 386–409.
15 Roemer, *A General Theory of Exploitation and Class*, p. 237.
16 Ibid., pp. 192–6.
17 Ibid., Chs. 7–9, especially pp. 265 ff.
18 Ibid.
19 B. Moore, *The Social Origins of Dictatorship and Democracy* (Harmondsworth, 1973), p. 471, and see Fenoaltea as in n. 14.
20 W. Langland, *Piers the Plowman* (Harmondsworth, 1974), p. 123.
21 K. Marx, *Capital*, vol. II (London, 1974), pp. 36–7.
22 Althusser & Balibar, *Reading Capital*, pp. 212–16.
23 Cohen, *Karl Marx's Theory of History*, pp. 63–6; J. Elster, *Making Sense of Marx* (Cambridge, 1985), p. 254; M. Finley, *The Ancient Economy* (London, 1979), p. 49.
24 Elster, *Making Sense of Marx*, p. 231; Cohen, *Karl Marx's Theory of History*, p. 73.
25 Marx & Engels, *Collected Works*, vol. V, p. 77 (*The German Ideology*); K. Marx, *The Poverty of Philosophy* (Moscow, 1973), p. 150.
26 Thompson, *The Poverty of Theory*, pp. 298–9; idem, *The Making of the English Working Class* (Harmondsworth, 1972), pp. 9–10.
27 Cohen, *Karl Marx's Theory of History*, pp. 73–7; P. Anderson, *Arguments within English Marxism* (London, 1980), pp. 39–43.
28 K. Marx, *Pre-capitalist Economic Formations* (London, 1975), pp. 68, 97–9; K. Marx, *Capital*, vol. III (London, 1974), pp. 614–15, 782–813, 878; Hindess & Hirst, *Pre-capitalist Modes of Production*, p. 221; M. Bloch, *Marxism and Anthropology* (Oxford, 1983), pp. 10, 151–2.
29 F. Engels, *The Origin of the Family, Private Property and the State* (Moscow, 1968), pp. 92, 95–8, 168–70, 174–5.

30 Bloch, *Marxism and Anthropology*, pp. 16–19, 54, 162.

31 Marx & Engels, *Collected Works*, vol. V, pp. 32–3, 42, 46, 50 (*The German Ideology*); Marx, *Pre-capitalist Economic Formations*, pp. 68–9, 90–1.

32 Bloch, *Marxism and Anthropology*, p. 257.

33 Engels, *The Origin of the Family, Private Property and the State*, especially Chs. 1–3, 9.

34 Marx & Engels, *Collected Works*, vol. V, p. 33 (*The German Ideology*); Marx, *Pre-capitalist Economic Formations*, pp. 69–70.

35 M. Godelier, *Perspectives in Marxist Anthropology* (Cambridge, 1977), pp. 51–8; Hindess & Hirst, *Pre-capitalist Modes of Production*, pp. 44–7.

36 Ibid., pp. 46–50; C. Meillassoux, *Anthropologie Economique des Gouru de Côte d'Ivoire* (Paris, 1964), especially pp. 98–9, 123–5, 172, 188; E. Terray, *Marxism and 'Primitive' Societies* (New York, 1972), pp. 93 ff.

37 M. Godelier, 'Social hierarchies among the Baruya of New Guinea' in A. Strathern (ed.), *Inequality in New Guinea Highland Societies* (Cambridge, 1982), especially pp. 6, 15–20.

38 Godelier, *Perspectives in Marxist Anthropology*, pp. 81–7, 115–16.

39 N. Modjeska, 'Production and inequality: perspectives from central New Guinea' in Strathern (ed.), *Inequality in New Guinea Highland Societies*, p. 51.

40 K. Marx, *A Contribution to the Critique of Political Economy* (London, 1971), pp. 21, 33; Marx, *Pre-capitalist Economic Formations*, pp. 69–70; Marx, *Capital*, vol. III, p. 634. See also A. M. Bailey & J. R. Llobera (eds.), *The Asiatic Mode of Production* (London, 1981); H. Lubasz, 'Marx's concept of the Asiatic mode of production: a generic analysis', *Economy and Society* XIII (1984), pp. 456–83; S. Avineri (ed.), *Karl Marx on Colonialism and Modernization* (New York, 1969).

41 Godelier, *Perspectives in Marxist Anthropology*, pp. 64, 116–17; M. Godelier, 'The Asiatic mode of production' in Bailey & Llobera, *The Asiatic Mode of Production*, p. 264; P. Anderson, *Lineages of the Absolutist State* (London, 1979), pp. 405–7, 486.

42 Anderson, ibid., p. 491; K. Marx, *Surveys From Exile* (Harmondsworth, 1973), p. 303.

43 Godelier, 'The Asiatic mode of production', p. 267.

44 Marx, *Capital*, vol. III, p. 791.

45 Anderson, *Lineages of the Absolutist State*, pp. 475, 482–3, 497, 518–19.

46 Marx explained the state ownership of land as the result of Islamic influence, rather than hydraulic agriculture, in a letter of 14.6.1853: K. Marx & F. Engels, *Selected Correspondence* (Moscow, 1975), p. 80.

47 F. W. Walbank, *The Decline of the Roman Empire in the West* (London, 1946); idem, *The Awful Revolution* (Liverpool, 1969). See also references in notes below. The spring 1975 edition of the journal *Arethusa* (volume VIII, no. 1) was devoted to the subject of Marxism and the Ancient World.

48 Marx & Engels, *Collected Works*, vol. V, pp. 32–3, 84, 89 (*The German Ideology*); Marx, *Capital*, vol. III, pp. 331–2; K. Marx & F. Engels, *Collected Works*, vol. IV (London, 1975), p. 113 (*The Holy Family*); K. Marx, *The Eighteenth Brumaire of Louis Bonaparte* (Moscow, 1972), p. 6.

49 Finley, *The Ancient Economy*, p. 49; Marx, *Pre-capitalist Economic Formations*, p. 87; K. Marx, *Wage Labour and Capital* (Moscow, 1970), p. 21.

50 G. E. M. de Ste Croix, *The Class Struggle in the Ancient Greek World* (London, 1981). For appreciative reviews see R. Browning, 'The class struggle in Ancient Greece', *Past and Present* 100 (1981), pp. 147–156; P. Anderson, 'Class struggle in the

ancient world', *History Workshop* 16 (autumn 1983), pp. 57–73; P. A. Brunt, 'A Marxist view of Roman history', *Journal of Roman Studies* LXXII (1982), pp. 158–63.

51 De Ste Croix, *The Class Struggle in the Ancient Greek World*, pp. 52, 54, 113, 179; E. Wood, 'Marxism and Ancient Greece', *History Workshop* 11 (spring 1981), pp. 10–11, 16–18; R. H. Hilton, *Bond Men Made Free* (London, 1977), p. 10; K. Hopkins, *Conquerors and Slaves* (Cambridge, 1980), p. 7. See Marx, *Capital*, vol. III, p. 806: peasant proprietorship was 'the economic foundation of society during the best periods of classical antiquity'. M. I. Finley argues that 'slaves provided the bulk of the immediate income from property … of the elites' in *Ancient Slavery and Modern Ideology* (London, 1980), p. 82.

52 De Ste Croix, *The Class Struggle in the Ancient Greek World*, pp. 39, 43, 44, 173, 179; P. Anderson, *Passages from Antiquity to Feudalism* (London, 1977), p. 22; B. D. Shaw, 'Anatomy of the vampire bat', *Economy and Society* XIII (1984), pp. 221–8.

53 De Ste Croix, *The Class Struggle in the Ancient Greek World*, pp. 52, 113, 173.

54 Ibid., pp. 149, 210, 222 ff.

55 Ibid., pp. 7–9; B. Hindess & P. Q. Hirst, *Mode of Production and Social Formation* (London, 1977), p. 41.

56 Marx, *Pre-capitalist Economic Formations*, pp. 71, 77–8; Marx & Engels, *Collected Works*, vol. V, pp. 33–4 (*The German Ideology*); Hindess & Hirst, *Pre-capitalist Modes of Production*, pp. 82–5; De Ste Croix, *The Class Struggle in the Ancient Greek World*, pp. 45–50, 85–95.

57 Hindess & Hirst, *Mode of Production and Social Formation*, pp. 40–1; Hindess & Hirst, *Pre-capitalist Modes of Production*, pp. 85–6; De Ste Croix, *The Class Struggle in the Ancient Greek World*, pp. 113, 149.

58 Ibid., pp. 114–20, 141.

59 Ibid., pp. 250–1; C. Wickham, 'The other transition: from the ancient world to feudalism', *Past and Present* 103 (1984), pp. 9, 20, 27–8.

60 S. Amin, *Unequal Development* (Hassocks, 1976), pp. 13–16.

61 D. Thorner, 'Peasant economy as a category in economic history', in T. Shanin (ed.), *Peasants and Peasant Societies* (Harmondsworth, 1975), pp. 202–8.

62 Marx, *Capital*, vol. III, pp. 616–17, 782–3, 790–1, 832, 883; Anderson, *Passages from Antiquity to Feudalism*, pp. 147–53.

63 R. H. Hilton, 'Introduction' to R. H. Hilton *et al.*, *The Transition from Feudalism to Capitalism* (London, 1976), p. 14; idem., 'Peasant movements in England before 1381', *Economic History Review* second series II (1949–50), pp. 117–22; E. A. Kosminsky, *Studies in the Agrarian History of England in the Thirteenth Century* (Oxford, 1956).

64 Marx, *Capital*, vol. III, pp. 615–25, 793–5, 799; J. E. Martin, *Feudalism to Capitalism* (London, 1983), Ch. 1; Hindess & Hirst, *Pre-capitalist Modes of Production*, Ch. 5.

65 Hindess & Hirst, ibid., p. 236.

66 A. Kuma, 'Agrarian class structure and economic development in pre-industrial Bohemia', *Past and Present* 85 (1979), pp. 52–3; C. Dyer, 'A re-distribution of incomes in fifteenth century England', *Past and Present* 39 (1969), pp. 11–33.

67 J. Hatcher, 'English serfdom and villeinage: towards a reassessment', *Past and Present* 90 (1981), pp. 21–7; Marx, *Capital*, vol. III, pp. 793–4.

68 Marx, *Capital*, vol. I, pp. 146–7, 151–2, 555, 558.

69 Marx, *Capital*, vol. III, pp. 325–6; M. Weber, *The Protestant Ethic and the Spirit of*

Capitalism (London, 1978), pp. 17, 21.

70 Marx, *Capital*, vol. III, pp. 325, 879; W. Kula, *An Economic Theory of the Feudal System* (London, 1976), p. 82; Marx, *Capital*, vol. II, p. 399.

71 Marx, *Pre-capitalist Economic Formations*, pp. 67, 99, 119–20; Marx, *Capital*, vol. I, pp. 165, 668; Marx, *Capital*, vol. III, p. 879; Marx, *Wage Labour and Capital*, pp. 28–9.

72 K. Marx, *Capital*, vol. I (Harmondsworth, 1976; Pelican edn), pp. 424–5, 448–51.

73 *Ibid.*, pp. 1020, 1023.

74 *Ibid.*, pp. 324, 1020–1.

75 *Ibid.*, pp. 495, 614, 1024–5, 1035; Marx, *Grundrisse*, p. 389.

76 Marx, *Capital*, vol. I (Pelican edn), pp. 439, 453, 456; A. Smith, *The Wealth of Nations* (Harmondsworth, 1974), pp. 109–10.

77 Marx, *Capital*, vol. III, p. 880.

78 Marx, *Capital*, vol. I (London, 1977), p. 253.

79 *Ibid.*, pp. 46–7, 51, 163.

80 *Ibid.*, pp. 164, 167, 202, 574; Marx, *Capital*, vol. III, pp. 157, 211 ff; 232 ff.

81 Marx, *Capital*, vol. III, pp. 142 ff. An initial difficulty with Marx's analysis is that he expresses outputs of the production process in prices of production, but expresses inputs in value terms. The problem is, of course, that the outputs of one industry are the inputs of another. Marx's scheme would thus require a particular product to have a different price when sold as an output, from when it is bought as an input, an impossibility, of course, as sale and purchase are two aspects of the same transaction. I. Steedman, *Marx after Sraffa* (London, 1977), pp. 43–4.

82 Marx, *Capital*, vol. I (London, 1977), pp. 45, 202; T. Morris-Suzuki, 'Robots and capitalism', *New Left Review* 147 (September–October 1984), pp. 110, 114.

83 E. von Bohm-Bawerk, *Karl Marx and the Close of his System*, edited by P. M. Sweezy (London, 1975), p. 75.

84 Steedman, *Marx after Sraffa*, pp. 30–1; I. Steedman *et al.*, *The Value Controversy* (London, 1981), p. 17.

85 G. Hodgson, *Trotsky and Fatalistic Marxism* (Nottingham, 1975), p. 71.

86 I. Steedman, 'Robots and capitalism', *New Left Review* 151 (May–June 1985), pp. 26–7.

87 I. Steedman, 'Value, price and profit', *New Left Review* 90 (March–April 1975), pp. 71–80.

88 S. Amin, *The Law of Value and Historical Materialism* (New York, 1978), pp. 3, 17–18.

89 K. Marx, *The Civil War in France* (Peking, 1970); K. Marx, *Critique of the Gotha Programme* (Moscow, 1971); A. Nove, *The Economics of Feasible Socialism* (London, 1983), part 1.

90 L. I. Brezhnev, *The Fiftieth Anniversary of the Union of Soviet Socialist Republics* (Moscow, 1972), pp. 83–4.

91 M. Salvadori, *Karl Kautsky and the Socialist Revolution 1880–1938* (London, 1979), Chs. 8, 9. For a general survey of such views see P. Bellis, *Marxism and the U.S.S.R.* (London, 1979).

92 L. Trotsky, *The Revolution Betrayed* (London, 1967), pp. 46–8.

93 *Ibid.*, pp. 248–9, 277–9; L. Trotsky, *The Death Agony of Capitalism and the Tasks of the*

Fourth International (London, 1970), p. 47; Bellis, Marxism and the U.S.S.R., p. 69.

94 Trotsky, The Revolution Betrayed, pp. 248–50.

95 Ibid., pp. 248–9; A. Nove, Political Economy and Soviet Socialism (London, 1979), pp. 213–14.

96 Trotsky, The Revolution Betrayed, pp. 248–50.

97 Ibid., pp. 249–54; Bellis, Marxism and the U.S.S.R., p. 236.

98 Although this was far too pessimistic an assessment of the possibilities for change within Soviet society, the analysis offered here does provide a valid description of the social relations of the Soviet Union at the time and of those societies which still claim to be socialist (S.R., 1998).

99 Ibid., Chs. 4–6; T. Cliff, State Capitalism in Russia (London, 1974); M. Djilas, The New Class (London, 1957).

100 Nove, Political Economy and Soviet Socialism, Ch. 12; V. K. Kusin, 'A propos Alec Nove's search for a class label', Soviet Studies XXVIII (1976), pp. 274–5.

101 Hindess & Hirst, Pre-capitalist Modes of Production, pp. 2–3.

CHAPTER 11

The political superstructure

The state as an 'instrument' of class rule

The state may be defined in terms of those institutions which go to make it up or in terms of the social functions which it serves. A classic definition of the former type is Weber's famous claim that the state is 'a human community that (successfully) claims the monopoly of legitimate use of force within a given territory'. Marxists have, on occasion, offered a similar institutional definition of the state. Weber himself cited Trotsky's comment at Brest-Litovsk that 'every state is founded on force', whilst Lenin defined the state as 'a special apparatus for the systematic application of force and the subjugation of people by force'. In *The Origin of the Family, Private Property and the State*, Engels offers a definition of the state similar to that of Weber. The state is a special authority with its army, prisons, taxes and officials, a separate public power, distinct from the mass of the people. Like Weber, Engels stressed that territory distinguishes a state from the social organisation of the tribe, whose members are united by ties of kinship.[1]

Where Marxism differs from other forms of social theory is in the emphasis which it gives to certain of the state's functions. Marxism offers a functional, as well as an institutional, definition of the state. Weber denied that the state can be defined in terms of its functions, since political institutions could carry out almost any task, and there is no task which is exclusive and peculiar to political organisations.[2] Marxists, however, have argued that despite the range of tasks undertaken by the state, it does have one primary and defining function: 'the state is a machine for maintaining the rule of one class over another';[3] the state gives the economic interests of the ruling class 'a universal expression as the will of the state, as law, an expression which is always determined by the relations of this class';[4] the state is 'the state of the most powerful, economically dominant class, which, through the medium of the state, becomes the politically dominant class, and thus acquires new means of holding down and exploiting the oppressed class'.[5]

It is useful to distinguish between two Marxist approaches to the state. The first of these approaches is to see the state as, in normal circumstances, the instrument of the ruling class: 'the state of antiquity was above all the state of the slave owners for holding down the slaves, as the feudal state was the organ of the nobility for holding down the peasant serfs and bondsmen ...'.[6] The social power of the propertied class of each mode of production thus 'has its practical-idealistic expression in each case in the form of the state, and therefore every revolutionary struggle is directed against a class which till then has been in power'.[7] The second approach, which Draper labels Marx's 'general theory of the state', is not that the state is always the direct instrument of the propertied class, but that, in general, the nature of the state is determined by the prevailing social conditions; political forms 'correspond' to the form taken by social relations. Those cases where the state is a direct instrument of the ruling class are merely special instances of this general determination of the political by the social.[8]

Miliband has argued that the first of these approaches, the instrumentalist conception that the state acts 'at the behest' of the dominant class, is 'a vulgar deformation of the thought of Marx and Engels'. When Marx and Engels argued that the modern state is 'but a committee for managing the common affairs of the whole bourgeoisie', they made a distinction between the interests of the individual capitalist and the capitalist class as a whole. The state can only meet these common interests if it enjoys a certain degree of autonomy from the bourgeoisie; the notion of a certain degree of autonomy of the state is 'embedded in the definition' of the state as an intrinsic part of it.[9]

In fact it would not be a vulgarisation of the thought of Marx and Engels to argue that, in some of their works, they offer an analysis which allows the capitalist state only a minimal autonomy with regard to the capitalist class and that these writings present the state as 'an instrument of exploitation of wage labour by capital'.[10] This is particularly true of their analysis of the bourgeois state which they offered in the years before Marx's *Eighteenth Brumaire of Louis Bonaparte* (1852). In the 1840s Marx and Engels argued that the fusion of bourgeois interest and state power was the norm in the more advanced capitalist societies: 'the independence of the state is only found nowadays in those countries where the estates have

252

not yet fully developed into classes', that is, where the legal orders of feudalism have not given way to the economic classes of capitalism. The modern state is thus 'nothing more than the form of organisation which the bourgeoisie is compelled to adopt, both for internal and external purposes, for the mutual guarantee of their property and interests'. The state is the form of political organisation through which the capitalist class asserts its common interests, and through which their rule is given general expression. Marx was concerned to refute Stirner's claim that the state is a 'third force' over and against the ruling class, that 'the state alone is the mighty one'. On the contrary, Marx argued that the modern state lacks independence and has to beg from the bourgeoisie who, eventually, 'buy up' the state.[11] Through the bourgeois revolutions the capitalist class established political constitutions most suitable for its own development and a form of law which was the will of that class 'made into a law for all'. Political power, in short, 'is merely the organized power of one class for oppressing another'.[12]

This 'instrumentalist' view of the state can be seen in Marx's *The Class Struggles in France* (1850), where Marx argues that the French state was unstable after 1815 precisely because it was not the expression of the general needs of the bourgeoisie, a class which was riven by economic and political divisions. Under the restored monarchy it was the large landed proprietors who exercised their influence through the Bourbon rule. Under the July monarchy created by the 1830 revolution it was, above all, the finance aristocracy which used the state for its own interests, interests which led to opposition not only from peasants, workers and the petty bourgeoisie, but also from within the bourgeoisie, and in particular from the industrial bourgeoisie. The task of the revolution of February 1848 was thus to create a republic in which all of the propertied classes entered into political power. Bourgeois rule thus obtained a complete rather than merely a partial form, a form which was 'the perfected and clearly expressed rule of the whole bourgeoisie' which allowed it to neutralise the economic and political divisions which threatened to undermine its own rule.[13]

Thus when Miliband argues that a certain degree of autonomy is built into the concept of the state, he faces the danger of lapsing into tautology. The so-called 'autonomy' of the state becomes, in this case, not an autonomy of interest or of personnel, but merely an institutional separation between the individual members of the bourgeoisie and the institutions of the state: 'The relative autonomy of the bourgeois state is, in other words, nothing more than the relative autonomy enjoyed by virtually any "executive committee" *vis-à-vis* the wider constituency or body whose purposes it serves.'[14] The autonomy of the state becomes nothing more than a functional specialisation, inherent in the idea of the state as a separate public institution. This notion can hardly be used to refute the claim that Marx and Engels offered, at least in their writings of the 1840s, a fairly straightforward 'instrumentalist' conception of the bourgeois state.

The social determination of the political

In addition to his 'instrumentalist' approach to the state Marx also offers the broader claim that even where the state is not the direct instrument of the ruling class its nature is determined by society's relations of production and its productive forces. These economic relations 'are in no way created by the state power' but on the contrary create it and form the 'real basis of the state'.[15] In this general claim the state expresses, in political form, the prevailing social and economic situation. Those cases where the state is the direct instrument of the ruling class are only a particular example of the more general, social determination of the political by the social: 'Assume a particular civil society and you will get particular political conditions which are only the official expression of civil society.'[16]

The difference between the 'instrumentalist' and the 'expressive' conceptions of the state is apparent in the contrast between the analysis of the bourgeois republic which Marx offers in *The Class Struggles in France*, and that of *The Eighteenth Brumaire of Louis Bonaparte*. In the former work the bourgeois republic is seen as the 'most potent and complete' form of the rule of the bourgeoisie, the form which allows its rule the most general expression and which permits the bourgeoisie to overcome the economic and political divisions which had previously threatened to undermine its rule.[17] In *The Eighteenth Brumaire* Marx emphasises that the most complete form of the rule of the bourgeoisie also presents dangers of its own; in particular, the very completeness of its rule now presents its enemies with a clear target for their opposition, a target unobscured by the existence of the monarchy and the internal quarrels of the capitalist class. It is dangerous for a faction of the bourgeoisie to take state power, yet it is also dangerous for the entire bourgeoisie to take power. The result is the opening of a gap between state and bourgeoisie, a gap which allows the state an unprecedented degree of autonomy.[18] It is not simply that Marx dropped his 'instrumentalist' concept of the state after

1850; on the contrary in The Eighteenth Brumaire Marx refers to the French state betweeh 1815 and 1851 as 'the instrument of the ruling class however much it strove for power of its own'.[19] Marx did not abandon his belief that the state could be the instrument of the ruling class, but rather turned his attention to a situation where, because of the conditions of civil society, this was not the case. He continued to stress that 'the state power is not suspended in mid-air', that it is determined by the prevailing social conditions. But he also emphasised that these conditions may lead not to a simple and direct correspondence between the economically dominant class and the personnel and policies of the state, but to an increasing independence of the state from the class which holds economic sway.[20]

Marx distinguishes two ways in which the state can achieve an increased degree of independence from the ruling class. The first is where the state is able to increase its autonomy by playing off one class against another in a situation where two (or more) classes are balanced. The second is where the economically dominant class abdicates from direct political power in order to guarantee its long-term economic and social supremacy.[21] Marx emphasised the potential for state independence arising from class balance as early as The German Ideology (1845–6). In a situation where feudalism is on the decline, and yet the capitalist class is not yet strong enough to assert its sway, the state, in its absolutist form, is able to obtain an independence 'because no section of the population can achieve dominance over the others'. This 'abnormal independence' was effected by the absolutist rulers using the emergent bourgeoisie 'as a counterpoise against the nobility', although Marx also qualifies the extent of this autonomy: the state can obtain only 'some appearance of independence' from both classes in such a situation of class balance.[22] Marx applied a similar analysis to Austria, where Metternich achieved the most complete form of absolute monarchy by balancing the nobility, peasantry and bourgeoisie in a 'reciprocal stalemate', and to Germany, where Bismarck played off the Junkers, bourgeoisie and proletariat against one another.[23]

Marx's analysis of the independence achieved by the regime of Louis Napoleon is often seen as the classic example of the state humbling the ruling class because of the stalemate reached in the class struggle: 'It was the only form of government possible when the bourgeoisie had already lost, and the working class had not yet acquired, the faculty of ruling the nation.'[24] Engels also included the Second Empire as one of those 'exceptional' periods when the state ceases to be a direct instrument of class rule, a period when 'the warring classes balance each other so nearly that the state power, as ostensible mediator, acquires, for the moment, a certain degree of both'.[25]

Yet much of Marx's analysis of the independence of the Bonapartist state is based not on a theory of class balance, where the state is able to assert its own wishes against the propertied classes because of the class stalemate, but rather on a theory of ruling class abdication, where the propertied class allows that state an increased autonomy in order to guarantee its own long-term economic and social interests. Marx argued that Bonapartism was the result of a situation where the bourgeoisie could no longer directly wield state power through the democratic republic. The very completeness of the bourgeoisie's control of the state revealed that state for what it was: the 'terrorism of class rule', a direct and confessed antagonism to the emancipation of the masses.

Destabilised by partial power, threatened by total power, the bourgeoisie's only solution was to abdicate from power altogether. The direct parliamentary rule of the bourgeoisie through its traditional political representatives had become incompatible with its own interests; the bourgeoisie thus turned to Bonaparte who offered strong government, tranquillity and the guarantee of industrial and commercial prosperity. Bonaparte broke the immediate political power of the ruling class, destroyed the influence of the bourgeoisie's own political and literary representatives and turned for support to the peasantry, the proletariat and his own lumpenproletarian entourage. Yet, even though the bourgeoisie appeared humbled before Bonaparte's rifle butt, the Second Empire guaranteed the order which allowed the continued dominance of the capitalist and landlord over the producer. The bourgeoisie thus attained a degree of development unexpected even by itself. Bonaparte's regime thus seemed independent of bourgeois society but was (Marx wrongly claimed) the last and only possible form of modern bourgeois rule.[26]

Marx offered a similar analysis of the British state in the mid-nineteenth century, where the industrial and commercial bourgeoisie formed the 'ruling class', but the landed aristocracy constituted the 'official government'. The bourgeoisie allowed an oligarchy of landed Whigs to monopolise government and office on condition that they represented and defended the interests of the bourgeoisie. By making concessions to the bourgeoisie (such as the repeal of the Corn Laws in 1846) the Whigs were able to limit the extent of reform and to safeguard their own position; by making concessions to the Whigs, the bourgeoisie were able to avoid the need to forge an alliance with the mass of the English people. This union of landlords and capitalists was made easier by the gradual and prolonged development of the bourgeoisie and the aristocracy's own conversion, at an early date, to capitalist forms of property.[27]

Marx and Engels did offer an 'instrumentalist' analysis of specific states, of the French Republic as the 'national war engine of capital against labour', or the Paris Commune as 'a lever for uprooting the economical foundations upon which rests the existence of classes'. Yet they were also aware of the gap which could be opened up between state and ruling class, that the state could strive for 'power of its own' and that the personnel of the state could see government revenues as their personal treasury, as a form of pelf, as well as an organised force for the subjugation of the producers.[28] Whether they regarded the autonomy of the Bonapartist state as the norm, as Engels claimed in 1866, or whether they saw such periods as exceptions, as Engels claimed in *The Origin of the Family, Private Property and the State*, is impossible to say. Nevertheless, even where Marx stressed the degree of independence enjoyed by the Bonapartist state, he also emphasised that the state's apparent victory over the ruling class appeared as such only to the eye of the uninitiated. Bonaparte's regime remained a form of class rule, a rule which guaranteed the material interests of the French bourgeoisie.[29] The absolutist state enjoyed only 'some appearance of independence' from the bourgeoisie and nobility and so appears as 'an ostensible mediator, for the moment'. Similarly, the Whigs only held onto power in Britain by granting all the concessions made unavoidable by the course of economic development.[30] The fact that Bonaparte played off the proletariat against the bourgeoisie did not make the proletariat into a ruling class in nineteenth-century France. The state remained an institution which helped guarantee the continued economic and social dominance of the propertied, as did absolutism and the British state of the nineteenth century. The state is, Marx claims, beneficial for the long-term general interests of the ruling class, even when it is obliged to resist the short-term interests of individual capitalists.[31] The state exists as a separate interest group within the social division of labour, an interest group which 'strives for as much independence as possible' but which nevertheless cannot resist the pressure of economic development and class interest. States which do attempt to resist the flow of economic change 'will go to pieces in the long run'.[32] If the state is not always optimal for the interests of the ruling class then it is, in general, functional for those interests.

34

34

Why is the state a 'class state'?

Marx and Engels did argue, then, that the state could act at the behest of the ruling class. Miliband prefers to see the state as acting 'on behalf' of the ruling class, rather than directly at its command, but, nevertheless, agrees that 'the state indeed is a class state, the state of the "ruling class"'.[33] For Marxists the state is, with greater or lesser qualification, a class state. But why should the state act on behalf of a particular class? Why should we prefer to see the state as an expression of some outside force (the ruling class), rather than as an independent and separate source of power? Miliband usefully distinguishes three possible answers to this question: the first is that the personnel of the state explains its class bias; the second is that the class nature of the state may be explained in terms of the structural constraints of the social order; and the third is that the ruling class is the most powerful interest group in society.

The first explanation of the class nature of the state is that its upper bureaucracy, general staff, judiciary and government, are themselves drawn from the ruling class. This form of explanation has the theoretical advantage that it explains why the state is functional for the ruling class in terms of the intentions of the actors involved.[34] In this case it is the common background, education, family ties, values and ideological presuppositions of the governing caste and the ruling class, which explain why the state apparatus is predisposed to favour the propertied, and will tend to merge the interests of the 'nation' (and hence the state) with those of the economically dominant class.[35] Marx and Engels certainly offered analyses of the state which stressed the class origin of its personnel. In *Condition of the Working Class in England*, for instance, Engels argued that the state is the bourgeoisie 'organized as a party' to defend itself through laws which protect its own property. These laws are themselves administered by members of the propertied classes, the Justices of the Peace, who 'see the foundation of all true order in the interests of their class'.[36] Marx similarly argued that the Factory Acts which were intended to restrict the capitalists were administered by tribunals in which 'the masters sat in judgement on themselves'.[37] Local government in nineteenth-century England remained in the hands of the middle class in the towns and the landlords in the countryside, the political self-government of the propertied.[38] In France after 1830 it was the finance aristocracy which directly headed the administration of the state and had command of the public authorities.[39]

The less developed the state in terms of its revenues and bureaucracy, the more apparent is the merger of the personnel of the governing caste with the ruling class. The feudal state of medieval England is a classic example where the landed magnates not only had an institutionalised form of power in their own private courts, but also dominated royal and public institutions, offices and jurisdictions. Thus, when the landlords were faced with a shortage of labour and tenants after the Black Death of 1348, they were able to resist their tenants' and employees' attempts at self-improvement not only through their own manorial courts but also, in their role as royal justices, as administrators of the wages freeze of 1351, a wage freeze made law by a parliament itself dominated by landlords. 'Government was by the rich and to a great extent for the rich.'[40] Similarly, in early modern England the government, parliament, local government, bureaucracy, army, navy and church were all dominated by members of the landlord class. Even in modern capitalist states the personnel of the state is drawn predominantly from members of the business, propertied and professional classes.[41]

There are problems, however, with attempts to explain the class nature of the state purely in terms of the social origin of its personnel. The state has not always been manned by members of the economically dominant class. An extreme example is that of Nazi Germany, where the traditional governing and ruling class had its power dramatically curtailed and 'in some crucial areas, notably foreign policy, altogether nullified'. Even in more conventional bourgeois states there can be a profound hostility between the state and the business elite. Capitalist opposition to Roosevelt's New Deal or to social democratic reform programmes are cases in point.[42] Of course, it could be argued that in all these cases the state defends the long-term interest of the capitalist class, but if this is so we need to show how, and why, the state is able to act as the guiding intelligence of the bourgeoisie, even when the bourgeoisie itself opposes the state. The instrumentalist claim that the state is, to a greater or lesser extent, 'privatised' in the hands of the economically dominant class is thus a powerful, but not conclusive, explanation of the class nature of the state.

The second form of explanation of why the state defends the interests of the ruling class is that based on structural determination. The nature of and policies adopted by the state are explained by their functional benefits for the ruling class, benefits which are guaranteed by the state's location within a particular society and constrained by the relations of production of the dominant mode of production.[43] Poulantzas argues, for instance, that the participation of members of the ruling class in the state apparatus is not the cause, but the effect, of the state's class nature. The state cannot be reduced to a subjective relation between the bureaucracy and the ruling class. The state is an institution whose function is to guarantee the cohesion and reproduction of the class system, a function which flows from its position as a specific instance of the social whole within which it has an objective role: 'If the functions of the state in a determinate social formation and the interests of the dominant class in this formation coincide it is by reason of the system itself.'[44]

The problem with this form of structural determination by the system is that it is not really a form of determination at all, but rather a conditional statement. In effect Poulantzas is claiming that if a specific class system is to be reproduced, then the state must carry out certain functions. But it is precisely why the state *does* carry out these functions that we are seeking to establish. Structural determination turns out to be a restatement of the very problem which we are trying to solve. It offers a tautology in the place of explanation: the state carries out certain functions, because it is these functions which objectively define the state. The social formation is thus reified into an historical actor which produces its own effects, and assigns the state a specific role. The personnel of the state then become mere bearers of this objective function. In effect, Poulantzas's argument is the sophisticated expression of a simple economism: the state must carry out certain tasks because of its insertion within a specific class structure.

The final explanation of why the state acts as a guarantor of the propertied class is that this class is able, through its resources, strength and influence, to act not only as a 'pressure group' on the state, but as the most powerful of all pressure groups.[45] Through this influence the ruling class is able to pass off its interest as the 'national' interest and so is able to command the attention and sympathetic response of the state. A clear example of this is Tony Benn's contrast between the state's attitude to industrial unrest and to financial speculation:

> Certainly my own direct experience of the potential role of the services during the oil tanker drivers' dispute of 1978–79 suggested strongly that the armed forces saw their role as preparing a military operation against trade union adversaries which required, for its success, a detailed knowledge of what the 'enemy' were planning. How different it is when pressure is brought to bear on Government by the forces of Capital. In 1976 when there was a run on the pound, in which the City of London and the Banks were playing a leading part, and as a result of which the British national interest was threatened most directly, there

260

was no evidence whatsoever that the security services were at all interested in the activities of those who were speculating against our clear national interest.[46]

This influence, which the propertied are able to bring to bear on the capitalist state, does not merely flow from a shared ideological outlook of government and business, nor from the links of family, friendship and social background which unite the two, nor from the fact that business interests form well-organised lobbies with vast resources. Quite apart from these subjective influences which tend to ease the partnership of state and capital, there is the simple fact of the massive constraint imposed on the state's actions by the capitalist class's control of the economy, of investment, production, finance and trade, its power to make decisions which determine where, what and how commodities are produced, decisions which influence wages, prices, profits and the balance of trade. It is this economic power which forms the basis of the pervasive influence of 'capital', an inert power which obliges the state to win the confidence and co-operation of 'business'. In order to carry out its functions of maintaining social order, furthering economic prosperity and defending national security, the government is vitally dependent upon the success of the economy, not least because it is this economy which forms the state's own fiscal base. It is not mere prejudice which leads to the identification of the national interest with that of private enterprise. Given the context and constraints within which the state operates, this identification has, to say the least, a large degree of plausibility.[47]

The constraints faced by the state in its relations with the ruling class vary from society to society. In medieval England, for instance, the 'subjective' constraint on the state's autonomy was its lack of a monopoly of armed force, and the fact that the nobility could, and did, threaten armed rebellion against those rulers whose policies appeared to infringe its privileges. The 'objective' constraint on the autonomy of the medieval state was simply the limited surplus produced by the feudal economy and the consequent restrictions placed on resources available to the state. Given these limited resources the state was unable to develop a large bureaucratic and military power of its own and so was dependent for its success upon the co-operation of the elites of town and (particularly) country. The deposition and murder of Edward II and Richard II revealed the fate in store for those monarchs who disregarded these constraints.

Together, the subjective constraints of the ruling class as pressure group and the objective constraints imposed by the social and economic

261

order (constraints which should not be confused with Poulantzas's tautological structural determination) account for why the state acts to defend the fundamental interests of the ruling class. That the state is distinct from the ruling class is inherent in its definition as a 'separate entity along and outside civil society'; all states enjoy some autonomy or independence 'from all classes, including the dominant classes'.[48] It was precisely because the dictatorship of the proletariat began to break down this separation that Marx considered it to be the dissolving form of the state.[49] The separation of state and ruling class does not mean, however, that the state enjoys an absolute independence, since any institution that was totally autonomous of others would, by definition, have no connection with them in the first place.[50] The state is thus incapable of total submergence within the ruling class, and equally incapable of total autonomy. In this light the much vaunted 'relative autonomy' of the state becomes rather banal since the state is, by definition, autonomous and this autonomy must, in practice, be relative and conditional.

The state is not totally independent of society, yet neither is it the mere instrument of the ruling class. A more useful model of the relation between the state and the ruling class is thus 'one of *partnership* between two different sets of forces, linked to each other by many threads yet each having its own separate sphere of concerns'.[51] To assert the relative autonomy of the state is vacuous. The key issue is what are the factors which alter the terms of this partnership of state and ruling class, allowing the state now more, and now less, room for independent manoeuvre? Marx offers one answer in *The Class Struggles in France*: the power of the state tends to grow in proportion to the growth in the number of challenges to the power of the ruling class and the conditions of that class's existence. Where a ruling class enjoys a relatively unchallenged hegemony over society, the relationship between state and class will be relatively close; where the ruling class is challenged from below, the autonomy of the state will be correspondingly enhanced and authoritarian forms of government will prevail.[52] Other factors influencing the extent of the state's autonomy include external pressure (a vital factor, as we shall see, in the case of absolutism) and the extent of the bureaucratic and financial resources which allow the state to rule without entirely depending on the good will of the dominant class.

Marx and Engels offered a number of metaphors with which to express the relationship between state and society, including that of the state as the 'instrument' of the ruling class and that of the state as the 'expression' or 'reflection' of civil society. All of these metaphors are problematic in that they cannot deal with the autonomy of the state, or its active historical role. Most useful is the metaphor of an 'alliance' between the state and the ruling class.[53] The state cannot for long rule against society, as Charles I discovered when he attempted to rule without the co-operation of the propertied classes of seventeenth-century England. The state cannot survive in spendid isolation, but must seek allies. Its natural ally is the class with the greatest economic and social power, the class which places the greatest constraints upon the autonomy of the state and whose interests seem to coincide with those of the nation as a whole. The fate of the Allende government in Chile is a tragic illustration of what may happen when the partnership between the state and the existing ruling class is broken, but the state is unable to forge a new social alliance upon which to base its power.[54] The state is a separate force within society, not an independent force from without. The state attempts to make its own history but not, as Allende discovered to his cost, just as it pleases or under circumstances of its own making.

The state and functional explanation: the case of absolutism

That the state machine and parliament 'are not the real life of the ruling classes, but only the organized general organs of their dominion, the political guarantees and forms of expressions of the old order of things' is, of course, a functional explanation of the state. Political institutions are explained in terms of their benefits for the continued supremacy of the dominant class.[55] This type of argument may be used to explain why the state carries out certain tasks (such as the guarantee of social order and the defence of property), or why the state takes a specific form. An example of the functional explanation of the form taken by the state is Miliband's and Poulantzas's claim that the interests of capital require the state to have a 'relative autonomy', in order to resolve the differences of interest within the capitalist class and to ensure that the long-term interests of the ruling class prevail over the short-term interests of its individual members.[56]

As always the problem with this form of explanation is the difficulty of specifying the mechanism which guarantees that a form of state functional for the ruling class will come into existence. Indeed, such functional explanations can, as long as the ruling class continues to exist, easily lapse into tautology: that the state is functional for the ruling class is 'proved' by the continued dominance of that class. It would be difficult to disprove this hypothesis since almost anything that the state does could, in the long term, be shown to be functional for the ruling class, given that it does continue to rule. We need, in fact, to distinguish two functional theses about the state: the first is that the state is beneficial for the ruling class in that it does not threaten the ruling class's continued social and economic supremacy, i.e. the state is not dysfunctional; the second is that the form and actions of the state are optimal for the ruling class, i.e. they allow that class to maximise its benefits. The difficulties of applying either form of functional explanation are clearly illustrated in Perry Anderson's account of the rise of the absolutist state.

Marx and Engels's own comments on absolutism tend to be rather contradictory, perhaps because they saw absolutism itself as a rather contradictory phenomenon. On the one hand they presented absolutism as a 'progressive' force which was both produced by, and in turn hastened, the development of capitalism. Absolutism encouraged the decay of feudalism; it was 'a weapon of nascent modern society in its struggle of emancipation from feudalism'. The French Revolution of 1789 was thus not simply the antithesis of the absolutist state which it overthrew but, on the contrary, furthered the centralisation of the state and the development of capitalism which had already begun. On the other hand, absolutism did eventually prove to be a fetter on the bourgeoisie, a class which found itself in opposition to the alliance of state and aristocracy in defence of the old order.[57] Marx and Engels thus argued that the absolutist state was the form of the state in the era of the transition from feudalism to capitalism, and was able to achieve its independence precisely because of its ability to play off the power of the class which represented a rising capitalism against that which represented a decaying feudalism.[58]

Anderson would agree with Marx and Engels that absolutism was the form of the state in the era of the transition to capitalism, but would not accept the conclusion that its independence was the result of a 'class balance', or that there was a plurality of ruling classes in the absolutist state. Engels's rather different interpretation of absolutism offered in *Anti-Dühring* is closer to Anderson's position: the growth of capitalism from within feudal society was 'not followed by any immediate corresponding change in its political structure. The state order remained feudal while society became more and more bourgeois.'[59] Anderson's argument is that, in western Europe, the development of the absolutist state was a response to changes in the form taken by feudal class relations. With the end of labour services, the commutation of rents, the decline of serfdom and the withering away of the landlords' manorial rights, the feudal ruling class was obliged to find new forms of social control which ensured their continued appropriation of peasant surplus labour: 'Absolutism was just this: a redeployed and recharged apparatus of feudal domination, designed to clamp the peasant masses back into their traditional social position – despite and against the gains they had won by the widespread commutation of dues.' The landlords compensated for a decline in their local political manorial power with a new form of centralised and militarised state apparatus: 'the political carapace of a threatened nobility'. The absolutist state thus has a functional explanation: it developed because of the landlords' need to maintain feudal relations of production and surplus extraction despite the changed conditions of early modern Europe.[60]

The theoretical difficulty of Anderson's case is its reliance on functional explanation, a difficulty which also leads to a number of empirical problems. Anderson assumes that absolutism was the only answer to the nobility's dilemma, i.e.

(1)   the social position of the nobility is threatened;
(2)   therefore it adopts absolutism.

In fact, other options were theoretically open to the landlords. In Poland, for instance, the landlords managed to secure their position by asserting their manorial control and enserfing the peasantry, rather than resorting to a centralised state. In other words, we first need to explain why the French landlords were obliged to adopt a particular solution to their problems – assuming, of course, that absolutism was such a solution.

The main weakness of Anderson's case, however, is his assumption not merely that the landlords would prefer a particular solution but, also, that they would necessarily be able to impose their preference. However, if we do not assume that the needs of the landlords would automatically be met by historical development, then Anderson's apparent functional explanation ((1) and (2) above) becomes a conditional statement:

(1)   the social position of the nobility is threatened;
(2)   therefore if it is to maintain its position it must attempt to develop a form of centralised state power to guarantee its extraction of surplus.

A conditional statement is not a form of explanation. The fact that the nobility had certain needs does not mean that those needs would automatically be met. Even if we agreed that absolutism was a solution to the landlords' problems, we would have to explain how, and why, they were able to impose their preferred solution. Functional argument cannot be a substitute for concrete historical explanation since, in practice, it only redefines the historical outcome which is to be explained in the first place.

The empirical problem with Anderson's argument is one of chronology, a problem which makes us question whether absolutism can be seen primarily as a response to the commutation of labour services and the growth of money rents in the first place. In France, for instance, labour services underwent a lengthy decline from as early as the mid-tenth century and by the early fourteenth century were virtually a thing of the past; the decline of serfdom was underway from the mid-thirteenth century and was completed well over a century before the decisive shift to absolutism in the early seventeenth century. It is thus difficult to show that there was any causal link between the end of serfdom and the rise of absolutism. Anderson fails to locate his explanation of absolutism within a detailed account of the transformation of feudal rent. As a result *Lineages of the Absolutist State* provides a brilliant survey of political developments in early modern Europe, but fails to prove the theoretical claims for the causal primacy of class relations, which was its initial purpose.

These theoretical and empirical weaknesses of Anderson's explanations of the rise of absolutism in western Europe are emphasised by his analysis of the development of centralised state power in the east. At one point he does claim that eastern European absolutism was a 'device for the consolidation of serfdom' but is forced to admit that Prussian serfdom spread a century before the emergence of absolutism, whilst in Poland the peasants were enserfed despite the total failure to develop a native absolutism. Why then did absolutism develop in the east? Why did the east's political superstructure converge with that of the west whilst their economic bases diverged and the east became increasingly feudal? Anderson's answer is to be found not in the internal class struggle or economic change, but rather in the arena of international conflict and diplomacy. The construction of Prussian absolutism, for instance, was a response to the growth of the Swedish military threat; the growth of absolutism in Russia was similarly forged in the struggle with Sweden and with the Crimean Tartars.[61]

In a sense Anderson again offers a functional explanation of absolutism; eastern absolutism is explained by its benefits for national security in a time of international warfare and growing external threats. But this form of functional explanation is made valid by Anderson's emphasis on human intention, and on the existence of a selection mechanism which allows us to explain an institution in terms of its benefits. The absolutist states were the conscious creations of their rulers who aimed to gather the military and fiscal power to resist their rivals; the example of Poland, dismembered between its neighbours, showed what would happen to those countries which failed to develop such a state. Just as the market selects those firms which are most efficient and punishes those which are inefficient, so international competition allows us to give a functional explanation of eastern absolutism. The 'need' for an absolutist state was not a need which had to be fulfilled but specifies the conditions which had to be met in order for the state to survive:

(1)   the state faced challenges in a time of international rivalry;
(2)   therefore if the state is to survive it must develop absolutist institutions.

The development of absolutism is historically contingent and must be explained in terms of the rulers' intentions, and the resources available to fulfil those intentions. The 'need' for absolutism is not in itself an explanation of why absolutism develops, as the example of Poland shows.

Anderson's argument, that eastern absolutism was 'centrally determined by the constraints of the international political system into which the nobilities of the whole region were objectively integrated', is thus a convincing one. Indeed, it is precisely such a *political* explanation of the rise of absolutism which Anderson offers in his detailed analysis of the west, despite his general theoretical claims for the primacy of changes in feudal class relations. The three great accelerators of French absolutism, he claims, were the Hundred Years' War, the religious wars of the sixteenth century and the Fronde in the seventeenth century, none of which would seem to offer a class-based explanation of the form taken by the French state. From these crises emerged the archetypal absolutism of Louis XIV which, Anderson argues, had the specific goal of military expansion. The development of royal absolutism went hand-in-hand with the need to levy troops and finances for foreign war. In the sixteenth century the French army had numbered 50,000 combatants; by the 1630s the figure was 150,000 or more. Absolutism was thus a regime 'born out of warfare'. As Anderson himself points out, the absolutist state was a machine built for war. Dynastic warfare is not, of course, divorced from the class nature and social structure of early modern societies, but it is a rather different explanation of absolutism from the changes in the form of feudal rent which Anderson orginally invoked.[62]

The degree of relative autonomy enjoyed by the state cannot be explained merely in terms of the internal class struggle and the social hegemony of the ruling class. Emphasis must also be placed on external threats to the state, such as foreign war, or on non-class internal crises, such as the French wars of religion, which provoke a crisis of the state and thus the possibility of an authoritarian response and the growth of state power. Such crises cannot be seen merely as a threat to the ruling class. In Poland, for instance, the failure to develop absolutism may have led to the end of the 'national existence' of the nobility within a separate Polish state, but this did not mean the end of the nobility *per se*. On the contrary, in the area of Poland seized by Russia (the greater part of the country's land and population) the landlords fared well and their economic prosperity continued, or even increased, with the introduction of the severe Russian law of serfdom.[63] Neither internally, nor externally, can the state merely be seen as an expression of ruling class interest.

This does not mean that relations between rulers and the landlord class were irrelevant to the nature or functioning of the absolutist state. In Prussia the taxes for a standing army, the vital component of the absolutist machine, were voted for by the nobility in return for tax exemptions on the Junkers themselves, and for land laws which more firmly bound the peasants to the soil. In France, the attempt of Louis XIII, Richelieu and Mazarin to overcome the combined threat of popular disorders, noble revolts, foreign invasion and religious separatism through the assertion of the central royal power, tended to undermine its own success by provoking resistance from France's traditional privileged elite. The success of Louis XIV's absolutism came not from a victory over the landlord class, but by coming to terms with that class's power and collaborating with it. The Fronde revealed to the aristocracy the futility and danger of resisting the French monarchy, they revealed to the monarchy the impossibility of imposing its control without the cooperation of the provincial elites. 'Despite the undoubted growth of royal power the absolutism of Louis XIV did not rest on bureaucratic efficiency but on a compromise with the dominant social classes on which the government depended.' The absolutist state cannot be reduced to an instrument of the ruling class, yet it was an important factor in the defence of the latter's status, privilege and income.[64]

The state as an 'expression' of social relations: the case of absolutism

The absolutist state has been used here as a test case of Marxist approaches to the state. Absolutism was not merely an instrument of the feudal ruling class. On the contrary the landlords, threatened by the incursions of a centralising state with which it competed for peasant surplus, resisted the development of central power and attempted to cling onto their local authority, a resistance with which the absolutist state was finally obliged to come to terms and which forced the state to win the confidence of the propertied.[65] The absolutist state certainly cannot be seen as nothing more than an instrument of class oppression,[66] nor can it be explained in terms of the functional requirements of the feudal mode of production, a form of explanation which is both theoretically and empirically inadequate.

If the absolutist state cannot be understood in 'instrumentalist' or functional terms, neither is it helpful to see it as an 'expression' of civil society as Marx claimed. The difficulty with this formulation is that it tends, once more, to render the state passive in the process of historical change. The state becomes merely the surface expression of some deeper, and more fundamental, change. Brenner, for instance, argues (like Anderson) that the establishment of secure forms of peasant proprietorship forced the landlord to rely increasingly on the centralised extraction of surplus from the peasants, in the form of taxation. Absolutism was thus not merely a guarantee of traditional forms of feudal surplus extraction, but 'rather it came to *express* a transformed version of the old system'.[67] Brenner's case for the importance of centralised surplus extraction is a powerful one, given that much of the state's taxation was directly passed into the hands of provincial notables, quite apart from their proceeds of office and state patronage.[68] The problem lies not with his analysis of the alliance which was reconstructed between the state and the ruling class, but rather with his metaphor of the state as merely the 'expression' of social change.

The basis of Brenner's analysis is the ability of the French peasantry to retain possession of the land. He argues that the peasantry of France, unlike that of England where agrarian capitalism developed, remained entrenched because of the help of the state. The state not only allowed the peasants to make short-term victories against the landlords, but also to establish these gains on a secure, in effect freehold, basis. The state had a vested interest in securing peasant property rights in order to levy its own demands on the peasant surplus; a secure peasantry and the absolutist state thus developed hand in hand in mutual dependence.[69] But, if the nobility's reliance on the state was the result of secure peasant tenure, and if this tenure was largely created and maintained by the actions of the state, then the state itself becomes a major historical actor with interests of its own. The state did not merely reflect, or 'express', social change, but was itself one of the agents of that change. The nobility's reliance on the state was thus partly produced by the actions of the state itself. Neither the instrumentalist, the functional nor the 'expressive' metaphor allows us to understand the active historical role of the state, a role in which it found itself in competition with the landlords for the peasants' surplus.

Neither does Brenner's analysis tell us why the state wished to extend its power and to secure a sound fiscal basis. As we have seen, the explanation for this need cannot be found in the realms of the internal class struggle. On the contrary: 'it was war and preparations for war that provided the most potent energizing stimulus for the concentration of administrative resources and fiscal reorganization that characterised the rise of absolutism'.[70]

The 'relative autonomy' of the absolutist state cannot be passed off as a functional requirement of the prevailing social relations, as Porshnev and Anderson tend to do.[71] The autonomy of the state must be taken seriously to mean that the state not merely expressed social change, but was itself a major agent of that change. The absolutist state was not, and could not be, totally independent of the propertied classes; neither were the two fused so that the state was purely an instrument of class rule. The relationship between the two was that of a negotiated partnership in which both sides found themselves defending the same basic social order: the nobility found profit, power and status through its growing involvement in the expanding state apparatus; the monarchy found that an excessive autonomy from the propertied tended to undermine its own ability to rule successfully. The outcome was an alliance of state and landlords, an alliance whose terms were determined by the internal and external threats faced by each and by the resources available to each. The establishment of absolutism must, like any other form of historical change, be explained in terms of the intentions (both conscious and unconscious) and actions of the historical agents, of the determinants of those intentions, the constraints of their actions and the consequences (intended and unintended) of those actions. In this explanation the state itself is one of the historical actors; it cannot be reduced to merely a 'reflection' or 'expression' of social change, an 'instrument' of the ruling class or a 'functional' response to changes in the form of feudal class relations.

What are the implications of this discussion of the state for Marx's metaphor of 'base and superstructure'? As we have seen the base cannot be defined as some pre-existing economic level, to which a political superstructure is added. On the contrary, politics and the state may form constitutive elements of the relations of production, and thus of the base. This 'interpenetration' is most apparent in the cases of the 'tributary' mode of production and post-capitalist societies, where relations of production have no existence independent of the state which is itself the extractor of producers' surplus labour. Even if we redefine the 'base' to include all of the social elements which function as relations of production, it is still difficult to retain the metaphor of base and superstructure, since it cannot be shown that the remaining political 'superstructure' is functionally explained by the 'needs' of the base, or that the superstructure is merely a 'reflection' or an 'expression' of the base. Yet, in practice, the state is normally functional for the interests of the ruling class. The problem is how to emphasise this functionality whilst retaining a sense of the state as an active historical agent which is influenced by a range of considerations besides that of the interest of the ruling class. The prevailing social relations of production are a crucial constraint on the actions of the state but, nevertheless, this does not mean that 'base and superstructure' is the best metaphor with which to express their interaction. It is the metaphor of alliance, or of partnership, between the state and the ruling class which best captures the relationship between the two. The 'relative autonomy' of the state, its room for independent manoeuvre within this partnership, cannot be defined in advance, but only be specified by consideration of particular historical moments. The relationship between the state and society can only be expressed through a metaphor and yet, in a sense, all metaphors are unsatisfactory. The metaphor of 'alliance' has weaknesses of its own, in particular its tendency to convert the state and the ruling class into homogeneous historical actors, rather than emphasising their own internal divisions. Nevertheless it is this metaphor which least problematically expresses the relationship between the economically dominant class and society's political institutions.

Notes

1 M. Weber, 'Politics as a vocation', in A. Pizzorno (ed.), Political Sociology (Harmondsworth, 1971), p. 28; F. Engels, The Origin of the Family, Private Property and the State (Moscow, 1968), pp. 95, 115–16, 167–8; V. I. Lenin, 'The state', in C. Wright Mills (ed.), The Marxists (Harmondsworth, 1969), p. 213.

2 Weber, 'Politics as a vocation', p. 27.

3 Lenin, 'The state', p. 217.

4 K. Marx & F. Engels, CollectedWorks, vol. V (London, 1976), p. 329 (The German Ideology).

5 Engels, The Origin of the Family, Private Property and the State, p. 168.

6 Ibid.

7 Marx & Engels, Collected Works, vol. V, p. 52 (The German Ideology).

8 H. Draper, Karl Marx's Theory of Revolution, vol. I (New York, 1977), pp. 584 ff; K. Marx, A Contribution to the Critique of Political Economy (London, 1971), p. 21; K. Marx, The Class Struggles in France 1848 to 1850 (Moscow, 1972), p. 62.

9 R. Miliband, Class Power and State Power (London, 1983), p. 47; K. Marx & F. Engels, The Communist Manifesto (Harmondsworth, 1970), p. 82.

10 Engels, The Origin of the Family, Private Property and the State, p. 168.

11 Marx & Engels, CollectedWorks, vol. V, pp. 90, 92, 355–6, 361 (The German Ideology).

12 Marx & Engels, The Communist Manifesto, pp. 85, 100, 105; Marx, The Poverty of Philosophy (Moscow, 1973), p. 137.

13 Marx, The Class Struggles in France, pp. 28, 30, 32, 35, 81, 102, 121–3; K. Marx, The Revolutions of 1848 (Harmondsworth, 1973), p. 261.

14 F. Parkin, Marxism and Class Theory: A Bourgeois Critique (London, 1979), p. 82.

15 Marx & Engels, CollectedWorks, vol. V, p. 329 (The German Ideology).

16 Marx, The Poverty of Philosophy, p. 156.

17 Marx, The Class Struggles in France, p. 122. See also the references in n. 13, above.

18 K. Marx, The Eighteenth Brumaire of Louis Bonaparte (Moscow, 1972), p. 105.

19 Ibid.; J. Elster, Making Sense of Marx (Cambridge, 1985), p. 408.

20 Marx, The Eighteenth Brumaire of Louis Bonaparte, p. 105.

21 Elster, Making Sense of Marx, Ch. 7.

22 Marx & Engels, Collected Works, vol. V, pp. 90, 92, 195, 361 (The German Ideology); Marx & Engels, The Communist Manifesto, p. 82.

23 Marx, The Revolutions of 1848, p. 216; Draper, Karl Marx's Theory of Revolution, pp. 327–9, 417–24.

24 K. Marx, The CivilWar in France (Peking, 1970), p. 66.

25 Engels, The Origin of the Family, Private Property and the State, pp. 168-9; and see his 'Introduction' to Marx, The Civil War in France, p. 5.

26 Marx, The CivilWar in France, pp. 66, 137, 162, 165, 167; Marx, The Eighteenth Brumaire of Louis Bonaparte, pp. 39, 88–91, 98, 103–4, 112–13.

27 K. Marx, Surveys from Exile (Harmondsworth, 1973), pp. 182, 254, 259–60, 279, 282.

28 Marx, The CivilWar in France, pp. 65, 72, 165; Marx, The Eighteenth Brumaire of Louis Bonaparte, pp. 105, 113.

29 K. Marx & F. Engels, Selected Correspondence (Moscow, 1975), p. 166 (letter of Engels to Marx, 13.4.1866); Engels, The Origin of the Family, Private Property and the

State, pp. 168–9; Marx, *The Eighteenth Brumaire of Louis Bonaparte*, p. 105; Marx, *The Civil War in France*, p. 165.

30 Marx & Engels, *Collected Works*, vol. V, p. 361 (*The German Ideology*); Engels, *The Origin of the Family, Private Property and the State*, p. 168; Marx, *Surveys from Exile*, p. 259.

31 Marx & Engels, *Collected Works*, vol. V, p. 180 (*The German Ideology*); K. Marx, *Capital*, vol. I (London, 1977), pp. 229, 461.

32 Marx & Engels, *Selected Correspondence*, pp. 398–9 (Engels to Schmidt, 27.10.1890).

33 R. Miliband, *Marxism and Politics* (Oxford, 1978), p. 74.

34 Above, pp. 87–8.

35 Miliband, *Marxism and Politics*, pp. 68–9.

36 K. Marx & F. Engels, *Collected Works*, vol. IV (London, 1975), pp. 567–8 (*The Condition of the Working Class in England*).

37 Marx, *Capital*, vol. I, p. 274.

38 Marx, *The Civil War in France*, p. 141.

39 Marx, *The Class Struggles in France*, p. 30.

40 R. H. Hilton, *A Medieval Society* (London, 1967), p. 268; idem, *Bond Men Made Free* (London, 1977), p. 172; J. R. Lander, *Conflict and Stability in Fifteenth Century England* (London, 1971), p. 172.

41 R. Miliband, *The State in Capitalist Society* (London, 1973), p. 55 and see ibid., Ch. 3 *passim*.

42 Ibid., pp. 84, 106; Miliband, *Marxism and Politics*, pp. 69–71.

43 Ibid., pp. 72–4.

44 N. Poulantzas, 'The problem of the capitalist state', in R. Blackburn (ed.), *Ideology in Social Science* (London, 1972), pp. 245–7.

45 Miliband, *Marxism and Politics*, pp. 71–2.

46 Tony Benn, *Guardian*, 8.12.1980.

47 Miliband, *The State in Capitalist Society*, Ch. 6; J. Westergaard & H. Resler, *Class in a Capitalist Society* (Harmondsworth, 1976), pp. 244–77; A. Giddens, *A Contemporary Critique of Historical Materialism* (London, 1981), pp. 210–19.

48 Marx & Engels, *Collected Works*, vol. V, p. 90 (*The German Ideology*); Miliband, *Marxism and Politics*, p. 83.

49 Marx, *The Civil War in France*, pp. 69–71, 168.

50 Giddens, *A Contemporary Critique of Historical Materialism*, p. 217.

51 Miliband, *Class Power and State Power*, p. 72.

52 Ibid., pp. 67–8; Marx, *The Class Struggles in France*, p. 104.

53 Engels, *The Origin of the Family, Private Property and the State*, p. 169.

54 Miliband, *Class Power and State Power*, p. 74.

55 Marx, *The Civil War in France*, p. 171.

56 Miliband, *Marxism and Politics*, p. 74; N. Poulantzas, *Political Power and Social Classes* (London, 1973), p. 287.

57 Marx, *The Class Struggles in France*, p. 104; Marx, *Capital*, vol. I, p. 672; Marx, *The Civil War in France*, pp. 162–3; Marx & Engels, *The Communist Manifesto*, p. 89; K. Marx, *The Revolutions of 1848* (Harmondsworth, 1973), pp. 189, 250, 259-63; F. Engels, *Herr Eugen Dühring's Revolution in Science* (London, Lawrence & Wishart, n.d.), pp. 186–7.

58 Engels, ibid.; Marx, *The Civil War in France*, p. 195; Marx & Engels, *The Communist Manifesto*, p. 82; Engels, *The Origins of the Family, Private Property and the State*, p. 168.

59 Engels, *Herr Eugen Dühring's Revolution in Science*, pp. 120–1. See also P. Sweezy, 'A rejoinder', p. 108, and C. Hill, 'A comment', pp. 118–21, in R. H. Hilton et al., *The Transition from Feudalism to Capitalism* (London, 1976).

60 P. Anderson, *Lineages of the Absolutist State* (London, 1979), Ch. 1.

61 Ibid., pp. 195–202, 212–16.

62 Ibid., pp. 29–33, 38–9, 102, 202; D. Parker, *The Making of French Absolutism* (London, 1983), pp. 60–4, 148–9.

63 Anderson, *Lineages of the Absolutist State*, pp. 196, 297; P. S. Wandycz, *The Lands of Partitioned Poland 1795–1918* (Seattle, 1974), p. 18.

64 Anderson, *Lineages of the Absolutist State*, p. 203; Parker, *The Making of French Absolutism*, pp. 86, 143, 151; R. Bonney, 'Cardinal Mazarin and the great nobility during the Fronde', *English Historical Review* XCVI (1981), pp. 818–33; W. Beik, *Absolutism and Society in Seventeenth Century France* (Cambridge, 1985), pp. 31–2, 327–37.

65 Parker, *The Making of French Absolutism*, pp. 329–37; A. D. Lublinskaya, *French Absolutism: The Crucial Phase 1620–1629* (Cambridge, 1968), especially pp. 2, 331; R. Brenner, 'The agrarian roots of European capatalism', *Past and Present* 97 (1982), pp 58, 80.

66 Engels, 'Introduction' to Marx, *The Civil War in France*, p. 17.

67 Brenner, 'The agrarian roots of European capitalism', p. 81. My emphasis.

68 Beik, *Absolutism and Society in Seventeenth Century France*, pp. 331–2.

69 R. Brenner, 'Agrarian class structure and economic development in pre-industrial Europe', *Past and Present* 70 (1976), pp. 69–71; Brenner, 'The agrarian roots of European capitalism', pp. 50–9, 79–82.

70 A. Giddens, *The Nation State and Violence* (London, 1985), p. 112.

71 Anderson, *Lineages of the Absolutist State*, p. 108; B. Porchnev, *Les Soulèvements Populaires en France de 1623 à 1648* (Paris, 1963), p. 563.

CHAPTER 12

The 'idealistic superstructure'

Marx claims that society's relations of production constitute the base not only for its political institutions, but also for its characteristic forms of thought and ideology: social being determines social consciousness. In this chapter we examine Marx's claims for the social determination of consciousness and argue that Marx's case is more complex than his critics have often realised. Marxists have been particularly concerned with ideological forms of consciousness, ideology being used in a critical sense to mean a distorted representation of social reality. Here we examine the nature of such distortions and argue that whilst Marxists have usefully described the workings of ideology their attempts to use the concept as an explanation of the continued dominance of the ruling class have been less successful. Finally, functional explanations of ideology are assessed and we argue that in this area functional ideology can have a limited validity, at least in those cases where human intention is specified as the feedback mechanism through which a social institution (in this case a specific body of thought) is brought into existence because of its tendency to produce certain effects.

The social determination of consciousness

In the 1859 'Preface' Marx claims that the relations of production constitute the 'economic structure of society, the real foundation on which arises a legal and political superstructure, and to which correspond definite forms of social consciousness'.[1] Lukes and Plamenatz interpret this to mean that social consciousness is derived from the political and legal superstructure, but this is a rather convoluted reading of this passage.[2] The 'Preface' is best understood to mean that both the state and social consciousness correspond directly to the economic foundation of society. Repeatedly, Marx makes clear his argument that, just as the relations of production correspond to the productive forces, so humans 'produce also their principles, ideas and categories in conformity with their social relations'.[3] Typically, Marx elsewhere also argues for a *direct* determination of consciousness by the productive forces *and* for a joint determination by the productive forces and the relations of production, which together constitute the social basis of the 'idealistic superstructure'. In general, though, his emphasis is on the social, rather than the 'technological', determination of ideas: 'It is not the consciousness of men which determines their existence, but their social existence which determines their consciousness.'[4]

The difficulty with such formulations, as we have already seen, is that not all forms of consciousness can be located in the 'superstructure', distinct from the productive forces or the relations of production. On the contrary, ideas can form part of the productive forces (e.g. science), or of the relations of production (e.g. kinship in Aboriginal society). The distinction between the social 'levels' is not one of separate institutions, or between the 'material' and the 'ideal'. The distinction between the separate aspects of social structure is one of *function*. It cannot be claimed that ideas are merely a secondary effect of social relations, since ideas themselves may function as part of the relations of production. The ability to think, and to possess consciousness, is as inherently a human trait as the ability to produce. Indeed, Marx makes the use of consciousness into one of the distinguishing features of specifically *human* production.[5] Ideas are not, in general, part of the superstructure and so dependent on the base, rather *certain* ideas are seen (metaphorically) as part of the idealistic superstructure because they are determined by the base. The 'idealistic superstructure' is thus a residual category consisting of those ideas (legal, political, moral, aesthetic, philosophical and so on) which do not constitute part of the productive forces, or of the relations of production. It is ideas in this more limited sense which we are concerned with in this chapter.

Marx emphasised, time and time again, that ideas and consciousness cannot form the starting point for an analysis of humanity, society or the state:

> Does it require deep intuition to comprehend that man's ideas, views and conceptions, in one word, man's consciousness, changes with every change in the conditions of his material existence, in his social relations and in his social life? What else does the history of ideas prove,

than that intellectual production changes in proportion as material production has changed?[6]

When we seek to explain why, for instance, the principle of authority
was manifested in the eleventh century or the principle of individualism
in the eighteenth century:

> we are necessarily forced to examine minutely what men were like in
> the eleventh century, what they were like in the eighteenth century,
> what were their respective needs, their productive forces, their mode of
> production, the raw materials of their production - in short what were
> the relations between man and man which resulted from all of these
> conditions of existence.[7]

In this sense Marx offers a functional explanation of intellectual development:

> All epoch-making systems have as their real content the needs of the
> time in which they arose. Each one of them is based on the antecedent
> development of a nation, the historical growth of its class relations with
> their political, moral, philosophical and other consequences.[8]

This is not to say that ideas are merely a reflection of existing social relations; they can in practice have a continuing influence, even when the
circumstances which generated them have disappeared. Each age creates
its own philosophy, but it must take as its starting point the body of
thought passed down by the previous age. In this sense 'the economy
creates nothing anew, but it determines the way in which the body of
thought found in existence is altered and further developed'. Socialists
and communists are, Marx claims, the theoreticians of the proletariat
but, nevertheless, they can only develop their theory through an
encounter with existing philosophical, political and economic systems.
Like every new theory, socialism 'had first to link itself on to the intellectual material which lay ready at hand, however deep its roots lay in
economic facts'.[9]

Ideas have no independent existence or history, says Marx, because
they arise not in some ideal heaven, but in the brains of concrete individuals as sublimates of their 'material life process'. As this life process
alters so does its 'ideological reflexes and echoes': 'It is not consciousness that determines life, but life that determines consciousness.'[10] This
does not mean, however, that humans are merely the passive puppets of
circumstances. Marx himself protested against Feuerbach's materialism
which forgot that 'men' are not only changed by circumstances, but that
'circumstances are changed by men'. From the very passage where he

argues that ideas can only be explained by their social environment Marx draws the conclusion that 'men are both the authors and actors of their own history'.[11] Certainly, Marx was well aware of the active role of ideas in history, of, for instance, the stimulus to capital accumulation provided by Protestantism.[12] But, given the circumstances in which Marx formed his views, this could never be his main emphasis. Marx's earliest intellectual opponents were the Hegelian thinkers, whom he condemned for presenting ideas as the dominant force in history, for their separation of thought from thinker and for their consequent presentation of intellectual history as the self-development of concepts. In *The German Ideology*, 'ideology' is simply the term Marx uses to critically characterise such idealism. Marx's mature thought was formed through a critique of contemporary political economy which, in its 'vulgar' form at least, he accused of proclaiming as everlasting truths the complacent views of the capitalists about their own world. 'Ideology' here comes to have a more general sense of apologia written from a particular class viewpoint. In such encounters Marx was bound to emphasise not the active role of ideas, but rather that ideas are not self-developing and that particular bodies of thought give a theoretical expression to the position and interests of particular classes.[13]

Marx presents his claims for the social determination of consciousness through the same metaphors that he used to illustrate the relationship between state and society. Ideas are described as the 'reflexes', 'reflections' and 'echoes' of social activity although, as we shall see, he believed that such reflections could take a distorted form. Human consciousness is described as the 'superstructure' which arises upon the 'basis' of civil society. Ideas are the 'outgrowth' of social conditions to which they 'correspond' or 'conform'.[14] In particular, Marx employs the metaphor of expression: consciousness is said to be an 'ideal expression' of material social relations; economic categories are 'but the theoretical expression', 'the abstraction' of the social relations of production.[15]

Class and ideology

As we have seen, Marx not only rejected the idealist notion that the realm of consciousness is independent and self-developing, but also attacked those such as Feuerbach who employed an abstract materialism. Feuerbach, like Marx, wanted to demonstrate the secular basis of religious thought, but in doing so he resolved the essence of religion into an abstract 'human essence'. Marx replied that it is not abstract individuals who produce religion and other forms of consciousness, but concrete individuals who belong to a specific society: 'the human essence is no abstraction inherent in each single individual. In its reality it is the ensemble of social relations.'

Ideas are neither the product of 'human nature' nor of the abstraction of 'society'. Rather, 'a definite consciousness is appropriate to a definite people and definite circumstances'.[16] Within a given society there will, therefore, be a diversity of competing ideologies. In France, in the first half of the nineteenth century, for example, a number of classes, and fractions of classes, produced their own corresponding form of political ideology:

> Upon the different forms of property, upon the social conditions of existence, rises an entire superstructure of distinct and peculiarly formed sentiments, modes of thought and views of life. The entire class creates and forms them out of its material foundation and corresponding social relations.[17]

Landed property found its expression in the ideology of the Bourbon party, finance capital in the Orleanists, the industrial bourgeoisie in Republicanism and the petty bourgeoisie in Social Democracy, which expressed the petty-bourgeois desire to harmonise the relations of capital and labour. The elections of 4 May 1848 thus brought to the National Assembly not the abstract, political citizens of Republican ideology, but rather concrete, social individuals who acted as the 'representatives of the different classes'.[18]

Marx recognised, however, that there is no simple correlation between the social origin of intellectuals and the class which they 'represent'. The Social Democratic representatives of the French petty bourgeoisie, for instance, were not necessarily shopkeepers themselves, or even the enthusiastic champions of shopkeepers. In their education and social position thinker and class may be as far apart as heaven and earth:

> What makes them (the Social Democrats – S.R.) representatives of the petty bourgeoisie is the fact that in their minds they do not go beyond the limits which the latter do not go beyond in life, that they are consequently driven, theoretically, into the same problems and solutions to which material interest and social position drive the latter practically. This is, in *general*, the relationship between the political and literary representatives of a class and the class they represent.[19]

Marx certainly did not explain his own revolutionary views in terms of his particular social situation, but by that of the proletariat, since communist consciousness, he claimed, could arise amongst those intellectuals who contemplated the position of the proletariat in modern society.[20] Similarly, the literary representatives of the propertied classes need not be propertied themselves. Quesnay, whose economic system 'represented the imminent and certain triumph of the French bourgeoisie', was himself a physician to Louis XV.[21] Thomas Malthus, a cleric, provided an apologia for the landlordism which the Ricardians saw as a hindrance to capitalist development yet Malthus's own views were hardly a direct expression of his own economic interests. As he said when contrasting his own position with that of his friend Ricardo: 'it is somewhat singular that Mr. Ricardo, a considerable receiver of rents, should have so much underrated their importance, while I, who have never received nor expect to receive any, shall probably be accused of overrating their importance'.[22] Within the ruling class there is thus a division of labour between the ideologists 'who make the formation of the illusions of the class about itself the chief source of their livelihood' and the active members of the class, a division of labour which 'can even develop into a certain opposition and hostility between the two parts'.[23]

Marx's recognition of the possible distance between the social position of the thinker and the class-position which his or her thought represents, should preclude any interpretation of this theory of ideology as simply a cynical deception created by a vested interest. At times Marx did lapse into such a cynicism: 'The Tories in England long imagined that they were enthusiastic about monarchy, the church and the beauties of the English constitution until the day of danger wrung from them the confession that they were enthusiastic only about ground rent.'[24] Marx also referred cynically to the Bourbons as 'merely the political expression of the hereditary rule of the lords of the soil' and to the Orleanists as 'only the political expression of the usurped rule of the bourgeois *parvenus*'. Yet he went on to say that such individual political loyalties were also the expression of 'old memories, personal enmities, fears and hopes, prejudices and illusions, sympathies and antipathies, convictions, articles of faith and principles', i.e. in short, were not 'merely' the result of material social interest.[25] Marx offered a similarly uncynical interpretation of the world-view of the petty bourgeoisie: 'One must not form the narrow-minded notion that the petty bourgeoisie, on principle, wishes to enforce an egoistic class interest. Rather it believes that the special conditions of its emancipation are the general conditions within the frame of which alone modern society can be saved and the class struggle avoided.'[26] Marx argues, in general, that ideas are determined by social circumstances. Nevertheless, the inheritance of past ideas, the division of labour between thinkers and the class to which their ideas are best suited, the complexity of personal motivations and the fact that ideas are an important influence on social development, all mean that there can be no one-to-one correlation of social class and ideology, nor a simple one-way determination of ideas by society.

Marx opened up a further distance between a class and its ideology when he drew a distinction between the forms of consciousness which are in a class's best interest and the ideology which it actually adopts in practice. This is not, for Marx, such a problem with the ruling class who, he believed, would naturally come up with ideologies defending their own power and privilege, whether through the feudal emphasis on hierarchy (which justified social inequality), or the bourgeois emphasis on the equality of worker and capitalist as buyers and sellers in the market-place (which in effect denies any fundamental social inequality).[27]

Marx did not, however, believe that the producing classes would arrive as easily at an ideology which expressed their own interests. Socialists and communists, for instance, may be the 'theoreticians of the proletarian class', but Marx was well aware that the proletariat need not share their theoretical outlook.[28] Indeed, Marx went so far as to claim that 'the ideas of the ruling class are in every epoch the ruling ideas'. The ruling class not only owns the means of material production but also the 'means of mental production' and so is able to 'regulate the production and distribution of the ideas of the age'.[29] As a result the producing class need not necessarily develop an outlook which corresponds to its own best interests. The French peasants of the nineteenth century, who turned to Louis Napoleon to restore their former glory, were embracing an ideology which was based on 'illusion' and 'absurdity', on 'hallucinations', 'superstition' and 'prejudice', produced in the death struggle of the peasantry.[30]

Similarly, Marx argued that the consciousness of the proletariat will not automatically express its real interests. The position of the working class in modern society forces it into contradiction with all other classes and gives it the potential to develop a revolutionary communist consciousness which seeks to abolish class. Yet this potential consciousness, which Lukács later labelled 'imputed consciousness', is not necessarily the consciousness which the proletariat actually has at all times and in all places.[31] Indeed, in 1850 Marx claimed that he had 'always resisted the momentary opinion of the proletariat'.[32] He thus distinguished between the consciousness which the working class has and the consciousness which it 'ought' to have: 'instead of the conservative motto "A fair day's wages for a fair day's work" they (the working class – S.R.) *ought* to inscribe on their banner the revolutionary watchword, "abolition of the wages system"'.[33]

This potential form of working-class consciousness can, Marx claimed, only emerge when bourgeois society has developed to its fullest extent and the clash of capitalism's productive forces with its relations of production leads to a new crisis; a crisis which originates in the realm of production, but which is fought out in legal, political, artistic, philosophic, 'in short, *ideological* forms'.[34]

Marx argues that the ideology of a particular class is determined by 'material interest and social position'.[35] The politics of the labour movement of the advanced capitalist countries have been steadfastly reformist in tactics and strategy. It follows that the failure of the working class to develop a communist consciousness and to struggle to abolish classes is the result, either of its material interest, or its social position. The reformist response is, of course, that the labour movement's consciousness has been in its own best interest, so that there is no real gap between the working class's interests and the politics it has adopted.

The revolutionary response to this problem is that reformist politics have *not* been in the working class's best interests. Some aspect of its social position must therefore have prevented the working class from arriving at the consciousness which its own interests would dictate. Candidates for the factor which prevents the development of a revolutionary working-class consciousness fall into two main categories: divisions in the working class (such as the privileges of the labour aristocracy; the power and status enjoyed by men within the family; the advantages of sharing in the exploitation of the Third World) and the distortions produced by the dominant ruling-class ideology (commodity fetishism which obscures the true nature of capitalist exploitation; nationalism, which encourages inter-class unity; the power of the capitalist and state-owned mass media; the illusions of equality generated by political democracy, where capitalist and worker have an equal vote in the ballot box; the paternalism of factory owners; and so on). In so far as these arguments function as explanations of the consciousness which workers *do* have, rather than as answers to the pseudo-problem of why workers do not have the form of consciousness which revolutionaries think they *should* have, they are useful. The problem with this perspective is not the historical one of explaining working-class consciousness, but the *political* one of how this consciousness is to be overcome; a problem which condemns revolutionary groups to being propaganda sects on the fringes of the labour movement, attempting to counter the consciousness generated by the working class's social position with the power of 'correct' ideas.

The claim that 'the ruling ideas of the age are the ideas of the ruling class' is used by Althusser as a functional explanation of how the ruling class maintains its supremacy. Althusser argues that the reproduction of society's relations of production is secured not only by the legal-political, repressive state apparatus, but also, crucially, by the ideological state apparatuses: education, the family, political parties, trade unions and so forth. Ideology is vital in perpetuating class society: 'no class can hold state power over a long period of time without at the same time exercising its hegemony over and in the State Ideological Apparatuses'.[36] The problem with such 'hegemonic' explanations of the reproduction of class relations is that, in effect, they merely rephrase the question which is to be answered, since why the producers accept ruling-class ideas is the very problem which is to be solved in the first place. A description of the mechanisms through which the ruling class attempts to secure its hegemony is not, in itself, an explanation of why such mechanisms are so successful.

A further problem is to what extent the ideas of the ruling class are accepted by members of the producing class. Did, for example, the working class of the nineteenth and early twentieth century adopt, in practice, the free-market, individualistic ideology of the bourgeoisie? The working class may not have developed the communist consciousness which Marx had hoped for but, nevertheless, its collective struggles did play a part in bringing about massive social change. The 'dominant ideology' is thus not merely imposed from above. It is subject to struggle, resistance and negotiation. This problem is particularly apparent in pre-industrial societies where the limited social role of the state and the absence of the mass media make it particularly difficult for the ruling classes to propagate their ideology. The persistence of feudal class relations may not have been the result of any hegemonic ideology, but rather of the peasants' preoccupation with the 'dull, economic compulsion' of scraping together a living and their isolation within local communities which prevented the formation of a national class 'for itself', united against a common enemy. Peasant victories in the class struggle were therefore local and piecemeal, rather than the result of national revolts which could only gain a unity through an attack on the corruption and financial exactions of the national government.[37] Thus the fact that the ruling class manages to maintain its supremacy does not, in itself, mean that its ideology enjoys active support amongst the mass of population.

The distortions of ideology

So far, we have used the term 'ideology' in a loose sense, to mean a set of ideas and assumptions about the nature of society. Lenin uses the word in this way when he says that 'the only choice is either bourgeois or socialist ideology'. Other Marxists have, however, given the term a more specific meaning. Larrain, for instance, argues that an ideology is not merely the consciousness of a particular class, but is a body of thought which has particular effects: it conceals social contradictions and so serves the interests of the ruling class. Ideology thus comprises only a part of society's idealistic superstructure and can, for instance, be distinguished from the 'free spiritual production' of an age. Both arise from the base of the productive forces and relations of production but, in itself, the fact that an idea is socially determined is not enough to define it as ideological. Marx claimed that *all* ideas are socially determined, including his own: 'the existence of revolutionary ideas in a particular period presupposes the existence of a revolutionary class'.[38] Elsewhere Marx gives a looser determination to revolutionary ideas. Such ideas do not require the presence of a revolutionary class for their existence, but they do depend upon such a class in order to have any *efficacy*. (Presumably this is why Marx's own revolutionary ideas have had so little impact in the advanced capitalist countries.) The idea of a communist Utopia may arise over and over again but, without sufficient development of the productive forces and the corresponding development of a revolutionary class, this idea will have no practical impact. Nevertheless, even these early communist schemes were not produced in isolation from society. They were the products of a capitalism where the proletariat was still in its infancy and existed for philosophers only as the most suffering class, rather than as the agent of revolution.[39] Marx argues, therefore, that both the generation of specific ideas, and their historical impact, are socially determined.

Those Marxists who use the term 'ideology' in a specific, critical sense argue that not only are ideological ideas socially determined, they are also an inadequate, partial or distorted picture of the world. Paul Hirst has rejected this view of ideology as a form of 'false consciousness': 'ideology is not illusory … because how can anything which has effects be false? It would be like saying that a black pudding or a steamroller is false.'[40] However, the fact that something has effects does not mean that it cannot be false. The anti-Semitic ideology of the Middle Ages, which held that the Black Death was caused by the Jews poisoning wells, certainly had effects (attacks on the Jews) and yet can still be seen as false. Unlike steamrollers and black puddings, ideology makes claims about the nature of society. Unless we adopt the relativist position that all such claims are equally valid, it is possible to distinguish between them. Certainly, an assessment of the adequacy of an idea is an implicit part of historical explanation: how we account for the belief that the plague was caused by the Jews poisoning wells will depend, to a large extent, on whether or not we believe that the Jews poisoned wells in the first place.

Yet, in itself, error or inadequacy is not enough to define an idea as ideological since the history of science is, to a large extent, the history of error. An error is thus regarded by Marxists as ideological when it is socially motivated and, in particular, when it serves the purposes of the ruling class. In fact, whether or not we confine the label of 'ideology' only to those ideas which are erroneous and functional for the ruling class, is largely a semantic point.[41] If we use the term in this way, then we need other terms for ideas which are either not erroneous or which do not serve the interest of the ruling class. Ideologies in the broad sense of general claims about the nature of society and politics may be divided into four groups:

(1) Classic dominant ideologies which are inadequate accounts of reality and which defend the interests of the ruling class. The medieval claim that the feudal order was part of a divine plan in which social groups formed a complementary hierarchy is a typical example.

(2) Subversive ideologies which are inadequate accounts of reality and yet counter to the interests of the ruling class. A classic instance is that of radical religious movements. Thomas Munzer's belief that the godly elect should prepare for the Millennium by killing off the ungodly, including priests and princes, was hardly a force for ruling-class hegemony in sixteenth-century Germany, yet neither was it an entirely adequate account of social reality.

(3) Subversive ideologies which are adequate accounts of reality and counter to the interests of the ruling class. Trotsky's theory of 'permanent revolution', which correctly predicted that a revolution in Russia would not be led by the bourgeoisie or be restricted to bourgeois aims, could be given as an example.

(4)   Post-revolutionary ideologies which are adequate accounts of real-
      ity and which serve the interests of the new ruling class, e.g. for
      Marxists, scientific socialism after the proletarian revolution. As no
      proletarian revolution has yet established socialism in the form in
      which Marx envisaged it, we would have to include the official
      ideologies of 'actually existing' socialist societies in category (1),
      as inadequate accounts of reality which serve the ruling class. The
      Soviet bureaucracy's denial of its own class existence is a typical
      example of this.

Marxist accounts of ideology have tended to stress the scientific short-
comings of ideology, particularly those ideas which serve the dominant
class. The subtitle of *The German Ideology* is 'A Critique of Modern German
Philosophy'; the subtitle of *Capital* is 'A Critique of Political Economy'. In
both works, Marx expounds his own view of social reality through a critique of the inadequacies of competing systems of thought. In the former work, Marx tackles the explicit ideas expounded by philosophers;
in the later he is also concerned with the implicit assumptions which
form the 'common sense' of the agents involved in the production
process. In *The German Ideology*, Marx's emphasis is on the distorting inversion performed by ideology: 'in all ideology men and their relations
appear upside down as in a *camera obscura*'; in *Capital* he is more concerned
with the distinction between misleading outer appearances and inner
reality (or essence) which science allows us to understand.[42] What is
noticeable, however, is the continuity in Marx's analysis of ideology
between the two works.

In *The German Ideology* Marx's emphasis is on the distorting inversion of
reality performed by Hegelian thought. Both the conservative Hegel and
the radical Young Hegelians dissolved human existence into consciousness. According to the Young Hegelians, 'the relations of men, all their
doings ... are products of consciousness'. For Hegel, ideas are the bonds
which hold society together; for the Young Hegelians they are the fetters
which chain humanity, fetters which will only be overcome by a change
in consciousness. The Young Hegelians thus criticised the conceptions
and ideas produced by oppressed humanity, rather than the conditions
which created such conceptions. Marx argued that this was to turn reality upside down; it is not ideas which are the basis of society, but social
relations which are the basis for politics and ideas. The Hegelians forget
that ideas are the products of real humans in specific societies and so
present ideas as independent entities; the creations of the human brain
are perceived as something distinct and separate from their creators.[43]

286

Just as the fetishism of primitive tribes ascribes powers to inanimate objects so, in religion and philosophy, 'the productions of the human brain appear as independent beings endowed with life and entering into relations with one another and the human race'. Marx applied this concept of fetishism to capitalist commodity production: 'in religion man is governed by the products of his own brain, so in capitalist production he is governed by the products of his own hand'. Capitalism thus appears as relations between commodities which are, in reality, only the product of human labour and social relations.[44]

Ideology thus inverts reality and, in doing so, reifies the products of the human brain and hand into independent, fetishised objects. The concrete social relations which form the empirical basis of human history are thus turned into the predicate of 'the Idea', of the state, or of the commodity.[45] The problem remains, however, of why philosophers, economist and agents of the production process produce or accept this distorted inversion of reality. Marx's answer is that the distortion is not the result of human idiocy, but results from the fact that reality itself appears in a distorted form. Ideology is a 'reflection' of the human situation, but it is a reflection of the misleading outer appearance of social relations, rather than their inner reality, the appearance, for example, that the rule of a particular class is only the rule of particular ideas.[46] Similarly, in his critique of political economy, Marx argues that 'vulgar economy' sticks to the realm of appearances instead of revealing the underlying laws which regulate and explain those appearances:

> Vulgar economy actually does no more than interpret, systematize and defend in doctrinaire fashion the conceptions of the agents of bourgeois production who are entrapped in bourgeois production relations. It should not astonish us, then, that vulgar economy feels particularly at home in the estranged outward appearance of economic relations. ... But all science would be superfluous if the outward appearance and the essence of things coincided.[47]

Ideology is thus a 'fantastic reflection' of the world, rather than a faithful one. It is the task of the ideology of the ruling class to mask the true nature of social relations: the fact that they are human products and thus capable of human change. All ruling classes thus attempt to eternalise their social relations, not only in reality, but also in the realm of thought.[48] Feudal ideology, for instance, legitimised feudal social relations by presenting them as ordained by God.[49] Modern political economy eternalises social relations by presenting capitalism as the expression of 'inviolable natural laws': 'just as theologians present every religion which is not their own as an invention of man, so economists present the institutions of capitalism as natural and those of other social orders as "artificial".The age of history, of change, is now over since capitalist social relations are held to be natural and, as such, eternal.'[50] In this way, dominant ideologies attempt to reduce class conflict by harmonising social relations with some wider abstraction, such as the divine will, human nature (if they are pessimistic), human reason (if they are optimistic) or the national interest.

Marx's emphasis on ideology as a misrecognition and as the 'common sense' of the age is developed in Althusser's theory of ideology. As we have seen, Althusser's account of ideology poses problems in so far as it attempts to explain why class relations are reproduced but, nevertheless, Althusser's description of how ideology works has much to offer the historian. Firstly, ideology is not merely a body of abstract ideas, it is a set of material actions, practices and rituals. Puritan ideology, for example, was not merely embodied in the books of Calvin or William Perkins, but was also a 'lived reality' in the actions of the Puritans: preaching, family worship, observance of the Sabbath, rejection of traditional sports and so on. Secondly, ideology is not merely a passive reflection of social relations. Ideology is an active process with its own effects: the formation of human consciousness. Ideology constitutes concrete individuals as subjects. It is through ideology that individuals acquire their social identity (as, for instance, Protestant Englishmen) and fulfil their place within the social structure. Nevertheless, although ideology is a 'lived reality' for those who experience it, it is an inadequate account of reality and as such constitutes the *imaginary* relationship of individuals to their *real* conditions of existence.[51]

It is precisely because ideology is an inadequate account of social relations that it cannot, for Marxists, provide the key to an understanding of an epoch: 'whilst in ordinary life every shopkeeper is very well able to distinguish between what somebody professes to be and what he really is, our historiography has not yet won this trivial insight. It takes every epoch at its word and believes that everything it says and imagines about itself is true.'[52] Like Durkheim, Freud and Pareto, Marx explains social life 'not by the notions of those who participate in it, but by more profound causes which are unperceived by consciousness'.[53] Winch has objected to this approach and argues that social explanation must be in terms of concepts which are familiar to the observed as well as to the observer. It is the task of philosophy to compare the ways in which different ways of thinking make the world intelligible, but it is not its task to enshrine any particular form of enquiry as the key to reality: 'it is not its business to award prizes to science, religion or anything else'.[54]

It is difficult to imagine a history which kept to these precepts. Take, for instance, the accusations of witchcraft made in early modern England. Our explanation of such accusations is directly dependent upon an assessment of whether witches did exist and whether they were able to produce the effects of which they were accused. If we award a prize to science and assume that witches did not possess a magical power, we are free to suggest other reasons why people made such accusations. One such social explanation is that accusations of witchcraft arose from the anxieties caused by the competing claims of communal charity and individual accumulation, a conflict which led to the hostility felt by those who refused charity being projected onto those who were refused help.[55] This explanation invokes concepts not familiar to the observed (the unconscious, projection) and claims to have a superior key to reality to those who made the witchcraft accusations. Whether we accept this particular explanation of witchcraft is immaterial. It merely illustrates that historical explanations of witchcraft rest on the assumed inadequacy of magical accounts of reality. If we refuse to make such an assessment then we cannot move beyond our starting point: people made witchcraft accusations because they believed in witches. In this sense Marxism represents part of the achievement of nineteenth- and early twentieth-century social science which saw that ideas are not only historical explanations, but themselves require social explanation.

Social explanation, functional explanation and ideology: the case of Protestantism

Marx provides, in a sense, a functional explanation of ideology: 'all epoch-making systems have as their real content the needs of the time in which they arose'.[56] A functional explanation is one where 'the *consequences* of some behaviour or social arrangement are essential elements of the causes of that behaviour'. In other words, 'it is always a good bet in trying to explain a social phenomenon, to look at its consequences'. Stinchcombe claims that ideology may be functionally explained in terms of its beneficial consequences for the prevailing relations of production: 'the approach is summarised in the famous phrase, "The ruling ideas of any age are the ideas of the ruling class"'.[57] Certainly, the ruling class's adoption of a particular ideology may be explained in terms of its benefits, either for the ruling class's own internal cohesion, or for the maintenance of its supremacy over other classes. Marx argues, for example, that religion helps to legitimise the privileges of the ruling class and to preserve social inequality.[58] But, as with most functional explanations, this claim has merely reformulated the very question which we were trying to answer, i.e. why is religion able to carry out the function of maintaining social inequality so effectively (assuming that it does have this function)? In particular, why do the ruled accept an ideology which is functional for their rulers but unbeneficial for themselves? Elsewhere, Marx explains the attraction of religion in terms of its consoling effects for the poor and powerless.[59] Once more, Marx offers a functional explanation; the producers adopt a particular ideology because of its benefits, the consolation of knowing that they will be rewarded in the next world for their sufferings in this world. In such cases functional explanation is legitimate because human intention is specified as the mechanism which explains why people adopt ideas which will have beneficial consequences for them. This does not necessarily mean that people consciously sit down and assess the benefits of competing systems of thought. Rather, in practice, people will adopt the ideas which their social position drives them towards.[60]

But if this is the case, we cannot claim that religion exists in order to cement social relations, however much this is the intention (conscious or unconscious) of the ruling class. The conservative effects of religion are an unintended consequence of its consoling effects for the poor. Such unintended consequences constitute the weak point of the case for functional explanations which assume, because x is followed by y, that x occurred in order to bring about y. If invoking human intentions makes functional explanation legitimate, then unintended consequences must present it with massive problems.

The problems involved in giving a functional explanation of ideology are apparent in Cohen's account of the rise of Protestantism:

> Protestantism arose when it did because it was a religion suited to stimulating capitalist enterprise and enforcing labour discipline. ... When Marx says that 'Protestantism, by changing almost all traditional holidays into workdays, plays an important part in the genesis of capital' he is not just assigning a certain effect to the new religion, but proposing a (partial) explanation of its rise in terms of its effect.[61]

Let us, for the moment, assume that there is some causal link between Protestantism and the rise of capitalism.[62] How have historians and social scientists expressed this relationsip? What are the implications of their accounts for the validity of functional explanation?

290

The classic Marxist account of Protestantism is that the new religion, particularly in its Calvinist form, was the effect of the economic and social change accompanying the rise of capitalism: 'Calvin's creed was one fittest for the boldest of the bourgeoisie of his time. His predestination doctrine was the religious *expression* of the fact that in the commercial world of competition success or failure does not depend upon a man's action or cleverness but upon circumstances uncontrollable by him.' In an age of economic revolution the emerging capitalist class adopted an ideology which not only reflected its social positoin but also, in turn, actively furthered its economic and political interests.[63]

This interaction of society and ideology is emphasised in Christopher Hill's accounts of English Puritanism. Hill is well aware that religion was not just a social rationalisation which acted as a cloak for vested interests. Puritanism was a system of thought involving deep spiritual questioning and principles for which people were prepared to kill and be killed. Yet in order to explain the attraction of this body of thought we still need to identify its social roots: 'to understand Puritanism we must understand the needs, hopes, fears and aspirations of the godly artisans, yeoman gentlemen and ministers and their wives, who gave their support to its doctrines. ... It seemed to point the way to heaven because it helped them to live on earth.' Early studies of Puritanism tended to concentrate on its social and economic doctrines, such as its slight relaxation of the prohibition of usury. Hill argues, like Weber, that Puritans were more concerned with the salvation of the soul than with lower interest rates. It is the basis of Puritan theology, rather than its secondary economic doctrines, which is the centre of his analysis in *Society and Puritanism*. The Puritan insistence on observing Sunday as a day of rest, for instance, could be seen as irrational Bibliolatry, as witnessed by the fierce discussions as to whether Saturday or Sunday should be kept as the sabbath. Yet the Bible had been read for centuries without the issue being perceived as important: 'the Bible is a large book in which men find different things in different ages in different circumstances'. Hill explains the new concern with the regular observation of weekly rest in relation to the needs of the yeomen, artisans and merchants, the 'industrious sort of people', who formed the backbone of Puritanism. This middle class found in Sabbatarianism an appealing doctrine which helped to overcome the irregular work routines of medieval society with its many saints' days: in 1561, in Geneva, the apprentices' traditional Wednesday holiday was abolished for being against the will of God; by the late seventeenth century, an English economist was calculating that every holiday cost the nation £50,000. Puritanism did not, however, only 'reflect' the growth of capitalism. It was also an active force, facilitating the transition from a society where labour was seen as the curse of Man, to one where devotion to one's calling was a means of glorifying God, a society where poverty was no longer seen as a holy state but was regarded as a sign of wickedness, a society where the sin of avarice had become the virtue of thrift and where indiscriminate alms-giving had been replaced by the search for the 'deserving poor'.[64]

It could, of course, be argued against Hill that Sabbatarianism was merely part of a wider Protestant attack on the 'superstition' of the Catholic church whose ceremony and devotion to saints came between God and the individual believer. But even if this were the case, we would still be left with the problem of explaining why the piety of one age became the superstition of another. Nor can it be objected that Hill's argument means that Puritanism only appealed to a capitalist middle class. Hill argues that the Puritan insistence on inner faith could provide a justification for resistance to a variety of forms of traditional authority: it could appeal to the rebellious gentry of Scotland or Hungary, or to the lower classes of the Dutch towns.[65] Just as Marxism in twentieth-century China has at various times been the ideology of revolutionary intellectuals, of the urban working class, of peasant revolt, of nationalist resistance and, finally, a means of legitimising the rule of the Communist Party bureaucracy, so Protestantism could carry out a number of functions and appeal to a variety of classes. It could be the 'political religion of intellectuals and gentlemen' as well as the social religion of yeomen and merchants. It could offer the promise of social order and discipline, as well as forming the basis for a radical individualism.[66]

The important point, for our purposes, is that the logic of Hill's argument is a valid one; the industrious, middling sort of people adopted Puritanism because of its benefits for them, its suitability for their interests and social position. The weakness of his analysis is not methodological, but empirical. It founders on a vague definition of the 'middling sort', a group which had its own internal divisions of interest. In practice, despite Hill's own intentions, his analysis seems to show that Puritanism appealed to the gentry, common lawyers and richer merchants and that Sabbatarianism had to be imposed on the middling sort by the JPs and municipal authorities.[67] Whether Hill's account of Puritanism is empirically valid or not, is not our concern here. It simply provides us with a classic example of the social explanation of the appeal of a specific ideology to a particular social group. If this is the argument favoured by Cohen, it gains nothing by being expressed in functional form (i.e. Protestantism is explained by its effects) since, in practice, it is merely an argument from intention (i.e. people adopt certain ideas within the limits of their social position and interests).

Weber's analysis of the relationship between Protestantism and capitalism is often seen as the opposite of Marx's, but in fact the two are not so dissimilar.[68] Weber argued that Protestantism played a vital role in the development of a rational, capitalist spirit of accumulation through its emphasis on thrift, hard work and devotion to one's calling. Whether Calvinism did promote a spirit of endless accumulation is not our problem here.[69] What is important is Weber's emphasis on the capitalist spirit as an unintended and even unwished-for result of the Reformation. Calvinist asceticism was actually *less* open-minded than late medieval theology about the pursuit of wealth. Weber's point is that the Calvinist doctrine of predestination produced an anxiety about personal salvation in the next world which was overcome by activity in this world. The Calvinist condemnation of idleness thus tended to encourage the personal accumulation of capital whose effects the Calvinists themselves warned against.[70]

Weber's essay is not a history of the rise of capitalism and needs to be seen in the context of his wider purpose of tracing the effects of religion on economic change. However, this purpose meant that Weber paid little attention to the question of why Puritanism was attractive and to what extent it was itself influenced by economic and social change. In practice, Weber simply assumes that Puritanism was to be found amongst the middle classes; the small bourgeois and farmers whose emphasis on thrift and sober domesticity formed a mark contrast with the conspicuous consumption of the aristocratic household.[71] The problem is that without some analysis of why and to whom Puritanism was attractive, Weber's account lapses into a circular argument: the activity of the Puritans was a response to their sense of anxiety, but their anxiety was itself induced by the Puritan doctrine of predestination.[72] The question remains of *why* specific groups adopted this doctrine in the first place, a question to which Marxism has at least offered some answer. Like Marx, Weber believes that Protestantism stimulated the rise of capitalism but he sees this as an unintended effect of Protestant theology. As such, these effects cannot function as an explanation of Puritanism, since they offer no feedback mechanism whereby the tendency of *a* to promote *b* guarantees the existence of *a* in the first place.

Fromm and Walzer have offered an account of Protestantism which, in many ways, synthesises the Marxist and the Weberian approaches. Fromm agrees with Weber that Protestantism was a response to a situation of anxiety, worry and confusion, but argues that the causes of this personal insecurity must be found in the social change of the early modern period, particularly in the rise of capitalism, commerce and competition, with their resulting dangers and opportunities. The new religion offered solutions which enabled the individual to cope with an otherwise unbearable anxiety but, for Fromm, as for Weber, this was actually a conservative response to an era of change. Yet the forms of behaviour encouraged by the new religion had the paradoxical effect of encouraging the further development of capitalism. Like the Marxists, Fromm seeks the social roots of Protestantism; like the Weberians, he stresses its unintended effects.[73]

It is difficult to see which of these historical accounts would be compatible with Cohen's functional explanation of Protestantism. If, like Weber or Fromm, he sees the encouragement which Protestantism gave to capitalism as an unintended effect, he cannot invoke functional explanation since unintended consequences provide no mechanism through which Protestantism was brought into existence in order to produce certain effects. If Cohen believes that capitalism had not developed prior to the Reformation he would have to specify the mechanism which brought Protestantism into being because of its functional effects for future capitalist development. He makes no attempt to do this. Finally, Cohen could adopt the classical Marxist position that as capitalism began to develop the emerging bourgeoisie adopted Puritanism as the outlook best suited to its interests. This is an intentional argument which is logically valid, but which gains nothing from being expressed in functional terms. Invoking human intent does not so much disprove functional explanation, as make it totally redundant.

Conclusion

Marx's claims for the social determination of human consciousness are, perhaps, the least controversial aspects of his historical materialism. The social relativism of ideas is now the commonplace of history and social science. Ideological change and the impact of such change can only be fully accounted for in terms of contemporary social structure, but this does not mean that ideas are merely the passive reflections of their age. Ideologies are active historical forces producing both intended and unintended consequences. The social determination of consciousness may be expressed in functional form (an ideology is attractive because of its benefits for a particular social group) provided that we emphasise that such formulations invoke human intention as the mechanism linking cause and functional effect. Where the effects of ideology are not intentional, as in the conservative effects of religion's consolation for the poor, functional explanation is not legitimate even when ideology can be shown to have functional effects for the prevailing relations of production. We may disagree with Marxist accounts of the attractions of particular ideologies, such as Hill's analysis of Puritanism, but the task remains of explaining the generation and impact of ideas in terms of the contemporary social structure. It is not enough, for instance, to see Puritanism as 'an obstinately religious phenomenon', adopted according to 'taste and choice', particularly in a period when religion did not exist as a 'private' sphere, divorced from the social, political and cultural issues of the day.[74] Social explanations deal, of course, in probabilities; Hill's argument does not mean that all members of the middling sort found Puritanism attractive nor that all those attracted to Puritanism were of the middling sort. They remind us, however, that the study of history is the study of causes and that in explaining the ideologies of an age we cannot merely accept the opinion of that age about itself. In this assumption at least, Marx's historical method has become an integral part of modern social science.

Notes

1 K. Marx, *A Contribution to the Critique of Political Economy* (London, 1971), p. 20.
2 J. Plamenatz, *Man and Society*, vol. II (London, 1963), p. 274; S. Lukes, 'Can the base be distinguished from the superstructure?' in D. Miller & L. Siedentop (eds.), *The Nature of Political Theory* (Oxford, 1983), pp. 103–4.
3 K. Marx, *The Poverty of Philosophy* (Moscow, 1973), p. 95.
4 K. Marx & F. Engels, *Collected Works*, vol. V (London, 1976), pp. 36, 74, 159 (all references to *Collected Works*, vol. V are to *The German Ideology*); K. Marx, *Theories of Surplus Value*, part I (London, 1969), p. 285; Marx, *A Contribution to the Critique of Political Economy*, p. 21; K. Marx, *Grundrisse* (Harmondsworth, 1974), p. 540.
5 Above, pp. 28–9.
6 K. Marx & F. Engels, *The Communist Manifesto* (Harmondsworth, 1970), p. 102.
7 Marx, *The Poverty of Philosophy*, p. 100.
8 Marx & Engels, *Collected Works*, vol. V, p. 462.
9 Ibid., p. 438; Marx, *The Poverty of Philosophy*, p. 109; F. Engels, *Herr Eugen Dühring's*

Revolution in Science (London, Lawrence & Wishart, n.d.), p. 23; K. Marx & F. Engels, Selected Correspondence (Moscow, 1975), p. 401 (letter of Engels to Schmidt, 27.10.1890).
10 Marx & Engels, Collected Works, vol. V, pp. 36–7.
11 K. Marx, Early Writings (Harmondsworth, 1975), p. 422 (Concerning Feuerbach); Marx, The Poverty of Philosophy, p. 100.
12 Marx, Grundrisse, p. 232.
13 Marx & Engels, Collected Works, vol. V, pp. 62, 154; K. Marx, Capital, vol. I (London, 1977), p. 85; B. Parekh, Marx's Theory of Ideology (London, 1982), Ch. 1.
14 Marx & Engels, Collected Works, vol. V, pp. 36, 53, 159, 183–4, 189, 193; Marx, The Poverty of Philosophy, p. 95; Marx, A Contribution to the Critique of Political Economy, p. 20; Marx & Engels, The Communist Manifesto, p. 99.
15 Marx & Engels, Collected Works, vol. V, p. 59; Marx, The Poverty of Philosophy, pp. 91, 95, 161, 164; Marx, Grundrisse, p. 489.
16 Marx & Engels, Collected Works, vol. V, pp. 183, 250.
17 K. Marx, The Eighteenth Brumaire of Louis Bonaparte (Moscow, 1972), p. 37.
18 Ibid., pp. 37–8, 40; K. Marx, The Class Struggles in France 1848 to 1850 (Moscow, 1972), pp. 33, 48.
19 Marx, The Eighteenth Brumaire of Louis Bonaparte, pp. 40–1. (My emphasis.)
20 Marx & Engels, Collected Works, vol. V, p. 52; Marx & Engels, The Communist Manifesto, p. 91.
21 Marx, The Poverty of Philosophy, p. 90.
22 K. Marx, Theories of Surplus Value, part III (London, 1968), pp. 51-2; W. J. Barber, A History of Economic Thought (Harmondsworth, 1977), p. 79.
23 Marx & Engels, Collected Works, vol. V, pp. 60, 92.
24 Marx, The Eighteenth Brumaire of Louis Bonaparte, p. 38.
25 Ibid., p. 37. (My emphasis.)
26 Ibid., p. 40.
27 Marx & Engels, Collected Works, vol. V, p. 176; Marx, Capital, vol. I, pp. 172, 547–8.
28 Marx, The Poverty of Philosophy, p. 109.
29 Marx & Engels, Collected Works, vol. V, p. 59; Marx & Engels, The Communist Manifesto, pp. 100–2.
30 Marx, The Eighteenth Brumaire of Louis Bonaparte, pp. 105–12.
31 Marx & Engels, Collected Works, vol. V, p. 52; T. Lovell, 'Ideology and Coronation Street' in R. Dyer et al., Coronation Street (London, 1981), p. 42.
32 K. Marx, The Revolutions of 1848 (Harmondsworth, 1973), p. 343.
33 K. Marx, Wages, Prices and Profit (Moscow, 1970), p. 55. My emphasis.
34 Marx & Engels, Collected Works, vol. V, p. 52; Marx, A Contribution to the Critique of Political Economy, p. 21 (my emphasis); K. Marx, Surveys From Exile (Harmondsworth, 1973), p. 131.
35 Marx, The Eighteenth Brumaire, pp. 40–1.
36 L. Althusser, Lenin and Philosophy and Other Essays (London, 1971), pp. 137–41. Althusser's theory is well summarised by T. Bennett, Formalism and Marxism (London, 1981), pp. 112–18.
37 Marx, Capital, vol. I, p. 689; Marx, The Eighteenth Brumaire of Louis Bonaparte, pp. 105–6; N. Abercrombie, S. Hill & B. S. Turner, The Dominant Ideology Thesis (London, 1980), especially Ch. 3.

38 V. I. Lenin, *What is to be Done?* (Moscow, 1973), p. 40; J. Larrain, *The Concept of Ideology* (London, 1979), pp. 60–3, 210; Marx, *Theories of Surplus Value*, part I, p. 285.
39 Marx & Engels, *Collected Works*, vol. V, pp. 54, 60; Marx & Engels, *The Communist Manifesto*, pp. 114–18.
40 P. Q. Hirst, *Problems and Advances in the Theory of Ideology* (Cambridge, 1976), p. 16.
41 T. Lovell, *Pictures of Reality* (London, 1980), pp. 41, 51–3; J. McCarney, 'Recent interpretations of ideology', *Economy and Society* 14 (1985), pp. 77–93.
42 Marx & Engels, *Collected Works*, vol. V, p. 36.
43 Ibid., pp. 23–4, 28–30, 36, 54–7, 62, 154, 159.
44 Marx, *Capital*, vol. I, pp. 77, 582.
45 Marx, *Early Writings*, pp. 62, 65, 80 (Critique of Hegel's Doctrine of the State); Marx, *Capital*, vol. I, p. 29.
46 Marx, *Collected Works*, vol. V, pp. 36, 61.
47 Marx, *Capital*, vol. I, p. 291; K. Marx, *Capital*, vol. III (London, 1974), p. 817.
48 Engels, *Herr Eugen Dühring's Revolution in Science*, p. 353; Marx & Engels, *The Communist Manifesto*, pp. 100–2.
49 Marx & Engels, *Collected Works*, vol. V, p. 154.
50 Marx, *Grundrisse*, pp. 85–7; Marx, *The Poverty of Philosophy*, pp. 105–6.
51 Althusser, *Lenin and Philosophy*, pp. 153–62. See also n. 36 above.
52 Marx & Engels, *Collected Works*, vol. V, p. 62; Marx, *The Eighteenth Brumaire of Louis Bonaparte*, p. 28; Marx, *A Contribution to the Critique of Political Economy*, p. 21.
53 Durkheim quoted in P. Winch, *The Ideal of a Social Science and its Relation to Philosophy* (London, 1977), p. 23.
54 Ibid., pp. 48, 102–3.
55 K. Thomas, *Religion and the Decline of Magic* (Harmondsworth, 1973), p. 670.
56 Marx & Engels, *Collected Works*, vol. V, p. 462.
57 A. L. Stinchcombe, *Constructing Social Theories* (New York, 1968), pp. 80, 93–9.
58 Marx & Engels, *Collected Works*, vol. V, p. 159.
59 Ibid., p. 188.
60 Stinchcombe, *Constructing Social Theories*, p. 86; Marx, *The Eighteenth Brumaire of Louis Bonaparte*, pp. 40–1.
61 G. A. Cohen, *Karl Marx's Theory of History: A Defence* (Oxford, 1978), p. 279. The quotation is from Marx, *Capital*, vol. I, p. 262.
62 Brenner's recent studies of the transition to capitalism simply ignore this issue. See Ch. 8.
63 Engels, 'Introduction' to the English edition of *Socialism: Utopian and Scientific* in L. Stone, *Social Change and Revolution in England 1540–1640* (London, 1970), p. 3, my emphasis; Marx, *Capital*, vol. I, p. 262; Marx, *Grundrisse*, p. 232.
64 C. Hill (ed.), *The English Revolution of 1640* (London, 1940), pp. 44–5; C. Hill, *Puritanism and Revolution* (London, 1969), pp. 21, 215; C. Hill, *Change and Continuity in Seventeenth Century England* (London, 1974), pp. 82, 89; C. Hill, *Society and Puritanism in Pre-revolutionary England* (London, 1969), pp. 131, 142, 145, 494–5; M. Weber, *The Protestant Ethic and the Spirit of Capitalism* (London, 1978), p. 89.
65 Hill, *Change and Continuity in Seventeenth Century England*, p. 99; Weber, *The Protestant Ethic and the Spirit of Capitalism*, p. 108.
66 M. Walzer, *The Revolution of the Saints* (New York, 1974), p. 328; P. Collinson, *The Religion of Protestants* (Oxford, 1982), p. 150.

67 See the review of Hill's *Society and Puritanism* by B. Manning in *English Historical Review* LXXXI (1966), pp. 358–60.

68 G. Marshall, *In Search of the Spirit of Capitalism* (London, 1982), pp. 140–3; A Giddens, 'Marx, Weber and the development of capitalism', *Sociology* IV (1970), p. 302.

69 M. Walzer, 'Puritanism as a revolutionary ideology', *History and Theory* III (1964), pp. 66–7.

70 Weber, *The Protestant Ethic and the Spirit of Capitalism*, pp. 90, 112–14, 157, 175.

71 Ibid., pp. 83, 91, 171–2, 174, 179.

72 Walzer, 'Puritanism as a revolutionary ideology', p. 71.

73 Ibid., pp. 71, 76, 89; E. Fromm, *The Fear of Freedom* (London, 1975), pp. 53, 62, 68, 74, 78, 86–8; Weber, *The Protestant Ethic and the Spirit of Capitalism*, pp. 116–17.

74 Collinson, *The Religion of Protestants*, p. 241; P. Collinson, *English Puritanism* (Historical Association Pamphlet, general series 106; 1983), pp. 5–6.

Conclusion:
Marxism, politics and history

The time is long past when we should feel obliged to conclude with a Cold War-style affirmation or rejection of Marx's claims in their entirety. It is futile to decide for or against 'Marx' when it is possible to construct a number of textually-authorised Marxes, some of which can be refuted by others. There is Marx the productive force determinist and Marx who emphasised the primacy of class. There is Marx the economic fundamentalist and Marx who emphasised the dialectical interaction between the 'economic base' and the political and ideological 'superstructure'. There is Marx the structuralist, who presents humans as merely the personifications of economic relations, and there is Marx who regards humans as the authors and actors of their own history. It is equally futile to ask which of these is the 'real' Marx. The key task is to ask which is the most *useful* Marx.

The most profitable reading of Marx is one which stresses the primacy of society's relations of production over its productive forces. It is the relations of production which allow us to distinguish between societies and which govern the pace and development of the productive forces. The productive forces do act as an important influence on the nature of society's relations of production. In particular they act as a 'negative' determination,[1] setting borders and limits to which relations of production cannot come into existence: a society with net-hunting technology will have different social relations from one with micro-chip computers. But this does not mean that society's relations of production 'correspond' to the level of the productive forces, that the relations of production are functionally explained by the needs of the productive forces or that the productive forces are the prime movers of social change through their alleged inherent tendency to develop. It is impossible to offer any single, general explanation of the form taken by society's relations of production.

Historical materialism can legitimately be read as such a philosophy of history, which automatically provides the answers to questions as soon as we have asked them, but it is more useful when it is seen as a historical theory which allows us to ask questions and to construct hypotheses, rather than as a means of supplying ready-made answers. It is its concepts and questions which distinguish 'Marxist' history from other histories, rather than its forms of research and validation.

Marx's central contribution to the social sciences is his classification of societies according to their relations of production. It must, however, be emphasised that these relations of production cannot plausibly be seen as society's *economic* foundation, since they include those elements of politics and ideology which function as relations of production. Marx presents his classification of social types in terms of their specific forms of exploitation or 'surplus' labour but such concepts must be rejected, for our present purposes, because of their reliance on subjective moral criteria. The core of Marx's historical theory is a typology of class relations. Whether we consider such relations to be 'exploitative' is of vital importance in our roles as 'citizens', but such judgements cannot function as the basis of a shared typology of social relations.

Indeed, in more general terms, it is important to distinguish between Marx's politics and Marx's history. Acceptance of Marx's historical claims entails no commitment to his revolutionary politics, nor are his revolutionary politics guaranteed by his historical method. It would thus be quite possible to accept Marxist accounts of the transition to capitalism or of the social appeal of Puritanism and yet to vote Conservative tomorrow. The basis for Marx's social analysis was his wider concern with the possibility of human liberation but, nevertheless, his analysis must be judged on its own merits, rather than in terms of the revolutionary motivation which produced it. The original impetus to Marx's social theory came from his revolutionary politics, but Marxist social science has often come to suffer through its political associations with the conversion of Marx's hypotheses into tenets of faith (e.g. the labour theory of value) or into the over-simplifications of political propaganda (e.g. the state is merely an instrument of class oppression).[2]

In a recent article Professor Peter Abell asks if making sense of Marx is worth the effort. Why study nineteenth-century ideas when so much needs to be done to lay the foundations for a genuine social theory of our own century?[3] One answer to this question is that, whatever the state of social theory, the condition of much historical writing remains at a pre-Marxist stage of development. In particular, whilst much of the most interesting Marxist historical work is concerned with pre-industrial society, it is precisely in this area of historiography that Marxism, with its emphasis on the social constraints on politics and ideology, has had least impact. An encounter with Marx's diverse and contradictory claims sharpens the historian's questions, concepts and awareness of the forms of explanation implicit in all historical writing. We may emerge from this encounter perched on Marx's shoulders, or standing on the ruins of his system. Either vantage point allows us to see further and more clearly. It is an encounter which many historians have yet to undertake.

Notes

1 R. Williams, *Marxism and Literature* (Oxford, 1977), pp. 84–7. See pp. 144–6, above.
2 I. Steedman, *Marx after Sraffa* (London, 1977), pp. 21–6; F. Engels, 'Introduction' to K. Marx, *The Civil War in France* (Peking, 1970), p. 17.
3 P. Abell, 'Sorting out Marx's confusing legacy', *The Times Higher Education Supplement* 689 (17 January 1986), p. 18.

Bibliography

(Place of publication is London, unless otherwise stated.)

I Works by Marx and Engels

K. Marx, *Early Writings* (Harmondsworth, 1975).
K. Marx & F. Engels, *Collected Works*, vol. III (1975).
K. Marx & F. Engels, *Collected Works*, vol. IV (1975).
K. Marx & F. Engels, *Collected Works*, vol. V (1975).
K. Marx, *Wage Labour and Capital* (Moscow, 1970).
K. Marx, *The Poverty of Philosophy* (Moscow, 1973).
K. Marx & F. Engels, *The Communist Manifesto* (Harmondsworth, 1970).
K. Marx, *The Revolutions of 1848* (Harmondworth, 1973).
K. Marx, *Surveys from Exile* (Harmondsworth, 1973).
K. Marx, *The Class Struggles in France 1848 to 1850* (Moscow, 1972).
K. Marx, *The Eighteenth Brumaire of Louis Bonaparte* (Moscow, 1972).
K. Marx, *Grundrisse* (Harmondsworth, 1974).
K. Marx, *Pre-capitalist Economic Formations* (1975).
K. Marx, *A Contribution to the Critique of Political Economy* (1971).
K. Marx, *Capital*, vol. I (London, Lawrence & Wishart edn; 1977) (Harmondsworth, Pelican edn; 1976).
K. Marx, *Capital*, vol. II (London, Lawrence & Wishart; 1976) (Harmondsworth, Pelican; 1978).
K. Marx, *Capital*, vol. III (London, Lawrence & Wishart; 1979) (Harmondsworth, Pelican; 1981).
K. Marx, *Theories of Surplus Value*, part I (1969); part II (1969); part III (1972).
K. Marx, *The First International and After* (Harmondsworth, 1974).
K. Marx, *Wages, Price and Profit* (Moscow, 1970).
K. Marx, *The Civil War in France* (Peking, 1970).
K. Marx, *Critique of the Gotha Programme* (Moscow, 1971).
S. Avineri (ed.), *Karl Marx on Colonialism and Modernization* (New York, 1964).

T. B. Bottomore & M. Rubel (eds.), *Karl Marx: Selected Writings in Sociology and Social Philosophy* (Harmondsworth, 1970).

F. Engels, *Herr Eugen Dühring's Revolution in Science* (London, Lawrence & Wishart; n.d.).

F. Engels, *The Origin of the Family, Private Property and the State* (Moscow, 1968).

F. Engels, *Ludwig Feuerbach and the End of Classical German Philosophy* (Moscow, 1969).

F. Engels, 'Introduction' to *Socialism: Utopian and Scientific* in L. Stone (ed.), *Social Change and Revolution in England 1540–1640* (1970).

K. Marx & F. Engels, *Selected Correspondence* (Moscow, 1975).

K. Marx & F. Engels, *Selected Works*, vol. II (Moscow, 1962).

II Works by other writers

P. Abell, 'Sorting out Marx's confusing legacy', *The Times Higher Education Supplement* 689 (17 January 1986).

N. Abercrombie, S. Hill & B. S. Turner, *The Dominant Ideology Thesis* (1971).

P. Abrams, *Historical Sociology* (Shepton Mallet, 1982).

H. B. Acton, *The Illusion of the Epoch* (1951).

L. Althusser, *Lenin and Philosophy and other Essays* (1971).

——, *For Marx* (1977).

L. Althusser & E. Balibar, *Reading Capital* (1975).

S. Amin, *Unequal Development* (Hassocks, 1976).

——, *The Law of Value and Historical Materialism* (New York, 1978).

P. Anderson, *Passages from Antiquity to Feudalism* (1977).

——, *Considerations on Western Marxism* (1977).

——, *Lineages of the Absolutist State* (1979).

——, *Arguments Within English Marxism* (1980).

——, 'Class struggle in the ancient world', *History Workshop* 16 (autumn 1983).

R. Aron, *Main Currents in Sociological Thought*, vol. I (Harmondsworth, 1965).

J. Baechler, *The Origins of Capitalism* (Oxford, 1975).

A. M. Bailey & J. R. Llobera (eds.), *The Asiatic Mode of Production* (1981).

W. J. Barber, *A History of Economic Thought* (Harmondsworth, 1977).

J. Barnave, *Power, Property and History* (New York, 1971).

W. Beik, *Absolutism and Society in Seventeenth Century France* (Cambridge, 1985).

P. Bellis, *Marxism and the U.S.S.R.* (1979).

C. Belsey, *Critical Practice* (1980).

T. Bennett, *Formalism and Marxism* (1981).

C. Bettelheim, *Class Struggles in the U.S.S.R. 1917–23* (Hassocks, 1976).

I. Blanchard, 'Population growth, enclosure and the early Tudor economy', *Economic History Review* Second Series XXIII (1970).

M. Bloch, *Land and Work in Medieval Europe* (1967).

M. Bloch, *Marxism and Anthropology* (Oxford, 1983).

M. M. Bober, *Karl Marx's Interpretation of History* (Cambridge, Mass., 1962).

R. Bonney, 'Cardinal Mazarin and the great nobility during the Fronde', *English Historical Review* XCVI (1981).

P. Bowen, 'Agriculture, prices, farm profits and rent' in H. P. R. Finberg (ed.), *The Agrarian History of England and Wales*, vol. IV, 1500–1640 (Cambridge, 1967).

R. Brenner, 'Agrarian class structure and economic development in pre-

industrial Europe', *Past and Present* 70 (1976).
——, 'The origins of capitalist development: a critique of neo-Smithian Marxism', *New Left Review* 104 (July–August 1977).
——, 'Dobb on the transition from feudalism to capitalism', *Cambridge Journal of Economics* II (1978).
——, 'The agrarian roots of European capitalism', *Past and Present* 97 (1982).
L. I. Brezhnev, *The 50th Anniversary of the Union of Soviet Socialist Republics* (Moscow, 1972).
A. R. Bridbury, review of L. White, *Medieval Technology and Social Change* in *Economic History Review* Second Series XV (1962–3).
A. Briggs, *Victorian Cities* (Harmondsworth, 1978).
R. Browning, 'The class struggle in ancient Greece', *Past and Present* 100 (1981).
P. A. Brunt, 'A Marxist view of Roman history', *Journal of Roman Studies* LXXII (1982).
N. Bukharin, *Historical Materialism* (Michigan, 1969).
R. N. Carew-Hunt, *The Theory and Practice of Communism* (Harmondsworth, 1969).
E. H. Carr, *What is History?* (Harmondsworth, 1970).
T. Carver, *Marx's Social Theory* (Oxford, 1982).
S. Clark (ed.), *One Dimensional Marxism* (1980).
J. Caughie (ed.), *Theories of Authorship* (1981).
T. Cliff, *State Capitalism in Russia* (1974).
G. A. Cohen, 'On some criticisms of historical materialism', *Proceedings of the Aristotelian Society* XLIV (Supplement, 1970).
——, 'Being, consciousness and roles: on the foundations of historical materialism' in C. Abramsky & B. J. Williams (eds.), *Essays in Honour of E. H. Carr* (1974).
——, *Karl Marx's Theory of History: A Defence* (Oxford, 1978).
——, 'Functional explanation: a reply to Elster', *Political Studies* XXVIII (1980).
——, 'Reply to Elster on "Marxism, functionalism and game theory"', *Theory and Society* XI (1982).
——, 'Functional explanation, consequence explanation and Marxism', *Inquiry* XXV (1982).
——, 'Forces and relations of production' in B. Matthews (ed.), *Marx: A Hundred Years On* (1983).
J. Cohen, review of G. A. Cohen, *Karl Marx's Theory of History: A Defence*, *Journal of Philosophy* LXXIX (1982).
G. D. H. Cole, *Socialist Thought: The Forerunners 1789–1850* (1953).
R. G. Collingwood, *The Idea of History* (Oxford, 1976).
K. Collins, 'Marx on the English agricultural revolution: theory and evidence', *History and Theory* VI (1966).
P. Collinson, *The Religion of Protestants* (Oxford, 1982).
S. Connor, *Charles Dickens* (Oxford, 1985).
J. P. Cooper, 'In search of agrarian capitalism', *Past and Present* 80 (1978).
J. Cornwall, 'English population in the early sixteenth century', *Economic History Review* Second Series XXIII (1970).
G. Dalton, 'How exactly are peasants "exploited"?', *American Anthropologist* LXXVI (1974).
R. Davis, *The Rise of the Atlantic Economies* (1977).
G. E. M. De Ste Croix, *The Class Struggle in the Ancient Greek World* (1981).

I. Deutscher, *The Prophet Armed* (Oxford, 1954).

M. Djilas, *The New Class* (1957).

M. Dobb, *Studies in the Development of Capitalism* (1975).

——, 'Historical materialism and the role of the economic factor', *History* XXXVI (1951).

H. Draper, *Karl Marx's Theory of Revolution*, vol. I (New York, 1977).

C. Dyer, 'A redistribution of incomes in fifteenth century England', *Past and Present* 39 (1968).

T. Eagleton, *Literary Theory* (Oxford, 1983).

N. Elias, *What is Sociology?* (1978).

J. Elster, *Ulysses and the Sirens* (Cambridge, 1979).

——, 'Reply to comments', *Inquiry* XXIII (1980).

——, 'Cohen on Marx's theory of history', *Political Studies* XXVIII (1980).

——, 'Marxism, functionalism and game theory: the case for methodological individualism', *Theory and Society* XI (1982).

——, *Sour Grapes* (Cambridge, 1983).

——, *Explaining Technical Change* (Cambridge, 1983).

——, *Making Sense of Marx* (Cambridge, 1985).

S. Fenoaltea, 'The rise and fall of a theoretical model: the manorial system', *Journal of Economic History* XXXV (1975).

F. Ferrarotti, 'Notes on Marx and the study of technical change' in D. McQuaire (ed.), *Marx: Sociology, Social Change, Capitalism* (1978).

M. I. Finley, 'Technical innovation and economic progress in the ancient world', *Economic History Review Second Series* XVIII (1965).

——, *The Ancient Economy* (1979).

——, *Ancient Slavery and Modern Ideology* (1980).

E. Fromm, *The Fear of Freedom* (1975).

E. Gellner, *Thought and Change* (1964).

——, 'The Soviet and the savage', *The Times Literary Supplement* 3789 (18 October 1974).

N. Geras, *Marx and Human Nature: Refutation of a Legend* (1983).

A. Giddens, 'Marx, Weber and the development of capitalism', *Sociology* IV (1970).

——, *The Class Structure of the Advanced Societies* (1978).

——, *Capitalism and Modern Social Theory* (Cambridge, 1979).

——, *Central Problems in Social Theory* (1979).

——, *Studies in Social and Political Theory* (1979).

——, *A Contemporary Critique of Historical Materialism* (1981).

——, *The Nation State and Violence* (1985).

M. Godelier, *Perspectives in Marxist Anthropology* (Cambridge, 1977).

——, 'Infrastructures, society and history', *New Left Review* 112 (November–December 1978).

——, 'The Asiatic mode of production' in A. M. Bailey and J. R. Llobera (eds.), *The Asiatic Mode of Production* (1981).

——, 'Social hierarchies among the Baruya of New Guinea' in A. Strathern (ed.), *Inequality in New Guinea Highland Societies* (Cambridge, 1982).

R. S. Gottlieb, 'Feudalism and historical materialism: a critique and a synthesis', *Science and Society* XLVIII (1984).

H. J. Habakkuk, 'The economic history of modern Britain', *Journal of Economic History* XVIII (1958).

S. Hall, 'Re-thinking the "base and superstructure" metaphor' in J. Bloomfield (ed.), *Class, Hegemony and Party* (1977).

F. Halliday & M. Molyneux, *The Ethiopian Revolution* (1981).

N. Harris, *Of Bread and Guns* (Harmondsworth, 1983).

J. Hatcher, *Plague, Population and the English Economy 1348–1530* (1977).

——, 'English serfdom and villeinage: towards a re-assessment', *Past and Present* 90 (1981).

O. Henderson, *The Life of Friedrich Engels* (1976).

C. Hill (ed.), *The English Revolution of 1640* (1940).

——, *Puritanism and Revolution* (1969).

——, *Society and Puritanism in Pre-revolutionary England* (1969).

——, *Change and Continuity in Seventeenth Century England* (1979).

——, 'A comment', in R. H. Hilton et al., *The Transition from Feudalism to Capitalism* (1976).

R. H. Hilton, 'Peasant movements in England before 1381', *Economic History Review* Second Series II (1949–50).

——, *A Medieval Society* (1967).

——, *The Decline of Serfdom in Medieval England* (1969).

——, 'Introduction' and 'A Comment' in R. H. Hilton et al., *The Transition from Feudalism to Capitalism* (1976).

——, *Bond Men Made Free* (Cambridge, 1977).

——, *The English Peasantry in the Later Middle Ages* (Oxford, 1979).

R. H. Hilton & P. H. Sawyer, 'Technical determinism: the stirrup and the plough', *Past and Present* 24 (1963).

B. Hindess & P. Q. Hirst, *Pre-capitalist Modes of Production* (1975).

——, *Mode of Production and Social Formation* (1977).

M. Hirsowicz, 'Is there a ruling class in the U.S.S.R.? – a comment', *Soviet Studies* XXVIII (1976).

P. Q. Hirst, *Problems and Advances in the Theory of Ideology* (Cambridge, 1976).

——, *Marxism and Historical Writing* (1985).

Q. Hoare & G. Nowell Smith, *Selections from the Prison Notebooks of Antonio Gramsci* (1973).

E. J. Hobsbawn, *The Age of Revolution* (1969).

——, *Industry and Empire* (Harmondsworth, 1972).

——, 'Karl Marx's contribution to historiography' in R Blackburn (ed.), *Ideology in Social Science* (1973).

G. Hodgson, *Trotsky and Fatalistic Marxism* (Nottingham, 1975).

K. Hopkins, *Conquerors and Slaves* (Cambridge, 1980).

G. Ionescu (ed.), *The Political Thought of St. Simon* (Oxford, 1976).

S. Jenkins (ed.), *Fritz Lang: The Image and the Look* (1981).

E. John, 'Some questions on the materialist interpretation of history', *History* XXXVIII (1953).

C. Johnson, 'The problem of reformism and Marx's theory of fetishism', *New Left Review* 119 (January–February 1980).

R. Johnson, 'Reading for the best Marx: history writings and historical abstraction' in R. Johnson & G. McLennan (eds.), *Making Histories* (1982).

E. L. Jones, *Agriculture and the Industrial Revolution* (Oxford, 1976).

G. S. Jones, 'Engels and the genesis of Marxism', *New Left Review* 106 (November–December 1977).

K. Kautsky, *Ethics and the Materialist Conception of History* (Chicago; n.d.).

——, *Thomas More and his Utopia* (1927).

M. Kidron, *Western Capitalism since the War* (Harmondsworth, 1970).

A. Klima, 'Agrarian class structure and economic development in pre-industrial Bohemia', *Past and Present* 85 (1979).

L. Kolakowski, *Main Currents of Marxism*, vol. I (Oxford, 1978).

E. A. Kosminsky, *Studies in the Agrarian History of England in the Thirteenth Century* (Oxford, 1956).

W. Kula, *An Economic Theory of the Feudal System* (1976).

V. K. Kusin, 'A propos Alec Nove's search for a class label', *Soviet Studies* XXVIII (1976).

E. Le Roy Ladurie, *The Peasants of Languedoc* (Illinois, 1976).

J. R. Lander, *Conflict and Stability in Fifteenth Century England* (1971).

W. Langland, *Piers the Plowman* (Harmondsworth, 1974).

J. Larrain, *The Concept of Ideology* (1979).

V. I. Lenin, *The Three Sources and Component Parts of Marxism* (Moscow, 1969).

——, 'The state' in C. Wright Mills, *The Marxists* (Harmondsworth, 1969).

——, *What is to be done?* (Moscow, 1973).

A. Levine & E. O. Wright, 'Rationality and class struggle', *New Left Review* 123 (September–October 1980).

D. Levine, *Family Formation in an Age of Nascent Capitalism* (New York, 1977).

G. Lichtheim, *From Marx to Hegel* (1971).

T. Lovell, *Pictures of Reality* (1980).

——, 'Ideology and Coronation Street' in R. Dyer *et al.*, *Coronation Street* (1981).

H. Lubasz, 'Marx's concept of the Asiatic mode of production', *Economy and Society* XIII (1984).

A. D. Lublinskaya, *French Absolutism: The Crucial Phase 1620–29* (Cambridge, 1968).

G. Lukács, *Political Writings 1919–29* (1972).

S. Lukes, 'Can the base be distinguished from the superstructure?' in D. Miller and L. Siedentop (eds.), *The Nature of Political Theory* (Oxford, 1983).

R. Luxemburg, *Social Reform or Revolution* (Colombo, 1969).

T. Malthus, *An Essay on the Principle of Population* (1973).

B. Manning, review of C. Hill, *Society and Puritanism in Pre-revolutionary England* in *English Historical Review* LXXXI (1966).

P. Mantoux, *The Industrial Revolution in the Eighteenth Century* (1947).

F. E. Manuel, *The New World of Henri Saint-Simon* (Notre Dame, 1963).

G. Marshall, *In Search of the Spirit of Capitalism* (1982).

J. E. Martin, *Feudalism to Capitalism* (1983).

J. McCarney, 'Recent interpretations of ideology', *Economy and Society* XIV (1985).

T. McCarthy, *Marx and the Proletariat* (Westport, 1978).

B. J. McCormick *et al.*, *Introducing Economics* (Harmondsworth, 1977).

D. McLellan, *Karl Marx* (1976).

G. McLennan, *Marxism and the Methodologies of History* (1981).

J. McMurtry, *The Structure of Marx's World View* (Princeton, 1978).

R. Meek, *Social Science and the Ignoble Savage* (Cambridge, 1976).

F. Mehring, On Historical Materialism (1975).

C. Meillassoux, Anthropologie Economique des Gouru de Côte D'Ivoire (Paris, 1964).

J. Merrington, 'Town and country in the transition from feudalism to capitalism' in R. H. Hilton et al., The Transition from Feudalism to Capitalism (1976).

R. K. Merton, Social Theory and Social Structure (Glencoe, 1962).

R. Miliband, The State in Capitalist Society (1973).

———, Marxism and Politics (Oxford, 1978).

———, Class Power and State Power (1983).

R. Mishra, 'Technology and social structure in Marx's theory: an exploratory analysis', Science and Society XLIII (1979).

M. Modjeska, 'Production and inequality perspectives from central New Guinea' in A. Strathern (ed.), Inequality in New Guinea Highland Societies (Cambridge, 1982).

T. Moi, Sexual Textual Politics (1985).

B. Moore, The Social Origins of Dictatorship and Democracy (Harmondsworth, 1973).

T. Morris-Suzuki, 'Robots and capitalism', New Left Review 147 (September–October 1984).

G. E. Mumy, 'Town and country in Adam Smith's "The Wealth of Nations"', Science and Society XLII, 4 (winter 1978–9).

D. C. North & R. P. Thomas, 'The rise and fall of the manorial system', Journal of Economic History XXXI (1971).

A. Nove, 'Is there a ruling class in the U.S.S.R.?' in A. Nove, Political Economy and Soviet Socialism (1979).

———, The Economics of Feasible Socialism (1983).

P. O'Brien, 'European economic development: the contribution of the periphery', Economic History Review, Second Series XXXV (1982).

P. Oliva, Panonia and the Onset of Crisis in the Roman Empire (Prague, 1962).

B. Parekh, Marx's Theory of Ideology (1982).

D. Parker, The Making of French Absolutism (1983).

F. Parkin, Marxism and Class Theory: A Bourgeois Critique (1979).

H. Pirenne, Economic and Social History of Medieval Europe (1968).

J. Plamenatz, Man and Society, vol. II (1963).

G. V. Plekhanov, Fundamental Problems of Marxism (1969).

———, The Development of the Monist Conception of History (Moscow, 1972).

B. Porshnev, Les Soulèvements populaires en France de 1628 à 1648 (Paris, 1963).

M. M. Postan, The Medieval Economy and Society (1972).

———, Essays on Medieval Agriculture and General Problems of the Medieval Economy (Cambridge, 1973).

N. Poulantzas, 'The problem of the capitalist state' in R. Blackburn (ed.), Ideology in Social Science (1972).

———, Political Power and Social Classes (1973).

N. J. G. Pounds, An Economic History of Medieval Europe (1974).

A. M. Prinz, 'Background and ulterior motive of Marx's Preface of 1859', Journal of the History of Ideas XXX (1969).

M. Rader, Marx's Interpretation of History (New York, 1979).

Z. Razi, Life, Marriage and Death in a Medieval Parish (Cambridge, 1980).

J. E. Roemer, A General Theory of Exploitation and Class (Cambridge, Mass., 1982).

N. Rosenberg, 'Factors affecting the diffusion of technology', Explorations in

Economic History X (1972–3).
——, 'Marx as a student of technology' in L. Levidow & B. Young (eds.), *Science, Technology and the Labour Process* (1981).
M. Sahlins, *Stone Age Economics* (Cambridge, 1983).
M. Salvadori, *Karl Kautsky and the Socialist Revolution 1880–1938* (1979).
J. Saville, 'Primitive accumulation and early industrialization in Britain', *The Socialist Register* (1964).
S. Sayers, 'Marxism and the dialectical method: a critique of G. A. Cohen', *Radical Philosophy* (spring 1984).
E. Searle, *Lordship and Community: Battle Abbey and its Banlieu 1066–1538* (Toronto, 1974).
T. Shanin (ed.), *Late Marx and the Russian Road* (1983).
B. D. Shaw, 'Anatomy of the vampire bat', *Economy and Society* 13 (1984).
W. H. Shaw, *Marx's Theory of History* (1978).
——, '"The handmill gives you the feudal lord": Marx's technological determinism', *History and Theory* XVIII (1979).
R. Simon, *Gramsci's Political Thought* (1982).
A. Skinner, 'A Scottish contribution to Marxist sociology' in I. Bradley & M. Howard (eds.), *Classical and Marxian Political Economy* (1982).
P. Sloan, *Marx and the Orthodox Economists* (Oxford, 1973).
A. Smith, *The Wealth of Nations* (Harmondsworth, 1976).
——, *The Wealth of Nations*, vol. II (Oxford, 1979).
H. Spencer, 'The study of sociology' in K. Thompson & J. Tunstall, *Sociological Perspectives* (Harmondsworth, 1971).
J. V. Stalin, 'Dialectical and historical materialism' in *Problems of Leninism* (Peking, 1976).
I. Steedman, 'Value, price and profit', *New Left Review* 90 (March–April 1975).
——, *Marx after Sraffa* (1977).
——, et al., *The Value Controversy* (1981).
——, 'Robots and capitalism', *New Left Review* 151 (May–June 1985).
A. L. Stinchcombe, *Constructing Social Theories* (New York, 1968).
——, 'Merton's theory of social structure' in L. A. Coser (ed.), *The Idea of Social Structure* (New York, 1975).
P. Sweezy, 'A critique' and 'A rejoinder' in R. H. Hilton et al., *The Transition from Feudalism to Capitalism* (1976).
P. Sztompka, *Structure and Function* (New York, 1974).
R. H. Tawney, *Religion and the Rise of Capitalism* (Harmondsworth, 1972).
E. Terray, *Marxism and 'Primitive' Societies* (New York, 1972).
K. Thomas, *Religion and the Decline of Magic* (Harmondsworth, 1973).
E. P. Thompson, *The Making of the English Working Class* (Harmondsworth, 1972).
——, *The Poverty of Theory* (London, 1978).
D. Thorner, 'Peasant economy as a category in economic history' in T. Shanin (ed.), *Peasants and Peasant Societies* (Harmondsworth, 1975).
J. Z. Titow, *English Rural Society 1200–1350* (1969).
E. Tomlinson, 'Althusser, Balibar and production', *Capitalism and Class* 4 (1978).
J. Topolski, 'Economic decline in Poland from the sixteenth to the eighteenth century', in P. Earle (ed.), *Essays in European Economic History 1500–1800* (Oxford, 1974).

L. Trotsky, *The Permanent Revolution and Results and Prospects* (1971).
——, *The Revolution Betrayed* (1967).
——, *The Death Agony of Capitalism and the Tasks of the Fourth International* (1970).
——, *Marxism in our Time* (New York, 1970).
P. van Parijs, 'Functionalist Marxism rehabilitated', *Theory and Society* XI (1982).
E. von Bohm-Bawerk, *Karl Marx and the Close of his System* (1975, ed. P. Sweezy).
F. W. Walbank, *The Decline of the Roman Empire in the West* (1946).
——, *The Awful Revolution* (Liverpool, 1969).
I. Wallerstein, *The Modern World System* (1974).
M. Walzer, 'Puritanism as a revolutionary ideology', *History and Theory* III (1964).
——, *The Revolution of the Saints* (New York, 1974).
P. S. Wandycz, *The Lands of Partitioned Poland 1795–1918* (Seattle, 1974).
M. Weber, *The Protestant Ethic and the Spirit of Capitalism* (1978).
——, 'Politics as a vocation' in A. Pizzorno (ed.), *Political Sociology* (Harmondsworth, 1971).
J. Westergaard & H. Resler, *Class in a Capitalist Society* (Harmondsworth, 1976).
L. White, *Medieval Technology and Social Change* (Oxford, 1971).
C. Wickham, 'The other transition: from the ancient world to feudalism', *Past and Present* 103 (1984).
G. Williams, '18 Brumaire: Karl Marx and defeat' in B. Matthews (ed.), *Marx: A Hundred Years On* (1983).
R. Williams, 'Base and superstructure in Marxist cultural theory', *New Left Review* 82 (November–December 1973).
——, *Marxism and Literature* (Oxford, 1977).
E. Wilson, *To the Finland Station* (1966).
P. Winch, *The Idea of a Social Science and its Relation to Philosophy* (1977).
E. Wood, 'Marxism and ancient Greece', *History Workshop* II (spring 1981).
——, 'The separation of the economic and political in capitalism', *New Left Review* 127 (May–June 1981).
C. Wright Mills, *The Marxists* (Harmondsworth, 1969).
H. Wunder, 'Peasant organisation and class conflict in east and west Germany', *Past and Present* 78 (1978).

Index

Index of names

The names of Marx and Engels have been omitted. For their views on particular topics, see the subject index.

Abell, P., 300
Acton, H. B., 189–92, 194
Althusser, L., 3, 4, 35, 177, 182,
    194–8, 202, 283, 288
Amin, S., 228–9
Anderson, P., 39, 127, 198–201,
    224–5, 264–8

Balibar, E., 22–3, 197
Benn, T., 260–1
Bloch, M., 217
Bois, G., 3
Brenner, R., 3, 10, 11, 161, 165–70,
    269–70
Bukharin, N., 27, 62, 66–7

Cohen, G. A., 3–4, 12–14, 17, 23, 27,
    29, 33, 41, 82, 84–90, 92, 94,
    96–126, 143–6, 190–1, 290–4
Collingwood, R. G., 8
Comte, A., 71

Darwin, C., 61, 71, 89, 106, 202
De Ste Croix, G. E. M., 3, 193, 224–7
Deutscher, I., 11
Dobb, M., 160–5
Draper, H., 2–3, 252
Durkheim, E., 288

Elster, J., 84–90

Feuerbach, L., 8–9, 31, 75, 277, 278–9
Foster, J., 3
Fourier, C., 71
Freud, S., 288
Fromm, E., 293–4

Giddens, A., 84
Godelier, M., 3, 190, 192–3, 221
Gramsci, A., 61–2
Guizot, F., 62

Hegel, G. W. F., 3, 8, 71, 75, 286–7
Helvétius, C., 62
Hill, J. E. C., 3, 290–5
Hilton, R. H., 3, 10, 109, 166, 230
Hindess, B., 111, 219, 223–4, 226–8
Hirst, P. Q., 111, 198, 219, 223–4,
    226–8, 284–5
Hobsbawm, E. J., 3
Hodgson, G., 51
Holbach, P., 62

Kautsky, K., 13, 34, 53, 60–6, 241

Larrain, J., 284
Lenin, V. I., 11, 13, 46, 62, 68–9, 72,
    158, 160
Lukács, G., 3, 60, 281
Lukes, S., 275

311

Index

McCarthy, T., 54
McMurtry, J., 12, 17, 23, 27, 33, 41, 51, 66
Malthus, T., 73, 152, 280
Mantoux, P., 110
Meek, R. L., 72
Mehring, F., 8
Mignet, F., 62
Miliband, R., 252–3, 258, 263
Millar, J., 72
Morgan, L., 36–7, 218

Pareto, V., 288
Parijs, P. van, 88–9
Pirenne, H., 163
Plamenatz, J., 107, 189–92, 194, 275
Plekhanov, G. V., 13, 60–6, 68–9, 72
Poulantzas, N., 259–60, 262–3
Proudhon, P. J., 3, 31–3

Rader, M., 182–3, 186–8, 194, 201
Ricardo, D., 3, 280
Robertson, W., 72, 74
Roemer, J., 210–14
Rosenberg, N., 27, 52–4, 77

Sahlins, M., 117–18

Saint-Simon, H., 63, 71, 73–4
Shaw, W. H., 12, 13, 21, 23, 27, 37, 82, 92, 94–6, 103–5, 120–2
Smith, A., 14, 23, 53, 69, 72–3, 157
Spencer, H., 71
Stalin, J. V., 62, 67–8
Stinchcombe, A. L., 88–9, 289
Sweezy, P., 14, 160–4
Sztompka, P., 86–7

Tawney, R. H., 14
Thompson, E. P., 3, 12, 201–2, 215–16
Trotsky, L., 9–11, 13, 62, 68–9, 242–4, 251, 285

Walbank, F. W., 224
Wallerstein, I., 160, 164–5
Walzer, M., 293
Weber, M., 232, 236, 251, 293–4
White, L., 109
Wickham, C., 224, 228
Williams, G., 185
Winch, P., 288–9
Wood, E., 225

Index of subjects

absolutism, 167, 180, 255, 257, 263–70
absorbing Markov machine, 88–9
Ancient mode of production, 9, 37–8, 40, 45, 68, 97, 130–1, 133, 149–50, 153–5, 192, 198, 215, 219, 224–9
Asiatic mode of production, 9, 39, 46, 48, 97, 123–4, 155, 219, 221–4, 229

barbarism, 37, 110, 218–19 see also primitive communism
base and superstructure, 14–15, 46–7, Ch. 9 passim, 221, 244–5, 271, 276
  fundamentalist version of, 177, 182–4, 187

dialectical version of, 177, 182, 184–8, 190
  interpenetration of, 188–93, 270
Bonapartism, 242–3, 253–6
bourgeois revolution, 180, 183, 185

capital, distinguished from capitalism, 232
  constant and variable, 237
capitalist mode of production, 20, 22, 24, 48–50, 68, 97–100, 113, 120–1, 124, 128–9, 132–7, 145–6, 149–51, 155–6, 180, 188–9, 199, 209, 210–13, 215, 229–30, 232–40
class and class conflict, 101, 105,

161–2, 165–70, 188, 215–17, 224, 245
complex redistribution in primitive
    societies, 220
consciousness, human, 8–9, 18–19,
    29–31, 93, 276–7

distribution, distinguished from
    production? 34–5, 147

economic reductionism, 8, 10–12,
    184–6, 194–5
exploitation, 20–1, 209–14, 237, 300
external relations, 182–4, 188

fetishism, 100–3, 107, 286–7
feudal mode of production, 19–21, 25
    n. 15, 38–9, 45–6, 53, 68,
    119–22, 129–30, 149–50,
    154, 160, 161, 164–5, 180,
    196–7, 199, 209–11, 228–33,
    259, 264–5, 285
forms of intercourse, 21
four stage theory, 72–3
functional explanation, 15, 32, 82–90,
    100–3, 111–12, 117, 119–26,
    164–5, 181, 263–8, 277,
    283–4, 289–95

Germanic mode of production, 9, 40

historical method, 104–7, 159, 170
human nature, 28–9, 75, 93–4, 118
hydraulic agriculture, 221–2

idealistic superstructure, 47, 178,
    180–1, 184–6, 275–95
ideas,
    functioning as a relation of
        production, 191–4, 198–9,
        276, 300
    role of in history, 8–9, 275–8
ideological state apparatus, 283
ideology, 47, 180–2, 184–6, 191–2,
    278–95
individual, role of in history, 10–11,
    201–4
industry *see* manufacture

inevitability, historical, 9
internal relations, 182–3, 188

kinship, as a relation of production,
    191–2, 198, 218–21

labour, human, 18–19, 28–9, 75, 92–4
labour theory of value, 236–40
laws of historical development, 151–2

Manchester, influence of on Marx and
    Engels, 75–6
manufacture and industry, 22, 98–100,
    145–6, 151, 235
material content of production, 143–6
merchant's capital, 232
mode of production, 24, 148–9, 196,
    198–201, Ch. 10 *passim*

necessary labour, 19–20, 237

organic totality, society as an, 177,
    182, 186–99, 201–4

political implications of Marxist
    history, 14, 300
political superstructure *see* state
population, as explanation of economic
    change, 162, 165–6
post-capitalist societies, 240–4, 271 *see
    also* socialism and socialist
    revolution
pre-capitalist modes of production, 97,
    102, 112, 119–24, 126–8,
    132, 146, 153–5, 188–9, Ch.
    10 *passim*, especially pp. 216–32
primitive accumulation of capital, 158
    see also transition from feudalism
    to capitalism
primitive communism, 9, 36–7, 44–5,
    48, 68, 97, 110–12, 198, 199,
    209, 217–21
production, as a social activity, 146–8,
    151–2
productive forces, 17–19, 21–4
    as basis for socialism, 48–52,
        133–7, 242
    development of, 41–2, 63–9,

82–3, 116–26, 153–9, 163–5, 299

    fettered by social relations, 43–6, 126–33

    primacy of, 4, 12–15, 27–41, 46–7, 52–5, 60–9, 72–7, 82, 85–6, 90, 92–116, 133, 143–6, 148–9, 163–4, 242, 299–300

progress, historical, 71, 74 *see also* productive forces, development of

Protestantism, 47, 180–1, 278, 288, 289–94

rate of profit, alleged tendency to fall, 49–50, 128, 135, 237–9

reformism, 136–7, 281–3

relations of production, 19–25, 43–6, 126–33, 148–51, 194, Ch. 10 *passim*, 299–300

revolution, 179, 195 *see also* bourgeois revolution; socialism and socialist revolution

savagery, 37, 110, 218–19 *see also* primitive communism

serfdom, 228, 231–2 *see also* feudal mode of production

simple redistribution of product in primitive societies, 219

slavery, 37–8, 97, 215, 224–6

Slavonic mode of production, 40

social form of production, 143–6

social formation, 200, 228

socialism and socialist revolution,

48–52, 97, 114–16, 131–7, 240–4, 277, 281–3, 285–6

society, seen as a game, 203–4

state, the, 11–12, 30–1, 46–7, 111–12, 159, 178–80, 184–5, 192–6, 198–200, 240–1, 243–5, Ch. 11 *passim*, 300

state capitalism, 242–4

structuralism and structural causality, 195–8, 202–4, 259–60

subsumption of labour, formal and real, 234–6

surplus labour, absolute and relative, 19–21, 111–12, 120–1, 209–14, 237

surplus value, absolute and relative, 20, 120–1, 124, 234–7

tax, as surplus labour, 222–3, 228 *see also* absolutism; Asiatic mode of production

trade, as explanation of transition to capitalism, 53, 157–9, 162–5

transition from feudalism to capitalism, 11, 13, 45–6, 102–5, 132, 156–70, 180–1, 185, 264, 290–4

tributary mode of production, 228–9, 271

workers' state, deformed, 242

work relations, 21–4, 108–10, 147

Young Hegelians, 31, 278, 286–7